IMAGINATIVE METHODOLOGIES IN THE SOCIAL SCIENCES

Classical and Contemporary Social Theory

Series Editor: Stjepan G. Mestrovic, Texas A&M University, USA

Classical and Contemporary Social Theory publishes rigorous scholarly work that re-discovers the relevance of social theory for contemporary times, demonstrating the enduring importance of theory for modern social issues. The series covers social theory in a broad sense, inviting contributions on both 'classical' and modern theory, thus encompassing sociology, without being confined to a single discipline. As such, work from across the social sciences is welcome, provided that volumes address the social context of particular issues, subjects, or figures and offer new understandings of social reality and the contribution of a theorist or school to our understanding of it. The series considers significant new appraisals of established thinkers or schools, comparative works or contributions that discuss a particular social issue or phenomenon in relation to the work of specific theorists or theoretical approaches. Contributions are welcome that assess broad strands of thought within certain schools or across the work of a number of thinkers, but always with an eye toward contributing to contemporary understandings of social issues and contexts.

Also in the series

The Gift and its Paradoxes
Beyond Mauss
Olli Pyyhtinen
ISBN 978-1-4094-5097-9

The Puritan Culture of America's Military
U.S. Army War Crimes in Iraq and Afghanistan
Ronald Lorenzo
ISBN 978-1-4724-1982-8

A Genealogy of Social Violence
Founding Murder, Rawlsian Fairness, and the Future of the Family
Clint Jones
ISBN 978-1-4724-1722-0

Imaginative Methodologies in the Social Sciences
Creativity, Poetics and Rhetoric in Social Research

Edited by

MICHAEL HVIID JACOBSEN
Aalborg University, Denmark

MICHAEL S. DRAKE
University of Hull, UK

KIERAN KEOHANE
University College Cork, Ireland

ANDERS PETERSEN
Aalborg University, Denmark

ASHGATE

© Michael Hviid Jacobsen, Michael S. Drake, Kieran Keohane and Anders Petersen 2014

All rights reserved. No part of this publication may be reproduced, stored in a retrieval system or transmitted in any form or by any means, electronic, mechanical, photocopying, recording or otherwise without the prior permission of the publisher.

Michael Hviid Jacobsen, Michael S. Drake, Kieran Keohane and Anders Petersen have asserted their right under the Copyright, Designs and Patents Act, 1988, to be identified as the editors of this work.

Published by
Ashgate Publishing Limited
Wey Court East
Union Road
Farnham
Surrey, GU9 7PT
England

Ashgate Publishing Company
110 Cherry Street
Suite 3-1
Burlington, VT 05401-3818
USA

www.ashgate.com

British Library Cataloguing in Publication Data
A catalogue record for this book is available from the British Library

The Library of Congress has cataloged the printed edition as follows:
Jacobsen, Michael Hviid, 1971-
    Imaginative methodologies in the social sciences : creativity, poetics and rhetoric in social research / by Michael Hviid Jacobsen, Michael S. Drake, Kieran Keohane and Anders Petersen.
        pages cm. -- (Classical and contemporary social theory)
    Includes bibliographical references and index.
    ISBN 978-1-4724-0992-8 (hardback) 1. Social sciences--Research--Methodology. 2. Social sciences--Study and teaching. I. Title.
    H62.J2963 2014
    300.72--dc23

2013033633

ISBN 9781472409928 (hbk)

Printed in the United Kingdom by Henry Ling Limited,
at the Dorset Press, Dorchester, DT1 1HD

Contents

Acknowledgements	*vii*
List of Contributors	*ix*

	Introduction: Imaginative Methodologies: Creativity, Poetics and Challenges to Conventional Social Science *Michael Hviid Jacobsen, Michael S. Drake, Kieran Keohane and Anders Petersen*	1

PART I READING

1	Chicago Vice and Virtue: The Poetic Imagination Meets the Sociological Imagination *Michael Hviid Jacobsen, Rasmus Antoft and Anja Jørgensen*	23
2	Bacon, Kundera, Bauman *Keith Tester*	55
3	José Saramago's Sociology *Michael S. Drake*	69

PART II WRITING

4	Reading and Writing the Experimental Text *Norman K. Denzin*	93
5	On Writing: On Writing Sociology *Zygmunt Bauman*	109
6	Alice in Computerland *Laurel Richardson*	121

PART III EXPLORING

7   Getting in Touch with the World: Meaning and Presence
in Social Science   133
Svend Brinkmann

8   Theatricalized Reality and Novels of Truth: Respecting
Tradition and Promoting Imagination in Social Research   155
Arpad Szakolczai

9   Creative Methods: Oracles, *Poiesis* and Epiphanies as
Metaphors of Theorizing   177
Kieran Keohane

PART IV TEACHING

10   Creativity in the Classroom: The Poetics of Pedagogy
and Therapeutic Shock in Teaching Sociology   197
Anders Petersen, Michael Hviid Jacobsen and Rasmus Antoft

11   Inspiring 'The Methodological Imagination': Using Art
and Literature in Social Science Methods Teaching   217
Julie Seymour

12   Imagining the Outsiders: Exploring Literary Representations
of 'the Other' as Pedagogic Practice   235
Louise Sturgeon-Adams

13   The Uses of Literary and Cinematic Characters in
Teaching Sociology   251
Lisbeth B. Knudsen

Index   *267*

Acknowledgements

This book is the outcome of the editors' aspiration imaginatively to rethink and rearticulate the notion of 'methodology' within the social sciences. Moreover, the book is a concrete materialization of a budding collaboration between the universities of Aalborg, Cork and Hull, which has gradually developed over the last few years. We wish to thank contributors for insightful and inspirational contributions. We also wish to thank Neil Jordan, Senior Commissioning Editor at Ashgate Publishing, for solid encouragement and professional guidance throughout the process of completing this book. With this book we hope to contribute to the ongoing and indeed valuable discussion about social science 'methodology' and how this can be continuously developed, challenged and improved. It is indeed an impoverished soul that cannot appreciate the multiplicity of methodologies.

Aalborg, Cork and Hull, Spring 2014
Michael Hviid Jacobsen
Michael S. Drake
Kieran Keohane
Anders Petersen

List of Contributors

Rasmus Antoft is Associate Professor of Sociology and Head of the Department of Sociology and Social Work at Aalborg University, Denmark. His main areas of research are: qualitative research methods, the sociology of professions, creative methods and the sociology of health and illness. He has co-edited *Den poetiske fantasi* (with Michael Hviid Jacobsen and Lisbeth B. Knudsen, 2010).

Zygmunt Bauman is a world-renowned and award-winning sociologist who for more than half a century has critically contributed to the development of sociology. His writings comprise more than 40 books and he is still publishing extensively. Some of his most important contributions to social theory are: *Modernity and the Holocaust* (1989), *Intimations of Postmodernity* (1990), *Postmodern Ethics* (1993), *Liquid Modernity* (2000), *Society under Siege* (2002) and more recently titles such as *44 Letters from a Liquid Modern World* (2010) and *Collateral Damage* (2011). A recent interview book *What Use Is Sociology?* (with Michael Hviid Jacobsen and Keith Tester, 2013) summarizes Zygmunt Bauman's vision of sociology.

Svend Brinkmann is Professor of Psychology at Aalborg University, Denmark. His main areas of research are: qualitative inquiry, cultural psychology, philosophy of science and ethics. He is currently studying the impact of psychiatric diagnoses on individuals and society. His books in English include: *InterViews* (2nd Edition) (with Steinar Kvale, 2008), *Psychology as a Moral Science: Perspectives on Normativity* (2011), *Qualitative Inquiry in Everyday Life* (2012) and *Qualitative Interviewing* (2013).

Norman K. Denzin is Distinguished Professor of Communications and Research Professor of Communications, Cinema Studies, Sociology, Criticism and Interpretive Theory in the Sociology Department at the University of Illinois, USA. His academic interests include interpretive theory, performance studies, qualitative research methodology and the study of media, culture and society. His publications include: *The Cinematic Society* (1995), *Interpretive Ethnography* (1996), *Interpretive Interactionism* (2001), *Performance Ethnography* (2003), *Flags in the Window* (2007), *Searching for Yellowstone* (2008) and he is co-editor of the *Handbook of Qualitative Research* (several reprints).

Michael S. Drake is Lecturer in Sociology at the University of Hull, UK. He is the author of *Problematics of Military Power: Government, Discipline and the Subject of Violence* (2001) and *Political Sociology for a Globalizing World* (2010). He has also published on the war dead and the body politic, on the representation and contention of social identity, and on power, resistance and the state. His current research includes musical cultures, social conditions of creativity, the political body, literature as sociology, and social theory.

Michael Hviid Jacobsen is Professor of Sociology at Aalborg University, Denmark. His main areas of research are: death and dying, criminology, social theory, creative methods, everyday life and utopia. Some of his most recent books in English include: *The Contemporary Goffman* (edited, 2010), *Utopia: Social Theory and the Future* (edited, 2012), *What Use Is Sociology?* (with Zygmunt Bauman and Keith Tester, 2013), *Deconstructing Death* (edited, 2013), *Poetics of Crime* (edited, 2013), *The Social Thought of Erving Goffman* (with Søren Kristiansen, 2014) and *Social Science Fiction* (edited with Keith Tester, forthcoming).

Anja Jørgensen is Associate Professor of Sociology at Aalborg University, Denmark. Her main areas of research are: urban sociology, human ecology, the Chicago School of Sociology, (local) communities, belonging and everyday life. She is currently studying the interconnections between local communities, mobility and belonging. Her books published in Danish include: *Når kvarteret opdager sig selv* (2006) and *Betingelser for fællesskab* (with Anne-Kirstine Mølholt, 2007).

Kieran Keohane is Senior Lecturer in Sociology in the School of Sociology and Philosophy at University College Cork, Ireland. He is the author of *Symptoms of Canada* (1997), *Collision Culture: Transformations in Everyday Life in Ireland* (2005) and co-author of *Cosmopolitan Ireland: Globalization and Quality of Life* (with Carmen Kuhling, 2007) as well as author of articles that have been published in journals such as *Cultural Politics, Theory Culture & Society*, and *Philosophy & Social Criticism*.

Lisbeth B. Knudsen is Professor of Sociology and is co-heading the research group on 'Demography, Social Geography and Health' at Aalborg University, Denmark. Her main areas of research are: socio-demography, reproduction, fertility regulation, family formation, population development in rural and urban areas, health, quantitative methods and register based research. She is the author of an introductory text book in demography and has written a number of contributions to textbooks in Danish. Her most recent book project in English is: *Our Demographic Future – A Challenge* (co-edited, 2010).

Anders Petersen is Associate Professor of Sociology and Head of School at Aalborg University, Denmark. His main areas of research are: social theory, social pathologies, creative methods, sociological perspectives on the self and the sociology of diagnosis. His current research project can be follow at www.dc.aau.dk and his most recent book in English is: *The Social Pathologies of Contemporary Civilization* (edited with Kieran Keohane, 2013).

Laurel Richardson, Professor of Sociology at Ohio State University, USA, is an internationally renowned qualitative researcher with specialties in arts-based research, writing-issues, gender and contemporary theory. She has modelled alternative modes of representing research through writing by publishing her work as poetry, ethnodrama, essay and autoethnography. She is currently writing a series of ethnographic essays, *Seven Minutes from Home*, and a nonfiction novel, *Kisses in the Dark*.

Julie Seymour is Senior Lecturer in Medical Sociology at Hull York Medical School, UK. Her main areas of research are: family and childhood practices particularly in the allocation of material, labour, spatial and emotional resources within the household, disability, caring relationships in the home and research methodologies. Recent publications include *Displaying Families: A New Concept in the Sociology of Family Life* (edited with Esther Dermott, 2011) and articles in the journals *Sociology* and *Childhood*.

Louise Sturgeon-Adams is Lecturer in Community Justice at the University of Hull, UK. Her main research interests are: illegal drug use, offending behaviour and probation practice. She originally trained as a probation officer and counsellor for people with alcohol problems and has been involved with training probation officers for the past ten years, alongside teaching undergraduate and postgraduate criminology students. Publications have included contributions in *Understanding Offending Behaviour* (2008) and *British Journal of Community Justice* (2013).

Arpad Szakolczai is Professor of Sociology in the School of Sociology and Philosophy at University College Cork, Ireland. His books include *Max Weber and Michel Foucault: Parallel Life Works*; *Reflexive Historical Sociology* (1998), *The Genesis of Modernity* (2002), *Sociology, Religion & Grace: A Quest for the Renaissance* (2006) and *Comedy and the Public Sphere: The Re-Birth of Theatre as Comedy and the Genealogy of the Modern Public Arena* (2013) all with Routledge, as well as numerous articles in such journals as *History of the Human Sciences*, *Theory Culture & Society*, and *European Journal of Social Theory*.

Keith Tester is Professor of Sociology at the University of Hull, UK. He has published widely on the work of Zygmunt Bauman, including *Conversations with Zygmunt Bauman* (2001) and *The Social Thought of Zygmunt Bauman* (2004). Other books include: *Eric Rohmer: Film as Theology* (2008), *Humanitarianism and Modern Culture* (2010) and *Panic* (2013).

Introduction
Imaginative Methodologies: Creativity, Poetics and Challenges to Conventional Social Science

Michael Hviid Jacobsen, Michael S. Drake, Kieran Keohane and Anders Petersen

Against 'Methodology'

According to the American sociologist Peter L. Berger, in his classic introduction to sociology, social scientists in general and sociologists in particular are a peculiar breed because their scientific disciplines are 'spacious playgrounds' and since they, as compared to many other scientists and researchers, have the golden opportunity to look beyond the restrictive confines of conventional sources of scientific practice for inspiration and expansion of their disciplinary scope:

> The sociological perspective is a broad, open, emancipated vista on human life. The sociologist, at his best, is a man [or woman] with a taste for other lands, inwardly open to the measureless richness of human possibilities, eager for new horizons and new worlds of human meaning. (Berger 1963: 67)

Looking for this 'measureless richness of human possibilities' and such 'new horizons' and 'new worlds of human meaning' often requires that the researcher or social scientist allows him/herself to step outside his/her own natural habitat, as it were, in order to be inspired, provoked, moved or persuaded by insights and ideas found at the outskirts of or even outside the immediate confines of his/her own scientific discipline. American cultural anthropologist Mary Catherine Bateson thus once rightly proposed that 'the most creative thinking occurs at the meeting places of disciplines. At the center of any tradition, it is easy to become blind to alternatives. At the edges, where lines are blurred, it is easier to imagine that the world might be different' (Bateson 1989: 73). Armed merely with the conventional methods, concepts, theories and analytical strategies of one's own discipline, researchers risk becoming narrow-minded and lose sight of the creative possibilities and unexplored alternatives of neighbouring scientific disciplines or – as British physicist and novelist Charles P. Snow (1959/1993) once called them – 'cultures'. However, by linking to, getting acquainted with, borrowing from, playing with or sucking the marrow out of the insights and ideas of other disciplines and cultures, and even outside the realm of science, one as a social scientist becomes better equipped to discover new land and to understand that one's own professional practice and perspective is merely one among many.

As compared to other and more creatively based branches of investigation or insight into the social world (often called 'literature', 'art' or 'poetry'), what conventionally characterizes and indeed distinguishes science is often referred to as 'methodology'. 'Methodology', in short, is the study of methods, for example, the methods used to study the social world. By 'methodology' is meant the stringent and followable (and often technical) itinerary from initial hunches, guesswork or utter ignorance into certified and infallible knowledge – an itinerary often described in great detail in textbooks on 'research methods'. However, the notion and practice of 'methodology' is not unproblematic. According to American sociologist C. Wright Mills (1959), in the social sciences methodology often becomes an end in itself rather than, as it was supposed to, a means to an end, for example, to obtain knowledge or in order to guide action. Methodology, Mills claimed, is increasingly worshipped by the proponents of the so-called 'Scientific Method' who believe that methodology – instead of the social world it is aimed at investigating – is itself of the utmost importance. This regrettable tendency Mills described as the 'methodological inhibition' (Mills 1959: 50).[1] An accompanying consequence of this 'methodological inhibition' was the denigration of other ways of understanding or capturing the social wold than those regarded as 'certified', 'proven', 'correct' or the like. Polish sociologist Stanislav Andreski thus once observed how 'the worshippers of methodology turn like a vicious hunting pack upon anybody branded as impressionistic, particularly if he writes well and can make his books interesting' (Andreski 1972: 117). 'Methodology' thus sometimes unfortunately becomes a strait-jacket for social scientists inhibiting instead of promoting the production of interesting, valid and useable knowledge. Therefore, we as social scientists need to allow ourselves to extend and expand our understanding of 'methodology' – we need to play with our methodological imagination, as it were, obviously without losing sight of the fact that methodology is only and remains a means rather than an end in itself. As Bill Nichols rightly argued in his introduction to a book aimed at showing the importance of film as a creative means to understand social life:

---

1 In his famous *Sociology as an Art Form* Robert Nisbet began his argument by claiming on the creative restrictiveness of the so-called 'Scientific Method': "It occurred to me a number of years ago while I was engaged in exploration of some of the sources of modern sociology that none of the great themes which have provided continuing challenge and also theoretical foundation for sociologists during the last century was ever reached through anything resembling what we are today fond of identifying as 'scientific method'. I mean the kind of method, replete with appeals to statistical analysis, problem design, hypothesis, verification, replication and theory construction, that we find described in our textbooks and courses on methodology" (Nisbet 1976/2002: 3).

> Methodologies cannot be allowed to become ends. They are means, tools to help construct models of how things work. In the hands of the crude or dogmatic, a methodology can be worse than nothing. It can become a rationale for banality, a justification for self-righteousness. But when used with care, methodologies can be of great value. (Nichols 1976: 1)

We need to acknowledge that the tree of knowledge has many branches, some of which are more crooked than others. We thus need to move from the 'methodological inhibition', as Mills described it, to a 'methodological imagination'. Methodology is not merely about measuring things, counting incidents or slavishly following prescribed steps in a research process. In fact, a too narrow focus on 'methodology' understood in this way may be counterproductive to scientific endeavours. As Peter L. Berger once poignantly observed: 'In science as in love a concentration on technique is quite likely to lead to impotence' (Berger 1963: 24). Methodology or the methodological imagination more broadly understood is about how we may possibly obtain interesting knowledge – 'stories' and not just dull 'information', as C. Wright Mills (1959) famously stated – about social life. Being aware of – and indeed curious about and interested in how this knowledge may be obtained – is part and parcel of what Mills famously described as 'intellectual craftsmanship'. Intellectual craftsmanship, Mills insisted, requires that the social scientist moves from an obsession with theoretical abstraction or methodological rigorousness and fetishism to a more comprehensive understanding of the world in which we live and which ambitiously aspires 'to make a difference in the quality of human life in our time' (Mills 1959: 226). By insisting that methodology can make a difference and that it is necessarily more than just crammed mechanical procedures or detailed technical instructions, we may also learn to focus more creatively on the problem, topic or phenomenon in question instead of focusing on the procedures, techniques or instruments intended to measure, explain or understand the problem, topic or phenomenon at hand. This is indeed the purpose and the promise of the imaginative methodologies contained in this book.

The 'Literary' and 'Poetic' Turn in Social Science

The metaphor of a literary or poetic 'turn' in the social sciences is not really adequate to conceptualize the plurality of processes through which literary and other artistic sources have become increasingly legitimate reference points and sources. We could better conceptualize the plural routes as a convergence, though even that does not do the trend justice, since the different strands frequently do not mingle, but retain diverse, if parallel, courses. Rather, the shift may be effectively conceived as a change of terrain, a 'groundshift', a paradigmatic revolution or a fundamental transformation of the very ontology of the social sciences as we reorient ourselves in a world that is undergoing rapid and fundamental change at all levels, from the personal to the planetary.

In geography, the 'turn' has proceeded along at least two paths, through attention to the subjective and even affective human sense of place as a particularity, and through fundamental critical re-engagement with the very notion of space itself (Massey 1994, 2005). Anthropology has aspired to transcend the historical divisions between the social and the human sciences, and between the sciences and the arts, but while the reflexive critical turn of much of the discipline against its own origins in the colonial and orientalist project produced writing that can be anti-scientistic in both form and content, the simultaneous drive to develop the discipline methodologically has produced writing at the opposite end of the stylistic spectrum (for example, Pierre Bourdieu's reflections on the methodology and philosophy of social science). For sociology, the sources have been even more diverse, from the influence of post-structuralism, to the recognition of gender as a central category and the epistemological debates around how to develop more emotionally engaged methodologies which can capture the quality of lived experience, through to the influence of cultural and media studies.

This realization brings the phenomena under discussion in this book closer to the wider 'cultural turn' in the social sciences, though representing its reflexive aspect, in which culture no longer figures only as data but becomes recognized as both constitutive of the social and as a mode of analysis of the social itself. There are of course implicit links between this and the contemporaneous movements in the arts from the 1960s turn away from 'art for art's sake' towards social and political engagement, which has produced a spectrum of practices extending from community theatre, art and writing projects, where subjects are encouraged to explore their own social situation and sense of identity, through the medium of artistic expression, through to the more ambivalent and opaque critical practices of art-practitioners like Joseph Beuys. The further radicalization of the avant-garde arts project of the 20th century carried over into the social sciences, most explicitly in the call for the critique and revolution of everyday life (Lefebvre 1961/2002; Vaneigem 1967/1983) in which social critique was to provide the basis for the self-transformation of society, but there were other convergences between the arts and social science in feminist practice around politicizing the personal, and appearing through a logic of the social sciences in which everyday life came to appear as a field of action rather than structure (Berger and Luckmann 1967/1991; Melucci 1989).

There is a politics of this phenomenon, represented on the side of the arts stream in the debates around creativity, between those who see the enfolding of critical art practice into everyday life and the extension of the definition of art to encompass everyday life as inherently emacipatory, experiments in new ways of living, thinking and being (Raunig 2007, Raunig, Ray and Wuggenig 2011; Berardi 2012), and those who see it as functional in a more conventionally productive, economic sense (Ray and Anderson 2000; Florida 2002). On the side of the social sciences, the perceived incursion of the arts upon their 'proper' domain has produced a backlash. Attempts to separate 'art critique' from 'social critique' see the former as compromised by its perceived critical betrayal of the social-democratic project in favour of a libertarianism which opens the door to corporate capitalism and neo-liberalism (Boltanski and Chiapello 2007), recycling some of the 1980s arguments against postmodernism (Jameson 1984; Callinicos 1990).

The debates around postmodernism, although today silenced by almost unanimous consensus, produced deep underlying shifts in sociological perception. The irreversible effects of that debate are secured by social and cultural changes, in which social reality has become thoroughly permeated with representations and everyday life is conducted increasingly through mediated forms. In this context, it seems futile to continue to treat representations as second-order reflections of an underlying social reality that can only be perceived through specialist methodological tools. Rather than displacing social reality, as in Jean Baudrillard's (1981/1994) incisive postmodernist mobilization of Jorge Luis Borges' fable of the map-makers, representation today constitutes an integral part of that reality. In this recognition, however, we have returned to the original premises of sociology – the realization that when we talk of the social we are always speaking of an imaginary which is real in so far as people act as though it is.

Wolf Lepenies (1988) once argued that sociology originated out of literature, though as he shows, in aspiring to instead become a science, sociology became unable to recognise itself in its original forms, and came to categorically mistake literature as its object rather than its subject, perceiving in it only data. The discipline deals with exceptions (such as the work of Erving Goffman) as though these were anomalies, contingent deviations which can be accommodated as such without disturbing methodological hegemony. However, in an increasingly mediated society, where representation is ubiquitous, rather than exceptional, and becomes itself an increasingly significant factor in everyday life, the paradigm of methodological orthodoxy is becoming progressively strained. In clinging to methodological postulates outmoded by the mediated development of social life itself, sociology risks an obsolescence that recalls that of the alchemists of early modernity, cast adrift outside a new paradigm.

The 'Art' of Social Science Research

Social science sometimes suffers from the conceit that it is 'science' modelled on the Natural Sciences' positivist epistemology and empirical methods, but social science is in many respects more comfortably at home with the Arts and Humanities. Like the study of language, literature, philosophy, religion, and the visual and performing arts, social science is interested in broadening, deepening and expanding the universe of human understanding. Speaking of the social sciences perhaps most problematically implicated in 19th century projects of modernization through imperial domination, Clifford Geertz says that anthropology 'is not an experimental science in search of law but an interpretive one in search of meaning' (Geertz 1973: 5). The anthropologist, that most characteristic practitioner of the 'field methods' of empirical social science, in fact works with

> a multiplicity of complex conceptual structures, many of them superimposed upon or knotted into one another, which are at once strange, irregular, and inexplicit, and which he must contrive somehow first to grasp and then to render. And this is true of at the most down-to-earth, jungle field work levels of his activity: interviewing informants, observing rituals, eliciting kin terms, tracing property lines, censusing households ... writing his journal. Doing ethnography is like trying to read (in the sense of 'construct a reading of') a manuscript -foreign, faded, full of ellipses, incoherencies, suspicious emendations, and tendentious commentaries, written not in conventional graphs of sound but in transient examples of shaped behaviour. (Geertz 1973: 10)

The methods of social science are akin to literary criticism, deciphering codes and translating languages. Walter Benjamin, a fellow traveller on Geertz's road, likens his own method to Rabbinical hermeneutics: 'I have never been able to do research and to think in a way other than, if I may so put it, in a theological sense – namely, in accordance with the Talmudic teaching of the forty-nine levels of meaning of every passage in the Torah' (Benjamin in Jay 1973: 17). Of Benjamin's many models, two that will interest us in the present context of imaginative methods of social science as art are his spirit guide the poet Charles Baudelaire, and his teacher Georg Simmel, whose lectures at the University of Berlin Benjamin attended occasionally. A particularly imaginative aspect of Benjamin's method – one of his 'little tricks of the trade' as he called them – was to transport himself imaginatively as though in a waking dream back in time to the world of Baudelaire and his friends Edouard Manet, Edgar Degas and the Impressionists, *flâneurs* in Paris, capital of the 19th century, immersing himself in its scenes of squalor and poverty, luxury and conspicuous consumption, *avant garde* bohemianism and refined intellectual cultures. 'The painter of modern life', Baudelaire says (he may have said 'social scientist' though the vocabulary had not been coined yet), concentrates his vision and his energy on 'its fashions, its morals, its emotions' on 'the passing moment and all the suggestions of eternity that it contains' (Baudelaire in Berman 1988: 133). Georg Simmel, once disparaged as an 'impressionist sociologist' (though he would have been pleased with the moniker), is now widely read and recognized as the most imaginative classical sociologist, one who has provided us with a treasure trove of methods for the study of contemporary late-modern/postmodern society. Simmel's methods emerged from his lifelong love of music and art, Ludwig von Beethoven and Rembrandt being amongst his inspirational touchstones. Beethoven's Symphony no. 9, for instance, can be heard as a musical representation of the dialectics of Enlightenment, G.W.F. Hegel's (1977) *Phenomenology of Spirit* expressed musically: beginning in revolutionary cacophony emanating from diverse and contrasting instruments and voices, clashing, then synthesizing, then decomposing, harmonizing again in higher and higher resolutions of the sublime and beautiful: human history united symphonically in the ideals of Enlightenment, Democracy and Progress. Similarly, in a different artistic medium, Rembrandt's numerous self-portraits over the course of his life, with its many triumphs and tragedies, his gaze turned inward on his own soul, is a prototype of Simmel's methodological reflexivity, an artistic representation of subjective inner experience of external history as objective culture. Beethoven and Rembrandt are the artistic sources of Simmel's own portraits, his essays depicting the types of people and forms of life that express the conflict in modern culture. Simmel's beautiful essays – and they are beautiful, masterpieces, a signal distinction that Simmel enjoys with only a few scholarly writers, Friedrich Nietzsche, for instance – are written with a characteristic style that imaginatively links the most subtle phenomenological detail with epic and abstract themes of history and philosophy. Simmel's sociological genius is built on disarmingly simple methodological principles, as he explains in "Sociological Aesthetics": 'the type appears in the individual, the law in the contingent and the essence and the significance of things in the superficial and fleeting' (Simmel 1968: 69).

Following Simmel's lead, Walter Benjamin sought 'to capture the portrait of history in the most insignificant representations of reality, in its scraps as it were' (Benjamin in Arendt 1992: 17). As 'reality' in modernity (and post-modernity) has become increasingly phantasmagoric, constantly shifting scenes of real and imagined images and illusions, Benjamin, along with his artist contemporaries, knew that we need to develop ways of seeing that are appropriate to this reality. The cubist artist Ferdinand Léger, for instance, says that

> as one crosses a landscape by automobile or express train, it becomes fragmented; it loses in descriptive value but gains in synthetic value. The view through the door of the railroad car or the automobile windshield, in combination with the speed, has altered the habitual look of things. A modern man registers a hundred times more sensory impressions than an eighteenth-century artist; so much so that our language, for example, is full of diminutives and abbreviations. (Léger 1973: 11)

In *The Sociological Imagination* C. Wright Mills advises us to 'let your mind become a moving prism catching light from as many angles as possible' (Mills 1959: 214) – his principle of imaginative method rhyming beautifully with how Jean Metzinger, Georges Braque and Pablo Picasso conceived of their method of cubism; as though the artist and the viewer (or the social scientist) were moving around the object, seeing it from many perspectives simultaneously; a cinematic, mobile perspective enabling a representation of a total image as remembered from successive and subjective experiences within the context of both space and time (Antliff and Leighten 2008). Incidentally, cubism's multi-perspectivalism was revolutionary not only in art but in science (Miller 2002), enabling Danish quantum physicist Niels Bohr to postulate that an electron could be both a particle and a wave simultaneously, heralding a postmodern epistemology of natural – and social – science: 'Depending upon our arbitrary point of view ... we must, in general, be prepared to accept the fact that a complete elucidation of one and the same object may require diverse points of view which defy a unique description' (Bohr 2011: 96). Social science's methods, born of a marriage between stern parents of science on the one hand and liberal arts and humanities on the other are characteristic children of the modernist *avant-garde*. Constitutionally ambivalent, critical-reflexive-hermeneutic artful and imaginative methods explore and press beyond the outer limits of individual and collective experience on the one hand, while, on the other hand and at the same time they are seeking to unite the diversity, intensity and seemingly random thrownness of modern existence into a coherent whole that can be grasped completely, articulated precisely and correctly represented. Three classical sociologists, Karl Marx, Max Weber, and Émile Durkheim (who, unlike Georg Simmel, we do not ordinarily think of in terms of their being 'artists') work with some of the most astounding and imaginative images and metaphors: Marx, as though anticipating Surrealism and Salvador Dali's melting clocks and liquid landscapes, describes in *The Communist Manifesto* a weird world of alchemy and sorcery where everything is pregnant with its contrary and where 'all that is solid melts into air' (Marx in Berman 1998: 95); Weber, seeking to grasp and express the bleak future for those condemned to live in an iron cage of rationalized acquisitiveness and mechanized petrification borrows imaginatively from Johann Wolfgang von Goethe's poetry: 'Specialists without spirit, sensualists without heart; this nullity imagines that it has attained a level of civilization never before achieved' (Weber 1958: 182); and Durkheim, frequently misunderstood as a purveyor of a dry, scientific sociology of 'social facts,' but his formulation of social facts as 'collective representations' constituting society's mind is an astonishingly rich and complex image of the human cosmos: 'a vast cooperative effort that extends not only through space but over time; their creation has involved a multitude of different minds associating, mingling, combining their ideas and feelings – the accumulation of generations of experience and knowledge. A very special knowledge, infinitely richer than that of the individual is concentrated in them' (Durkheim 2001: 18).

The Greek root of 'method' is *hodos*, meaning a road, a path; metaphorically: 'a course of conduct'; 'a manner of doing things'. Imaginative methods and methodologies are ways of doing things that can take us, if we want to go there, as far as the outer horizons of knowledge of the human world. Palaeoanthropology speculates that the first action that raises us from animal to human life is not tool-making, or even language, for before language there is emotion, affection between mothers and infants or between lovers, expressed as a sweet tone of voice, a smile, a caress or a graceful gesture transforming affection into a sign to represent an idea that transcends the brute reality of the world (Greenspan and Shanker 2006). From the creation of this first world-transcending idea springs the symbolic order, the Name of the Father, the Divine, and divinity, in Durkheim's formulation, is 'society configured and expressed symbolically' (Durkheim 1974: 52). Unlike a flint axe, the primordial love song (perhaps it was a lullaby?) is lost to our ears forever, but it suggests that not Hobbesian war but a constant striving towards beauty and the good life is what defines the course of human development. An imaginative *hodos* that follows the path of civilization back towards the creation of the first sign is the same path that Martin Heidegger (1989: 265) identifies as 'the way back into the ground of metaphysics'; the pathway through the forest where we may glimpse the meaning of Being as being-with-others, a method that always lies near at hand; or as Simmel, once again, places his finger upon it: 'From each point on the surface of existence – however closely attached to the surface alone – one may drop a sounding into the depths of the soul, so that all the most banal externalities finally are connected with the ultimate decisions concerning the meaning of life' (Simmel 1964: 413).

'Paying It Forward' – Imaginative Teaching

As already emphasized, this book intends to ignite the creative and poetical sparks when thinking about and doing social and sociological research. The complex social predicament we find ourselves in certainly calls for sociological research that is able grasp this in a creative and poetic manner. If social researchers, in what has come to be known as the age of austerity in most European societies, succumb to more traditional ways of investigation, there is a good chance that we miss out on solving, understanding and explaining the problems with which we are faced. Social research, in so many ways, therefore cries out for creative approaches. However, one thing is doing creative and poetic research another thing is to teach this research imaginatively. The main question seems to be how we are capable to transfer our research to the ways in which we teach and hence pedagogically seek to inspire students to think about social issues in novel and thought-provoking ways? By and large, universities are quite conservative when it comes to teaching. Lectures in large theatres are more often than not the standard way of teaching. The teaching often takes the form of monologue rather than dialogue, and of podium teaching rather than seminar activity, because the location and the actual form of the teaching do not permit more active involvement on the part of the students, or because curriculum pressures lead to everything being targeted and focused on providing relatively specific keywords or concepts that are easy to remember. This format has a hard time being particularly creative. That is, when teaching takes the form of monologue it is rather difficult to inspire students and satisfy, stimulate and intensify their creative appetite. And students do have such an appetite. They really have a deep felt appetite for wanting to learn about how to use sociological theories and methods in a creative way in order for them to get a firm grip of the social problems they are struggling to comprehend. It would be a shame if university teaching hindered this.

One of the ways in which university teaching can try to accommodate this – try to install a more imaginative teaching to stimulate student creativity – is by changing their modus vivendi. But not just any form of change will do. As Howard Cannatella argues:

> Certainly, all creativity invokes changes of thought, a striving for new ways to communicate that draws upon changes in one's personal consciousness and

emotional states. However, changing the appearance of an object for the sake of change may require little skill in execution and perception. (Cannatella 2004: 62)

What Cannatella directs our attention to is the fact that creativity cannot be used as a means to an end, where it only has instrumental value. Hence, what we refer to as imaginative teaching has little to do with changing the appearance of something for the sake change per se, but rather to change our perception of how to communicate teaching that enables us to internalize and embody the subject matter into the students. In a perfect world, the students should be 'allowed' to feel, taste and smell that which the lecturer is teaching them. They should be enabled to sense sociology. This is not an easy task. Imaginative and creative teaching is not a spread-on that one can use at one's pleasure. It is hard work. Cannatella again:

> With no direct significance, decisive disturbance of mind, and no hard thought imaginatively resolved crisis in the work, creativity may be viewed as an afterthought. Creativity, as so described, looks like wayward embellishment rather than coming from and being taken forward through the challenges of subject knowledge, provocative impressions, and bedazzled sensory experiences. If no particular abiding interrelation with a discipline exists, creativity leads nowhere and this is particularly so when there appears to be no embodied relevance to the work. (Cannatella 2004: 66)

When thinking about teaching ones subject matter creatively, one is surely forced to thinking about the content of the work one shall teach. It would be hard to imagine, for example, that one could teach Talcott Parsons' theory of the social system by dancing the functional imperatives of social systems – the so called AGIL schema. This 'creative' endeavour would most likely be the subject of ridicule on the part of the students (and probably from the university as such) and hence have a counter-productive effect. That is not to say, however, that other creative tools cannot be used when teaching Parsons. In fact, one could actually state that teaching Parsons requires creative imagination of some sort in order to make his theory relevant for the students. What we are espousing in this volume is thus not the idea of creative and imaginative teaching for the sake of the idea. We are rather trying to put focus on the immense benefits of using a structured creativity in order for university teachers to be aware of the huge potential of a more imaginative approach to the endeavour of teaching social science.

Structure and Content of the Book

This book consists of a range of chapters that in various ways describe how to develop, expand and challenge conventional social scientific methodology by way of literary, poetic and other alternative or unusual sources of inspiration. The book contains chapters by a host of scholars working within disciplines such as sociology, social work, demography, gender studies, anthropology, criminology and psychology all trying to rethink, provoke and reignite imaginative social scientific methodology and move it beyond the aforementioned 'methodological inhibition'. Chapters deal with how social research (in its uncovering of problems as well as in its analysis, representation and report of findings) as well as teaching endeavours may be enhanced or rethought by importing ideas, stylistic ploys (for example, analogies and metaphors) and critical social commentary from literature, poetry, music, drawings, film and other sources of material not conventionally regarded as part and parcel of the social scientific methodology toolbox.

Expressions like 'poetics for sociology' (Brown 1977), sociology as an 'art form' (Nisbet 1976/2002), 'passionate sociology' (Game and Metcalf 1996), 'anti-methods' (Roderick et al. 2000), 'arts based research' (Barone and Eisner 2012), 'creative factors in research' (Porterfield 1941), 'sociology through stories' (Schoepflin 2013), 'poetic imagination' (Antoft, Jacobsen and Knudsen 2010), 'artistic approaches' (Eisner 1981) or 'anarchistic methods' (Feyerabend 1975) – or what we collectively characterize as 'imaginative methodologies' – might give the impression that we are dealing here with utterly unscientific, speculative or pseudo-scientific endeavours that not only provoke but also undermine time-honoured understandings of science, validity, certified knowledge and authority. However, as the chapters in this book will show, dealing creatively, poetically and indeed imaginatively with methodology is not equivalent to mere playfulness or the abandoning of conventional criteria for social research – rather, it is a matter of admitting that there is not one single linear road leading to knowledge about the social world and that detours, shortcuts, excursions and roundtrips are an integral and imaginative part of the development of scientific knowledge.

This book is about some of the many so-called 'expressive forms' with which one can study and understand society (see, for example, Roderick et al. 2000). The purpose of this book has been to gather a variety of insights from different social scientific disciplines and applicable to different stages in the process of developing, revising or using knowledge. The book is divided into four parts that each deal with reading, writing, exploring and teaching about social issues.

Part I of the book, Reading, centres on how we may read the social sciences as a variety of disciplines that in certain ways are closely related to and quite often borrow from more artistic forms of expression such as literature. There is, as Joan Rockwell (1974) once proposed, most definitely fact to be found in fiction but simultaneously there is also fiction or poetics to be uncovered in those texts we conventionally regard as fact (see also Krieger 1983). Taking a new look at the history of, for example, sociology, one may discover that the texts that we conventionally label or approach as 'theory' might in fact be seen as small and sometimes even beautiful pieces of art. There is thus a dialectical relationship between social science and art in that both, as Robert Nisbet (1976/2002) once reminded us, provide portraits, landscapes and situational descriptions of human action that in many ways have more in common than normally meets the eye.

Chapter 1 by Michael Hviid Jacobsen, Rasmus Antoft and Anja Jørgensen takes us back to the early formative years of sociology when the discipline was officially founded at the University of Chicago. The chapter revisits some of the pioneers and their predecessors of the so-called 'Chicago School of Sociology' in order to tease out the particular poetic and creative edge to the works of Robert E. Park, Everett C. Hughes, Erving Goffman and Howard S. Becker. The authors show how this poetic and creative edge mixes with a profound sociological imagination of these writers, and how such an unmistakable 'poetic imagination' is, for example, evident in their journalistic curiosity, essayistic predilection, rhetorical and textual techniques such as the narrative, storytelling, metaphors, irony and sarcasm as well as in plain writing styles and performance science.

Chapter 2 by Keith Tester begins from the premise that social thought is not an isolated activity. It takes place in a broader cultural context, and it is possible for bodies of work from outside of social theory to cast light on some of its themes. This chapter establishes a conversation between the social thought of Zygmunt Bauman, the literature of Milan Kundera and a painting by Francis Bacon. It is contended that bringing these three bodies of work together shows how they share a common concern to recover the alterity of human existence from intimations of necessity. The wider stake of the paper is the extent to which it can encourage thinking about the relationships between social thought and other modes of creative activity.

In Chapter 3, Michael S. Drake takes up Wolf Lepenies' challenge to recover our understanding of literature as sociology and to work our way back to a literary or poetic, sociology, through an analytical overview of novels by the global Portuguese author José Saramago. The novels analysed here all mobilize and play out sociologically-informed speculative scenarios, suggesting that fiction can provide the missing half of the sociological enterprise, the experimental dimension, from the micro-social level of the self to the macro-social dimension of the state and globalization. The stature of Saramago's contribution as experimental sociology is underlined by methodological reflections and an ongoing critical engagement with 'common sense' throughout his novels.

In Part II, Writing, we encounter perspectives on how the writing of social science, and perhaps particularly sociology but also criminology (see, for example, Jacobsen 2013), may indeed benefit from experimenting with a more literary style and rhetorical representational form. At the end of the day, science and literature, fact and fiction, both are textually and rhetorically framed endeavours aiming at tearing down the wall between perceived and imagined reality and providing the reader with visions not only of how the world is but also of how it could be. Obviously, science and fiction are not the same – their claims to (re)presenting reality are not identical. However, despite its continuous claims to value-neutral and 'objective' knowledge, reporting science is not a neutral endeavour and need not be phrased in a purely clinical or distanced manner (see, for example, Clifford and Marcus 1986; Gusfield 1976; Locke 1992). As the chapters in this section all show, writing social science can be made more inspirational, more moving, more poignant, more relevant and even more fun reading if inspired by the language and representational form of novelists and poets. Moreover, writing social science in creative ways may also result in the researcher being able to reach audiences outside the realm of science thereby making his/her research relevant to wider publics (Richardson 1990).

In Chapter 4 by Norman K. Denzin, a discussion of the reading and writing of the so-called 'new experimental text' testifies to the fact that social science, and in this case sociology, may be conducted in ways that are opposed to conventionalized standards for academic publishing. Based on the experience with and critique of a specific journal's guidelines for submitted articles, the author argues that a new literary interpretivist mode of writing social science is gradually replacing and indeed challenging the classic 'realist' text and that we need to recognize and welcome the fact that such a mode of representation that plays with narrative, poetry and creativity has important contributions to social science. Following this, the author presents a short one-scene play and based on this discusses tenure and the politics of publishing, including citation analyses. The chapter is concluded with a discussion of how to create a safe space for writing and publishing the new experimental text.

Chapter 5 by Zygmunt Bauman commences with Milan Kundera's assertion that it is the job of the true poet to uncover the otherwise hidden human possibilities by demolishing the walls behind which the unchangeable hides. Following this poetic notion, Bauman states that the sociologist 'ought to come as close as the true poets do to the yet hidden human possibilities. For that reason we need to pierce the walls of the obvious and self-evident'. Writing sociology, like writing poetry, is thus aimed at disclosing common-sense and ideology and in the process uncovering forgotten hopes, hidden promises or concealed possibilities. As Zygmunt Bauman shows in this chapter, it is precisely the 'calling' of sociology to separate fate from destiny, to show to men and women that what they see – and are taught to see – as inevitable is in fact amenable to alteration and can be subjected to acts of free choice. The job of writing sociology is to show to men and women that everything remains possible because, despite everything, fate can always be transcended. Sociology is always engaged writing – non-committal sociology is an utter impossibility.

In Chapter 6 by Laurel Richardson – who was a published poet before turning to sociology – the reader by way of a personal everyday life story is presented with a creative way of writing that lingers between poetry and social commentary. The story presented revolves around a personal experience with a computer breakdown that takes the author into a spiral of interactions with computer-competent family members, sales personnel at the local computer store and other customers. Although the story builds on an utterly personal experience and a selection of personal dialogues that to the naked eye perhaps appears devoid of sociological insight, it nevertheless – in content and representational form – presents a challenging sociologically relevant account about our society, technology, gender stereotypes, etc. The chapter thus shows how personal experience – wrapped in a poetic framework – may be reported in an unconventional representational form that reveals something interesting about contemporary society.

In Part III of the book, Exploring, contributors delve into discussions and exemplifications of how to comprehend and to analyse social as well as social philosophical issues through more literary or poetically inspired means and how there is an unmistakable affinity between the meaning-making of social science and that of more artistic endeavours. In a culture of convergence, like ours, it is only to be expected that various branches of social life, for example, science and art, start to communicate and borrow from each other. As Wolf Lepenies (1988) and Richard H. Brown (1977) many years ago have shown, historically as well as regard to content and methods the social sciences are closely related and indeed indebted to their colleagues working within the literary realm. Chapters illustrate how notions of rationality, truth and theory are not necessarily at odds with narrative, dramaturgy, metaphors, epiphanies and other poetically laden concepts. In fact, in order to explore and understand the social world more fully, social scientists may find valuable inspiration in more creative methodologies than those conventionally taught and recommended.

In Chapter 7 by Svend Brinkmann, focus is placed on how interpretation of meaning has been highly successful in establishing the qualitative corners of the social sciences on a firm hermeneutic footing. It has brought us the linguistic, discursive, literary, postmodern and other similar turns. In this chapter, however, Brinkmann questions the almost exclusive focus on meaning and interpretation in today's qualitative social science. By doing so, Brinkmann contrasts a meaning-centred approach with what he calls a presence-centred approach to qualitative social science, drawing in particular on Hans Ulrich Gumbrecht's recent work on presence. The presence-centred approach leads to a more poetic and lyrical idea of social science, which adds to more conventional narrative and interpretive ideas. Presence is a much more bodily and almost materialist concept than meaning, and in the chapter Brinkmann presents some ideas of how to analyse concretely the layer of presence in cultural phenomena.

Chapter 8, by Kieran Keohane, challenges the conventional differentiation between 'theory' and 'methods' by exploring the deep grammar of their usage in the ancient practice of going on pilgrimage to consult the Oracle at Delphi. This practice, which to a contemporary eye may seem to be anachronistic, esoteric, and irrational, turns out on closer examination to have a great deal in common with modern methods of theorizing. Max Weber, Émile Durkheim and indeed much of modern theorizing and philosophizing involves going on a journey, a *hodos*, solemnly undertaken by *theorai* and systematically pursued to a point where we stand in radical astonishment at the threshold between what we know already and what lies beyond our grasp, and glimpsing an idea that may transcend the gulf between them. Contemplating that epiphany, grasping and expressing a unifying idea glimpsed in a fleeting moment is what the method of theorizing is, and *poiesis,* the creative bringing to light, articulating and representing transcending ideas is the language of theory as a form of life. These themes are explored in a discussion of continuities and affinities from the Greeks, through sociology's classic texts by Durkheim and Weber, to the creative poetics of James Joyce.

In Chapter 9, Arpad Szakolczai locates the concern with imaginative methods in terms of Modernity's obsession with innovation. From the outset the social sciences have been permanently in need of new and innovative methods, desperately trying to discover the magic wand that would make their efforts truly scientific. But this search for new methods is symptomatic of a deeper problem of Enlightenment and modernity's reckless pursuit of innovativeness and creativity at any price, combined with ideologies of progress and the self-flattering belief that finally the time has come for truly scientific or innovative methods, triumphantly throwing into the wastebasket the wisdom of previous ages. As a result, just as in other areas of the modern world, conventional wisdom, the 'canon' or the 'tradition' has very little traditional or even wise about it, being rather the ossified, dogmatic remains of the 'revolutions' accomplished in the previous generations. The cumulative outcome of such revolutions, apart from a genuine increase in technical know-how, is rather a sad state of confusion concerning the basic aims of intellectual endeavour. Innovativeness is indeed needed today; but, while this must challenge and question assumptions of the past centuries, it should be combined with a return to and restoration of the genuine traditions of knowledge, going back to the Presocratics and especially Plato.

In Part IV, Teaching, the chapters all concentrate on how the poetic imagination is not merely a matter of reading, writing or exploring social issues creatively or, in other words, to conduct social research in a poetically inspired manner. Also teaching practice and the passing on of knowledge and inspiration to students within the social sciences may be stimulated and guided by a more imaginative approach than merely presenting dull theoretical stuff or statistical diagrams in the lecture theatre. There is a longstanding tradition dating almost half a century back for using fiction and even science-fiction as a creative source in teaching social issues (see, for example, Wohlfeil 1970), and in contemporary society with its abundance of visual images in films, television series and the internet, such sources may fruitfully be included in teaching social issues at introductory as well as advanced educational levels.

In Chapter 10 by Anders Petersen, Michael Hviid Jacobsen and Rasmus Antoft, the authors set out to demonstrate that communication of sociological knowledge to a broader audience than sociologists and academics per se can (and should) utilize and incorporate a broad variety of inspirational sources and pedagogical tools. Whether it be literature, films, music, performances, effects of therapeutic shock, etc., the claim of the chapter is that they help to create a pedagogical space through which researchers can enter into dialogue with their audience. When the arts and fiction mediate our sociological knowledge, theories, findings etc. that creates the communicative and interactional space that not only enables a proliferation of sociological research but also the creation of new insights. This entails, the authors state, that researchers must be more aware of their communicative tool-kit if they wish to interact more with a broader audience. In the chapter the authors call for a more 'poetic' approach to communicating sociological insights, something which they believe will enable a more dynamic, nuanced, precise communication but also a funnier and more interesting one.

Chapter 11 by Julie Seymour addresses issues in teaching social research methods, which can be seen by students as abstract and unrelated to the substantive topics of sociology. This chapter discusses ways in which popular culture (for example, cartoons, advertisements) as well as literature and music, provide sources for material which can be incorporated in such modules to enliven the delivery of methods training and methodology. Such material can not only be used to illustrate important points by way of example or counter-example, but also more importantly to lead participating students to greater theoretical and analytical understanding of the totality and interrelatedness of the research process.

In Chapter 12, Louise Sturgeon-Adams addresses some key pedagogical issues in teaching sociology. The chapter identifies the need to meet student expectations by moving beyond a 'transmission model' of teaching and learning which replaces student fascination and interest in human behaviour in social context with explanations pre-packaged as formulaic fixed ideas reduced to doctrinal precepts. Using as a case-study a criminology module about drugs in society, the chapter explains how reading Thomas De Quincey's *Confessions of an English Opium Eater* can reintroduce the human experiential dimension into the study of the 'drugs problem', in place of the reified subject of social science discourse, 'the individual' or 'the actor'.

In the final Chapter 13, Lisbeth B. Knudsen, from a personal perspective, addresses how she uses literature and films as illustrations or as images of societal conditions and changes and how these illustrations and images are valuable and sometimes necessary artefacts to use when teaching. She particularly does so in relation to her own research areas, covering topics such as the family, fertility, abortion and the use of birth control. What she emphasizes is the empirical connection that these illustrations and images must have in order for them to be useful tools when trying to explain and make societal phenomena understandable to students. In the chapter, the author also raises a voice of caution when using these tools, particularly if there is a discrepancy between the lectures and the students' perception of what the images or the illustrations actually show.

We hope this book and its chapters may stimulate and inspire the poetic imagination and the development of, experimentation with and not least utility of imaginative methodologies within the social sciences which allows for more pertinent, sometimes more precise and definitely more readable research. We began this introductory chapter by quoting American sociologist Peter L. Berger and his self-proclaimed 'humanistic perspective' on sociology, and we will conclude it with his appropriate observation on how the increasing maturity of the social science disciplines (perhaps particularly sociology) may result in a welcome openness towards diverse epistemological and methodological ways of capturing, exploring, writing and teaching about human life:

As the social sciences move from their enthusiastic puberty to a mellower maturity, a ... degree of detachment from one's own game may be expected and, indeed, can already be found. One can then understand sociology as one game among many, significant but hardly the last word about human life, and one can afford not only tolerance but even an interest in other people's epistemological entertainments. (Berger 1963: 187)

References

Andreski, S. (1972): *Social Science as Sorcery*. London: Penguin Books.
Antliff, M. and P. Leighten (2008): *A Cubism Reader: Documents and Criticism, 1906-1914*. Chicago, IL: University of Chicago Press.
Antoft, R., M. Hviid Jacobsen and L.B. Knudsen (eds) (2010): *Den poetiske fantasi – om forholdet mellem sociologi og fiktion*. Aalborg: Aalborg Universitetsforlag.
Arendt, H. (1972): "Introduction: Walter Benjamin 1892-1940", in *Illuminations*, edited by W. Benjamin. London: Fontana Press.
Barone, T. and E.W. Eisner (2012): *Arts Based Research*. Thousand Oaks, CA: Sage Publications.
Bateson, M.C. (1989): *Composing a Life*. London: Grove Press.
Baudrillard, J. (1994): *Simulacra and Simulation*. Detroit, MI: University of Michigan Press.
Berardi, F. (2012): *The Uprising: On Poetry and Finance*. Los Angeles: Semiotext(e).
Berger, P.L. (1963): *Invitation to Sociology: A Humanistic Perspective*. London: Penguin Books.
Berger, P.L. and T. Luckmann (1991): *The Social Construction of Reality: A Treatise in the Sociology of Knowledge*. London: Penguin Books.
Berman, M. (1988): *All that is Solid Melts into Air: The Experience of Modernity*. New York: Penguin Books.
Bohr, N. (2011): *Atomic Theory and the Description of Nature*. Cambridge: Cambridge University Press.
Boltanski, L. and E. Chiapello (2007): *The New Spirit of Capitalism*. London: Verso.
Brown, R.H. (1977): *A Poetic for Sociology*. Cambridge: Cambridge University Press.
Callinicos, A. (1990): *Against Postmodernism: A Marxist Critique*. Cambridge: Polity Press.
Cannatella, H. (2004): "Creativity in Teaching and Learning". *Journal of Aesthetic Education*, 38(4): 59-70.
Clifford, J. and G.E. Marcus (eds) (1986): *Writing Culture: The Poetics and Politics of Writing Ethnography*. Stanford, CA: University of California Press.
Durkheim, É. (1974): *Sociology and Philosophy*. New York: Free Press.

Durkheim, É. (2001): *The Elementary Forms of Religious Life*. Oxford: Oxford University Press.
Eisner, E.W. (1981): "On the Differences between Scientific and Artistic Approaches to Qualitative Research". *Educational Researcher*, 10(4): 5-9.
Feyerabend, P.K. (1975/2010): *Against Method: Outline of an Anarchistic Theory of Knowledge*. New York: Verso.
Florida, R. (2002): *The Rise of the Creative Class ... And How It's Transforming Work, Leisure, Community and Everyday Life*. New York: Basic Books.
Game, A. and A. Metcalfe (1996): *Passionate Sociology*. London: Sage Publications.
Greenspan, S. and S. Shanker (2006): *The First Idea: How Symbols, Language and Intelligence Evolved from our Primate Ancestors to Modern Humans*. Cambridge, MA: Da Capo Press.
Gusfield, J.A. (1976): "The Literary Rhetoric of Science: Comedy and Pathos in Drinking Driver Research". *American Sociological Review*, 41(1): 16-34.
Hegel, G.W.F. (1977): *The Phenomenology of Spirit*. Oxford: Oxford University Press.
Heidegger, M. (1989): "The Way Back into the Ground of Metaphysics", in *Existentialism from Dostoevsky to Sartre*, edited by W. Kaufmann. New York: Meridian.
Jacobsen, M. Hviid (ed.) (2013): *Poetics of Crime: Excursions in Cultural, Critical and Creative Criminology*. Farnham: Ashgate.
Jameson, F. (1984): "Postmodernism, or: The Cultural Logic of Late Capitalism". *New Left Review*, 1(146): 59-92.
Jay, M. (1973): *The Dialectical Imagination: A History of the Frankfurt School and the Institute of Social Research, 1923-1950*. Boston, MA: Little, Brown & Co.
Krieger, S. (1983): "Fiction and Social Science", in *The Mirror Dance: Identity in a Women's Community*, edited by S. Krieger. Philadelphia, PA: Temple University Press.
Lefebvre, H. (1961/2008): *Critique of Everyday Life* (Volume I-III). London: Verso.
Léger, F. (1973): *Functions of Painting*. London: Thames & Hudson.
Lepenies, W. (1988): *Between Literature and Science: The Rise of Sociology*. Cambridge: Cambridge University Press.
Locke, D. (1992): *Science as Writing*. New Haven: Yale University Press.
Massey, D. (1994): *Space, Place and Gender*. Cambridge: Polity Press.
Massey, D. (2005): *For Space*. London: Sage Publications.
Melucci, A. (1989): *Nomads of the Present: Social Movements and Individual Needs in Contemporary Society*. London: Hutchinson.
Miller, A., (2002): *Einstein, Picasso: Space, Time and the Beauty that Causes Havoc*. New York: Basic Books.
Mills, C.W. (1959): *The Sociological Imagination*. New York: Oxford University Press.

Nichols, B. (1976): "Introduction", in *Movies and Methods, Volume 1*, edited by B. Nichols. Berkeley, CA: University of California Press.

Nisbet, R. (1976/2002): *Sociology as an Art Form*. New Brunswick, NJ: Transaction Publishers.

Porterfield, A.L. (1941): *Creative Factors in Scientific Research*. Durham, NC: Duke University Press.

Raunig, G. (2007): *Art and Revolution: Transversal Activism in the Long Twentieth Century*. Los Angeles: Semiotext(e).

Raunig, Ge., G. Ray and U. Wuggenig (2011): *Critique of Creativity: Precarity, Subjectivity and Resistance in the 'Creative Industries'*. London: MayFlyBooks.

Ray, P.H. and S.R. Anderson (2000): *The Cultural Creatives: How 50 Million People are Changing the World*. London: Crown Publications.

Richardson, L. (1990): *Writing Strategies: Reaching Diverse Audiences*. Newbury Park, CA: Sage Publications.

Rockwell, J. (1974): *Fact in Fiction*. London: Routledge & Kegan Paul.

Roderick, I. et al. (2000): *Anti-Methods: Expressive Forms of Researching Culture*. Ottawa: Carleton University.

Schoepflin, T. (2013): *Sociology in Stories: A Creative Introduction to a Fascinating Perspective*. Dubuque: Kendall Hunt Publishing Company.

Simmel, G. (1964): "The Metropolis and Mental Life", in *The Sociology of Georg Simmel*, edited by K.H. Wolff. New York: Free Press.

Simmel, G. (1968): "Sociological Aesthetics", in *The Conflict in Modern Culture and other Essays*, edited by P.K. Etzkorn. New York: Teachers' College.

Snow, C.P. (1959/1993): *The Two Cultures*. Cambridge: Cambridge University Press.

Vaneigem, R. (1967/1983): The *Revolution of Everyday Life, or Knowing How to Live*. London: Rebel Press.

Weber, M. (1958): *The Protestant Ethic and the Spirit of Capitalism*. New York: Charles Scribner's Sons.

Wohlfeil, A.W. (1970): "Science-Fiction Stories in the Social Studies". *The Clearing House*, 44(5): 300-4.

PART I
Reading

Chapter 1

Chicago Vice and Virtue:
The Poetic Imagination Meets
the Sociological Imagination

Michael Hviid Jacobsen, Rasmus Antoft and Anja Jørgensen

We don't give a damn for logic around here. What we want to know is what people do!

Robert E. Park

Introduction: The Art of Sociology

There can be little doubt that one of the most influential currents in the early and formative years of sociology, as well as through most of the 20th century, has been the sociological tradition evolving at the University of Chicago in the late 1900s and early 20th century. The hallmark of this tradition, to be presented in more detail below, was its combination of a unique perspective on how to practice sociology and a unique style of communicating sociological knowledge. Over the years, the Chicago School of Sociology has been subject to many and varied interpretations and evaluations. However, it is a fact that the Chicago School strongly emphasized the importance of venturing out into the empirical reality to explore it there. And although most tend to associate the Chicago School with primarily qualitative methods like observations, interviews or analysis of diaries and letters (Kurtz 1984: 84ff), there was in fact a considerable interest in using quantitative data in the Chicago School as well (Platt 1995). Thus, the Chicago School was a positivistic-naturalistic science preoccupied with fieldwork and direct observation, as well as a creative, artistic and poetically inspired tradition, which, in addition to its emphasis on empirical fieldwork, argued in favour of as well as practiced a more literary approach to sociology. Martin Bulmer said about this inherent duality:

> [All the Chicago sociologists were] in some ways empiricists, keen upon the use of hypotheses and experimental verification ... Axioms, postulates, rational deductions, ideas and ideals are all deemed valuable when they can be made to function in actual experience, in the course of which they meet with constant modification and improvement ... All display the attitude of enquirers rather than of expositors of absolute knowledge; their most confident affirmations are

expressed in a tone that shows that they do not regard them as final. (quoted in Bulmer 1984: 32)

Another characteristic of the Chicago School was, and still is, its emphasis on understanding and writing – and especially communicating – sociology in a way that unites communicative and analytical aspects in a unique stylistic, aesthetic and poetic text format, not merely as superficial embellishment of the text, but actually being a 'hybridization' of sociological and literary imagination (Toscano 2008: 201). Referring specifically to the Chicago School sociologist Harvey Warren Zorbaugh's book *The Gold Coast and the Slum*, Andrew Abbott remarked on the effect such a work may have on the reader:

> He [Zorbaugh] rather looks at a social situation, feels its overpowering excitement and its deeply affecting human complexity, and then writes a book trying to awaken those feelings in the minds – and even more the hearts – of his readers. This recreation of an experience of social discovery is what I shall here call *lyrical sociology*. (Abbott 2007: 70)

This description – and the term 'lyrical sociology' – more or less sums up the hallmark of so many of the other Chicago School sociologists, explaining their unparalleled ability to portray and communicate human conditions in such a way that their readers feel and truly comprehend the research findings presented. That this was in fact an ability characteristic of the Chicago School of Sociology was also the conclusion that Carla Cappetti arrived at in her book *Writing Chicago* (1993), in which she describes the origins of the Chicago School of Sociology with particular emphasis on the various 'extra-scientific' sources of inspiration that many of the early Chicago School sociologists relied on and were influenced by. In fact, much of early sociology was inspired by literature and journalism, and this is particularly true of many of the Chicago School sociologists (Strong 1988/2006: 119ff).

Obviously, sociology did not begin with the Chicago School of Sociology, even though the School is often regarded as the launch-pad of institutionalized sociology. At least half a century before the foundation of the department of Sociology at the University of Chicago in 1892 – that is, in the early and mid-1800s – sociology was already beginning to establish itself as an academic discipline in Europe. But the seeds of sociology can be traced even further back. One of the characteristics of very early sociological reasoning was that, contrary to what later turned into sociology, it had no qualms about manifesting its scientific status by relying on a wide variety of inspirational sources (White 1975). Karl Marx, for instance, often turned to Honoré de Balzac, Émile Zola, Bernard Mandeville, Charles Dickens and other great contemporary writers for inspiration. Also Émile Durkheim used literary sources as inspiration in his studies of suicide; Georg Simmel's writing style was clearly inspired by contemporary essayists, and Max Weber was well versed in the literary works of his day and drew inspiration for his ideal types from the way novelists were able to capture their fictional universes. In his book *Between Literature and Science*, Wolf Lepenies (1988) analyses the budding sociology as a hybrid between science and literature, describing the delicate balancing act that the emerging scientific discipline sociology had to perform:

> From the moment of its inception sociology became both a competitor and a counterpart of literature. On the one hand, when sociology desired to be sociography it came into conflict above all with the realistic novel over the claim to offer an adequate reproduction of the 'prose of everyday circumstances'; when, on the other, it claimed to be social theory it incurred the suspicion of degenerating into a 'closet' science. (Lepenies 1988: 12-13)

Robert E. Park, one of the most central figures of the Chicago School, whom we will return to later in the chapter, commented on the debt owed by many of the early Chicago School sociologists to literary writers: 'We were particularly indebted to the novelists for our intimate knowledge of contemporary urban life; but understanding urban life requires a far more distanced and investigative attitude than what Émile Zola has to offer in his 'experimental' novels' (Park 1915/1974: 3). Park also said it was reading Goethe's Faust that inspired him to study sociology, and later in life he developed a keen interest in the works of Walt Whitman. So, in a way literature and early sociology were Siamese twins as well competitors – a source of initial inspiration, and a distant relative, but not immediate family.

Just as many have sought to trace and map sociology's literary beginnings (Irving 1983; Lepenies 1988; Nisbet 1976/2002), over the years others have pointed out that social science and journalism are two disciplines whose paths have often crossed and enriched each other (Lindner 1996; Marx 1972; Schudson 2003; Svith 2006; Zelizer 2004). Some of the best sociologists display a decidedly journalistic flair in their style of communicating, while some of the best journalists base their work on sociological concepts and methodology. Just think of Günther Wallraff, the archetypical investigative journalist; his approach basically involves using conventional sociological methods to explore conventional sociological themes. Park, who had a background in journalism, used to recommend his sociology students to use their senses and 'write down only what you see, hear and know, like a newspaper reporter' (Park in Cappetti 1993: 24).

In this chapter we will demonstrate how the poetic imagination stemming from the Chicago School's reliance on literature and journalism for inspiration can be traced across several generations of Chicago sociologists, and how the intersecting circles of sociology, journalism and literature have resulted in the unique way in which Chicago sociology is practiced and communicated, which justifies its lasting impact on and relevance to contemporary sociology.

The 'Chicago School' and Chicago Poetics

Before presenting a number of specific examples of the poetic sense of the Chicago School of sociology, we would like to give a brief outline of the origins of the Chicago School, the persons behind it and what it stood for. Starting with the term itself, the 'Chicago School', it needs to be pointed out that the term is often used as an umbrella for a number of social scientists who, linked through their association with the University of Chicago, produced a wide range of empirically-based urban studies of Chicago and its inhabitants during the period of its urban expansion from the 1890s up through the first half of the 20th century. It was in Chicago that Albion W. Small (1854-1926) in 1892 opened the world's first department of sociology, and it was here that the sociologists carried out their studies on social conditions in the following decades. The 'Chicago School of Sociology' is sometimes referred to as the 'School of Human Ecology' because it aimed to study and understand people in relation to and as conditioned by their physical surroundings; also, several of the Chicago sociologists were interested in evolutionary thinking. Some of the most important members of the Chicago School tradition include Louis Wirth (1854-1926), William I. Thomas (1863-1947), Robert E. Park (1864-1944), Ernest W. Burgess (1886-1966), Florian Znaniecki (1892-1958) and Everett C. Hughes (1897-1983). In addition, George Herbert Mead (1863-1931), Erving Goffman (1922-1982) and later Howard S. Becker (b. 1928) must be included as some of the outstanding sociologists who found inspiration in and later contributed substantially to the development of the Chicago School (Andersson 2003; Bulmer 1984; Harvey 1987; Tomasi 1998).

The starting point for most of the sociology practised at Chicago School was a perception that sociological knowledge should make a difference and have practical consequences. Many of the early sociologists were inspired by pragmatic philosophy, just as many of them were deeply involved in voluntary social work. The most important works from the early Chicago School include *The Polish Peasant in Europe and America* (1918-1920) by Thomas and Znaniecki, and *The City* (1925) by Park and Burgess. Chicago sociologists also conducted research into alcoholism, gambling, homelessness, suicide, homicide, leisure, poverty and immigration into the big city – generally speaking, they were mainly interested in exploring deviancy and differentness. After the Second World War, a 'Second Chicago School' of researchers emerged, who, from a starting point primarily in symbolic interactionism, continued and further developed the Chicago School perspective in sociology. In general, the Chicago School is characterized by having a distinct qualitative and ethnographic orientation, focusing on studying people in their natural surroundings (the city), being critical of non-empirical research and theory, and being driven by a desire to uncover and understand patterns of human interaction. There are different strands within the Chicago School: the human ecology strand, the (dis)organization strand, the social psychology strand, and the action research strand used especially within social work (Jørgensen 2005). Thus, it would seem relevant to ask whether the Chicago School was, in fact, one school, since the scope of the work that the Chicago sociologists were involved in seems to indicate a high degree of internal heterogeneity, despite some overlap and shared platforms. According to Howard S. Becker (2003), the Chicago School should not be seen as an institutionalized school, but rather as an 'activity group' sharing a specific mind-set and certain research interests. This is also how we understand the Chicago School in this chapter: a shared mind-set spanning several generations of sociologists associated for a shorter or longer period with the University of Chicago, and not as a firmly rooted paradigm.

One of the characteristics of the work of the Chicago School sociologists was their methodological openness towards a diversity of documentary material: letters, diaries, newspaper articles, various statistical materials and transcripts from courtrooms, associations and organizations, as well as autobiographies, literary and other types of fiction and poetry (Cappetti 1993: 22-3). The Chicago School sociologists let themselves be inspired by journalism, literature and literary criticism, treating these sources as supplements to their sociological knowledge. As Carla Cappetti noted: 'Beneath their [the Chicago sociologists'] scholarly practice lay the perception that sociological life history and literary autobiography, sociology and literature, belong on the same continuum rather than separate spheres' (Cappetti 1993: 31). As the opening quotation of this chapter by Robert E. Park reveals, the main purpose of the Chicago School was not to develop a highly abstract logic about social life but rather to assist in understanding what people actually do.

In short, the Chicago School sociologists were interested in anything that might give them an insight into human life, without religiously swearing by the dogmatic rules on legitimate source material. Another characteristic of these sociologists was fact that they often looked outside their own discipline to find inspiration for their analyses. To give a few examples: Thomas was originally a teacher of classical and modern languages, Park worked as a journalist, Robert Redfield had poetic aspirations and wrote novels, Becker cultivated his jazz career alongside sociology, Herbert Blumer used to be a professional American football player, while Goffman originally worked in the Canadian film industry. All in all, this should give an idea of the multifaceted creativity and variety of inspiration from all walks of life that these sociologists brought with them into their research into sociology. Moreover, there was an open-minded tradition for and fascination among many of these sociologists to mingle and socialize with a variety of literary Chicago writers during the first half of the 20th century – for example, the story goes that when Park met with the Chicago-based African-American and Communist novelist Richard Wright (who became famous for his detailed depiction of racial issues), he muttered: 'I want to shake hands with a great writer. I don't agree with much that you write but it's honest and great writing' (Park in Bone 1986: 446). In fact, the Chicago sociologists – and most notably Park, see below – had a strong aversion to abstract intellectualism and academic thinking detached from concrete social conditions, dissociating themselves from deductive logical and philosophical claims. As Fred H. Matthews said, Park's work was permeated by his abhorrence for 'the pretentious ... the self-conscious intellectuals and social climbers who deliberately separated themselves from the majority' (Matthews 1977: 17). Like most of the Chicago School sociologists, Park sympathized with and was interested in ordinary men and women. In general, from the earliest representatives via Hughes and up to and including Goffman and Becker, the Chicago School has been imbued with a profound humanism, understood as a broad humanistic understanding of applicable methods, a desire to describe and communicate with ordinary people as well as an ambition to contribute towards solving the concrete societal problems experienced by real human beings. As Ken Plummer stated about what he perceived to be a particular 'Chicago Vision':

> The approach of the Chicagoans shunned analytic abstractions, deductive logic, philosophical dualisms or truths ripped from their very contexts: in place of the philosophical games which philosophers play (and which may or may not be true, we have no way of telling) the Chicagoans substituted a concern with concrete experience embedded in problem-solving. (Plummer 1983: 53)

However, this deliberate distancing from abstract or academic science and deductive logic that a number of the Chicago School sociologists enjoyed cultivating through their impressionistic and poetic creativity, positioning themselves in opposition to the positivist line of thinking predominant in the first half of the 20th century, also attracted criticism. As Stanislav Andreski stated in his *Sociology as Sorcery* about the relationship between on the one hand methodology fetishism and worship of rigid scientific standards, and on the other more impressionistic methods of analysis and communication: 'The worshippers of methodology turn like a vicious hunting pack upon anybody branded impressionistic, particularly if he writes well and can make his books interesting' (Andreski 1972: 117). As can be seen from this quote, there has been a tendency to question the scientific standard of any publication that manages to reach beyond narrow academic circles and attract the attention of a wider audience. In this chapter, we will argue that it takes courage to think and practice sociology in alternative ways, and that those who do so should be applauded and encouraged rather than besmirched and criticized.

In the following, we will introduce a number of examples from the historic development of the Chicago School, its leading characters, and the special way of thinking, understanding, practicing and communicating sociology that has come to be associated with the Chicago School of sociology. Although there is no direct continuity between all of the sociologists chosen, they have one thing in common: a willingness and ambition to engage in and practise sociology in a way that was markedly different and in opposition to mainstream science at the time.

Robert E. Park's 'Super Journalism'

Robert Ezra Park (1864-1944) was one of the most prominent sociologists at the Department of Sociology at the University of Chicago from 1914–1936. He was a strong advocate of communicating the findings of sociological studies in a way that ensured that they reached and were read by the general public. According to Park, this implied that sociologists must deliberately strive to write in a straightforward and readable manner, just as they should use journalistic methods when collecting their data. While traditional journalists should describe and analyse specific phenomena and events, it was Park's belief that sociologists should use their superior analytical training and skills to carry out in-depth analyses, put things into perspective and the proper context, and in some cases also even predictions. As he put it: '[The sociologist] must be a kind of super journalist, like those who write for *Fortune Magazine*. However, he must report his findings a little more accurately with slightly more distance than the average news reporter' (Park 1950: viii). According to Park, sociological studies should help inform the public about society, and preferably in such a way that it read like a good story. Even though Park himself did not make any great contributions when it came to realizing these goals, he is often pointed out as the main reason why so many of his students later succeeded in doing so (Lindner 1996: 82). In addition to this journalistic perspective on communication, Park was strongly inspired by the literary way of observing, understanding and describing things. As has been noted: 'In his studies of urban life, Park was driven not only by the obsessive curiosity of the metropolitan reporter, but also by the romantic sensitivity gradually emerging among poets and novelists after a century of observing the sprawling industrial metropolises with fascinated horror' (Matthews 1979: 121). It was these two currents – journalism and literature – that eventually merged to become Park's brand of sociology.

Society as Communication

To Park, the concept of 'communication' was the very key to understanding what society is: how it is established, how it is maintained, and how it is passed on. The very fact that people communicate and interact is the foundation on which society comes into existence. When people communicate, they acknowledge each other's existence, interests and goals, and they start to overcome distances – both geographic and in the social sense. What precedes society, says Park, is an unreflective community, an 'ecological community', characterized by individuals living in an unconscious but fundamentally competitive situation which forms the basis of, or is an important aspect of society. At this stage, there is no conscious and reflective communication; only the kind of communication that is driven by instincts. When society – that is, conscious and reflective communication – is added on top of community, the ecological level does not disappear; rather, it is overshadowed by other, more conscious ways of interacting. Park says about the relationship between community and society:

> Now, it is an indubitable fact that societies do have this double aspect. They are composed of individuals who act independently of one another, who compete

and struggle with one another for mere existence, and treat one another, as far as possible, as utilities. On the other hand, it is quite as true that men and women are bound together by affections and common purposes; they do cherish traditions, ambitions, and ideals that are not all their own, and they maintain, in spite of natural impulses to the contrary, a discipline and a moral order that enables them to transcend what we ordinarily call nature and, through their collective action, recreate the world in the image of their collective aspirations and their common will. (Park 1952: 180)

According to Park, the way in which people communicate in society, that is, reciprocally and consciously, evolves through different phases, assuming different forms: an economic phase marked by conflict, a political phase marked by adaptation, and a moral phase characterized by assimilation. Human geographers study the basic competition characteristic of the ecological community whereas economists are concerned with the way in which money mediates conflicts between people. Political scientists focus on how political institutions and laws contribute towards making people adapt to society; and finally sociologists and social anthropologists explore the forms of communication or interaction taking place in the moral phase; that is, when people interact in situations not based on politically determined rules and regulations or the economic laws of supply and demand. So, it is communication based on norms and values that constitutes the field of sociology.

When Park chooses to make communication the pivotal element of his description of society, it has to do with the fact that Park perceived society to be an essentially organic process in which the dynamics are driven by communication and interaction. Park distanced himself from perceptions of society as an established structure, arguing instead that society progresses through the above four phases (which, according to Park, can also be traced geographically). This means that in principle it is always possible to influence and change society, depending on the courses that communication and interaction are taking. Communication can take place more or less freely and unrestrainedly. From time to time, social and ecological structures and conditions may change so drastically that the communication and interaction processes are disturbed – for example, the impact of war, outbreak of serious diseases and other types of crises may disturb the so-called biotic or natural equilibrium. Introducing his concepts of invasion, succession and dominance, Park offered some tools for understanding the structural barriers and conditions for communication in society (Park 1952: 229). It follows as a logical consequence of the perception of society as a dynamic process rather than a rigid structure that it becomes highly relevant to look into how researchers can either directly or indirectly influence and/or change society. If society can indeed be influenced and changed, then it obviously becomes a matter of immense interest to place oneself in a position to communicate the knowledge one acquires in such a way that it optimizes the chances of influencing society. For Park, it was essential as well as natural that sociology should be in close dialogue with society;

but the proximity that Park strived for was of a kind that needed to be practiced in a specific way.

Merging Sociology and Journalism

Park believed that sociologists should on the one hand be engaged in and preoccupied with society, but on the other stay clear of normative and moral judgments in their sociological analyses. Park thought that moral and normative judgments could block interesting observations and detection of important phenomena. At the same time, Park was adamant that sociologists had to make observations and collect empirical evidence as closely to the relevant people and events as at all possible. Park distinguished between the terms 'acquaintance with' and 'knowledge about' (Park 1955: 5f). Whereas the former represents an approach in which the researcher allies himself with the objects to be explored, even in some cases having a specific political agenda for his research (action research), the latter reflects a more 'disinterested' observer of social phenomena in society – still managing, however, to be involved and engaged in the specific field. Park had worked as a journalist from time to time before taking up his position at the University of Chicago, and he was very interested in *New Journalism*, a new wave of journalism that changed and reformed journalism in the 1800s away from focusing mainly on the ordinary and general developments to a stronger focus on the unusual and surprising, and on extraordinary, atypical, infrequent events. *New Journalism* wanted to turn journalism into something other than a party-political pulpit from which the editor could preach his political gospel to his readers. *New Journalism* also implied a movement towards telling the story behind the story and putting a specific face to a general story. The overall intention was showing how little people are involved and affected by big stories, for example, famine, war, immigration; the point being that behind all great events there are people affected by them. And that it is this connectedness that is important, both for the individual and for the further course of events. As this interaction is so important, it needs to be told. *New Journalism* dramatically changed what was considered newsworthy, and it became increasingly common to find stories focusing on the unprecedented and unknown (Lindner 1996). Park was heavily inspired by *New Journalism* in his work as a journalist, and he carried this line of thinking and ideas with him in his work as a sociologist at the University of Chicago – both the idea of focusing on exceptions, the unusual and the unknown, and the idea of 'seeing the big story in the small' by putting concrete faces to stories of overall changes and phenomena in society. A catchphrase often associated with Park's perspective is the 'city as a social laboratory' (Park 1929). Park argued that it was possible to look at the modern city as a laboratory for studying social life and social relationships in a modern context, and he called for a sociology aiming to tell the many stories waiting to be told about social relations in the modern metropolis, and doing it in a way that provided insight into the new life forms and life situations occurring in the big city. The city offers new opportunities for individual development but also new kinds of social problems. As mentioned before, Park was a strong advocate of fieldwork as a methodological tool to achieve the necessary proximity to and insight into the many new phenomena and problems that living in a city involved:

> Go and sit in the lounges of the luxury hotels and on the doorsteps of the flophouses; sit on the Gold Coast setters and on the slum shake-downs; sit in Orchestra Hall and in the Star and Garter Burlesk. In short, gentlemen, go get the seat of your pants dirty in *real* research. (Lindner 1996: 82)

These strong words of advice were given by Park to his students in a lecture, and duly written down by Howard S. Becker. Here Park not only calls for sociological fieldwork, he also expresses a sharp criticism of distanced 'library-oriented' or 'armchair' sociology focusing more on methodological procedures, rules and techniques than on what he called 'the art of seeing' and the 'ability to sense that something new is happening'.

Communication as Storytelling/Narrative

To Park, communication of the findings of sociological studies was closely linked to considerations of how to tell a good, and preferably sellable, story. Park considered it a badge of honour if a sociological study was reported as an exciting story – and if the story could be sold, and thus told, to the general public, then all the better. This was not because Park was concerned about the earning potential of sociologists, but because – in line with his pragmatic approach to knowledge – he believed that the knowledge produced by sociologists through their research ought to reach the general public and as far as at all possible be put to practical use. To achieve this end – making certain that findings were read and understood by a wider audience – sociologists needed to be aware of the fundamental difference between descriptive and connotative or informative and expressive or poetic language: 'The distinction between language and communication forms that are descriptive, as in scientific descriptions, and language and communication forms that are symbolic and expressive, as found in literature and art' (Park 1950: 52). Park saw both functions of language as important tools to create, maintain and transform social relations as well as broader cultural processes. According to Park, science and journalism typically contribute with new knowledge and have a specific aim, whereas literature and art are designed to influence attitudes, feelings and opinions, but they do not usually contribute to any real increase in existing knowledge.

This brings Park in line with Charles K. Ogden and Ivor A. Richard's (1923/1949) classic distinction between 'symbolic language' and 'expressive language'. Whereas symbolic language is impersonal, as for example, in mathematics, expressive language is personal, and marked by factors like intonation, accent, etc. (Park 1950: 38). The reason why Park emphasizes the importance of this distinction lies in his somewhat contradictory idea of how sociology should be conducted in practice. On the one hand, Park subscribes to the very traditional scientific concept of the aloof but curious scientist exploring the world around him on a neutral basis. On the other hand, Park is controversial and almost rebellious in his dissociation of himself from the almost religious focus of the traditional scientific community on procedures, techniques and methodology. Park believes that this focus tends to stand in the way of gaining new knowledge and insights into the complexity of modern society, just as it prevents the scientific community's new knowledge from reaching the surrounding society. For Park it was therefore important to keep in mind at all times that generation and communication of new knowledge should be the central element of a sociologist's work, emphasizing that sociology is not a science merely interested in influencing people's feelings, perceptions and interpretations without offering actual new knowledge – because, Park said, that is what we have literature for!

Everett C. Hughes's Essayism

In a historical perspective, it is one of Park's students, Everett C. Hughes (1897-1983), who came to play the unique role in American sociology of acting as the bridge-builder between the founders of the Chicago School of Sociology and what later came to be known as 'The Second Chicago School' (Fine 1995). His influence and importance for sociology is the result of a combination of his rather provocative yet understated teaching, and his unique subtle yet penetrating essays. However, his essays constitute only a part of the writings for which he is renowned; Hughes also wrote numerous monographs, alone or with others, which have become almost classics, including his own *Frenchtown Canada in Transition* (1943), *Men and Their Work* (1958), and *Boys in White: Student Culture in Medical School* written together with Howard S. Becker, Blanche Geer and Anselm L. Strauss (1961). Both when teaching and in his essays, Hughes demonstrated a special talent for identifying similarities between patterns of social phenomena that at first glance seem very different – *mistakes at work, routinized emergency, bastard institution* and *dilemmas and contradiction of status* – as well as for inventing and constructing sociological concepts that are capable of shedding new light on everyday actions and events, precisely by seeing them as examples of more general phenomena.

Hughes was a student of Park, writing his dissertation under Park's guidance and influence. Although Hughes could be characterized as one of the students who went on to create his own intellectual products, there can be no doubt that he was strongly inspired by the themes Park was interested in, as well as his way of thinking and communicating sociology (Coser 1994). However, unlike Park, Hughes was first and foremost a brilliant essayist, who developed a special style that managed to capture and present social phenomena and sociological issues in an interesting and creative way.

Between Simmel and Park

When trying to capture Hughes's style, it needs to be underlined that there is no such thing as a Hughesian social theory in the vein of Weberian, Marxian or Parsonian social theory. Yet, Hughes's thinking is quite distinctive. It is a way of thinking and working akin to the sociologist he probably admired most after Park, that is, Georg Simmel. Hughes and Simmel are often described as unsystematic, or impressionistic, sociologists – although more recent sociologists have convincingly demonstrated that Simmel's work does indeed contain a good deal of systematic theory construction, and that a group of Hughes's dedicated students are arguing that the same goes for his work (Coser 1996).

The Spanish philosopher José Ortega y Gasset very aptly compares Simmel to a squirrel: jumping from one nut to the next, performing spectacular exercises when leaping from one branch to another, beaming with joy, it seems, when gracefully performing these acrobatic leaps (Gasset 1949). This poetic comparison describes qualities that should not only be attributed to Simmel, as they are evident in Hughes's work as well. Hughes did not develop his ideas through a linear progression of thought. His style and approach involved moving from a first observation on to a second – with the second observation often merely hinted or indicated in the initial observation without necessarily having a direct logical connection. Hughes himself characterized his style as a kind of 'free association'. He stated as follows:

> In my own work I have relied a great deal on free association, sometimes on a freedom of association that could seem outrageous to the defenders of some established interest or cherished sentiment. Wright Mills must be given credit for the phrase *the sociological* imagination. The essence of the sociological imagination is free association, guided but not hampered by a frame of reference internalized not quite into the unconscious. It must work even in one's dreams but be where it can be called up at will. (Hughes 1993a: xvi)

Hughes's fondness of the essay as his media for disseminating his research should, in our opinion, above all be seen as a product of his restless, never-ceasing interest in social life: so many things to observe about the human comedy unfolding, so many generalizations to be made, and such a great need for sociology to create order in the seemingly disorderly aspects of social reality. With the myriad of impressions inevitably and inescapably available once you start observing social life, exploring and reporting the details of just a few social phenomena seemed far too narrow and restrictive for Hughes (Coser 1994: 13).

Almost all of Hughes's essays are written in the same style: A writing style that often confuses the reader; first of all because it ignores traditional editorial conventions, and secondly because it apparently sidesteps the empirical research foundation otherwise characteristic of the sociological tradition he came from. This is not, however, merely a case of stylistic eccentricity: Hughes's writing style simply reflects his work approach and ideas on how best to communicate sociology. In order to better understand his writing style, the first thing to bear in mind is that many of the essays he wrote during his professional career were intended to be presented in a specific context: for example, as a speech given to a scientific society, a preface to a book or a special issue of a magazine or journal, or as lectures and talks. The interesting thing is that Hughes did not afterwards edit such manuscripts into proper articles. Quite the contrary, he made no effort to hide the original purpose of the essay in the final version. So, among the analyses and overall themes of his writings, we find remarks and comments on the methodology and field of sociology, observations on general scientific problems, personal anecdotes, references to the work of students and colleagues as well as current political and social events. In his article "Of Sociology and the Interview", originally published in 1956, Hughes (1993b) describes how sociology has come to be the science of and for the interview. On the one hand, he says that the interview has become the favourite digging tool of sociologists; on the other that the interview constitutes the frame of a key sociological theme: interaction. To illustrate this discussion, he includes an example from the media, describing how Margaret Truman was 'hired' by the TV host Ed Murrows to interview her parents – her father being President Harry S. Truman – in their own home for the TV show *Person to Person*. The point of using this example was that the interview is an apt illustration of the multiple role-plays unfolding in interaction: in the interview Margaret Truman plays the role of a professional interviewer as well as that of a daughter.

Free Association and Anecdotal Sociology

It is possible that the above description of the particular way of writing and conducting sociological research practiced by Hughes has left the reader with the impression that his essays spring from a few specific cases, and that his essayistic style is simply a trick employed to maintain the attention of his audience. But that is not the case. The elements mentioned should be seen as stylistic devices serving a specific purpose, used very deliberately, and to some extent explainable by his methods. Hughes's essays are often thematically constructed. As mentioned, his analysis develops through a kind of free association on an idea, pursuing a particular thread to its logical end. Once the thread ends – and the line of argumentation is exhausted – he takes up another thread, or issue, not necessarily logically connected with the preceding.

Hughes's stylistic approach is in stark contrast to that of other sociologists of his generation and the way they communicated their research findings and reflections on theories. Unlike many other social scientists, Hughes does not subscribe to the rhetoric of the natural sciences. Neither did he attempt to create his own terminology, as for example, Talcott Parsons did. Hughes's efforts point in a different direction: he wishes to demonstrate how to implement the basic principles of his way of conducting sociology research, and how to introduce ideas whose content is clear and precise yet originates in 'everyday' language instead of speculative *a priori* constructs (Chapoulie 1996: 26).

To sum up, Hughes's style could be said to combine two elements. In his essays, he connects the rather stringent development of his ideas with 'everyday' language, often based on fairly imprecise empirical references. However, this should not be seen as lack of consistency in his way of working, rather as a way of making sure that analyses are not exhausted too early or in order not to overlook or forget interesting aspects of social reality. An essential element of Hughes's style is his use of personal anecdotes to illustrate analytical points. Life in academia as well as the work of a village priest – two realities that he had a profound knowledge of – often formed the basis for his presentation of the analytical points of his stories. Through his father's work as a Methodist priest in various villages in the state of Ohio – and not least through his father's diaries – Hughes had developed a deep knowledge of the life of a priest in 'small town' America. The anecdotes are often used as a method of scientific communication. However, it is especially his stories about life in academia that are central in his essays, as many of Hughes's experiences can be seen as evidence of the common experiences of research communities. His use of personal anecdotes to illustrate abstract analysis also serves an educational purpose. For example, Hughes points out that beginners in the art of field study often have trouble connecting their observations to abstract sociological categories. By using simple and often personal examples in his own essays, Hughes demonstrates how the categories and concepts constructed by him work in practice, thus illustrating how his representation expresses his conceptualization, and thereby his version of sociology.

Hughes's distinctive style was not only characteristic of his written work. Two of his students, David Riesman and Howard S. Becker, have said that his lectures often perplexed even the most gifted of his students. Hughes's non-conformist ideas produced a stark contrast between the ideas resulting from his free association and his respectable and gentlemanly looks and manners, and this seems to have been characteristic of Hughes lecturing (Reisman and Becker 1993). So his use of intuitive, analogous connections and arguments, often based on rather unconventional metaphors, both shocked and inspired. However, his unconventional ideas were never provocative for the sake of provoking, or downright cynical. They always served a sociological purpose: producing new ways of reflecting on sociological problems or uncovering new dimensions of social phenomena. To give an example: Hughes pointed out that there are quite a few similarities between priests and prostitutes. This comparison was not intended to shock; Hughes merely wanted to illustrate the sociological point that people working in service trades learned, and had to learn, how to conceal confidential information about as well as from their clients. By using this comparison of extremes, Hughes managed, in an exemplary manner, to shed new light on Simmel's discussion about the importance of secrecy, confidentiality and information in social life.

Erving Goffman – A Poetics of Common Sense

The Canadian-American sociologist Erving Goffman (1922-1982) was a product of as well as a key contributor to the way of thinking characteristic of the Chicago School during the first decades of the 20th century (Wax 1990). Some of Goffman's main sources of inspiration – particularly his understanding of social interaction as a ritual ceremony – were Bertram W. Doyle, Park and Hughes (Jaworski 2000). Goffman's field of research was clearly inspired by the early Chicago School sociologists, which is why he is often described as one of the representatives of the 'second generation' of the Chicago School. Goffman based his studies directly on the focus areas established by the early sociologists, for example, Park and Hughes, including patterns of human interaction. However, he certainly also made his own important contributions to the area, for example, his unique perspective and development of conceptual frames.

Although strictly speaking Goffman cannot be characterized as a member of the Chicago School – he himself consistently refused to accept any theoretical label or affiliation to any paradigm – there can be no doubt that his work was heavily influenced by the sociological spirit of the Chicago School which dominated sociology for decades. To a large extent, Goffman owes his involvement in sociology to Hughes, who persuaded him to write his PhD thesis *Communication Conduct in an Island Community* at the University of Chicago. The dissertation was based on prolonged and intensely involved field studies on Unst, one of the Shetland Islands, where Goffman meticulously observed and reported the islanders' everyday life and routines (Goffman 1953). The first outline of what would later evolve into Goffman's renowned dramaturgical metaphor for studying social life (Goffman 1959) is already evident here. Actually, there is an almost unbroken line from Goffman's PhD to his very last writing three decades later "The Interaction Order", the manuscript for the speech he was supposed to give as President of the American Sociological Association but never did, due his advanced cancer (Goffman 1983). What the dissertation and the manuscript have in common, and for that matter the many books and articles published in between, is Goffman's preoccupation with the painstaking recording of all the seemingly insignificant and trivial interactions between people in their everyday lives.

Goffman is probably one of the most widely read sociologists of the 20th century. For a number of reasons: firstly, because he 'invented' the so-called 'interaction ritual', dealing as he did in his many books with topics that few others before him had taken seriously or explored in detail in sociology. Secondly, because he developed a comprehensive arsenal of precise and colourful concepts and useful typologies in order to describe and understand the actions and events unfolding in this interaction ritual. And thirdly, and in this context probably the most interesting, because he managed to communicate his research in a style full of empathy yet linguistically and rhetorically succinct and analytically easily accessible. When describing why Goffman's contribution to sociology is so highly original and thought-provoking, Thomas J. Scheff pointed out the following three characteristics of his work:

1. Goffman was a superb observer of the micro-social world and invented a variety of conceptual tools to capture it.
2. Goffman described not only human thought and action, but also feelings, and in doing so he often managed to appeal to the reader's feelings as well.
3. Goffman spearheaded an attack on ingrained notions and challenged a number of well-established myths, for example, in relation to self, deviation, gender, language, etc. (Scheff 2006: 15-16).

This challenge to entrenched ideas in social science research as well as popular common sense notions manifested itself both in the substance of Goffman's field of research – mainly studies of normality and deviation – but also in his way of communicating the findings of his research. As already mentioned, throughout his career human interaction in face-to-face contexts remained the focus of Goffman's research. All the same, his work never resulted in a coherent or comprehensive theory on interaction, rather in a string of concise concepts and understandings that not just described and illustrated the little strategies and habits people use in their everyday dealings with each other, but also managed to capture some fundamental characteristics of being a human being in the world. When Goffman died, Eliot Friedson said about the lasting legacy of Goffman's work, 'Goffman's work lives on and will live on, not as a contribution to the development of systematic sociological theory, but rather as a contribution to human consciousness' (Friedson 1983: 361). But why did Goffman not contribute by developing a systematic and formalized sociological theory? Probably because the way Goffman wrote about and studied human interaction was characterized by a distinctive and rebellious sense of the poetic, which is hard to incorporate in any systematic sociological theory.

What, then, is so poetic about exploring everyday life? Goffman's special gift was his ability to capture everyday life without ever succumbing to the mundaneness of it; by using his observations, concepts and metaphors he manages to rise above the trivial. As two interpreters of Goffman's work said about the 'formalism' detectable in his writings as a continuation of Simmel's work:

> By the very act of making trivia a topic of study and recognizing its prevalence and importance in everyday life, formal sociologists change the very thing they seek to study. That is, trivia is no longer trivial; it now becomes important. To the extent this is true, the sociologists' rendering of trivia in everyday life cannot by definition correspond to the actors' experience of trivia ... This is true of Goffman's work. While his analyses of forms of interaction in everyday life are engaging and insightful, they are not, in the sense described above, 'true to the phenomena'. In his work, these forms become key features of everyday life, while in the lives of those he describes, they are taken for granted and go unnoticed. (Schwartz and Jacobs 1979: 183)

The double movement that Goffman mastered so much better than most sociologists of his generation consisted in approaching a phenomenon without becoming part of it – describing everyday life while at the same time constructing it artistically by means of abstractions, metaphors and the concepts of sociology. In this respect, Goffman's approach was closely related to that of literary writers. His poetic style was prosaic because he examined the numerous prosaic episodes of everyday life and because it was neither simulated nor patronizing. Perhaps his method can best be described as 'socio-literary', being social scientific and poetic at the same time (Smith and Jacobsen 2010). In the following, we will briefly look into three selected aspects of his particular prosaic or mundane poetics – Goffman's essayism and alternative sources, his metaphors, and his irony.

Essayism and Alternative Sources

One of Goffman's greatest sources of inspiration was undoubtedly the writings of Georg Simmel – both in terms of his choice of field and focus area (human interaction) within sociological research and in terms of his way of writing and communicating sociology. In fact, Goffman acknowledged his debt to Simmel on the very first page of his PhD dissertation, quoting Simmel's statement about the necessity of investigating the invisible threads of microscopic interactions woven between people, forming the fabric holding society together. Simmel is mostly known for his impressionistic essays and for his meticulous and exquisite writing style, balancing between an elevated, scientific, abstract style of language and an equally down-to-earth interest in basic aspects of human life, be it human interaction, fashion, the stranger, or food. Like Simmel and Hughes – and many of the other Chicago School sociologists – Goffman preferred an essayistic style of presentation. Thus most of his books are collections of essays rather than systematically structured scientific papers reporting findings on a specific theme. When the great German writer Robert Musil tried to explain what is so special about the essay, he characterized it as being 'the unique and unalterable form that a person's inner life assumes in a decisive thought' (Musil 1953/1995: 301). For that reason Musil placed the essay between *amor intellectualis* on the one hand and poetry on the other, as both were equally necessary to understand the essential aspects of life.

In spite of the fact that the essay, in Musil's words, is a product of decisive thought, it is still – due to its conciseness and contrary to a logically structured scientific treatise – characterized by its professed aspiration to be essentially a sketchy outline or tentative suggestions. As a matter of fact, Goffman deliberately added understated subtitles to most of his works, for example, 'studies', 'essays' or 'notes', thereby supporting the impression that they were merely works in progress, essayistic assumptions or initial considerations. Goffman thus positioned himself as a sociologist who was writing in the style of serious literary writers, not over-duly worried about complying with the strict academic rules on representation at the time usually crystallizing into tables, figures, graphs and statistics. By contrast, the outcome of his essays was usually the generation of sociological concepts, which, with a poetic touch, managed to capture either a specific, or a general but often overlooked, phenomenon. Below, Randall Collins sums up some of the most famous and catching Goffmanian concepts:

> Face-work, deference and demeanor, impression management, and the presentation of self; frontstage and backstage, teams and team-work, discrepant roles; a typology of secrets: dark, strategic, inside, entrusted, and free; moral careers, total institutions, and ways of making out in them; commitment, attachment, embracement, engagement, and role distance; focused and unfocused interaction, face engagements, accessible engagements, situational proprieties and improprieties, and the tightness and looseness of situation rules; vehicular units and participation units; territories of the self; personal space, use space, turns, information and conversational preserves; territorial violations; markers and tie-signs; supportive interchanges (access rituals) and remedial interchanges (accounts, apologies, body gloss); frames, keyings, fabrications, frame-breaking and out-of-frame activity. (Collins 1981: 222)

All the above and many more of Goffman's concepts are 'sensitizing' in the sense of the word defined by another of the other great Chicago School sociologists of the time, Herbert Blumer (1954), because – in contrast to 'definite' concepts – they can be used in a variety of contexts. As Goffman remarked on the pros and cons of the essayistic approach and its sensitizing conceptual development perspective:

> This method of presenting material may be irksome to the reader, but it allows me to pursue the main theme of each paper analytically and comparatively past the point that would be allowable in chapters of an integrated book. I plead the state of the discipline. I think that at present, if sociological concepts are to be treated with affection, each must be traced back to where it best applies, followed on from there wherever it seems to lead, and pressed to disclose the rest of its family. Better, perhaps, different coats to clothe the children well than a single splendid tent in which they all shiver. (Goffman 1961: xiii-xiv)

This is not to say that Goffman's essays are basically a ragbag of more-or-less arbitrary concepts. Far from it. The vital difference between the scientific essay – for example, Goffman's – and purely literary essays is that as far as at all possible every attempt must be made to live up to the academic rules governing argumentation, objectivity, representation and making a contribution to the scientific discourse (Catano 1986). And this was what Goffman's essays did.

However, it was not just in his choice of format for representation or in his development of concepts that Goffman differed from most of his contemporaries. He also differed in his choice of illustrative source material – Goffman often let himself be inspired by poetic or literary sources, whether he was investigating 'total institutions' for psychiatric patients or chance meetings between strangers in public places. In many of his books, it is detective stories, books on etiquette or technical manuals that serve as exemplification of important points or as support for the development of his concepts. In his main work *The Presentation of Self in Everyday Life* (1959: xi), Goffman acknowledges that his source material adds up to mixed bag, explaining why he deliberately draws on a myriad of materials for inspiration – in this book about a third of the sources are 'alternative' rather than conventional scientific sources. In another of his major works, *Asylums* (1961), a count of the references shows that of the book's 292 references, 42 per cent come from other scientific works; 58 per cent come from autobiographies, novels, essays and personal interviews (Bynum and Pranter 1984: 98). This demonstrates that Goffman was an expert at drawing inspiration from all sorts of impressions which, coming from a multitude of heterogeneous genres, provide interesting and inspiring angles on sociological issues. Once he himself admitted on the sometimes dubious, yet still scientifically valid and useful character of his often impressionistic findings:

> Obviously, many of these data are of doubtful worth, and my interpretations – especially some of them – may certainly be questionable, but I assume that a loose speculative approach to a fundamental area of conduct is better than a rigorous blindness to it. (Goffman 1963: 4)

A Master of Metaphors

One of the most explicit and indeed original ways through which Goffman succeeded in structuring and embedding his often impressionistic empirical findings was by way of metaphors. Usually, we associate metaphors with the works of writers of literary fiction and poetry. However, one of the most characteristic poetic features of Goffman's sociology is the way he develops metaphors or metaphoric networks (Corradi 1990). His metaphors serve the purpose of re-describing or re-contextualizing the ordinary everyday life, which is so difficult to capture, exactly because it so, well, ordinary (Jacobsen and Kristiansen 2006). By using vivid, striking metaphors, Goffman manages to turn the trivial into something not at all trivial, and in Goffman's writings metaphors thus constitute a kind of 'idiosyncratic map' (Manning 1992: 15) of the actions people perform when interacting, as well as their underlying motives and understandings (Hopper 1981). Thus, the metaphor is used to rewrite and communicate what is going on, so that it perhaps takes on a new meaning when seen through the prism of the metaphor.

Goffman operated with four general overall metaphors in his works; or only three according to some (Kalekin-Fishman 1988). The first and undoubtedly most well-known and widely used is the theatrical metaphor developed in *The Presentation of Self in Everyday Life*, in which he introduced his dramaturgical, performative perspective on social life (Goffman 1959). At the centre of the metaphor lie the skills and abilities of people to act as performers, and his view of social life as essentially consisting of well-rehearsed performances. Together the concepts constitute a network of understandings and interpretations of this theatrical metaphor, and include: performance, front stage, settings, actors, backstage, script, impression management, team performance, disruption, dramaturgical impact, etc. The ritual is another colourful metaphor found in several of his works – for example, in *Interaction Ritual* (1967). Goffman's main point here is that many of the small inconspicuous acts of politeness that form part of everyday life can be understood as acts of ritual deference in the micro-social order. The concepts often used in this metaphor include civil inattention, ceremonial rules, signals of acceptance, opening moves, remedial rituals, maintenance work, deference, etc. A third metaphor that Goffman used for a while was the game metaphor from *Strategic Interaction* (1969), in which social interaction was interpreted by focusing on the strategic motives and actions that characterize the way people meet each other – acting as a sort of spies or agents. The concepts developed by Goffman in this metaphor include for example, strategic information management, secrecy, game rationality, bluffs, moves and countermoves, mutual monitoring, information manipulation, etc. Finally, the frame metaphor from his *Frame Analysis* (1974) deserves mention although it is not quite as well-developed as the other three. In the frame metaphor, which is more philosophically or phenomenologically abstract than the others, the way people understand and interpret the surrounding world is described on the basis of concepts like situational definition, social frame, natural frame, frame breaking, keying, organization of experience, primary framework, fabrication, etc. What all of Goffman's metaphors have in common is the fact that they are a hybrid between sociological science and art, which is precisely what makes them capable of offering us a refreshing new look at things we take for granted. Robin Williams captured this special quality of Goffman's metaphors in the following quote:

> The bulk of [Goffman's] concepts were generated, developed and elaborated through the use of metaphor ... Metaphor were used by Goffman not as imagery, nor for the purpose of embellishing some pre-existing text, but it was used *directly*, as a technique of research, and it is a commonplace to assert that he was a master of this trope. This was no accident of style of course, for metaphor is the most powerful of means to express the complexity of relations that are possible between concepts; not through adding power to language incrementally, but because it is itself constitutive of the power of language ... It is not then that Goffman's studies were made to appear innovative through the use of metaphor, but that his conceptual advances were accomplished in the only way possible, through the process of linguistic invention and development pressed into the service of a sociological perspective. (Williams 1983: 101, original emphasis)

When discussing Goffman's metaphors, it is important to bear in mind that he did not believe the social world *to be* a theatre play, a strategic game, a big ritual ceremony or a picture frame, but that we – as creative social scientists – can understand it *as if it were*. That is, there is considerable poetic potential in developing and using metaphors to capture what is happening in society, even though Goffman repeatedly stressed the importance of recognizing the analytical limitations involved in using metaphors vicariously (Goffman 1959: 246). Nevertheless, his own skilful use of metaphors has contributed greatly towards raising awareness of the metaphor as a powerful tool in sociology's big methodological toolbox.

Sensitizing and Sophisticated Irony

Having described Goffman's use of alternative source material, his essayism and remarkable use of metaphors, a description of his work would, however, not be complete without mentioning his humorous, ironic and satirical approach to writing and communicating sociology, which is a distinct undercurrent in most of his writings (Fine and Martin 1990). Generally speaking, sociology is not otherwise renowned for its humorous approach to things. As Peter L. Berger once wrote: 'It is quite possible that the total absence of any sense of humour actually interferes with the attempt to give an intellectually adequate picture of society' (Berger 1963: 67). By using humour and irony as an organic part of his way of writing and communicating research, Goffman managed not only to entertain his readers but also to enable them to see aspects of society and sociology in new, thought-provoking and sometimes surprising ways.

As a literary or rhetorical device, irony usually implies saying something you do not really mean, being hypocritical or deliberately playing tricks with the truthfulness of what is written. However, Goffman's sophisticated and sensitizing irony is used differently, as its main purpose is to make us realize things that we would otherwise not realize, by applying a casual and humorous but also rather calculated way of communicating with the surrounding world. The metaphors mentioned above are thus ironic ways of portraying the trivial events of everyday life in such a way that we understand them better. Essentially, Goffman's sociological irony strives to make the unfamiliar familiar – turn it into something we can relate to and understand – and vice versa, turn things we take for granted into something exotic, worthy of our interest and attention. As Ricca Edmondson once noted about this Goffmanian rhetorical 'common sense' strategy, which on the one hand presents things as common sense but on the other wishes to turn common sense upside down:

> Goffman differs from other sociologists chiefly in the *degree* to which he concerns himself with sensitising the reader to his arguments, and in a sense this strategy is forced upon the reader ... [Goffman] wishes to bring the reader eventually to explain as normal what he or she might once have rejected as bizarre, or to defend as reasonable conduct which might have seen absurd (occasionally, vice versa, Goffman attacks as absurd what once looked reasonable. (Edmondson 1984: 148-9)

This special knack of drawing attention to the duality of the seemingly trivial events of everyday life made Alan Dawe describe Goffman as a 'sociological jester' (Dawe 1973: 248) because he liked to tease or play tricks on colleagues as well as ordinary people, making them see the world in a new and different light through his sociological analysis, but he was probably also ironic about his own role – as we shall see later.

It is evident from Goffman's writings that he was a rhetorical genius. The way he communicates his sociological findings has so much depth and so many levels, but to most readers it still seems easily accessible and perfectly understandable. In many ways, Goffman's sociology is 'the sociology of the obvious', not just because it examined obvious, commonplace aspects of life, but also because he wrote in way that managed to include the reader in his line of argumentation. For example, many of his sentences begin with words like 'Obviously' or 'Of course', just as many of his phrases speak to the reader in an inclusive way by emphasizing the obvious, or at other times expressing arguments only tentatively (Smith and Jacobsen 2010: 128ff). This accommodating and inclusive technique was by no means arbitrary; its aim was to deliberately turn a statement into something so obvious that there was no reason to discuss it.

As mentioned, Goffman liked to be ironic also at the expense of his readers – for example, needling colleagues advocating the scientific or positivistic way of thinking as the ideal for sociology; and people reading his books would sometimes find themselves at the receiving end of his irony when they suddenly became painfully aware of their own bodily behaviour and defence mechanisms in everyday life. But Goffman probably used irony about himself too. He would for instance often deliberately understate or downplay the importance of his findings. This is what Goffman wrote in one of his books:

> Obviously, many of these data are of doubtful worth, and my interpretations – especially some of them – may certainly be questionable, but I assume that a loose speculative approach to a fundamental area of conduct is better than a rigorous blindness to it. (Goffman 1963: 4)

One of the most remarkable features of Goffman's work is that his sociology seems relevant. Readers are able to recognize themselves in the universe that Goffman describes so creatively and ironically, whether they have an academic background or not, which is hardly ever the case in the comprehensive, abstract, theoretical accomplishments of for example, Talcott Parsons, Niklas Luhmann or Jürgen Habermas. In Goffman's writings, the abstract gives way to the concrete, esoteric language to inclusive language, and humour and irony are complementary to analysis.

Besides being an excellent communicator in writing, Goffman is remembered by many of his students as a very creative teacher, who was always able to catch and hold his students' attention, using his satirical touch also to carry out experiments with social conventions in his social life. Despite being a very private person, Goffman was an expert when it came to testing his theories and concepts in practice in various social contexts. This ability, as well as the importance attached to performance, is also characteristic of one of the Chicago School sociologists who followed in Goffman's footsteps.

The Performer Howard S. Becker

Howard S. Becker (b. 1928) is one of the sociologists whom Gary Alan Fine (1995) identifies as belonging to the wave of sociologists previously described as the 'Second Chicago School'. Becker studied, did his PhD and later worked at the University of Chicago, while all the time also working as a professional jazz musician. And like many of his contemporary colleagues in Chicago, he spent parts of his career working outside academia. While Becker studied and worked in Chicago, Hughes was still active there, a great inspiration to many of the second generation of Chicago School of sociologists, and in many ways Becker owes his socialization as a sociologist to Hughes's influence. For instance, it was on Hughes's suggestion that Becker started studying jazz musicians as a professional group. Also, it was in collaboration with Hughes, Blanche Geer and Anselm L. Strauss that Becker conducted the renowned ethnographic study *Boys in White* (1961), today regarded as a classic in the sociology of professions, unfolding Hughes' and the Chicago sociologists' understanding of professions and offering inspiration on how to practice sociological research but, just as importantly, on how to communicate its findings. In an interview with Ken Plummer, Becker says that he sees his own sociological practice as a continuation of the legacy passed on from Simmel to Park to Hughes (Plummer and Becker 2003). As Becker himself has acknowledged Goffman's importance for his own work on several occasions (Becker 2003), it seems plausible to draw a direct line from Simmel via the early Chicago sociologists and Goffman to Becker's writings.

Readable Social Science

A recurring theme in Becker's sociological work is his dedication to, metaphorically speaking, having an ongoing conversation about how to produce sociological knowledge and not least how to communicate that knowledge. The outcome of his deliberations can be read in a commendable trilogy, consisting of the books: *Writing for Social Scientists: How to Start and Finish Your Thesis, Book, or Article* (1986), *Tricks of the Trade: How to Think About Your Research While You're Doing It* (1998) and *Telling About Society* (2007). The books reflect a conversation, often rather provocative, that he has had throughout his career, in educational, editorial and writing contexts. The discussions quite often use as a starting point his observations of how students fear and loathe writing about sociology, his colleagues' anxious wrestling with how to write readable scientific publications, and his own fights with editors of journals stubbornly insisting on rigid conventional guidelines favouring an 'objective' writing style; that is, a rather rigid idea of scientific presentation shaping the authors' understanding of what it takes to be published and how 'science' must be produced and presented.

In his book *Writing for Social Scientists* (1986), Becker dared tackle head on the woolly, obscure and often pretentious form of communication that, according to him, was characteristic of most sociological writing. The book offers practical advice on how a sociology student or sociologist overcomes his writer's block, accepts that the art of writing is risky business as it exposes the author to the 'public', communicates in a precise, vivid and understandable sociological language etc. The underlying theme of the book as well as his later works on scientific rhetoric is, implicitly, his rejection of the objective writing style. Because, as he writes:

> As demonstrated by Kuhn, Rorty and a number of literary researchers, language can never be neutral, a simple window on the world. Writing always implies writing from a particular perspective embracing a host of cultural, political and philosophical ideas. (Becker 1986: 26)

When reading Becker, it is immediately obvious who is writing: I (read: Becker) am, not a generalizing or objectifying 'we'. His prose flows easily – short, punchy, informal sentences, and he prefers simple, straightforward words and active verbs whenever possible. 'Plain language' is an appropriate label for Becker's writing style, just like Hughes's. Becker is an ardent advocate of using a 'plain style' as the platform for scientific representation. 'Plain style' or 'plain writing' refers to a puritanical style of communicating, usually contrasted with an elaborate academic style scoring high on any readability index. In 'plain style', the use of technical terminology and jargon is deliberately kept to a minimum, sentences are short and uncomplicated, and the writer aspires to convey his message to a wider audience by writing it in a clear and concise language.

An examination of Becker's way of writing reveals many similarities with Hughes's and Simmel's essayistic writing style. In reality, many of Becker's books are compilations of essays, conference papers, lectures, articles, etc. Just like Simmel, Becker wrote a number of short essays, which he then later combined into a proper monograph. For example, one of his most famous books *Art Worlds* (1982), which is based on a variety of fragments or short texts all springing from the same basic idea, but an idea that tends undergo certain changes during the work phase. In *Art Worlds* the overarching idea was that an art world consists of people who do certain things together. The story behind the book was that Becker had accepted to teach a course in art sociology. He recorded all his classes and had them transcribed, and these transcripts turned into the first chapters of the book. Other chapters grew out of his other work – conference papers, lectures etc. which he had been asked to contribute on the subject. Finally, he assembled all these fragments, adding what was missing to make it read as a whole book (Plummer and Becker 2003). One way of describing the process could be comparing it to a collage of pictures which, when put together, presents a comprehensive narrative about the art world. A collage creating coherence. This creative method of working was not at all rare in his production, quite the contrary. Another of his widely read books, the classic in deviation sociology *Outsiders: Studies in the Sociology of Deviance* (1963) grew out of a similar process. Although Becker strongly recommends that sociologists reflect a lot more on their writing style, he equally strongly emphasizes that it must never be at the expense of substance, 'Becker's thoughtful recommendations will, however, be no good to a writer who has inflated his obscure writing style into an intellectual vacuum' (Tilly 1986: 551). In other words, reflecting on your writing style and using creative language with active verbs, short and vivid sentences will never do the trick if your writing is basically all form and no substance.

But this is not the end of it, as far as Becker is concerned. To him, it is not just about writing style but more generally about how best to create representations of society; how do we create narratives about social life in such a way that they best represent knowledge about the social world. Depending on the position from where we look at reality, we create different representations of the same things: an artist will see one thing, a landscape architect another, and a sociologist something else again. And what is more, these representations are subject to interpretation processes (Becker 2007). Regardless of how accurately we as sociologists think we have interpreted and represented the unfolding of social life, however tenable we think our arguments are, it will still all form part of what Richard Rorty has metaphorically described as 'conversations'. Conversations that interpret the representation and assign meanings to it. In other words, sociological knowledge about the social world is a construction taking place through conversations with the reality studied, with other researchers and with the readers of the written scientific representation. Based on this insight, Becker experiments with alternative forms of representation which acknowledge the assumption of research as a social construction, thus inviting conversations about how to understand and interpret the social phenomena studied.

Sociology as Performance

In his methodological article "Performance Science", Becker in cooperation with Michal M. McCall and the theatre director Paul Meshejian introduces a new way of presenting sociological/ethnographic field studies (McCall, Becker and Meshejian 1990; see also Becker, McCall, Morris and Meshejian 1989). Instead of presenting their methodological reflections on using a play as sociological representation in a traditional research manuscript (to be read out monotonously at for example, a conference), they wrote the findings of their field studies as a script for a play, then 'acted out' their findings. Unfortunately, space does not allow a full account of their arguments for experimenting with this type of representation, and we will just briefly mention two of their arguments. Firstly, research becomes 'multi-vocal', meaning that it is not only the researcher's voice and his formation of meaning which is present in the representation. Since the informants are also actors in the play, there will be more voices demanding their say. In practice, this means that the researcher takes a step back in his representation, allowing the informants to step forward and be heard as well. This makes the data material stand out more clearly – less interpreted or even manipulated. By turning the researcher into just one actor among several in the script, his voice becomes less authoritative, making it easier to have a conversation about how to interpret the field studies:

> We give the audience so much data that they can do their own analysis. Remember after our first performance? Someone said she felt like she could do her own analysis, get her own meaning, maybe a different meaning from ours, out of our data. (McCall, Becker and Meshejian 1990: 129)

Secondly, this form allows the researcher to include more voices in his script: voices that often disagree with each other. One of Becker's criticisms against scientific representations is that they tend to delimit themselves, which he sees as a by-product of the logic of the argumentation used in traditional research papers: when building up an argument, scientists usually try to protect themselves by countering any potentially critical questions in advance. Or pushing it to the extreme: if your argument holds, there will be no questions. This kind of logic not only suppresses the voices of the informants, it also excludes alternative interpretations by assigning meaning to the text or even hammering home the meaning. By giving the researcher more voices, the script writers allow the researcher to express doubt and uncertainty about interpretations, which opens up for alternative interpretations that argue against or question the plot of the play. For Becker and his colleagues, the point of using a script for a play is that it works more like a narrative, whose open form, compared to a traditional research manuscript, creates the space in which interesting conversations can take place and questions be asked, which helps bring research forward. They do emphasize, however, that using a play as a sociological representation of research fits the content of their particular research interest: the study of American theatre. Other types of sociological studies will require other types of representations; other types of experiments to find suitable forms of communication.

It was their field studies of theatres and insight into the theatre as a format for art and representation that gave them the idea of how best to communicate their analyses of life on the stages of American theatre. They have described how they had discovered from their own previous writings on the rhetoric used in scientific communication that the conventions of scientific representation are more or less arbitrary. Realizing this made Becker and his colleagues open and sensitive to other ways of representing sociological knowledge. Because, as they put it in the concluding passage of their play:

> *Howie*: ... Performance formats ought to make everyone realize- it made us see it – how much we take for granted when we write or read or hear conventional scholarly papers.
> *Michal*: The omniscient analyst.
> *Howie*: The dominance of the analytic voice.

Michal: Ignoring the richness of mood and emotion.
Howie: Hiding the facts of fieldwork.
Michal: Being alienated from our own work.
Howie: Since we are always editing reality, we might as well experiment.
(McCall, Becker and Meshejian 1990: 132)

Arguably, it is Howard Becker's desire, ability and willingness to experiment, both with sociology as a scientific form and discipline and with the methods of producing sociological knowledge as representations of social life that constitutes the most characteristic aspect of his creative and poetic sociological practice. He constantly questions conventions and challenges the boundaries of the discipline's understanding of itself and way of communicating sociological knowledge to the scientific community as well as the wider public. But he does so out of an ambition to create more precise and nuanced analyses and representations of the social phenomena (for example, deviation, abuse, work, arts and collective action) that constitute social reality.

Conclusion

In this chapter we have sought to illustrate, by means of a selection of examples from a few central writers of sociology, how it is possible to trace the lasting influence of one of sociology's fundamental, greatest and most durable currents – the Chicago School – in a number of central sociological writers spanning nearly a century, as a distinct stratum of analytical as well as communicative approaches marked by strong poetic and aesthetic undertones, constantly striving in various ways to make scientific texts more comprehensible, interesting and readable. For more than 100 years, the Chicago School of Sociology has represented an approach to sociology that has always allowed creative, innovative and communicative aspects to take centre stage.

That explains why the Chicago School was in opposition to many other types of sociology. In his book *For Sociology: Renewal and Critique in Sociology Today*, Alvin W. Gouldner distinguishes between two main opposing perspectives or paradigms in sociology. On the one hand 'the classic paradigm', striving for logic, predictability and regularity, with its focus on normal and frequency distributions and averages and written in a language characterized by abstraction, logic, and distance. And on the other, 'the romantic paradigm', using poetics and literary flair to focus on the deviant, the exotic, the unusual, the valuable, with its understanding of the world as a place where chance or unpredictability do and should play a role as well (Gouldner 1973). The Chicago School – in substance as well as style – probably comprises elements of both paradigms; but when it comes to communicating sociological knowledge to the world, the Chicago School obviously belongs to romantic paradigm.

But what exactly has the kind of poetically inspired sociology that the Chicago School represents got to offer today's sociologists? One answer to that question is that it can inspire modern social scientists to experiment, both with their choice of subject and form of communication, as the Chicago School sociologists continued to do over the years. But it can also be used to show the surrounding society, which sociology has to relate to and communicate with, that sociology is more than dry logic, boring data, pedantic counts, inflated common sense or similar often voiced derogatory descriptions. The poetics of the Chicago School can help to demonstrate what sociology really is – a vibrant, passionate and sometimes even entertaining discipline, in which the study of the seemingly trivial or banal can turn into interesting, dramatic, thought-provoking and important insights. Also, in recent years there has been a growing trend in sociology to increase its focus on 'public sociology', demanding that sociological knowledge, experience and insight interact with and enter into active dialogue with the surrounding society (Carey 1975; Burawoy 2005; Jacobsen 2008). Sociology's mission and ambition must always be to communicate with the surrounding society which it draws on and is a part of – otherwise sociology will end up as nothing but desktop or library sociology, without any relevance or importance to anybody except sociologists themselves. Obviously, there are many ways in which sociology can communicate with the surrounding society and help bring about change and improvement or increase understanding in society. One way to make sociological knowledge interesting and relevant to academic circles as well as a wider community is to take care to communicate it in an easily understandable way; that is, always bearing in mind when writing and analysing that non-sociologist must be able to understand and relate to what is written.

The pragmatic approach to sociology founded and practiced by the Chicago School sociologists, which at the end of the day boils down to making their knowledge easily accessible and applicable, is an archetypical example of how sociological knowledge can be scientifically sophisticated and still appeal to a wider audience, no matter whether the subject is urban development, deviation, professions, social interaction or any of the other themes explored by the Chicago sociologists over the years. Both in terms of scope, way of collecting information, generating concepts and theories, and not least communicating the knowledge acquired, the Chicago School as it unfolded through most of the 20th century was in fact a shining example of public sociology, which, with its unmistakable poetic flair, has had a lasting impact on sociologists but also inspired anyone who has ever studied sociology however briefly. Thus, it seems safe to conclude that the legacy of the Chicago School reaches far beyond traditional, narrow academic circles and well into the surrounding society that sociology is part of.

Translated into English by Lis Sand

References

Abbott, A. (2007): "Against Narrative: A Preface to Lyrical Sociology". *Sociological Theory*, 25(1): 67-99.

Andersson, O. (2003): *Chicagoskolan – institutionaliseringen, idétraditionen och vetenskapen*. Lund: Lund Monographs in Social Anthropology.

Andreski, S. (1972): *Social Science as Sorcery*. Harmondsworth: Penguin Books.

Becker, H.S. (1963): *Outsiders: Studies in the Sociology of Deviance*. Glencoe, IL: Free Press.

Becker, H.S. (1982): *Art Worlds*. Berkeley, CA: University of California Press.

Becker, H.S. (1986): *Writing for Social Scientists*. Chicago, IL: University of Chicago Press.

Becker, H.S. (1998): *Tricks of the Trade*. Chicago, IL: University of Chicago Press.

Becker, H.S. (1999): "The Chicago School, So-Called". *Qualitative Sociology*, 22(1): 3-12.

Becker, H.S. (2003): "The Politics of Presentation: Goffman and Total Institutions". *Symbolic Interaction*, 26: 659-69.

Becker, H.S. (2007): *Telling About Society*. Chicago, IL: University of Chicago Press.

Becker, H.S., B. Geer, E.C. Hughes and A.L. Strauss (1961): *Boys in White: Student Culture in Medical School*. Chicago, IL: University of Chicago Press.

Becker, H.S., M.M. McCall, L.V. Morris and P. Meshejian (1989): "Theatres and Communities: Three Scenes". *Social Problems*, 36(2): 93-116.

Berger, P.L. (1963): *Invitation to Sociology: A Humanistic Perspective*. Garden City, NY: Doubleday.

Blumer, H. (1954): "What Is Wrong With Social Theory?". *American Sociological Review*, 19: 3-10.

Bone, R. (1986): "Richard Wright and the Chicago Renaissance". *Callaloo*, 128: 446-68.

Bulmer, M. (1984): *The Chicago School of Sociology*. Chicago, IL: University of Chicago Press.

Burawoy, M. (2005): "2004 ASA Presidential Address – For Public Sociology". *American Sociological Review*, 70(1): 4-28.

Bynum, J. and C. Pranter (1984): "Goffman: Content and Method for Seminal Thought". *Free Inquiry in Creative Sociology*, 12: 95-9.

Cappetti, C. (1993): *Writing Chicago, IL: Modernism, Ethnography and the Novel*. New York: Columbia University Press.

Carey, J.T. (1975): *Sociology and Public Affairs: The Chicago School*. Beverly Hills, CA: Sage Publications.

Catano, G. (1986): "El Ensayo Sociologico: Entre la ciencia y la literatura?". *Revista Universidad de Antioquia*, 206: 50-72.

Chapoulie, J.M. (1996): "Everett Hughes and the Chicago Tradition". *Sociological Theory*, 14(1): 3-29.

Collins, R. (1981): "Three Stages of Erving Goffman", in *Sociology Since Midcentury*. New York: Academic Press.

Corradi, C. (1990): "The Metaphoric Structure of Scientific Explanation". *Philosophy and Social Criticism*, 16(3): 161-78.

Coser, L.A. (1994): "Introduction", in *On Work, Race, and the Sociological Imagination*, edited by E.C. Hughes. Chicago, IL: University of Chicago Press.

Dawe, A. (1973): "The Underworld-View of Erving Goffman". *British Journal of Sociology*, 24: 246-53.

Edmondson, R. (1984): *Rhetoric in Sociology*. London: Macmillan.

Fine, G.A. (ed.) (1995): *A Second Chicago School: The Development of a Postwar American Sociology*. Chicago, IL: University of Chicago Press.

Fine, G.A. and D.D. Martin (1990): "Sarcasm, Satire, and Irony as Voices in Erving Goffman's *Asylums*". *Journal of Contemporary Ethnography*, 19(1): 89-115.

Friedson, E. (1983): "Celebrating Erving Goffman". *Contemporary Sociology*, 12(4): 359-62.

Gasset, J.O. y (1949): "In Search of Goethe from Within". *Partisan Review*, 16.

Goffman, E. (1953): *Communication Conduct in an Island Community*. Unpublished PhD thesis, Department of Sociology, University of Chicago.

Goffman, E. (1959): *The Presentation of Self in Everyday Life*. New York: Doubleday/Anchor Books.

Goffman, E. (1961): *Asylums: Essays on the Social Situation of Mental Patients and Other Inmates*. New York: Doubleday/Anchor Books.

Goffman, E. (1963): *Behavior in Public Places: Notes on the Organization of Gatherings*. New York: Free Press.

Goffman, E. (1967): *Interaction Ritual: Essays on Face-to-Face Behavior*. New York: Pantheon Books.

Goffman, E. (1969): *Strategic Interaction*. Philadelphia, PA: University of Pennsylvania Press.

Goffman, E. (1974): *Frame Analysis: An Essay on the Organization of Experience*. New York: Harper & Row.

Goffman, E. (1983): "The Interaction Order". *American Sociological Review*, 48: 1-17.

Gouldner, A.W. (1973): *For Sociology: Renewal and Critique in Sociology Today*. London: Allen Lane.

Harvey, L. (1987): *Myths of the Chicago School of Sociology*. Brookfield: Gower Publishing Company.

Hopper, M. (1981): "Five Key Concepts of the Dramaturgical Perspective". *Free Inquiry in Creative Sociology*, 9(1): 47-52.

Hughes, E.C. (1943): *French Canada in Transition*. Chicago, IL: University of Chicago Press.

Hughes, E.C. (1958): *Men and Their Work*. Glencoe, IL: Free Press.

Hughes, E.C. (1993a): *The Sociological Eye: Selected Papers*. New Brunswick, NJ: Transaction Publishers.

Hughes, E.C. (1993b): "On the Sociological Interview", in *The Sociological Eye: Selected Papers*, edited by E.C. Hughes. New Brunswick, NJ: Transaction Publishers.

Irving, D.C. (1983): "The Real World and the Made World: The Sociologist's Use of Literary Analogy", in *Publications of the Missouri Philological Association*, Volume 8. Warrensburg, MI.

Jacobsen, M.H. (ed.) (2008): *Public Sociology: Proceedings of the Tenth Anniversary Conference Celebrating Sociology in Aalborg*. Aalborg: Aalborg Universitetsforlag.

Jacobsen, M.H. and S. Kristiansen (2006): "Goffmans metaforer – om den genbeskrivende og rekontekstualiserende metode hos Erving Goffman". *Sosiologi i dag*, 36(1): 5-33.

Jaworski, G.D. (2000): "Park, Doyle and Hughes: Neglected Antecedants of Goffman's Theory of Ceremony", in *Erving Goffman* (4 volumes), edited by G.A. Fine and G.W.H. Smith. London: Sage Publications.

Jørgensen, A. (2005): "Chicagosociologi – hverdagslivets modernisering", in *Hverdagslivet – sociologier om det upåagtede*, edited by M.H. Jacobsen and S. Kristiansen. Copenhagen: Hans Reitzels Forlag.

Kalekin-Fishman, D. (1988): "Games, Rituals and Theater: Elements in Goffman's Grammar of Social Action". *Sociologia Internationalis*, 26(2): 133-46.

Kurtz, L.R. (1984): *Evaluating Chicago Sociology*. Chicago, IL: University of Chicago Press.

Lepenies, W. (1988): *Between Literature and Science: The Rise of Sociology*. Cambridge: Cambridge University Press.

Lindner, R. (1996): *The Reportage of Urban Culture: Robert Park and the Chicago School*. Cambridge: Cambridge University Press.

Manning, P. (1992): *Erving Goffman and Modern Sociology*. Stanford, CA: Stanford University Press.

Marx, G.T. (ed.) (1972): *Muckraking Sociology: Research as Social Criticism*. New Brunswick, NJ: Transaction Publishers.

Matthews, F.H. (1977): *Quest for an American Sociology: Robert E. Park and the Chicago School*. Montreal: McGill-Queens University Press.

McCall, M.M., H.S. Becker and P. Meshejian (1990): "Performance Science". *Social Problems*, 37(1): 117-32.

Musil, R. (1953/1995): *The Man Without Qualities, Volume I*. London: Minerva.

Ogden, C.K. and I.A. Richards (1923/1949): *The Meaning of Meaning: A Study of the Influence of Language Upon Thought and the Science of Symbolism*. London: Routledge and Kegan Paul.

Park, R.E. (1915/1974): "The City: Suggestions for the Investigation of Human Behavior in the Urban Environment", in *The City*, edited by R.E. Park and E. Burgess. Chicago, IL: University of Chicago Press.

Park, R.E. (1929): *The City as a Social Laboratory in Human Communities: The City and Human Ecology*. Glencoe, IL: Free Press.

Park, R.E. (1950): *Race and Culture: The Collected Papers of Robert Ezra Park*. New York: The Free Press.
Park, R.E. (1952): "Succession: An Ecological Concept", in *Human Communities: The City and Human Ecology*. Glencoe, IL: Free Press.
Park, R.E. (1955): "News as a Form of Knowledge", in *Society*. Glencoe: Free Press
Platt, J. (1995): "Research Methods and the Second Chicago School", in *A Second Chicago School: The Development of a Postwar American Sociology*, edited by G.A. Fine. Chicago, IL: University of Chicago Press.
Plummer, K. (1983): *Documents of Life*. London: Allen & Unwin.
Plummer, K. and H.S. Becker (2003): "Continuity and Change in Howard S. Becker's Work: An Interview with Howard S. Becker". *Sociological Perspectives*, 46(1): 21-39.
Riesman, D. and H.S. Becker (1993): "Introduction to the Transaction Edition", in *The Sociological Eye: Selected Papers*, edited by E.C. Hughes. New Brunswick, NJ: Transaction Publishers.
Scheff, T.J. (2006): *Goffman Unbound!: A New Paradigm for Social Science*. Boulder, CO: Paradigm Publishers.
Schudson, M. (2003): *The Sociology of News*. New York: W.W. Norton & Company.
Schwartz, H. and J. Jacobs (1979): *Qualitative Methods: A Method to the Madness*. New York: Free Press.
Smith, G. and M. Hviid Jacobsen (2010): "Goffman's Textuality – Literary Sensibilities and Sociological Rhetorics", in *The Contemporary Goffman*, edited by M. Hviid Jacobsen. London: Routledge.
Strong, P.M. (1988/2006): "The Rivals: An Essay on the Sociological Trade", in *Sociology and Medicine: Selected Essays by P.M. Strong*, edited by A. Murcott. Aldershot: Ashgate.
Svith, F. (ed.) (2006): *At opdage verden – research fra akademikere til journalister*. Århus: Forlaget Ajour.
Tilly, C. (1986): "Writing Wrongs in Sociology". *Sociological Forum*, 1(3): 543-52.
Tomasi, L. (ed.) (1998): *The Tradition of the Chicago School of Sociology*. Aldershot: Ashgate.
Toscano, G. (2008): "Artistic Performances and Sociological Research", in *Studies in Symbolic Interaction, Volume 31*, edited by N.K. Denzin. Bingley: JAI Press.
Wax, M.L. (1990): "Erving Goffman and Chicago Sociology". *Man (New Series)*, 26(1): 163-4.
White, H. (1975): *Metahistory: The Historical Imagination in Nineteenth-Century Europe*. Baltimore, MD: Johns Hopkins University Press.
Williams, R. (1983): "Sociological Tropes: A Tribute to Erving Goffman". *Theory, Culture & Society*, 2(1): 98-101.
Zelizer, B. (2004): *Taking Journalism Seriously: News and the Academy*. London: Sage Publications.

Chapter 2
Bacon, Kundera, Bauman

Keith Tester

Introduction: Bacon, Kundera, Bauman

In Francis Bacon's 1975 painting of *Two Figures* they twist around one another, their heads juddering against the acid green platform on which they are placed. Apart from a bruised leg their body parts are indistinct. They are reduced to a single entwined mass but their humanity is never lost because the face of one figure is slammed against the green base. The platform on which the figures writhe is raised in the air and the eye of the viewer is pulled towards it by the grid of lines which is so familiar in Bacon's work. The lines seem to turn the bodies into a specimen in a display case. This is an exhibit. The central point of the canvas is a reddish-black hole of flesh, and on the acidic base a fluid seeps from the figures. It could be semen, vomit, drawl, lard or just a light smear of grubby white paint. However the background of the painting raises a question. It is a deep curtain, like one lowered before an expectant audience. If this is an exhibit is it in a court, a circus, a peep show or theatre?

Milan Kundera has published a collection of essays called *The Curtain* in which he gives to the novel the task of pulling aside the drapes of self-evidence and preconception by which the reality of human lives is hidden away or denied (Kundera 2007). The novel, Kundera insists, has the job of showing what is really going on when all the grandiloquent pretensions of History and Necessity are pulled off the humans who are forced by power to struggle beneath their weight. As is the matter in the collection, *Encounter*, Kundera wants to use the novel to recover the truths of our human being which are otherwise 'veiled by our membership in a collectivity that blinds us with its dreams, its excitement, its projects, its illusions, its struggles, its causes, its religions, its ideologies, its passions' (Kundera 2010: 13). These are truths such as our fears, loves, laughter, hope and excrement. The truth of the frequent failure or refusal of humans to be what we are told we are 'meant to be'.

Bacon's curtain immediately raises a question: what side of the curtain was he showing with his *Two Figures*? Is he showing us the truth lurking behind the illusions of the lives we tell ourselves are the way they must be? Or are we also specimens in a row of little cases, waiting for the curtain to be pulled up so the voyeurs on the freak show of the lives of others might gawp and decide to do something to improve us (for our own good, of course)? Is Bacon showing us the human distorted by the 'it must be' of History, or the ambiguous indeterminacy of the human when it is left to itself? Meanwhile, recalling another work by Kundera, these two figures must be light because their acid green base is without firm support. It seems to be floating. Are they distorted because this lightness is unbearable? To whom is it unbearable? Bacon is too subtle to give answers. He forces us back to the canvas, back to the ever-hanging and indeterminate question.

Meanwhile, Zygmunt Bauman knows Kundera's work and has thought with it deeply. Indeed Bauman has taken up his pen in support of Kundera's vision of writing as an attempt to demolish the wall behind which human truths are hidden by those who say they know 'what must be' and who proclaim the necessity of the obvious and self-evident (Bauman 2000: 202). He has explicitly discussed *The Curtain*, and said Kundera's image of pulling it apart to look at what it hides is, 'eminently appropriate as the job description of the practitioners of the *sociological* vocation' (Bauman in Jacobsen and Tester 2007: 315). For Bauman, indebted to Kundera, sociology ought to be concerned with 'piercing through the 'curtain of prejudgements' to set in motion the endless labour of reinterpretation, opening for scrutiny the human-made and human-making world 'in all the comic nudity of its prose' and so drawing new human potentialities out of darkness in which they had been cast'. Bauman said: 'I do believe that by doing or failing to do such a job sociology ought to be judged' (Bauman in Jacobsen and Tester 2007: 315). Demolishing a wall, rending a curtain; in both cases the concern is to reveal what is kept hidden, to reclaim what is pushed away. But *what* is pushed away? *What* is hidden by the wall or the curtain?

Here a triangle – Bauman, Bacon, Kundera – links together. Kundera's *Encounters* contains a superb essay on Bacon which points to Bauman's themes.[1] Kundera sees Bacon asking a fundamentally *ethical* question. Bacon's art distorts the human figure but even when the distortion is most pronounced the face remains tangible, present. For example, one of the *Two Figures* has hair, eyes, teeth, a mouth. The other figure appears to be turned away from the viewer, but still their hair (hair cut and combed – hair made cultural and therefore transferred from the necessary to the contingent, hair shifted from the 'what must be' to the indeterminate 'it could be this or that') remains at the top of their foetally crunched form. For Kundera this is typical of Bacon since his art investigates the question: 'To what degree of distortion does a beloved person remain a beloved person? For how long does a cherished face growing remote through illness, through madness, through hatred, through death remain recognizable? Where is the border beyond which a self ceases to be a self?' (Kundera 2010: 7). Kundera's Bacon prods at this question by never losing sight of the face of the other, 'the face I gaze upon to seek in it a reason for living the 'senseless accident' that is life' (Kundera 2010: 15). In other words, Kundera's Bacon is asking a stark question: what does this other mean

---

1 Milan Kundera's essay points to Zygmunt Bauman's themes, but this is not to say that Kundera has any knowledge of Bauman's work. He might, he might not: I have absolutely no idea. Equally, I do not know Bauman's attitude to Francis Bacon. I am making connections at the level of published texts alone.

to me and what do I owe it? The answer is simple: the other means everything to me and I owe to her humanity; my own humanity, her humanity, and by extension a human world. I owe to her my actions of the reclamation of everything the curtain hides away. I owe to her the action of my loving gaze upon her face.[2]

Bauman stresses the face of the other in the ethical approach he derives from Emmanuel Lévinas and which he uses as a lever for an immanent critique of the obvious and taken for granted. The face of the other petitions for care and asks for the extension of my hospitality and sociability towards it. The face of the other pleads that I neither crush nor ignore it. The petition and plea follow from my free ability to extend either kindness or harm because we are in relationship with one another. Both being moral and being evil are possible only, 'under the ... condition in which we encounter human beings – under social conditions' (Bauman in Bauman and Tester 2001: 60). Consequently, the ethical is not about acting in terms of abstract ideals or according to rational criteria. The ethical is about what we do in our social relationships with one another. It is the *human condition* to be present in relationship with the other, the never-ceasing *moral choice* is how the condition will be played out, and the *drama* is that the self and the other can never be the same and remain human. Bauman said: 'The self and alterity are bound to meet while staying in different universes. They are not commensurable, just as infinity cannot be fathomed, let alone exhausted, by anything as finite as

---

2   To insist after Kundera that Bacon's art focuses on the face is to go in a direction contrary to the one asserted in Gilles Deleuze's book about Bacon. According to Deleuze Bacon paints heads not faces: 'As a portraitist, Bacon is a painter of heads, not faces', and the head 'is a spirit in bodily form, a corporeal and vital breath, an animal spirit. It is the animal spirit of man: a pig-spirit, a buffalo-spirit, a dog-spirit, a bat-spirit ... Bacon thus pursues a very peculiar project as a portrait painter: t*o dismantle the face*, to rediscover the head or make it emerge from beneath the face' (Deleuze 2005: 15). From this it is but the shortest of steps to Deleuze's claim that Bacon paints bodies as indeterminate meat. Whether this is human or animal meat is utterly besides the point because meat is meat and meat is, 'undoubtedly the chief object of Bacon's pity, his only object of pity' (Deleuze 2005: 17). To support this claim Deleuze cites Bacon's remark: 'If I go into a butcher shop I always think it's surprising that I wasn't there instead of the animal' (Bacon in Deleuze 2005: 17). But when Bacon made the remark he was making a point aesthetic and ethical not ontological: 'you go into a butcher's shop and see how beautiful meat can be and then you think about it, you can think of the whole horror of life – of one thing living off another' (Bacon in Sylvester 1992: 48). In other words, meat is *not* the 'object of Bacon's pity'. *If* it is possible to deduce so simple a sentiment from Bacon's work, his pity is focused on the horror which reduces everything to meat. And as soon as the matter is put in such a way, Bacon's project is clarified as one of recovering the face on the head. The human is *not* at all reducible to some 'animal-spirit' and to pretend it is part of the problem. Certainly, Kundera also knows from Bacon that we are potential meat – this is less a revelation than a historical banality – but he never takes the meat from the human body and therefore he never allows himself to forget the human face (Kundera 2010: 13). When all is said and done there are two main problems with Deleuze's reading of Bacon. First it is ethically lethal. Second it is not supported by Bacon's paintings or words.

the transient and mortal self. We cannot fulfil our desire, but neither can we stop trying to fulfil it. This is the breathtaking beauty and the heart-rending drama of the moral self's predicament' (Bauman in Bauman and Tester 2001: 133). Indeed: 'The Other, as long as she or he is approached as an exemplar of alterity ... is unknowable, but being human we cannot stop wishing to know' (Bauman in Bauman and Tester 2001: 133-4). Bacon's painting provokes because it raises a question about how far the two figures with two heads yet one judderingly visible face remain knowable as selves, as others to us and to one another, even as their bodies meld into one mass. Bacon's painting challenges the viewer and forces us to think about what we are seeing and how it is to be regarded.

It is the human truth and reality to have to choose how the other will be treated. I have to choose because I am possessed of free will, and so while the face of the other can insist, can petition, it cannot at all compel. If the face of the other were able to compel it would deny my alterity and, therefore, be a demand incompatible with what it means to be human. According to Bauman, establishments of necessity and self-evidence hide away the face of the other. They subordinate the indeterminate moral relationships flowing from the reality of our alterity to one another to instrumental rational calculations (Bauman 1989). Yet it is in this replacement that the attraction of claims to necessity and 'what must be' resides. As soon as we can proclaim the inevitability and necessity of something or other we can off-load our responsibility for what is done unto others, what we do to them. It stops being 'our fault' and a choice we freely made. We can live lightly without the burden of our moral responsibility. For Bauman it is the responsibility of sociology to pull the curtain away from the conceits of necessity and to give back to us our moral responsibility towards the other. This responsibility might well be unwanted, it might well be a heavy burden, but without it life cannot be called human (Bauman 2008). Or to quote Francis Bacon, the job is to 'open up or rather, should I say, unlock the valves of feeling and therefore return the onlooker to life more violently' (Bacon in Sylvester 1992: 17).

From this two questions arise. The first can be put in Bacon's terms: how have the 'valves of feeling' towards the face of the other been locked? Mixing metaphors, it can be said that the curtain has hidden the face of the other, but in precisely what does the curtain consist? The second question follows logically: how can the 'valves of feeling' be unlocked? Yes, the answer is by simply pulling aside the curtain, but *how* is it to be pulled?

Locking the Valves

Bacon himself once alluded to a kind of curtain. He said he wanted his paintings to get through to the violence at the heart of things: 'We nearly always live through screens – a screened existence. And I sometimes think, when people say my work looks violent, that perhaps I have from time to time been able to clear away one or two of the veils or screens' (Bacon in Sylvester 1992: 82). Kundera uses the novel to pull aside the curtain so the indeterminacies of human life can be seen, Bauman sees sociology as an activity destroying the walls separating the instrumental 'what has to be' from the freedom of human responsibility to make lives human, and Bacon sees his painting as a way of getting through the screen between our placid existences and the violence which he identifies as the truth of reality: 'When talking about the violence of paint, it's nothing to do with the violence of war. It's to do with an attempt to remake the violence of reality itself' (Bacon in Sylvester 1992: 81). What is this violence of reality? 'When I look at you across the table, I don't only see you but I see a whole emanation which has to do with personality and everything else. And to put that over in a painting ... means that it would appear violent in paint' (Bacon in Sylvester 1992: 82). The violence of reality is the existential encounter with the truth of alterity.

An ethic can be extracted from Bacon's proposition. He is emphasizing the relationship between himself and the alterity of the other. Despite the intimations of a quick glance at his canvasses Bacon is highly respectful of the human other and refuses to allow them to be merely what they appear to be or what they are for him. He accepts the human condition of alterity. There is more to being human than 'this'. Uncovering the extra ingredients requires the doing of a kind of violence to the face the other normally presents to the world. In response to a question by David Sylvester Bacon agreed that painting a portrait is a way of bringing someone back into reality (Sylvester 1992: 40). But for Bacon a kind of practical ethic followed from what he was trying to do in his portraiture. He preferred to work from photographs rather than the model because he did not want his subjects to see what he was doing to their image: 'they inhibit me. They inhibit me because, if I like them, I don't want to practise before them the injury that I do to them in my work. I would rather practise the injury in private by which I think I can record the fact of them more clearly' (Bacon in Sylvester 1992: 41). Of course, there is a degree of arrogance (Bacon would have probably said 'vanity') in this position because it does make the artist the revealer of a truth otherwise hidden. But perhaps more significant is the modesty of his argument, a modesty similar to the temper of the work of Kundera and Bauman. None of them claim to be in the business of invention. All of them are concerned to reveal what is already there, and consequently their work is put at the service of what can be discovered because it is other than them, because of its alterity. In short, all three are concerned to restore our humanity to us. This – humanity as the indeterminacy of alterity – is the truth about which they speak and paint. It is the feeling for the other which they seek to unlock and reveal.

The point is to recover the truth and to do so by 'unlocking the valves of feeling' or – to use another metaphor – by pulling aside the curtain or veil. The job has to be done with a kind of violence because in contemporary historical circumstances it is much easier to live with the valves locked than unlocked. Why?

Bacon was sure that existence is meaningless (Sylvester 1992: 133), but we cannot bear to live with this knowledge. His argument is very strongly drawn from *Burnt Norton* in T.S. Eliot's *Four Quartets*: 'human kind cannot bear very much reality' (Eliot 1969: 172). 'I think of life as meaningless', Bacon said, 'but we give it meaning during our own existence. We create certain attitudes which give it meaning while we exist, though they in themselves are meaningless really' (Bacon in Sylvester 1992: 133). As he put it: 'man now realizes that he is an accident, that he is a completely futile being, that he has to play out the game without reason' (Bacon in Sylvester 1992: 28). Yet, this increases the stakes of the game for the artist. According to Bacon, the realization of the meaninglessness of life leads to a quest for 'distraction' from the abyss (Sylvester 1992: 29). The distraction is of two sorts; first of all it can involve 'a kind of hedonistic and drifting life' (Bacon in Sylvester 1992: 134) or it can consist in the embrace of anything which causes diversion from the horror of the futility of existence. These diversions are the 'certain attitudes' to which he referred. This is the trap into which art can too easily fall: 'You see, all art has now become completely a game by which man distracts himself; and you may say it has always been like that, but now it's entirely a game' (Bacon in Sylvester 1992: 29). And so the artist who accepts the game as a diversion from meaninglessness but who wants to reveal the truth the diversion disguises has to play it against itself if he wants his work to be meaningful. Bacon had to accept the rules of art (he always placed himself in the tradition, insisting on the paraphernalia of gallery presentation for example), in order to ensure all the more violently that his work could not be one more cause of distraction, of one more locking of the valves. You can only work against the game if you have imbibed its rules.

One sign of Bacon's strategy in this regard is his use of the crucifixion motif. Bacon put his crucifixions in the tradition of Western art when he drew on Cimabue for the right hand panel of his own *Three Studies for a Crucifixion* of 1962 (Sylvester 1992: 13-15). But he did this in order to play against the game. He took up one of the dominant myths of Western culture and sought to unlock it. Bacon wanted to connect the image back to the reality of slaughter (Christ as meat), and he did this by referencing photographs of animal carcasses ('meat as Christ'; Bacon in Sylvester 1992: 23). Yet the attempt to unlock the horror of the Crucifixion might well have failed. As Bacon got older he painted fewer of them, and his explanation of the shift is interesting. In a rather grumpy conversation in which Bacon appears to have been in an alcohol-fuelled foul mood he said: 'I used to use the crucifixion, not because I believed in it, but as a myth on which I felt many things. But I would never use it or could never use it again because it's become – it was always dried up for me, but it's become impractical to even use it' (Bacon in Davies 2002: 64). The 'impracticality' presumably is due to the failure of Bacon's crucifixions to unlock the reality he wanted violently to reveal. Bacon seems to have developed much the same appreciation of the success of his series of Popes. These are now famous paintings, perhaps often no more than decorations, and for maybe precisely this reason Bacon regarded them as 'very silly' (Bacon in Sylvester 1992: 37). The acceptance of these paintings into the pantheon of 'Western art' had neutered their ability to reveal the true reality; their very success had transformed them into failures by Bacon's own standards. They had become just more distractions.

An important issue here is Bacon's refusal of nostalgia. His concern was to play against the game in which he was fated to participate, and he made no attempt to play another. The historical moment cannot be escaped: 'There's no century I want to live in. After all, I'm accustomed to today. There's nothing else I want to live in' (Bacon in Davies 2002: 53). A similar temper runs through Kundera and Bauman. They refuse nostalgia too. Nostalgia is the search for a determinate if not determining past in which everything is 'as it must be'. But for Kundera the past is never to be forgotten because without memory it is impossible to struggle against power. He uses memory as a lever to unlock what is announced by power presently to be necessary (Kundera 1996). With Kundera memory is for the sake of the present and future, not the past. Bauman is more concise: 'I know of no arrangement of human togetherness, present or past, which could be seen as an optimal solution to the aporia of human condition' (Bauman in Jacobsen and Tester 2007: 320). For all three it is necessary to confront the circumstances in which we live and seek to be human; not wish them away with dreams of a past in which all questions were answered. If nothing else, such a past would have been a human hell. Nostalgia is just one more distraction, and yet this is precisely its attraction. Nostalgia pulls the curtain in front of the truth of the reality of existential indeterminacy. To this extent one sign of the commitment running through the work of Bacon, Kundera and Bauman is their steadfast refusal of easy consolations. To paraphrase Eliot, they are trying to bear reality.

The attempt to unlock the truth of the indeterminacy of alterity explains Bacon's repudiation of narrative in his art. In one of their conversations David Sylvester pointed out to Bacon how most of his paintings are of single figures. Bacon accepted the observation and explained why: 'the moment there are several figures – at any rate several figures on the same canvas – the story begins to be elaborated. And the moment the story is elaborated, the boredom sets in; the story talks louder than the paint' (Bacon in Sylvester 1992: 22). Bacon went on to use this principle to explain why the different panels of his triptychs are separated by vertical breaks and so often painted on separate canvasses. As soon as figures are bought together, Bacon repeated, a story starts to be told (what is their relationship, what are they doing to one another and why? These questions are also provoked by the *Two Figures* but in this case the paint is powerful enough to negate them). But painting a triptych in three different sections and having only one figure in each disrupts the tendency towards narrative (Sylvester 1992: 23). The problem with narrative is the way it imposes a set of meanings on what for Bacon ought to be restored to indeterminacy, and moreover how it undermines potential ways of seeing the picture (van Alphen 1992: 21). Narrative transforms the image into the representation of a 'what must be', and in so doing locks down the violent feeling the painting might otherwise unleash. A good example of the rather deadening effect of narrative is provided by one of Bacon's own paintings, his 1965 *Crucifixion* which is in Munich. A figure in the third of the three panels is wearing a Nazi armband, and John Russell is right to call the painting 'flawed' on this account (Russell 1979: 128). The Nazi armband carries too much narrative weight, and it is impossible to see this particular *Crucifixion* as very much more than a portrayal of recent European history. The armband introduces a narrative and determines meaning because to some significant degree its obviousness makes it impossible to see the rest of the image.

Kundera also makes it possible to see why the Nazi armband is a flaw in the 1965 *Crucifixion*. Kundera once distinguished between the novel which examines 'the historical dimension of human existence' and that which 'is the illustration of a historical situation' (Kundera 1988: 36). Kundera committed himself to the first way of dealing with history. He explores *history as an existential situation*, and therefore he understands human existence historically, although his concern is always with the present in which he lives (Kundera 1988: 37-8). This is also what Bacon mostly achieves. For instance, although the rectangles surrounding figures in many of his canvasses (including the *Two Figures*) were identified by him as having no purpose other than to focus the eye on the figure (Sylvester 1992: 23), they do something else too. They also put the figure into an existential situation which is rendered historical by the presence of curtains, platforms or other artefacts which are distinctly mid-twentieth century. Meanwhile, the Munich *Crucifixion* is flawed because thanks to the obtrusive and largely unnecessary Nazi armband it is simply an 'illustration of a historical situation'. According to Kundera, novels which illustrate a historical situation merely 'translate non-novelistic knowledge into the language of the novel' (Kundera 1988: 36). By extension this *Crucifixion* can be said to translate non-figurational knowledge into the language of figuration to such an extent that the painting is incapable of escaping the burden of historical illustration placed upon it. It unlocks no valves. In fact when Bacon illustrates the historical situation he is, to use his own word, a little boring.

In Bauman's terms too, the Nazi armband is a flaw. The reason why is intimated by John Russell, for whom the armband means 'a loss of universality' (Russell 1979: 129). In his dealings with the Nazis, Bauman has always gone to great lengths not to lose the universality of the message of the Holocaust. If it is *only* seen as something done by Nazis or Germans to Jews then the Holocaust is if no great existential relevance to those who were not likely to be victims or perpetrators. But for Bauman the Holocaust is something with which we must all grapple, something we must all confront. The Holocaust has universal relevance because it shows where modern ideals and practices *can* lead, regardless of the identity of the parties involved (Bauman 1989). To quote Bauman: 'Germany's guilt is not a German affair ... Germany did what it did because of what it *shares* with the rest of us, not because of what makes it different from us ... The trouble with blaming Germany ... is that everybody else is exonerated' (Bauman in Bauman and Tester 2001: 85-6). We are all guilty; this is part of the historical dimension of today's human existence.[3]

---

3 In personal correspondence, Zygmunt Bauman has made much the same point about Michael Haneke's 2009 film *The White Ribbon*. To read Haneke's film about cruelty in a small German village just before the First World War as a reflection on the roots of

The Munich *Crucifixion* actually serves by its very flaw to throw into relief the wider universality of Bacon's project and the extent to which he shares a common concern with Bauman and Kundera. They are all explorers of the *historical dimension of human existence*.

Unlocking the Valves

For Francis Bacon then the locking of the valves of feeling has happened because of the characteristics of the present historical dimension of human existence. Existence has been shown to be meaningless and the loss of God has turned everything into a game. It is indeed noticeable how Bacon consistently talks about the 'current situation' and so forth. For instance his repudiation of narrative in painting is tied explicitly to the historical when he talks about 'the complicated stage in which painting is now' (Bacon in Sylvester 1992: 22). He identifies the existential aspect of the historical moment as one in which the religious has been 'cancelled out ... Now, of course, man can only attempt to make something very, very positive by trying to beguile himself for a time by the way he behaves, by prolonging the possibility of his life by buying a kind of immortality through the doctors' (Bacon in Sylvester 1992: 29). He was also very aware of the 'paradox about the survival of works of art – I mean in our society, where art doesn't serve any ritual or didactic purpose' (Bacon in Sylvester 1992: 89). Bacon insistently stresses the historical dimension in which he attempts to confront what he believes to be the reality of human existence. He largely succeeds when his art is without historically illustrative flaw.

According to Milan Kundera, the existential situation Bacon confronts is one in which the self has gone into hiding. Put another way, the existential situation is one in which indeterminacy has been overridden. In the *Encounter* collection, Kundera draws on a theme which is raised in his novel *Immortality*. He identifies how alterity is undermined by the extent to which it has become inescapably obvious that all of our features and gestures are shared with others. Alterity is diluted in the same (Kundera 2000, 2010: 6). Kundera's first collection of essays, *The Art of the Novel*, had already identified a historical process in which the ambition of the self became more and more restricted through the modern period, as individuals stopped being creators of the world and instead became passengers on a train of History from which it was impossible to get off and which charged them all the same price for a ticket (Kundera 1988). Consequently, it is possible to unlock the valves of feeling which follow from the indeterminacy of alterity only if there is a degree of distortion of the commonplace and, furthermore, an attempt to discover what might remain irreducibly other. This is what Bacon tries to do,

---

Nazism is, for Bauman, to completely lose its universal message. For Bauman the message of the film lies in its reinforcement of Haneke's career-long struggle to show effects without causes or, to put it another way, his attempt to uncover the historical dimension of human existence without falling into the trap of illustration.

and Kundera sees it as an attempt to recover, 'the face that harbors 'that treasure, that nugget of gold, that hidden diamond' that is the infinitely fragile self shivering in a body' (Kundera 2010: 15).

Bacon said he tried to do this by 'deform[ing] people into existence' (Bacon in Sylvester 1992: 146) and as an example of the strategy he cited portraits he made of the French writer Michel Leiris in 1976 and 1978. Bacon had already explained to Sylvester how easy it would be for him to make a 'literal portrait' of someone, but such a production would be uninteresting since it would not actually reveal the other's alterity (Bacon in Sylvester 1992: 121). To achieve a revelation of such an order something else was necessary; a degree of violent distortion which would try to unlock the indeterminacy of the other rather than merely record their direct appearance. This is the background against which Bacon discussed his two portraits of Leiris. He made the otherwise counter-intuitive claim that, 'the one I did which is less literally like him [the 1976 portrait] is in fact more poignantly like him' (Bacon in Sylvester 1992: 146). And the more distorted of the two paintings of Leiris could be judged to be more 'like him' because in the violence it did to Leiris's appearance it managed to unlock 'the pulsations of a person'. Bacon explained precisely what he was trying to unlock in his portraiture: 'The living quality is what you have to get ... The sitter is someone of flesh and blood and what has to be caught is their emanation' (Bacon in Sylvester 1992: 174). He is after their alterity. Bacon quickly ruled out any spiritual reading of his use of the word 'emanation' and instead started to talk about 'energy': 'There is the appearance and there is the energy within the appearance. And that is an extremely difficult thing to trap. Of course, a person's appearance is closely linked with their energy'. He continued: 'So far it seems that if you are doing a portrait you have to record the face. But with their face you have to try and trap the energy that emanates from them' (Bacon in Sylvester 1992: 175). In Kundera's terms this energy, this emanation, is the hidden diamond of the self in the shivering body.

The question is, of course, *how* to trap the energy. When Bacon explored the matter he highlighted the historical dimension of his existential investigations. As the portraits of Leiris demonstrate the formal means of unlocking the energy of the face of the other is through distortion. And Bacon was clear that he was working in a historical moment which required a high level of distortion thanks to the development and spread of the 'mechanical means of rendering appearances'. Kundera would doubtless identify these as the technologies which have taken the unique gesture and face away from the other, making us all more or less the same. According to Bacon, photography and movies mean 'that a painter, if he is going to attempt to record life, has to do it in a much more intense and curtailed way' than previously (Bacon in Sylvester 1992: 176). The point can be illustrated through a comparison of aspects of Bacon's own work with how Edgar Degas painted the spine in his *After the Bath* which is in the National Gallery, London. Bacon had obviously looked at the Degas very closely indeed and he noted how the top of the woman's spine almost protrudes from her skin. For Bacon this subtle move by Degas emphasized the vulnerability of the woman's body (Bacon in

Sylvester 1992: 47). In Zygmunt Bauman's terms, it might even be proposed that Degas' spine is a kind of petition for care, and in as much as the spine highlights vulnerability it most certainly intimates alterity to the viewer who is thereby called upon to do something with this knowledge of the fragility of the other. Yet, when Bacon paints spines, the subtlety has gone, and he would say this is because he *has* to be more intense than Degas if he wants to unlock alterity. Consequently, the spine is referenced in what Bacon judged to be the more successful of the two Leiris portraits, but it appears as the left cheek bone. The third panel of the 1964 *Three Figures in a Room* directly quotes the Degas spine, but now the curve is sharper, more like a wound on the body of the man sitting on the toilet.[4] The historical dimension of the existential situation demands a brutal art, a violent distortion of the other, if alterity is going to stand a chance of being unlocked and issued into the world as a principle of indeterminacy and possibility.

This is to focus on the formal properties of some of Bacon's late portraits, but throughout his mature career (after the mid 1940s) Bacon also relied on a *method* of work which sought to unlock feeling. His reliance on accident is a recurrent theme in the discussions with David Sylvester. Bacon's usual working method involved wiping the paint on the canvas with a rag; he would rub the canvas with something to hand, mix dust in the oils or throw paint. Why? It was a deliberate attempt to 'break the willed articulation of the image, so that the image will grow, as it were, spontaneously and within its own structure, and not my structure' (Bacon in Sylvester 1992: 160). The painter who seeks to unlock the valve of feeling must also seek to unlock the alterity of the painting, and this can only happen through the deliberate maximization of the accidental. The artist has to renounce control. For example, the 1979 painting *Jet of Water* was meant to be a picture of a wave, but after he had painted the background of the picture Bacon simply put a mix of paint into a pot and threw it at the canvas. Through the random impact of the paint the intended wave was transformed into a jet of water and this is what Bacon worked with; he respected the otherness which the accident had made possible (Bacon in Sylvester 1992: 162-4). Bacon also threw paint at portraits (one example of this almost certainly being the *Two Figures*). He was seeking to 'keep the vitality of the accident' (Bacon in Sylvester 1992: 17) because only in this way might the paintings have the ability to reveal alterity as the reality of existence: 'It's an illogical method of making, an illogical way of attempting to make what one hopes will be a logical outcome – in the sense that one hopes one

---

[4] Bacon's frequent allusions to the excremental can also be seen in terms of his concern to pull aside the curtain. They are not mere affects. Here bear in mind Kundera's announcement that kitsch is a 'categorical agreement with being' involving 'the absolute denial of shit, in both the literal and the figurative senses of the word' (Kundera 1984: 248). Bacon's confrontation with the excremental is a denial of the categorical agreement with being – it is an acceptance of indeterminacy. Or, as Kundera put it: 'Either/or: either shit is acceptable (in which case don't lock yourself in the bathroom!) or we are created in an unacceptable manner' (Kundera 1984: 248).

will be able to suddenly make the thing there in a totally illogical way but that it will be totally real' (Bacon in Sylvester 1992: 105).

Of course, neither Kundera nor Bauman embrace the accidental in precisely this way. But they do create space for their texts to be given a multiplicity of meanings, and therefore they allow for their work to become other than they might have intended. They let their work be used as levers on the recovery of alterity. Kundera's novels are exceptionally tightly and deliberately structured but this is done in the name of making the novel and its readers 'increasingly sensitive to the *poetry of the improbable*' (Kundera 2010: 171). This is the temper of the essays in *The Art of the Novel*. There Kundera put forward the argument that the novel explores *existence* not *reality* and 'existence is not what has occurred, existence is the realm of human possibilities, everything that man can become, everything he's capable of'. But this is always existence in the world and therefore the novel also has to be aware of the historical dimension in which these possibilities are discharged and lived (Kundera 1988: 42). Kundera points the novel in the direction of the possible, and therefore towards what is other to necessity and 'what must be'.

The style of Bauman's writing also increasingly seeks to create the space for readings other than he might have intended. Just as Bacon renounced his control over the canvas, Bauman gives up his authority over his authorship. He permits his work to become *other*. His *44 Letters from the Liquid Modern World* (which collects pieces written for *La Repubblica delle Donne*) deliberately plays on the accidental; the accident of being asked to write for an Italian newspaper, the accident of whether or not these 'letters' will be read (after all they cannot demand to be read), the accident of the time and place in which they were written. All of these historical dimensions of the letters' existence are emphasized. Their alterity is unlocked. But Bauman says it is not at all an accident that there are precisely 44 letters. Bauman wrote 44 letters in homage to the Polish writer Adam Mickiewicz who in one of his own works called a figure representing Freedom by the name of Forty-Four. Consequently, when Bauman uses Mickiewicz's number he is registering one strand of the historical dimension of his own existence. But of course this begs another question: why did Mickiewicz give Freedom the name Forty-Four? Bauman proposes that the name was chosen purely, 'in the heat of inspiration – motivated … by a care for poetic harmony rather than an intention to convey a cryptic message' (Bauman 2010: 4). For Bauman there is a truth to be unlocked from the name and number Forty-Four. It is the truth of alterity and the freedom of ethical responsibility following its being pulled out from behind the curtain.

Conclusion

Zygmunt Bauman, Francis Bacon and Milan Kundera are all concerned to pull aside the curtain of necessity in order to reveal the truth of human existence, the reality of alterity. Each does this in a different sphere of cultural activity, but each draws on inspiration from outside their own 'discipline' in order to try to unlock the valves of feeling and thus return us to the humanity which the contemporary historical moment otherwise denies. Bacon was inspired by poets like Eliot and Yeats, Kundera has been inspired by Beethoven and Schoenberg, Bacon and Bauman has drawn inspiration from a range of novelists, not the least of whom is Kundera. They are all playing the same game of trying to deny the hold of necessity over human indeterminacy. They are all concerned to do nothing less than play a part in making the world fit for humanity through the release of the *indeterminacy of alterity*.

And there is something else they share, something which also makes the work of one different from the work of the others. They all uphold the integrity of the tradition in terms of which they work. They all know that if the historical dimension of human existence is going to be their object of inquiry, and that if the release of alterity from the trap of history is going to be their concern, they need also to know the historical dimension of their own work. They need allies in the business of unlocking the valves of feeling. It is indeed noticeable how Bacon positioned himself in relation to Velazquez, Poussin, Degas and none of his contemporaries. 'Today there is absolutely no one to talk to', Bacon once remarked (Bacon in Sylvester 1992: 66). In his essay on Bacon, Kundera makes a comment which applies to his own work too: 'The twentieth century does not cancel our debts to Shakespeare' (Kundera 2010: 8). Kundera always carefully identifies his work as an instalment in the history of the novel and has announced: 'The only context for grasping a novel's worth is the history of the European novel. The novelist needs answer to no one but Cervantes'. Of course, this comment presupposes the novelist's knowledge of Cervantes and, by extension, of the history of the novel to which she or he contributes (Kundera 1988: 144). Meanwhile, Bauman's commitment to tradition was made quite clear when he said: 'Being part of the cultural tradition defines the fashion in which one seeks knowledge and understanding: respect for reality, self-control and self-criticism' (Bauman 1987: 1). Without an awareness of the tradition in which we work we actually cannot work – we can have no questions, no way of looking, no sense of the contemporary historical dimension of our explorations. Without tradition we cannot unlock the valves on our own feeling.

Commitment to unlocking the valves of feeling (feeling human, human feeling), and to the recovery of the indeterminacies of alterity from the necessary is therefore far too serious to be carried out under the sway of fashion or the banner 'anything goes'. The point is to be aware of the historical dimension of human existence, to be aware of what has happened to the face of the other and thereby to play better the existentially compelling game of its recovery as the freedom and responsibility of the truth of alterity. In the form and content of their work this is the shared message of Francis Bacon, Milan Kundera and Zygmunt Bauman. It is also the burden of responsibility they place on their audiences.

References

Bauman, Z. (1987): "The Importance of Being Marxist", in *Social Theory and Social Criticism: Essays for Tom Bottomore*, edited by W. Outhwaite and M. Mulkay. Oxford: Basil Blackwell.
Bauman, Z. (1989): *Modernity and the Holocaust*. Cambridge: Polity Press.
Bauman, Z. (2002): *Liquid Modernity*. Cambridge: Polity Press.
Bauman, Z. (2008): *The Art of Life*. Cambridge: Polity Press.
Bauman, Z. (2010): *44 Letters from the Liquid Modern World*. Cambridge: Polity Press.
Bauman, Z. and K. Tester (2001): *Conversations with Zygmunt Bauman*. Cambridge: Polity Press.
Davies, H.M. (2002): *Francis Bacon: The Papal Portraits of 1953*. San Diego, CA: Museum of Contemporary Art.
Deleuze, G. (2005): *Francis Bacon: The Logic of Sensation*. London: Continuum.
Eliot, T.S. (1969): *The Complete Poems and Plays*. London: Faber & Faber.
Jacobsen, M. Hviid and K. Tester (2007): "Sociology, Nostalgia, Utopia and Morality: A Conversation with Zygmunt Bauman". *European Journal of Social Theory*, 10(2): 305-25.
Kundera, M. (1984): *The Unbearable Lightness of Being*. London: Faber & Faber.
Kundera, M. (1988): *The Art of the Novel*. London: Faber & Faber.
Kundera, M. (1996): *The Book of Laughter and Forgetting*. London: Faber & Faber.
Kundera, M. (2000): *Immortality*. London: Faber & Faber.
Kundera, M. (2007): *The Curtain: Essays*. London: Faber & Faber.
Kundera, M. (2010): *Encounter: Essays*. London: Faber & Faber.
Russell, J. (1979): *Francis Bacon*. London: Thames & Hudson.
Sylvester, D. (1992): *The Brutality of Fact: Interviews with Francis Bacon*. London: Thames & Hudson.
van Alphen, E. (1992): *Francis Bacon and the Loss of Self*. London: Reaktion.

Chapter 3
José Saramago's Sociology

Michael S. Drake

Introduction

In one of the novels of the Portuguese author, José Saramago, the 'common-sense' of his leading character explains its own method in the succinct formulation that 'metaphors have always been the best way of explaining things' (Saramago 1999: 233). The statement is of wider import, indicating Saramago's own stance as a storyteller, using the device of fiction as a way of explaining the world. Common-sense is of course the bugbear of sociology, which demotes it to a part of that-which-is-to-be-explained, rather than according it the status of rival explanation. However, Saramago's statement does not infer that sociology per se is grounded on a category mistake. Rather, it suggests that we can differentiate between sociology as an empirical remapping of the social world, where it takes up cudgels against common sense in order to erect its own rival simulacra, and sociology as critical enquiry, which has an entirely different relationship to common sense as an element of the social world, as a factor to be taken into account, without imposing an ontological distinction between what is to be explained and the tools of explanation.

This chapter will consider some of the novels of José Saramago as critical sociology in another form. The use of literature for sociological insight has some precedent and important studies have used it as a source (see, for example, Sennett 1977, or Erving Goffman's frequent use of examples from literature, among a wide range of other sources, to illustrate his arguments). Wolf Lepenies (1988) has argued that sociology originated out of literature as commentary on society and the discourse that surrounded it, an argument resonant with Jürgen Habermas' (1989) analysis of the literary dimensions of the public sphere, often neglected in the take-up of that work by political sociology in favour of an understanding in which the public sphere functions to mediate civil society and the institutions of the state, with the resulting disappearance of the cultural politics of the public sphere which were integral to Habermas' original analysis. Jim McGuigan (2005) has pointed out how in Habermas, the literary dimension of the public sphere was integral to the function of the whole, because public critique of the cultural field constituted a forum for reflection on the relation between self and society, rather than simply on policies of the state. This was the public sphere that produced the 'prehistory' of sociology, in work extending across philosophy and literature. This public sphere preceded the separation of natural sciences, social sciences and humanities, the emergence of distinct disciplines, and the nineteenth century institutionalization of those divisions with the professionalization of the sciences. Lepenies demonstrates how sociology's subsequent aspiration to the status of a science in that later context rendered it unable to recognise itself in literary forms, with the result that literature (and indeed all cultural representation) became perceived by sociology only as data, as the object to be interpreted, for sociology, rather than as insightful sociological interpretation in itself.

This chapter takes up Wolf Lepenies' challenge to recover our understanding of literature as sociology and to work our way back to a literary, or poetic, sociology, through an analytical overview of novels by the José Saramago. Saramago is known as a politically motivated author, but I will show that in reducing his work to ideology we overlook its sociological import. Such a reductive operation is usually undertaken because we forget what sociology can be. If Lepenies is correct, a literary sociology would enable us to reconfigure our discipline, not only by redrawing boundaries, but requiring us to rethink what sociology is.

Saramago's sociology is not empiricist, but nor is it 'interpretive sociology'. Rather, his novels are sociology as speculative social thought, undertaken through the form of an imaginary which is able to get to the core of contemporary concerns normally concealed beneath the surface assumptions of social life. Saramago's sociology is undertaken in the form of novelistic explorations of tendencies within contemporary society. An often explicit and detailed typification of his protagonists (the clerk, the teacher, the doctor's wife, the prime minister, the mechanic) enables Saramago to investigate effects of social processes for situated subjectivity in the same way that Max Weber employs his ideal types in reference to the situated individual. Similarly, the relation of narrative developments to the subject is like Goffman's dramaturgies in relation to the actor. Just as the protagonists are generalizations, ideal types, so the settings Saramago describes are similarly sociological conceptualizations. There are no references to particular place or institution in Saramago's novels, but strong representations of the city, the state, the office, the schoolteacher's common room, the doctor's surgery, the doorstep, all as social locations or situations in Goffman's (1959) sense. At the same time, Saramago evades the tendency for such cultural commentary to become ideologically didactic by writing in a reflexive dimension, continually interrogating the everyday subjective conditions of knowledge and enquiry, and in that sense his novelistic methodology fulfils the function Habermas ascribed to the cultural public sphere of the 18th century.

Fiction as Experimental Sociology

The narrative of the novel form enables Saramago to think *experimentally*, in a way that is conventionally and methodologically foreclosed for the social sciences for both practical and ethical reasons. At the same time, however, this experimental sociology suggests that surface appearances can be more significant than we like to assume, since our definitive and overriding concern to get beyond the taken-for-granted aspects of social life leads us to dismiss such features, using a range of devices to downplay the everyday and the immediate in favour of a secretive reality to which our refined methodologies ostensibly give us unique and privileged access. As social scientists cut off from direct access to the interiority of the social subject, we habitually tend to look for hidden motivations, meanings and forces and neglect the superficial, the self-evident, which becomes recaptured by Saramago's experiment, generating sociological insight.

Saramago takes up the older engagement of sociologists such as Georg Simmel and Marcel Mauss in exploring 'the independent life of society' through metaphor, allegory, style and structure, which all bear sociological weight without ever carrying 'a message' in the sense of ideologically didactic 'realist' literature. In fact, the closest literary correlates to Saramago's work are probably the novel explorations produced as part of what Václav Havel called the 'unpolitical politics' of the underground and subversive traditions of the post war European Eastern bloc (Havel 1988), or the magical realism often produced by Latin American authors working under similarly authoritarian regimes. The ironic distanciation of such novels enabled their authors to escape the attention of the censors, who were looking for literature as didactic in its opposition as the laudatory accounts of politically-motivated achievement approved by the totalitarian party or junta. Saramago's long life under Portuguese fascism may have set a similar template for his thought, but he only began to write the novels we know in his disillusionment with both the 1974 'Carnation Revolution' that had overthrown the remains of the Salazar regime, and with the ideological and institutional forms of Marxism and the Communist Party in which he had invested his emancipatory humanism. If there is an evasion of censorship here, it is evasion of Saramago's own, internal censor, an ingrained habitus of the imagination – not only that internal to the subject formed under fascism, but also the censor in him, who during the Revolution purged the newspaper at which he worked of ideological opponents. The political task of the fiction he subsequently wrote was to evade both bad faith and cynicism, accomplished by developing a sociological imagination corresponding to C. Wright Mills' (1959) formulation, which enabled Saramago's fiction-writing to explore contemporary social trends and experience through ideal-type characters and settings. In Saramago's work, the resulting ironic distanciation serves to enable his fiction to freely explore the potential of the sociological imagination when emancipated from the self-imposed shackles of scientistic empiricism and abstractionist social theory.

The Global Condition of Literature

José Saramago's novels are widely translated. For this chapter I have read them in English translations. Rather than translation obscuring what the author 'really meant' (as though that is accessible anyway, since reading is an entirely different interpretive activity from writing and texts take on a life of their own once in print), we can instead understand translation and dissemination of works of literature, music, etc., into other cultural contexts as adding globalized, or 'hybrid' meanings. This conceptual approach to the effects of globalization on culture was first developed to explain the appearance of new youth sub-cultures of second and third generation immigrant minorities of global migration, as cultural innovation and diversification appeared when the apparently monolithic 'national' cultures of the old Western imperial nation-states began to fragment in the context of post-colonialization. The new cultural forms that emerged in the context of mass migrations, cultural fusion and diversification are usually described by terms such as 'hybrid' or 'mestizo'. The global dissemination of literature via its translation into English as an effective global language also has this effect. It is not so much the change of meaning in translation which adds to the layers, but the hybridization of meaning subsequent on our reading in a 'glocal' context (Robertson 1995; Pieterse 1995). Dis-embedding is equally a re-embedding, in new context.

Moreover, we need to be aware that an author such as Saramago, with his lifelong commitment to a humanist internationalism, wrote not only for an indigenous readership, but for global readers. Particularly toward the end of his life, when he was at his most prolific, Saramago knew that his novels would be translated. Nevertheless, sometimes, it seems clear that the text is introducing the reader to specific features of the Portuguese historical experience. Sometimes the references are to Lusaphone concerns, especially to do with language, in particular his subversion of grammatical conventions associated with cultural hegemony in the translation of social order onto the order of language. Saramago uses little punctuation, but rather than an avant-garde affectation, his aim is to capture the way that ordinary people speak. The artificial breaks introduced by grammatical devices which separate the speech of characters from authorial narration function to establish a centred authority in conventional forms and thus bear the ideological implication that both technical expertise and a distinct authoritative voice are necessary to tell a story (I thank Jimmy Turner for this point). Saramago's authorial intention is to carry into literature some legacies of the oral culture in which he was brought up as a child of an illiterate, but story-telling family. We can nevertheless read in Saramago common features of a European and even a global experience. That experience exemplifies C Wright Mills' (1959) concept of the 'sociological imagination', linking the individual and their experience (through a representational proxy, the character on whom the novels focus at any given time) to society (in an imaginary extrapolation of contemporary social forms, trends and relationships).

Saramago's characters are always embedded in the social, and the social is embedded in them, articulated through their inner voice, those internal dialogues which Saramago conjures up, where his omission of punctuation and paragraphing effectively replicates the chaos of internal dialogue, the rambling contradictory cascade of flow-of-consciousness, most especially in indecision and panic, conditions which his characters, like all of us, experience as part of the common fabric of their inner life in a context of chronic uncertainty.

Authorship, Analysis and Allegory

My aim here is not to situate José Saramago sociologically, treating his biography as data for the analysis of his texts, in either a psychoanalytic or a social determinist frame. The first frames an author's texts in terms of intrinsic meanings, of which the author themselves may be unaware; the second frames the text in terms of extrinsic meanings deriving from its relation to its contemporary social context, enquiring into its wider social function; the first privileges psychological context, the second social context. Both these approaches assume that there is a true meaning of the text to be inferred from its conditions of production. Sociologically, it does not matter what Saramago 'really meant', or what his novels 'really' express, rather, what matters is what his novels can tell us about our contemporary social condition.

Authorship, contextualization and relevance all play a part in that, but in this approach it is the texts themselves that have 'agency', producing meaning and insight, rather than their value being attributed, given by something outside them. In a sense, this depersonalizes Saramago's work, dispossessing the author as agent, but as fellow authors, we can recognise that texts take on their own life once they have left the author's pen, typewriter or hard drive. Not only do they cross oceans, cultures and histories, but they are edited, translated, published, marketed, read, reviewed, discussed, recontextualized and reframed at every stage. Our writings become, in Michel Foucault's terms, discourse.

It may seem odd to think of Saramago's work as beyond political ideology, since his own life was explicitly articulated ideologically. However, his turn from journalism to fiction indicates disillusionment with the forces and direction of the Portuguese revolution, in which he had played an explicitly ideological part as Communist Party member and newspaper editor. Undertaken much later in his life, but serving as a reflection on commitments and choices in his stance to the world, his *Notebooks* (2010) confirm his understanding of the inadequacy of ideology critique to grasp the contemporary world. In the *Notebooks*, that realization itself becomes the basis for critical conceptualization of the Left as a 'silent tomb', which undoes the animating work of ideological articulations of the world, representing them as ossified, dead, become (less than) myth rather than enlightenment: 'Nothing of anything at all, absolute silence, as if there were nothing but dust and spiders in the ideological tombs where they had taken refuge, or nothing more than an ancient bone which was no longer solid enough for a relic' (Saramago 2010: 21-2). This critical analysis, the literary form of his critique of ideology critique, reconfigures its object as something macabre, slightly surreal and inherently melancholic.

The world has changed radically since the age of ideology, which no longer relates contemporary concerns. The loss of security of self and social identity characteristic of a globalizing, liquid, post-ideological world propels Saramago's characters into adventure, whether willingly, in *All The Names* (1999), or unwillingly, in *The Cave* (2002). In those novels, his characters' explorations lead them to moments of enlightened clarity that are often no more than implicit in the text, unheralded, unannounced and hence resolutely secular, but which reinvoke the salvational religious narrative of redemption embedded within modern ideology and which even today permeates and gives meaning to consumer society. However, the powerful exceptions to this redemptive narrative strategy are the two sequential novels, *Blindness* (2005a) and *Seeing* (2007) which are at once Saramago's most political and most pessimistic works. There seems for Saramago the ideologist no way out of disenchanted and determinant modernity.

It was the realization of just such an impasse of ideological analysis which led Walter Benjamin into correspondence with the Frankfurt School in the 1930s, and which had driven him to develop his analysis of allegory (Benjamin 1998). Allegory is produced, Walter Benjamin argued, in what Slavoj Žižek (2010), in ironic parody of contemporary American fundamentalist Christian rhetoric, has called 'end times'. In times of terminal crisis of value-systems and world-views, when the organizing concepts of the era lose purchase on reality, but nothing else has yet appeared to replace them, the fantastic takes on the function of articulating the hopes, fears and desires of the epoch. Benjamin can help us to understand Saramago as just such an allegorist of the terminal crisis of the values of our era, which was built on the dual pillars of capital and the state, the two ill-favoured objects of Saramago's critical authorship.

Saramago's work in its sociological dimensions is often more than metaphor. He is a knowing allegorist, himself partaking of the 'enlightened false consciousness' characteristic of an age in which ideology no longer refers to a real order (Sloterdijk 1987; Žižek 1989), not because he wants to, but because he has no option not to, even as he addresses its falsehood. Allegory can no more lead us out of the forests of disenchantment than can the re-enchantments offered by ideology today, but Saramago implies that rather than turning back and seeking answers from the tombs of ideology, which have nothing new to say and merely echo the questions we throw into them, we can instead arrive at new understandings, renewed clarity, a post-postmodern enlightenment which is, however, always contingent, tacit, provisional, a moment in a world of shifting meanings which does not attempt to apprehend and freeze the world in reifying constructions. Benjamin similarly contrasted the aims of allegory with that of its contemporary sciences: 'The intention which underlies allegory is so opposed to that which is concerned with the discovery of truth that it reveals more clearly than anything else the identity of the pure curiosity which is aimed at mere knowledge with the proud isolation of man' (Benjamin 1998: 229). For Benjamin, in place of singular totalizing knowledge, allegory presents us with 'baroque polymathy'.

Jeremy Tambling (2010) reminds us of the 'danger' Benjamin identified of ascribing a singular overarching meaning to allegory, in other words, of reducing it to metaphor or symbol. Such a totalization textualizes (in the terms of Quentin Skinner's (1988) methodology for reading historical texts in political theory) in the sense that it removes a text from its immediate political *context* and instead reads it as addressing a putatively universal human condition which inevitably introduces historically anachronistic concerns reflecting the reader's own situational embeddedness. Skinner points out that a parallel process occurs with contextualizing analysis, when a text is read as an expression of its social and political context located within a historiographical framework such as historical materialism. In both cases, Skinner argues, analysis applies criteria of interpretation from outside the text itself. Instead, he wants to read texts in terms of what they *did* in their own context. Skinner therefore wants to take context (the conditions of production and reception of the text) into account, but does not accord it the privilege of determination of meaning. Texts do something, Skinner argues, and that is what we need to read. Rather than projecting our own concerns onto the text, we need to attend to what it does, to read it in terms of its effects, of what it constitutes.

Selection

Saramago's novels often exhaust his own ideological tendencies, expressed most strongly in the sentimental nostalgia for moral community and family of *The Cave* (2002). However, even there, Saramago is deliberately playing with the naive opposition between modernity and community, exhausting it, so that his work becomes a critique of the ideology critique that produces such crude oppositions. *All the Names* (1999), with its focus on the anachronistic status of the clerk, deploys its archaisms knowingly and meaningfully, rather than with the deliberate naivety of *The Cave*. The novels I have selected from his extensive oeuvre can also be described as post-ideological novels of the society of the self, but Saramago's scepticism over a selfhood that needs to continuously reaffirm itself through interior dialogue simply situates these novels as accounts of reflexivity in its complex, chronic, overfolded, uncertainty. In these novels, the attractions of both tradition and modernity are explored, exhausted, and exceeded.

My selection excludes Saramago's novels of 'alternative history', though those too offer commentary on our contemporary condition. The books selected for analysis in this chapter were all written within 10 years, along with others from 1995-2005, during the most prolific period of Saramago's mature literary production from the late 1970s, after his abandonment of institutional political activity and journalism. through to his death in 2009. My selection focuses on the novels in which Saramago traces versions of our present, extrapolating from tendencies within our contemporary reality and exploring dilemmas of the subject in the that condition. His typological settings also highlight the anomalies of our social present, the persistence of anachronism, even in the form of institutions and roles, depicting a contemporary society that is more like a socio-typological version of Leon Trotsky's economic diagnosis of 'combined and uneven development' than a uniform modernity or postmodernity.

Highlighting the disjuncture of modernities produces a quasi-magical-realist effect, but in this Saramago is simply exposing aspects of social reality that conventionally remain unremarked, under the wraps of the taken-for-granted. In

Saramago's novels, archaic institutions and social relations nestle within the heart of societies that are otherwise modern, individualized, and unremarkable to us. Different speeds and historical processes overlap in the novels, often contained within institutions that are almost ethnographically explored by the novels, and the his characters often move between them with no sense of disorientation, reminding us that our own lives intersect a plurality of life-worlds, including those of everyday lived reality within institutions that are often, in their internal mechanisms, very far from the rationalizing tendencies described by abstract theories of modernity.

However, Saramago's speculative experimental settings approximate to a universal modernity in the sense that the novels selected here take place within or around a city which is never given any more specificity. The setting is thus another ideal type, a modern trope that is familiar to a global readership through the everyday experience of urbanism and suburbanism in which Saramago situates his characters. 'The city' as a concept also refers to the *polis*, the archetypal political community, and the form thus provides Saramago with the scope for another layer of meaning in these novels, as explorations in political sociology.

Allegorical Reading

Disjuncture is particularly evident in *The Cave*, which functions as an exploration of the social and subjective consequences of the prevailing tendencies of contemporary global economic development, featuring a small rural family artisanal business faced with the indifference of corporate market monopoly which provides its customer-clients with everything they need, both managing and serving their consumerism in a totally integrated system. Even here, however, Saramago's analysis is complex, since his deliberately sentimental and patronizing characterization of the artisans seems intended to remind us of the tendencies of ideology to understand popular resistance only in terms of nostalgia or romanticism.

The Double (2005b) is about the insecurity of identity in a mediated age, a concern of modern fiction since the advent of mass society that is accelerated with digitization. The fear that we may encounter a simulacrum of ourselves is not in itself to be taken only at face value. While we can recognise the irrationality of the lead character's obsessive fears, these are merely an extrapolation of the concerns which lead us to use secure access codes for our personal data, for the realization that impersonation, and of course its criminal spectrum of identity theft, becomes so much more plausible when identity itself depends on mediated data. Those fears are of course marketized by the security industry and the novel, but the novel's insights transcend its pre-digital setting. It is about fears of identity which arise as a contradiction of the dominant ideology of consumer capitalism, the paradoxical realization of self-consciousness that in a society saturated with simulacra, one cannot be unique. The illusion of our particular individuality is given away in the internal conversation that the protagonist holds with his 'common sense' about this very problem, showing that even in the commonplace notion of 'common sense', we implicitly recognise our divided consciousness.

Seeing (2007) develops Saramago's critical political sociology beyond the vulgar anarchist opposition of community to the state. In the novel, the people refuse the contract of citizenship, refuse to play the game of constitutional politics while realizing their constituent power in Michael Hardt and Antonio Negri's sense (2001) by casting blank ballots, and thereby undermining the legitimation process on which power depends. However, this apparently anti-statist allegory contrasts with naive anarchist scenarios in which an organic and naturally communal community would appear spontaneously in place of the state. Rather, in the novel it is the ethos of public service and the discipline of everyday civility which ensures order. It is not so much the state that disappears from the city, but executive power. The novel clearly extrapolates contemporary tendencies of electoral disillusionment and falling polls that have been widely discussed in political sociology (Crook, Pakulski and Waters 1992; Crouch 2004; Hay 2007; Drake 2010). Beyond reflections on civil society, Saramago also explores the response of executive power and the 'political class' which lives off as well as for politics (Weber 1946). In the resulting scenarios, executive power reasserts itself by actively inciting (in this case actually staging) a threat to the security of civil society, in order to re-establish consensual acquiescence to domination by a sovereign, leviathan-like power over all, in an allegory that is frequently repeated on an international scale, most notably in response to 9/11. We can discount the paranoia of conspiracy theorists, but still recognise the response of the Bush regime and its allies in Blair and Berluscon as a coup d'etat in the public sphere (Agamben 2000, 2005).

Blindness (2005a) can be read as an allegorical critique of contemporary global neoliberalism and finance capital and as such, it correlates with a broad range of critical sociological analysis of the disastrously cannibalistic practices of the 'new capitalism' which had arisen on the ruins of industrialism (Sennett 2006; Klein 2008; Strange 1986; Boltanski and Chiapello 2006). Its scenario of a city in which everyone goes blind, quarantined by the rest of the world, depicts the Hobbesian world underpinning neo-liberal ideology. However, to this, Saramago's allegory adds the critical insight that in this society of competitive exchange and imperative consumption, the immediate maximization of profit precludes the key to the functioning of 'the hidden hand'; the capacity of actors to *see* (in the sense of knowing) where and how to satisfy one's desires and to *foresee* how to rationally advance one's own interests in the satisfaction of those desires, are both denied. In *Blindness*, the characters continue to pursue the same self-interest as before even though they can no longer foresee the consequences of their actions, in the same way that imperative immediate profiteering undermines the key to the operation of market economy in such a way that we do not adjust by modifying our behaviour, but continue to pursue the same ends, even though the medium of knowledge, of sight and foresight, which constituted those ends as rational, is no longer available to us. The human, social world of *Blindness* is the human, social world of neoliberal capitalism in which pursuit of self-interest is blind to the wider social conditions on which it acts, with the effect that short-term profit calculations functionally displace any longer-term strategic reasoning. This is a world in which we can no longer see (perceive, know) what we want, in which condition we therefore flounder and flail around, assuming that we desire most to satisfy the basest of pleasures because we cannot know anything else, anything beyond our own immediacy. In the novel, one character retains her sight, but far from the one-eyed becoming monarch in this land of the blind, in this context the ability to 'see' becomes socially dysfunctional and must be concealed, just as those who identified the impending disaster of credit capitalism were ignored, marginalized and even ridiculed.

What is more, as *Blindness* points out with an objectivity that is almost cruel, in short-term calculations we cannot 'see' the Other, except as the object of our desire, and since we can see (know, perceive) the Other only in the way that we can perceive anything in this apparently zero-sum world of imperative competitiveness, where any gain to one is loss to another, as an object for us to consume, we lose all sense of them even as a means for us. Saramago thus shows us how neoliberal capitalism has moved beyond the capacity of Kantian critique, into a new realm of nightmare, in which others are no longer even means, but become disposable objects for our consumption. We are now at two removes from the condition of the categorical imperative, which posits seeing (recognizing, understanding) the Other as an end. Our use of others in classical capitalism required that we allow for their reproduction and well-being, even if only to satisfy our own desire to use them again as means toward our own satisfaction. In neoliberal capitalism, our use of others can be terminal, without regard for their continuity even as an object for us. To extend the analogy and to crystallize it in concrete terms, in the classical capitalist exploitation of labour it was necessary to pay the worker a wage, in order for labour to reproduce itself for further exploitation; in neoliberal capitalism we see the reappearance of slavery, and slavery not of the plantation, which had its own conservative economy, but as a pure *extraction* of labour which will use up the bodies it consumes totally, leaving only what Giorgio Agamben (1998) terms *homo sacer*, bare life, a condition that appeared in the death camps and the gulag and is today reproduced in the mines and slave labour camps of the war-torn world, but also in the brothels of the 'black economy' expanding in the very midst of the world of rights.

Such a shift from exploitation to primary, destructive extraction is mirrored in both our approach to the environment and to each other. However, Saramago's novel shows how this can produce its own overcoming in a moment in which we are able, potentially to each and all realize the common vulnerability of each and all. Bryan S. Turner (2006) has explored similar ideas in his formulation of inescapable bodily vulnerability as grounding for universal human rights. In the novel, this condition is the city in which all become blind and know (one of the few things that can be known to each and every one of them) that all others are blind also; in the world, it is certain aspects of globalization which produce the realization of the possibility of reconstituting politics as an ethics of universal human rights, a notion that can be, as Turner has pointed out, underpinned by recognition of common human vulnerability. In the context of almost universal vulnerability to the effects of global financial crisis, this could have been a lesson learned, but, as in Saramago's imaginary city, we rather seem intent on reproducing the very same behaviour that has been exposed as self-destructive.

The shift from exploitation to extraction of labour, or in terms of capital accumulation a shift from calculably profitable investment to asset-stripping, has been remarked upon by many observers as the development within capitalism of a short-termist imperative for profit-taking that was hitherto strategically dysfunctional, in contrast to the long-term calculus of profitable investment. The selective smash and grab of destruction capitalism simply seizes whatever is proximate and of value in that moment, squeezes it of value, and it becomes a disposable brick to enable the next raid. Saramago's novel show how this occurs because we can no longer (fore)see consequences. In his novel, as in the real world of capital today, we, the blind, do not even clean up our own shit.

Names, Persons, Identities

We are discussing the work of an author whose name is known as the winner of a Nobel Prize for Literature. His books are widely available, translated into numerous languages, and can be found filed under his name, in high street and airport bookshops across the world. However, José Saramago's name was the result of the arbitrary authority inherent in one of the archaic institutions upon which modernity depends. He told in interviews how he himself had been told the story of his name by his grandparents. When his parents had taken the infant to be registered by the state, the Registrar inscribing his existence into state recognition appended to his illiterate landless peasant father's family name, the 'small name' by which that economically and socially insignificant man was known in the locality that constituted the horizons of his life, rendering it the name by which the child would be officially known. The problem of names recurs throughout many of Saramago's novels. His characters often have unlikely, almost unbelievable names, or names so ordinary they reflect their bearer's sparse, near social non-existence, arousing suspicion of inauthenticity. In this recurrent device Saramago highlights the continuous and ubiquitous insecurity of personal identity in modern and especially in 'liquid modern' society (Bauman 2000), where even a nuclear family unit may share no surname between them.

Naming is an ancient problem (Wilson 1998), but often remains sociologically unremarked. The absence of fixed surnames in medieval society created little cause for concern so long as it remained characteristic of the lower orders, while for the nobility, a name defined both character and fate. In early modern Europe, individual social mobility and the upward class mobility of the bourgeoisie meant increasing fixity of names, with the development of more rigorous and uniform naming systems, which, although differing from one culture to another, were all transmitted downwards in the trans-European civilizing process, increasingly policed by the growing surveillance apparatus of the state, and extruded beyond Europe by the administration of global empires. Genealogically, even where some aspects of identity were traced through the matrilineal line, these systems obliterated female personal lineage in deference to patriarchy. However, even in the early twentieth century, this identification was still avoidable, as we know from prominent examples of those who for one reason or another escaped its clutches, such as the obscurity that still surrounds the relation between name and person of the author who published novels and film scripts as B. Traven. However, that indeterminacy of identity had become foreclosed by the 1970s, when the radical US political activist Abbie Hoffman was able to escape arrest by the FBI only by resorting to cosmetic surgery, in addition to the more traditional means of fleeing the country and adopting a new named identity under forged papers.

Throughout the later 20th century, individual identity became increasingly forensic, with development of fingerprinting, genetic mapping, retinal scanning and most recently digital facial recognition technology which can be applied to the immense database available to the increasingly globally integrated intelligence apparatus, including CCTV footage from public streets and public buildings, media reportage, social media such as YouTube, as well as the footage recorded by the surveillance squads which are now part of every public order policing operation, everywhere. However, rather than subscribing to reactive paranoia, Saramago's fiction enquires into the nature of the insecurity represented by both ubiquitous surveillance and the public unease that gives it a grip on our fears.

Amongst the referents that today enable us to identify an individual as a particular person, the name is the *social* element. It is this social aspect of identity which is no longer trusted, which is considered inadequate. On Facebook, millions confront this fear on a daily basis, always with the background awareness that this imperative online buttress to our personhood may be withdrawn, disappear. It is in this knowledge that as persons we reinforce and reaffirm, on a daily if not an hourly basis, our faith in ourselves and our recognition by others. In *Blindness*, with the collapse of the social, names disappear completely as characters become known to each other through their place in each other's lives, through co-presence, and are differentiated or identified by reference to the work which they can no longer do (just as many modern names refer to trades long rendered obsolete).

Historically, as names became increasingly essential to the formation of modern society, the state became the arbiter of the connection between name and body. In *All the Names* (1999) Saramago explores that ontological function of the archive of the state, the simple physical location of paper records, of tattered, faded folders which provide the only ultimate verification of social reality. The clerk of that story, Senhor José, as his hobby, collects cuttings about famous compatriots, in a conscious mirroring of the function of the archive of the state which Saramago sees replicated in all the collecting characteristic of modern society, of what people 'believe to be their spare time'. Collecting, and likewise the surveillance operations of the state, have no instrumental purpose; their function is rather symbolic, even 'metaphysical': a barricade against 'the idea of chaos being the one ruler of the world' (Saramago 1999: 13). For Saramago's clerk, this 'leisure' is of course the mirror of his labour, just as his 'home' is a room adjoining the Central Registry of the state archive where he works.

This insignificant subaltern thus transpires not to be introduced to us by chance. Saramago has situated his character at the sociological fulcrum of modernity, as its precise point of articulation. As servant of the state, Senhor José is nothing but an extension of it, living through an ontological dependence that is the explicit and conscious consequence of his voluntary servitude. The story of *All the Names* is of his emancipation through transgression, driven by the internal struggle of the clerk to come to terms with the *value* of lives that are simultaneously signified and displaced by the names. The emancipation of one single subject of the archive from obscurity becomes his own emancipation from the ontological dependence of servitude. Ultimately, *All the Names* is an optimistic novel, with its denouement suggesting that the state can be saved from its depersonalizing tendencies, the implication that it can be benignly humanized, represented in Senhor José's redemption from his multiple sins of transgression. Saramago remained a modernist and a humanist despite his critical insights.

The Double (2005b) is also about fears about identity in public, the fear that one is perhaps not as unique as our dominant ideology of individualization tells us we are. Tertulliano Maximo Alfonso, the teacher protagonist of the novel, conducts conversations with himself, with his common sense, and even in that 'common sense' more than one self inhabits the body. It is a sociological commonplace to accept the multiplicity or intersectionality of social identities in late modern, or liquid societies, where different contexts constitute our social identity differently and require us to perform the appropriate role in order to retain recognition as an authentic agent, but Saramago's use of these interior conversations exposes as delusional the idea that social constraint to perform social identity means we are alienated from authentic selfhood. This function of interior dialogue is most particularly and ironically effective in *The Double*, where the basic premise of the book is the primary character's search for the actor who appears to be identical to him, his double, and who thereby, for the character himself alone (others find the likeness barely remarkable), threatens the integrity of his person. Self-identity is shown as also divided, even fragmentary. The teacher's common sense lays claim to some expertise in this (and in that claim subverts the conventional 'common sense' notion of common sense, which would suggest we are a coherent self), pointing out that it is in emergencies, crises, that the multiplicity of voices within us become aware of each other, enter into dialogue, contradict one another, with the effect that is commonly understood as a problematic splintering of ego, as confusion, but which is implied by this interior dialogue to be in fact a source of multiple views on a predicament, producing a potential source of insight through a Nietzschean perspectivalism (Saramago 2005b: 22).

The State and Bureaucracy

Through *All the Names*, Saramago explores the contradictory condition of subjectivity of the clerk, expected to perform impersonal objectivity toward the public with a bureaucratic disregard for persons which means all are to be treated equally, while himself subject to personal domination under the guise of that very same professional detachment, resulting in a subalternity which is even denied recognition as such.

The novel concerns the keeping of the records of the dead and the living, a role that the modern state took over from the medieval church, focusing particularly on that a role as custodianship of the memory of each and every 'soul'. The novel proceeds like an exploration of the subjectivity produced by an institution conforming to Max Weber's analysis of modern bureaucracy, from the point of view of the subaltern ranks of the hierarchy, with attention to the practical micro-details of pre-digital mass filing systems in terms of space, materials and the distribution of bodies, as a constitutive Foucaultian disciplinary apparatus. Saramago thus explores, through the clerk and his interior life, the subjective effects of this architecture of knowledge, explored here through fiction as an experimental method of speculative sociological imagination, extrapolating conditions into consequences in the lived context of the everyday life of an individual whose inner life is revealed by the techniques of the novelist.

It is significant that the self-appointed task of the clerk – to find a woman known to him only through chance misplacement of her state records (birth, marriage, divorce) – is, like his title, his status, his habitus and his very identity, redundant today, in the age of digital technology and online identities. The obsolescence of his work function implies the obsolescence of the clerk's entire personality formation. Moreover, that anachronism is instrumental. Saramago published the book in Portuguese in 1997, by which time he was already renowned in a globalizing, networked world, his work translated into English and published within two years for a global market. The book's anachronistic setting is thus deliberate, an indication of the social and cultural impoverishment of the clerk, the full extent of which is only highlighted for us the reader as it gradually unfolds for the clerk himself, as he ventures further into the outside world in search of his obsession, until it finally reaches a terrible, pathetic conclusion in the deceased woman's empty flat. The clerk is Saramago's contemporary everyman, the universal subject of a globalizing information society.

The pitiful poverty of the clerk's life becomes evident only gradually. Mid-way through *All the Names* we are given a detailed tour of the interior of his 'house' (which seems more like an English bedsit) when he considers where to hide something so that a visitor would not see it. We realize that he lives in one room, with a bed, table and one chair, a cubicle for a bathroom and a curtained niche used as a wardrobe. We only see this in his disengagement from his responsible, dutiful habitus, after and as a consequence of his committing burglary in his obsessive pursuit of the whereabouts of the real person whose archival record randomly caught his attention. It is only in this state of alienation from himself, in which he sees himself doubled (Saramago 1999: 100), that we see revealed the reality of his status expressed in his accommodation, his person a mere annex of the archive. We are used to thinking in terms of an opposition between relative and absolute conceptions of poverty, but Saramago here reminds us that these are not really opposites, but variations in measure of the same thing, of poverty considered as material resources, as income and wealth, and, even where we take into account *quality of life*, we reduce it to what can be measured and compared, and do not consider the *quality of living*.

Much later in the novel, after he has finally located the person he has been seeking, and has visited the deceased schoolteacher's relatively spacious, light modern flat, and has abandoned himself to the ruination of his own career, Senhor José himself reflects on the hovel-like character of what he calls his house, clinging to the edifice of the Central Registry in which he works. The point here seems political rather than sociological, or one of applied insight, in which precarity opens the possibility to see the actual poverty of our living lives as *qualitatively* cramped, impoverished and compromised by the routine security we come to think we need in the absence of alternative visions of how we might live. Such alternatives are conventionally envisaged through the medium of the state, which is perhaps the real subject of *All the Names*, if *Blindness* is about the individual and *Seeing* is about civil society. Writing in the context of the devastation produced by neo-liberal globalization, and again evading his own ideologically didactic censor, Saramago's mini-parable here, a story with a story, shows us that security under the state conceals our lives' qualitative confinement by lowering our horizons so that we can no longer see beyond the bars of our 'need' to be exploited, regimented, governed and reassured by continual disciplinary surveillance. Precarity is shocking because it shatters the cage of our illusions, but its risk may be a necessary condition of subjective emancipation.

Biopolitics: The State, the Body and Memory

In his illness, after being caught in a downpour when burgling the school in pursuit of further records on the trail of his obsession to somehow find the woman 'in person', as though she could be redeemed from the anonymity to which the state consigns her memory, the adjoining door between Senhor José's home and chamber-like open office floor of the Central Registry, this door between his public and private lives, comes into use. First, the clerk himself trespasses this symbolic public/private divide, taking a personal interest in the public archived records, selecting a particular person from the impersonal mass of individual records in which all are treated as a general category, and using his access to the public domain for his personal interest. As a consequence, the public domain, in the person of the Registrar himself, intrudes into the clerk's private domain. Saramago here offers us a realist sociological parable of political philosophy, extrapolating the consequences of the demands of an affectively sensitized society to 'humanize' the workings of the state in relation to its subjects, but rather than a normative account, his allegory produces a critical analysis of the outcome which parallels some of the work of theorists of biopolitics who have taken their lead from the later Foucault (Agamben 1998; Esposito 2008, 2012). If we receive from the state, as individual persons, we must expect that state to take an interest, beyond the impersonal, in our private life, since that is its ethical obligation in that exchange.

If we expect the impersonal state to become personal, to become interested in us, as feeling, living persons, we must also expect the less welcome corollary, that our private life becomes open to the state, our lives transparent to its surveillance and evaluation. The state in this parable is represented by the figure of the Registrar, benign but terrible, 'who knows all there is to know about the kingdoms of the visible and the invisible' (Saramago 1999: 110), and who, we and the clerk learn, collects all available information about his own subordinates, who, 'likes to know everything' (Saramago 1999: 113). The archives of the state, assumed a paragon of order, are revealed by the clerk's nocturnal incursions as chaotic in this basic function of monitoring the population in whose existence the state consists as a necessity. But as the clerk has discovered, the state (or the Central Registry) is not what it appears. The potential for a necessary unyielding rationality of state borne of its bureaucratic workings, theorized by Max Weber, is here undermined by an uncoordinated but nonetheless effective tangle of subversive petty interests – the egoistic whims of architects, the perversity of clerks infected with irrational desires by the 'disoriented society' (Saramago 1999: 148), by spiders, dust, and the limitations of physical space, all of which circumvent the realization of the omniscient metaphysical construct of 'the state'. However, we quickly learn that the power of the state lies not in its purported efficiency, but in its symbolic function, the 'miracle' it works of 'transforming life and death into mere paper' (Saramago 1999: 152), a secular transubstantiation producing the effect of an illusion of security, recognition, certainty, through which it totally possesses its subjects as the ultimate, ontological verification of their existing and of ever having existed. It is the archive, not the body, which in the modern state demarcates between life and death, which endows life with recognition, with social reality (Saramago 1999: 156).

In an unprecedented speech to the assembled administrative staff of the Central Registry, the Registrar makes explicit that symbolic function of the state as its primary rationale. Having first been drawn into its archaic and dismal operations, these have gradually been revealed as anachronistic even within the context of the novel, which is not set as we might initially have imagined in the early twentieth century, but much later, in a world that is, beyond the Registry, recognisably like our own. The Central Registry's technology and organization are, in terms of the outside world, obsolete, but in the Registrar's speech, that very anachronism grounds its authority in tradition, in a symbolic order rather than in the rational laws on which we assume its functions are grounded. Legitimation is therefore not quite what it seems. The tendency of legal-rational authority observed by Max Weber (1946) to ultimately supersede all tradition, is here reversed – the law is legitimate only because based in tradition, and tradition must maintain what is rationally obsolete in order to remain legitimate. Thus, the state, if an anachronism in a globalizing world, is nonetheless a necessary anachronism, and must, moreover, function through archaic practices, precisely in order to legitimate the rational-legal order. The law that is increasingly the law of the global requires the anachronism of symbolic nation-states, with all their fussing, petty regulations and divergences, however inconvenient and inefficient these appear to be.

The Registrar's speech suggests that the state's symbolic authority consists in the archive itself. Later, we find that this speech is made in response to the crisis that Senhor José's actions have revealed for the Registrar, who has (unbeknown to the clerk and to us, the readers) been monitoring his every move. In this speech he proposes, or declares, a revolution. Not of the kind that will abolish the nation-state, or the Central Registry, but a revolution which will reconstitute the social order in its representation of itself to itself. He proposes not that the Central Registry be reformed or modernized, but that the archive itself be re-organized, to reunite the files of the living with those of the dead in one single, unitary archive. His speech is essentially about the archive as repository of social memory, and of its inherent responsibility in that role for the function of representing society to itself, as if the archive were the Durkheimian totem of the nation-state considered as a unity of the metaphysical ideal, the offices of administration, and the people. His reasoning for this re-organization is that a change in the archive is therefore identical with a change in the state in that wider sense, in the social order which routinely disregards the dead, just as the archive routinely disregards them by removing them to the farther reaches of the labyrinthine corridors, enabling society to forget. Inspired (as we subsequently learn) by Senhor José's obsessive pursuit of one random sampled person from the archive- who by this time we learn is tragically dead by her own hand – the Registrar proposes no less a profound change for society than that it cease to forget. He speaks, emotively, to similarly inspire his staff, of the task of building a new symbolic order and thereby reconstituting society from within its sacred representation of itself to itself. In the context of post-fascist Portugal, proposing to reunite the dead and the living has serious implications, as the activity of the Association for the Recovery of Historical Memory has had in Spain, but Saramago's insight takes us well beyond such national particularities to consider a society beyond the 'denial of death' of modern conceit.

Learning that the subject of his obsession, the real woman whose card he inadvertently selected and that caught his eye and his conscience in a moment of distraction, is dead, Senhor José sets out to find her grave. The General Cemetery is superficially a mirror image of the Central Registry, its complementary institution, but the symmetry is only superficial. It has the same administrative structure, the same external facade, and has grown by the same process of accretion, which Saramago thereby points out as a feature of the modern state in general, at intervals, when it becomes overcrowded, breaking down the walls and rebuilding them further out (a process analogous with the scope of the state rather than, in most cases, its territoriality). In this way, both the cemetery and the registry have grown haphazardly, an effect that is common to the modern state in the general and universalized form in which it has developed from its medieval European origins.

However, the care of the bodies of the dead endows the General Cemetery with relatively lower prestige than the Central Registry is accorded for its archival custodianship of the paper records of dead. Marginality and neglect in this case, as so often, have produced a space in which innovation was possible. Centuries before the Registrar's recently announced decision, his counterpart, the Keeper of the Cemetery, had decided that walls produced social forgetfulness of the dead and so had them demolished, with the effect that the cemetery has subsequently expanded not radially but as a series of tributary developments. In an astonishing aerial image, Saramago shows us how this has the effect that in its extremities, its ever-branching and narrowing capillaries merge into the leafy suburbs, where the dead and living mingle in close proximity. In contrast to the monolithic and insular Central Registry, the General Cemetery as an institution has maintained pace with the world around it, becoming part of it rather than representing it. Here, Saramago's allegory offers us the vision of another kind of state, with a similar function but very different precepts, focused on the provision of care rather than the concentration of power.

The title of the book, *All the Names*, it transpires, is the motto of the General Cemetery (1999: 188), which presents itself in an ontologically affirmative sense, in contrast to the Central Registry's deductive ontological power, in the claim that a gravestone is the only material validation that a person has ever lived. This was alive, the gravestone says, in contrast to the archive's ultimate possession of the name and the life, consigning it, in death, to bureaucratic oblivion. In contrast to the nightmarish interior of the Central Registry's archive of the dead, the cemetery proves a place of beauty and delight, this grand garden of the bodies of all the dead, in contrast to the house of the records of subjects of the state, exuding calm rather than the terror invoked by the depths of the Central Registry.

Enlightened Disenchantment

The cemetery, like an enlightenment version of the enchanted garden of fairy tales, does not cast a magic spell over the clerk, but rather subversively *unworks* the spell of the symbolic power of the state, finally compounding his rebellion against the imagined need for career, discipline and professional detachment. When the clerk finds the grave, he sleeps the night there, and takes the next day off work, to visit the home of the dead woman, though he finds no revelation. The novel thus finally reveals it is about apparent disillusionment which turns out to be enlightenment, a negative dialectic in reverse. We have followed the clerk's slow, professional self-destruction, the gradual dismantling of the psychological apparatus of self-delusion that we call integrity, as the impeccably respectable professional becomes liar, forger, burglar, thief, impersonator, stalking a woman known to him only through the archival record and for whom he has, initially, no sense of personal respect, seeing her merely as an interesting specimen, an extension of his hobby of celebrity-watching. We watch his disintegration, his splitting in two, his increasing compromise of ethical conduct, his dissimulation, manipulation, and ultimately his abandonment to his expected dismissal.

In the long slow conclusion to the novel, after the preceding revelations, disillusionment, and abjection, a new enlightenment slowly unfolds for the clerk. First in the cemetery, when Senhor José discovers that the grave he has found is probably not that of the deceased woman he has been seeking, since the numbers on the graves do not correspond to the cemetery's records, and she could therefore be in any one of the plots reserved for suicides, producing a realization which unfolds more fully when he tenderly and carefully lies down in exhaustion on the dead woman's bed, when he realizes that he has never known her, cannot know her, that her suicide remains inexplicable and, contrary to all his expectations, finds that he already knows enough. Now, he realizes, he can now let go of the fetish for imperative acquisition of knowledge and power, in not needing to know any more than that she existed, that she had a life, just as we, the reader, never learn her name, even at the end of the book.

Research

At the end of *All the Names*, Senhor José seems to have finally escaped the conscientious superego of his 'common sense'. Common sense is of course a commonplace negative for sociology, against which we define our enterprise, as 'getting behind' common sense which tells us the world is as it is because it is that way. Saramago exposes that foundational fraud. The teacher, like most of us, prefers to act upon his hopes, rather than the message of his common sense. We rarely follow common sense. Like Saramago's characters, we proceed by analysis and intuition, by attempts to anticipate outcomes and consequences through precisely this kind of interior dialogue between what we know (evidence) and our intuitive hopes and hunches. In a sense, then, every member of society is at once a novelist and a sociologist. In its long critical opposition, a position that has often defined the discipline, sociology has been jousting at windmills, since no-one is duped for long by common sense, any more than we are empty vessels for ideology. As Anthony Giddens (1991) pointed out, reflexivity is integral to the contemporary human condition, not a privileged methodology of ethnographers. In this respect, Saramago the sociologist is also very close to Erving Goffman, who also incorporates commonplace insights into his analysis in books that sometimes appear as not much more than a scrapbook of cuttings, strung together with wry observation.

Other comparisons to Goffman arise throughout *The Double*, for instance in Saramago's drawing our attention to 'subgestures' which the novelist's craft conventionally reduces to singular signs, 'doubt always prudent, support always unconditional, warning always disinterested' when we actually attend to their 'multiple scintillations', which function 'like the small print in a contract' (Saramago

2005b: 35). While *The Double* is his most explicitly sociological novel, throughout that novel Saramago is also critically reflective of his own, the novelist's craft, thus methodologically strengthening the impression that the two are closely related.

As in *All The Names*, the lead character in *The Double* describes as 'research', and even as 'a sociological study' his haphazard and yet meticulous search for the real person who is the double he has seen as a bit-part actor in B movies (Saramago 2005b: 82). In fact, that explanation is intended to conceal his real purpose, but the deceit becomes refined into a full-blown proposal which effectively ridicules the absurdity of claims to systematically investigate social reality through its representations, to 'make a study of the tendencies, inclinations, intentions and messages, explicit, implicit and subliminal, in short, the ideological signals disseminated amongst its consumers, image by image, by the film production company' (Saramago 2005b: 84). It is clear here that representation and reality have become conflated such that the researcher has become concerned about the effect that representation has on social life, when in fact Saramago has already told us that representation and interpretation, the subtleties of the subgesture, far exceed the connivances of a company that would be, realistically, far more concerned with making money than with 'disseminating ideology' that is in any case a part of everyday life. Again, as in *All the Names*, the abstruse logic of an elaborate investigative methodology is undone by the suggestion that the investigator could use the data available in everyday life, and look up the name of the actor he is seeking in the telephone directory. There is serious methodological implication for us here. If print and analogue technology, in its social form, provides such a ready alternative for 'research', then aren't the much-vaunted, belaboured 'research methods', which we invest with such value, actually, effectively, all but redundant in the face of the vast data available through digital life?

Conclusion

Not only José Saramago's fiction can be considered as sociology. I have suggested here that any narrative fiction will by its very nature undertake experimental sociology, and will do so regardless of genre, because the allegorical form is a function of its conditions of production. Attention to those conditions of production of fiction can therefore help us to read narrative fiction as sociology without requiring us to reduce the work to a symptomatic expression of those conditions.

However, some experimental explorations are undertaken merely to confirm the reader's given understandings and social expectations. Those works may assist the individual consumer by providing a basis for reflection, and can provide cultural evidence in support of the empirical mapping of the world by mainstream social science, which seeks to verify what is, but other fictions begin from undecided, emergent tendencies, challenging or even alarming the reader with their narrative development and subjective consequences. Such differential value within literature can no longer, if indeed it ever could, be ascribed to a distinction between high and low culture. It does, however, replicate a fault line running through contemporary sociology itself, between research which seeks to identify key points of tension, characteristic tendencies, critical indices of contemporary society, and those which begin from the point of identifying a gap in the empirical description of the world produced by mainstream social science. Allegorical interpretation is simply one approach we can draw from literary theory without collapsing a sociological standpoint. On such a basis, we could begin to construct new affinities between literary theory and sociology which might enable us to find an alternative to the division of sociology between abstract social theory and the self-assigned role of empiricist social science as the equivalent of the map-makers in Jorge Luis Borges' fable.

References

Agamben, G. (1998): *Homo Sacer: Sovereign Power and Bare Life*. Stanford, CA: Stanford University Press.
Agamben, G. (2000): *Means Without End: Notes on Politics*. Minneapolis, MN: University of Minnesota Press.
Agamben, G. (2005): *State of Exception*. Chicago, IL: University of Chicago Press.
Bauman, Z. (2000): *Liquid Modernity*. Cambridge: Polity Press.
Benjamin, W. (1998): *The Origin of German Tragic Drama*. London: Verso.
Boltanski, L. and E. Chiapello (2006): *The New Spirit of Capitalism*. London: Verso.
Crook, S., J. Pakulski and M. Waters (1992): *Postmodernization: Change in Advanced Society*. London: Sage Publications.
Crouch, C. (2004): *Post-Democracy*. Cambridge: Polity Press.
Drake, M.S. (2010): *Political Sociology for a Globalizing World*. Cambridge: Polity Press.
Esposito, R. (2008): *Bios: Biopolitics and Philosophy*. Minneapolis, MN: University of Minnesota Press.
Esposito, R. (2012): *The Third Person*. Cambridge: Polity Press.
Giddens, A. (1991): *Modernity and Self-Identity: Self and Society in the Late Modern Age*. Cambridge: Polity Press.
Goffman, E. (1959): *The Presentation of Self in Everyday Life*. Harmondsworth: Penguin Books.
Habermas, J. (1989): *The Structural Transformation of the Public Sphere: An Inquiry into a Category of Bourgeois Society*. Cambridge: Polity Press.
Hardt, M. and A. Negri (2001): *Empire*. Cambridge, MA: Harvard University Press.
Havel, V. (1988): "Anti-Political Politics", in *Civil Society and the State: New European Perspectives*, edited by J. Keane. London: Verso.
Hay, C. (2007): *Why We Hate Politics*. Cambridge: Polity Press.

Klein, N. (2008): *The Shock Doctrine*. London: Penguin Books.
Lepenies, W. (1988): *Between Literature and Science: The Rise of Sociology*. Cambridge: Cambridge University Press.
Mills, C. Wright (1959): *The Sociological Imagination*. London: Penguin Books.
McGuigan, J. (2005): "The Cultural Public Sphere". *European Journal of Cultural Studies*, 8(4): 427-43.
Pieterse, J. Nederveen (1995): "Globalization as Hybridization", in *Global Modernities*, edited by M. Featherstone, S. Lash and R. Robertson. London: Sage Publications.
Robertson, R. (1995): "Glocalization: Time-Space and Homogeneity-Heterogeneity", in *Global Modernities*, edited by M. Featherstone, S. Lash and R. Robertson. London: Sage Publications.
Saramago, J. (1999): *All the Names*. London: Harvill Press.
Saramago, J. (2002): *The Cave*. London: Harvill Press.
Saramago, J. (2005a): *Blindness*. London: Vintage Books.
Saramago, J. (2005b): *The Double*. London: Vintage Books.
Saramago, J. (2007): *Seeing*. London: Vintage Books.
Saramago, J. (2010): *Notebooks*. London: Verso.
Sennett, R. (1977): *The Fall of Public Man*. New York: Knopf.
Sennett, R. (2006): *The Culture of the New Capitalism*. New Haven, CT: Yale University Press.
Skinner, Q. (1988): "Meaning and Understanding in the History of Ideas", in *Meaning and Context: Quentin Skinner and His Critics*, edited by J. Tully. Cambridge: Polity Press.
Sloterdijk, P. (1987): *Critique of Cynical Reason*. Minneapolis, MN: University of Minnesota Press.
Strange, S. (1986): *Casino Capitalism*. Oxford: Blackwell.
Tambling, J. (2010): *Allegory*. London: Routledge.
Turner, B.S. (2006): *Vulnerability and Human Rights*. Pennsylvania, PA: Pennsylvania State University Press.
Weber, M. (1946): *From Max Weber: Essays in Sociology* (edited by H.H. Gerth and C. Wright Mills). New York: Oxford University Press.
Wilson, S. (1998): *The Means of Naming: A Social and Cultural History of Personal Naming in Western Europe*. London: UCL Press.
Žižek, S. (1989): *The Sublime Moment of Ideology*. London: Verso.
Žižek, S. (2010): *Living in the End Times*. London: Verso.

PART II
Writing

Chapter 4
Reading and Writing the Experimental Text[1]

Norman K. Denzin

Introduction

In this chapter I want to create a space for reading and writing the new literary work in the social sciences (see Ellis 2009; Poulos 2009; Diversi and Moreira 2009; Goodall 2000, 2008; see also Morse et al. 2009; Thorne 2009; Charon 2006; Frank 1995, 2004a, 2004b; Richards 2008; Faulkner 2009). This space is required if the promises of the new experimental work are to be realized. The classic realist ethnographic text is now under attack. Global and local legal processes have erased the personal and institutional distances between researchers and those he or she writes about. Subjects now challenge how they have been written about. Writers can no longer presume to present an objective, non-contested account of the other's experiences.

The worlds we study are created through the texts that we write and perform. These texts make the world visible. A politics of representation shapes this process, nothing is ever just visible. We inhabit a second-hand, text-mediated world. Jacques Derrida (1973) reminds us that nothing exists outside the text. For nearly three decades we have been writing our way of James Clifford and George E. Marcus's (1986) *Writing Culture*. Narrative genres connected to ethnographic writing have 'been blurred, enlarged, altered to include poetry and drama' (Richardson 2000a: 929). This blurring has led to imaginative experimentations with messy texts, autoethnographies, ethnodramas, short stories, memoirs, personal histories, writing stories, layered texts, and creative nonfiction. These are all forms of performance writing (Pollock 1998). They trouble the edges between text, representation, criticism and personal experience.

The resistances to these new writing forms are considerable. These texts have been criticized for being non-objective, narcissistic, just plain bad writing, too reflexive, too personal, too political. Many reject the new writing out of hand (see Morse et al. 2009). There is little consensus concerning how to read, write or when and where to publish literary social science. This is ironic because, at one level most social science writing is storytelling, sometimes with numbers, sometimes with words. That is storytelling is a way of making sense of social phenomenon by weaving it into a coherent narrative.

---

1 This chapter draws from Denzin (2010: 85-100). I thank Michael Hviid Jacobsen for his comments and suggestions.

My argument in this chapter starts with guidelines for reading and writing the new work, the new interpretive formats, or CAP – Creative Analytic Practices – as Laurel Richardson and Elizabeth Adams St. Pierre (2005) call them. I next take up criticisms of the literary-narrative turn from within one branch of qualitative inquiry, qualitative health research (Morse et al. 2009; Thorne 2009). I counter this critique with a poetic exemplar. In a short one-scene play I discuss tenure and the politics of publishing, including citation analyses. I conclude with a discussion of creating a safe apace for the new writing.

But first consider these remarks from a correspondent from New Zealand. I had suggested some revisions of an article, based on a newly published book by a North American author. The correspondent responds:

> I find myself a bit resistant to the insistence of this form of North American 'post post anxiety'. Our anxieties down here are rather different, and I find myself not wanting to be swept in the centre.

I replied:

> I appreciate the resistance and confronting, but how do you
> Write against the centre when the centre no longer holds?

The New Zealand writer replied:

> Yes, well, despite the arguments to the contrary, from where we sit the Centre DOES hold. On the margins we feel the Centre's overwhelming disciplinary effects. The Centre is the place where anxieties and certainties about the centre not holding are of concern. And the center seems bent on pushing out all the performance, transgressive, indigenous writers.

There it is: centre/margin, disciplinary effects, journals, the politics of publishing, writing as performance, transgressive texts, being read, promotion, money, grants, tenure, power, influence.

There is an irony, a charade of sorts. Those who write outside the margins, or experiment with different writing formats, are accused of being difficult, of publishing their criticisms and their work in B-level journals, of being marginal voices. Audre Lorde may have been right. It is not possible to use the master's tools to dismantle his house.

This does not mean the experimentalists are forever banned to the margins, to launch their criticisms and their work from journals that do not count in the larger scheme of things. We have to build a different house. We cannot overcome the mainstream resistances to critical qualitative inquiry. The mainstream will never accept our political, performative, experimental forms of scholarship.

This means many different houses, many different tents, multiple centres, and each centre having its quality criteria and holding its members to those standards. Multiple mainstreams.

Reading and Writing the New Work

Several issues need to be addressed at the same time.[2] This kind of work is difficult. The writer has to be a better than average researcher, and a better than average writer. Then the writer has to be skilled enough to effectively link research and writing within a literary frame, as a performance text, short story, a poem, or an ethnodrama. Most social researchers are not literary writers, and they have been punished when they have tried to be literary. In order to develop the proper writing skills they need training in creative writing, they need to form, join and participate in writing groups. They are encouraged to invite literary co-authors, and they need to get their work critiqued by professional writers and editors.

Most journal editors are not capable or competent to review writing in this genre, including experimental performance narratives. Without a set of criteria that can be followed, they do not feel comfortable saying that something is a good piece of literary social science. They do not have the training to be able to do this on their own. Criteria need to be outlined, but a plurality of frameworks should be encouraged. Not all inquiry can be effectively represented within a literary format. Researchers need to fit their methods to their research questions. They also need to fit their writing genre to the topic at hand; that is what are they trying to report about? They must also fit their writing genre to their intended audience. Granting agencies probably do not want to read three-act ethnodramas. It may not be appropriate to shrink 1,000 pages of transcripts into a single poem. A single interview may not be appropriate for a dramatic reading involving multiple characters. A fictionalized short story might work well in a social work classroom but be completely ineffective in a presentation to policy makers or grant officers. The writer must ask: 'Does the literary format effectively communicate knowledge about the subject matter at hand? Would a traditional format do better?'. If so, then the literary format is not warranted.

A somewhat ambiguous set of criteria should operate. Sandra L. Faulkner (2009: 89), drawing on the work of Laurel Richardson (1992, 1994, 1997, 2000b, 2001), Carolyn Ellis (2000), Arthur P. Bochner (2000), Patricia Clough (2000) and others, sets out three criteria for evaluating research poetry:[3] scientific, poetic and artistic:

---

2 These points are all stolen from Mitch Allen (2008).

3 She uses the term research poetry to reference 'poems that are crafted from research endeavors' (Faulkner 2009: 20), work that turns interviews, transcripts, observations and personal experience into poetic form (on found poetry, see also Prendergast 2006).

Scientific Criteria: depth, authenticity, trustworthiness, understanding, reflexivity, usefulness, articulation of method, ethics.

Poetic Criteria: artistic concentration, embodied experience, discovery, conditional, narrative truth, transformation.

Artistic Criteria: compression of data, understanding of craft, social justice, moral truth, emotional verisimilitude, sublime, empathy.

Faulkner's first two categories are applied to any form of critical qualitative inquiry. Her third category can be extended. Is the literary, poetic statement effective aesthetically? Does it exhibit accessible literary qualities? Is it dramatically evocative? Is it lyrical? Does it invoke shared feelings, images, scenes, and memories? Does it express emotion effectively, economically? Does it establish *objective correlatives* for the emotions the writer is attempting to evoke (see Eliot 1920)? Does it meet the criteria attributed to Emily Dickinson: 'If I read a work and it makes my whole body so cold no fire can ever warm me, I know it is poetry'.

Reading the New Writing

Editors like writers need a framework for evaluating the new work. A two-sided thesis is suggested. First, experimental writing must be well crafted, engaging writing, capable of being respected by critics of literature as well as by social scientists. Second self-referential works must do more than put the self of the writer on the line, or tell realist emotional stories about self-renewal, crisis, or catharsis. These narratives should be a stimulus for social criticism, and social action. Much of what passes as new may, under another framework, is old hat.

In promoting the turn to narrative in the human disciplines, Richard Rorty (1989: 60) argued that our liberal society needs social texts that promote compassion, texts that encourage us to feel the sufferings of others. Ethnographic narratives, poems, performance texts ethnodramas become experimental ways of implementing Rorty's injunction. The narrative turn opens a wider space for experimental writers who tell critical realist tales, deploying multiple points of view, and various literary devices about life today.

These works push the boundaries of the traditional ethnography. They blur and shade into performance texts. They disturb the relationship between fact and fiction. They use scene setting, overlapping dialogue, multiple points of view, composite characters, flashbacks, foreshadowing, and interior monologues, parallel plots. The basis unit is the scene, the situation, not the fact. Stories and poems are written in facts, not about facts. They move outward from personal, epiphanic experience to a narrative description of the experience, and then a critique of the social structures that shaped it. This is not a retelling of experience. The telling creates the experience. It privileges emotion, so as to evoke emotional responses for the reader, thereby producing verisimilitude and a shared experience.

The writer asks the reader to submit to the text's causal version of how and why something happened. The poetic, narrative text makes public what many sociologists and anthropologists have kept hidden: the private feelings, doubts, and dilemmas, uncertainties that confront the field-worker. These doubts reveal that the field lies within us, not outside in some external site. In emphasizing the personal, the emotional, the new writers engage in a new kind of theorizing. Works are filled with biographical, not disciplinary citations. A minimalist kind of social science is created. Personal experience is not mediated complex theoretical terms.

These experimental texts break with the past, with timeworn traditions of using ethnography to present the experiences of others. Many of the experimentalists are writing cultural criticism as they fashion new understandings of the gendered self-writing its way into the second decade of this new century.

Criticisms

As noted above, the poetic, narrative text has been criticized on several grounds, and these criticisms are directly connected to the defining features of the genre, namely the emphasis on the personal, reflective text and the absence of a public method that would allow critics to assess the so-called validity of the author's assertions. These criticisms centre on the fact/fiction problem, and the attempts to be literary. They extend to charges of narcissism, self-indulgence, sloppy writing, the privileging of discourse over representation, description and analysis. Other critics assert that literary representations transform, or change the form and meaning of the empirical materials, raising validity issues (Morse et al. 2009: 1035). The absence of guidelines for doing nuts and bolts research, and for turning 'data' into poetry or narrative is also noted, and others lament the absence of social theory (see Denzin 1997: 215, 2010: 164-5; Ellis 2009: 230-3).

A responsible reflexive texts announces its politics, ceaselessly interrogates the realities it evokes. Such works make readers work. They are messy. They are local. They are historically contingent. They are risky.

There remains a pressing need to invent a reflexive form of social science writing that turns ethnography and experimental literary texts back onto one another. The goal is not be experimental for the sake of being experimental. The goal is to change the world through the way we write about it.

Editorial Resistance

The beat goes on. The criticisms do not go away. The editors of the journal *Qualitative Health Research* (QHR) recently published an editorial against transforming data into poetry or free verse (Morse et al. 2009). The editors assert that:

> You can find 'poetry' anywhere. And one of the latest trends in qualitative inquiry appears to be the transformation of data into poetry or free verse. In many cases this is a new form of an old dilemma – how do we present rich data in a way that captures the richness? (Morse et al. 2009: 1035)

The editors also observe that there has also been an increased use of the single case narrative report, either in the form of a case study, or a literary story (Thorne 2009).

The editors launch several criticisms against this recent poetic, narrative turn. The objections are by now quite familiar:

1. Formatting. Sometimes lengthy quotations extend forever in the results section.
2. On occasion the subject's voices present the analysis. There may be minimal commentary from the researcher.
3. Quotations are used to illustrate the analysis in various forms.
4. The data are presented raw, as if delivered directly from the transcriptions.
5. There may be random punctuation. The texts may be meticulously coded. Each pause and each utterance may be carefully marked and measured.
6. The point of this kind of micro-analysis is not apparent.
7. Converting a transcription into free verse confuses the goals of research.
8. There is no interpretation, no analysis, no theory, no concepts, no hypotheses.
9. Turning research into poetry or narrative does not enhance the depth of analysis nor add to the richness of the findings.
10. The single case only tells one story. Where is the theory? Where are the methodological guidelines? Where is the rigour?
11. Narrative inquiry is not scientific inquiry.

For the *Qualitative Health Research* editors interpretation and analysis have to be framed in terms of raw data, concepts, hypotheses, analysis, rigor, rich findings and theory construction. The meaning of a work is to be found in these terms Poetry, case studies, and stories do not address meaning at this level. Hence they have no place in their journal.

Closing the Door on Narrative

Having reviewed their own case against narrative, the editors of QHR state that they have made the decision to resist accepting manuscripts of this genre for publication (Morse et al. 2009: 1035). These are their reasons. First, QHR is only allotted 144 pages per issue, 12 times a year. If an article using free verse increases the length of an article by five pages, someone else loses five pages. Articles must earn their space, 'even to the extent that a 40-page article must be twice as significant, and of greater interest to the majority of our readership, than a 20-page article ... We cannot afford the additional space these works take up, unless it is justified' (Morse et al. 2009: 1035).

Second, experimental writers do not share their original transcripts. 'We suspect this is deliberate because transforming data into a poem-like structure does change the form of the data, even if it does not change the meaning in any significant degree' (Morse et al. 2009: 1035). Hence they cannot trust the findings reported in the poetry or the case study. Third, authors do not show how the data were transformed into poetry, or narrative. No guidelines are offered. Fourth, poetry and research are at odds with one another. This journal publishes research, not poetry Fifth, work cast as poetry focuses on literary representations, rather than the health research. Hence the meaning of the work remains ambiguous.

Learning from the Critics

There are several lessons to be learned here. Obviously experimental writers need to make a more effective case for their project, including outlining the range of interpretive criteria they use when fashioning their work. They should clarify what their goals are and how they hope to achieve them with their literary texts. They should highlight the features of a minimalist text, including why they want to show and not tell.

It bears repeating that all scientific writing is storytelling. The editors of QHR are telling a story about why they do not want to publish stories. Experimental writing is emic, not etic inquiry; it is humanistic and interpretive by nature. It should not be asked to answer to etic, hypothesis-testing criteria.

It's a little like first and second-order concepts, or Clifford Geertz's (1983: 57-9) experience-near and experience-distant writing. The poetic, performative form is experience-near, grounded in the concrete, the local, the immediate present, first-order textuality, flesh-and-blood human beings talking to one another. This is what Della Pollock (1998) calls 'performing writing'.

The editors of QHR want second-order, experience-distant writing. They envision a four-tiered interpretive structure: (1) the world of lived experience; (2) evidence from and about that world gathered through the use of research methodologies; (3) transcriptions, and analysis of these materials; (4) theoretical interpretations of those analyses.

This is a fine model, but it is not the only model. Others like Laurel Richardson (2000a) or Carolyn Ellis (2009) work with a three-tiered model: (1) lived experience and its meanings captured through observations, interviews and conversations; (2) transcriptions of interviews; (3) turned into poetry, or narrative. Other writers, poets, work with a single textual model; the narrative text that constitutes lived experience itself.

The two interpretive communities should find a respectful way to communicate with one another. Many experimentalists do work directly relevant to the health care field (Frank 1995, 2004a, 2004b; Charon 2006). The experimentalists are trying to create spaces for the voices and stories of those who have been objects of others' reports. This locates narrative and storytelling within an empowerment ethics of health care and narrative truth (Frank, 1995: xiii; Charon 2006: 208-9; Bochner 2007; Ellis 2009: 15). They do not want their work to be shut out because of methodological misunderstandings.

A Poetic Exemplar: Louisa May

Laurel Richardson's poem, "Louisa May's Story of Her Life" (Richardson 1992, 1997) provides a perfect example of how the poetic turn can work. The poem was created from the transcription of an in-depth interview Richardson had conducted with Louisa May, an unwed mother. In the poem Richardson used only Louisa May's words, syntax, an extract:

> The most important thing
> To say ... is that
> I grew up in the South.
> Being southern shapes
> Aspirations ... shapes
> What you think you're going to be ...
> I grew up poor in a rented house. (Richardson 1992: 20)

Richardson stated that she wanted a framework and a method that went beyond sociological naturalism, beyond positivistic commitments to tell an objective story. She wanted to use poetical devices like repetition, pauses, meter, rhymes, diction, tone to write Louisa May's life (Richardson 1992: 19-20, 24-6, 1997: 142-3). She transcribed Louisa May's interview into 36 pages of prose text. She then shaped it into a poem/transcript:

> What possessed me to do so was head wrestling with postmodern issues about the nature of 'data', the interview as an international event, the representation of lives. The core problems raised by postmodernism – voice, presence, subjectivity, the politics of evidence, the inability of transcripts to capture reflexive experience – seemed resolvable through the poetic form which re-creates embodied speech (Richardson 1992: 23, 1997: 143)

In moving from interview to the transcribed text, to the poetic representation Richardson kept the pauses, the line breaks, the spaces within and between lines, the places where to be quiet, when to be loud.

When performed the poetic representation opens up to multiple, open-ended readings, in the ways that straight sociological prose does not permit. This writing-performance text is reflexive, and alive (Richardson 1992: 25, 1997: 142-3; Richardson and St. Pierre 2005: 964). It is never transparent. It has to be read, performed. Thus does Richardson show how she did her work, noting, too, that she worked carefully with her wiring group as she moved from one step to the next in the production of this work.

The poetic representation of lives is never just an end in itself. The goal is political, to change the way we think about people and their lives, and to use the poetic-performative format to do this. The poet makes the world visible in new and different ways, in ways ordinary social science writing does not allow. The poet is accessible, visible, and present in the text, in ways that traditional writing forms discourage.

At this level, It is pretty obvious that all the forms of creative, analytic, interpretive practice outlined by Laurel Richardson and Elizabeth Adams St. Pierre (2005: 962) needs to be honoured:

> Performance writing,
> > autoethnography,
> > > literary and ethnographic fiction,
> > > > poetry
> > > > > ethnodrama,
> > > > > > writing stories,
>
> reader's theatre,
> > layered texts,
> > > aphorisms,
> > > > conversations, epistles, memoirs,
> > > > > polyvocal texts,
> > > > > > comedy, satire, allegory
>
> visual and multi-media texts,
> > dense theory,
> > > museum displays,
> > > > dance,
> > > > > choreographed findings

These performance texts are always:

> political,
> emotional,
> analytic,
> interpretive,
> pedagogical,
> local, partial,
> incomplete.
> painful to
> read,
> exhilarating.

The Experimental Text: A One-Scene Play

Characters:
Speaker One
Speaker Two

Staging Notes: Performers are seated around a seminar table on the third floor of Gregory Hall, a four story, 125-year-old brick classroom on the campus of the University of Illinois. There a 25 chairs along the walls and around a 40-foot long wood table. Two large nature paintings on loan from the art department hang on the north and east walls of the room. There is a pull down screen at the south end of the room for projecting video. Overhead lights are dimmed. Sun streams in through the two north windows. It is 1:00 in the afternoon. The time is the present. The text of the play is handed from speaker to speaker. The first speaker reads the text for speaker one. The second speaker reads the text for speaker two, and so forth, to the end.

Scene One: Getting Nailed by Those Citation Reports

Speaker One:

> Hey, I can't get to first-base with using these Creative Analytic Practices (CAP). Are you out of your mind! Poetry, drama, ethnodrama, dance, museum pieces, readers' theatre. My department has never heard of these forms.

Speaker Two:

> Hey, I'm in your corner. My department head and my dean say this kind of writing is not acceptable scholarship. They say they do not understand what I do when I write this way. And they say the journals where I publish do not have high enough International Bibliography of the Social Sciences (IBSS) or Journal Citation Reports (JCR) scores. My colleague who does the same kind of work I do did not get tenure.

Speaker One:

> I'm not defending anybody, but a lot of folks, like the libraries, use the Thomson Reuters Journal Citation Reports. They claim to be a systematic, objective means for critically evaluating the world's leading journals with quantifiable, statistical information based on citation data. They measure influence by compiling an article's cited references. This produces an influence or impact measure at the article and journal level.

Speaker One:

> I don't want an objective document. I want tenure. My colleague who was turned down for tenure never even got into one of these journals.

Speaker Two:

> Here is where the new writing connects to the politics of publishing. If traditional journals reject this work, then the experimental scholar's work does not find a home in the mainstream.

Speaker One:

> I'm terrified. My colleague lost her job. She is in a community college now, and will never again have time to write. This objective system did her in.

Speaker Two:

> Blame her department. Don't blame the industry. Blame the academy. It is the misuse by academics, members of tenure committees, and hiring committees, that is most problematic. Committees draw conclusions about the performance of an individual scholar based on these scores. But the JIF is not intended to he used as a surrogate for evaluating scholars. It should only be applied to journals, not individual scholars.

Speaker One:

> Yeah, Lotta help that is today!

Speaker Two:

> Evaluators are not doing their job, if they rate a paper more highly solely because it appears in a high-impact journal, regardless of what the paper actually says. (Monastersky 2005)

Speaker One:

> Citation scores cannot determine quality. Quality is complex and involves substantive contribution to a field, aesthetic merit, reflexivity and voice, and emotional impact on the reader (see Richardson and St. Pierre 2005: 964). Under these criteria, my colleague who did not get tenure was doing quality work.

Speaker Two:

Here are some rules of thumb for junior faculty, tenure committees and journal editors:

1. Only consider these scores in their proper context. They do not measure content;
2. Multidisciplinary journals must develop and be held to their own standards;
3. Do not use the Journal Impact Factor to assess the performance of individual scholars;
4. These scores can only legitimately be used to evaluate journals, and then only with great caution.

Speaker One:

We need to have our own social justice impact criteria, criteria that turn on moral terms, criteria that celebrate resistance, experimentation, conflict, empowerment, sound partisan work that offers knowledge-based radical critiques of social institutions, and social situations, while promoting human dignity, human rights, and just societies around the globe.

Speaker One:

And the victims? The non-tenured temps. The folks who wrote resistance texts that did not get published what about them?

Letting the Old Do the Work of the New

It is now possible to read the recent writing experiments and the criticisms of these attempts at genre bending as more than normal science inching its way forward. There is more going here then the vagrant efforts of a few who would dare to engage autoethnography, ethnopoetics, self-narratives, ethnodramas, performance texts, even poems, mysteries and novels. The boundaries of the traditional realist ethnographic text have been forever changed. The cause for optimism is premature. Granted the old way of doing ethnography or writing interpretively is being changed, and this is confirmed by the fact that innovative writing forms seem to be everywhere present. But this position ignores the recuperative and conservative elements of the traditional, hegemonic social science order, that order which insists on marginalizing the new, not treating it as a version of a new order of things.

Put bluntly, the verdict for many is in. The old, better than the new, can do the work of interpretation. So forget all of this experimental stuff. But there is more at issue then different ways of writing. The material and ethical practices of a discipline are on the line; no wonder the criticism is relentless.

Many of the critics of the new writing presume a universal ethnographic subject, the other who was not the ethnographer. These critics looked at society from the outside, contending that objective accounts of society could be given by objective observers. This observer was able to write in a way that did not require the presence of a real subject in the world. Social experience and real people were irrelevant to the topic at hand. This lead to the production of an interpretive structure that said social phenomena should be interpreted as social facts (Smith 1989: 45).

This structure shifted arguments about agency, purpose, meaning and intention from the subject to the phenomena being studied. It then transformed those phenomena into texts about society. The phenomena were then given a presence that rested in these textual descriptions (Smith 1989: 45). Real live people entered the text as a part of discourse in the form of excerpts from field notes, or the casual observations of the theorist, or as 'ideal types' (Smith 1989: 51, 1996). These are the real people the editors of *Qualitative Health Research* want to hear from, but only their terms.

The new writers wish to overturn this picture of social science writing. This view of social science writing has generated the by now familiar litany of criticisms of the new writing discussed in this and previous chapters. The traditional critique focuses on issues of method, truth, and verification, challenging the new writing because it fails to use agreed upon methods of verification, including random samples, representative texts, and so-called unbiased methods of interpretation.

The traditionalists reject the criteria of evaluation used by the new writers, seeing them as assaults on the pursuit of truth. These methods, these strategies of writing, and the persons who use them, constitute grave threats to the social sciences. For some the new writing, and its politics, explains the dire straits that fields like sociology and education now confront. The traditionalist's solution is to silence the new writers; use traditional methods to develop a central core of knowledge collect solid facts about society. These moves cut to the core of the politics that are involved in the new writing.

Coda

To summarize the many points from this chapter, writers and editors need to work together if the new writing is to find its place in the current discourse. Writers need to produce better work by doing the kinds of things previously noted: attending workshops, creating writing groups, working with literary co-authors, sharing the interpretive, poetic and artistic criteria they use in their work. Editors need to attend workshops on the new work and read more widely on the genre. They need to show how their criteria for judging the new work compare to the criteria endorsed by Sandra L. Faulkner (2009) and others. They need to add poets and fiction writers to their editorial boards. They need to be willing to take chances, even when they do not fully appreciate or understand a new experimental work.

Let us go back to the beginning of this chapter. We need to find spaces for experimental work when the mainstream refuses to accept our scholarship. We need our own mainstream, our own blue-ribbon journals, our own prestigious book series, our own interpretive criteria, our own international congresses, our networks, our mentors, and our own departments.

References

Allen, M. (2008): "Academic Journals and the Politics of Publishing". Paper presented at the Fourth International Congress of Qualitative Inquiry, Urbana, Illinois.
Bochner, A.P. (2000): "Criteria Against Ourselves". *Qualitative Inquiry*, 5(2): 278-91.
Charon, R. (2006): *Narrative Medicine: Honoring the Stories of Illness*. New York: Oxford University Press.
Clifford, J. and G.E. Marcus (1986): *Writing Culture: The Poetics and Politics of Ethnography*. Stanford, CA: University of California Press.
Clough, P. Ticineto (2000): "Comments on Setting Criteria for Experimental Writing". *Qualitative Inquiry*, 6: 278-91.
Denzin, N.K. (1997): *Interpretive Ethnography*. Thousand Oaks, CA: Sage Publications.
Denzin, N.K. (2009): *Qualitative Inquiry Under Fire: Toward a New Paradigm Dialogue*. Walnut Creek, CA: Left Coast Press.
Denzin, N.K. (2010): *The Qualitative Manifesto: A Call to Arms*. Walnut Creek, CA: Left Coast Press.
Derrida, J. (1973): *Speech and Phenomena*. Evanston: Northwestern University Press.
Diversi, M. and C. Moreira (2009): *Betweener Talk: Decolonizing Knowledge Production, Pedagogy and Praxis*. Walnut Creek, CA: Left Coast Press.
Ellis, C. (2000): "Creating Criteria: An Autoethnographic Story". *Qualitative Inquiry*, 5(2): 273-7.
Ellis, Ca. (2009): *Revision: Autoethnographic Reflections on Life and Work*. Walnut Creek, CA: Left Coast Press.
Eliot, T.S. (1920): *The Sacred Wood: Essays in Poetry and Criticism*. London: Meuthen.
Faulkner, S.L. (2009): *Poetry as Method: Reporting Research through Verse*. Walnut Creek, CA: Left Coast Press.
Frank, A. (1995): *The Wounded Storyteller: Body, Illness and Ethics*. Chicago, IL: University of Chicago Press.
Frank, A. (2004a): *The Renewal of Generosity Illness, Medicine and How to Live*. Chicago, IL: University of Chicago Press.
Frank, A. (2004b): "Moral Non-Fiction: Life Writing and Children's Disability", in *The Ethics of Life Writing*, edited by P.J. Eakin. Ithaca, NY: Cornell University Press.
Geertz, C. (1983): *Local Knowledge: Further Essays in Interpretive Anthropology*. New York: Basic Books.

Goodall, H.L. (2000): *Writing the New Ethnography*. Walnut Creek, CA: AltaMira Press.

Goodall, H.L. (2008): *Writing Qualitative Inquiry: Self, Stories and Academic Life*. Walnut Creek, CA: Left Coast Press.

Monastersky, R. (2005): "The Number That's Devouring Science". *Chronicle of Higher Education*, 14 October.

Morse, J.M., J. Coulehan, S. Thorne, J.L. Bottorff, J. Cheek and A.J. Kuzel (2009): "Data Expressions or Expressing Data". *Qualitative Health Research*, 19(8): 1035-6.

Pollock, D. (1998): "Performing Writing", in *The Ends of Performance*, edited by P. Phelan and J. Lane. New York: New York University Press.

Poulos, C.N. (2009): *Accidental Ethnography*. Walnut Creek, CA: Left Coast Press.

Prendergast, M. (2007): "Found Poetry as Literature Review: Research Poems on Audience and Performance". *Qualitative Inquiry*, 12(3): 369-88.

Richards, R. (2008): "Writing the Othered Self: Autoethnography and the Problem of Objectification in Writing about Illness and Disability". *Qualitative Health Research*, 18(12): 1717-29.

Richardson, L. (1992): "The Poetic Representation of Lives: Writing a Postmodernist Sociology". *Studies in Symbolic Interaction*, 13: 19-27.

Richardson, L. (1994): "Writing as a Method of Inquiry", in *The Handbook of Qualitative Research*, edited by N.K. Denzin and Y.S. Lincoln. Newbury Park, CA: Sage Publications.

Richardson, L. (1996): "Educational Birds". *Journal of Contemporary Ethnography*, 25: 6-15.

Richardson, L. (1997): *Fields of Play*. New Brunswick, NJ: Rutgers University Press.

Richardson, L. (2000a): "Writing: A Method of Inquiry", in *Handbook of Qualitative Research* (2nd Edition), edited by N.K. Denzin and Y.S. Lincoln. Thousand Oaks, CA: Sage Publications.

Richardson, L. (2000b): "Evaluating Ethnography". *Qualitative Inquiry*, 6: 253-5.

Richardson, L. (2001): "Poetic Representation of Interviews", in *Handbook of Interview Research*, edited by J.F. Gubrium and J.A. Holstein. Thousand Oaks, CA: Sage Publications.

Richardson, L. and E. Adams St. Pierre (2005): "Writing: A Method of Inquiry", in *Handbook of Qualitative Research* (3rd Edition), edited by N.K. Denzin and Y.S. Lincoln. Thousand Oaks, CA: Sage Publications.

Rorty, R. (1989): *Contingency, Irony and Solidarity*. Cambridge: Cambridge University Press.

Smith, D.E. (1989): "Sociological Theory: Methods of Writing Patriarchy", in *Feminism and Sociological Theory*, edited by R.W. Wallace. Newbury Park, CA: Sage Publications.

Thorne, S.E. (2009): "Is the Story Enough?". *Qualitative Health Research*, 19(9): 1183-85.

Chapter 5

On Writing: On Writing Sociology[1]

Zygmunt Bauman

The need in thinking is what makes us think

Theodor W. Adorno

Quoting the Czech poet Jan Skácel on the plight of the poet (who, in Skácel's words, only discovers the verses which 'were always, deep down, there'), Milan Kundera comments (in *L'Art du roman*, 1986): 'to write, means for the poet to crush the wall behind which something that 'was always there' hides. In this respect, the task of the poet is not different from the work of history, which also discovers rather than invents'. History, like poets, uncovers, in ever new situations, the human possibilities heretofore hidden. What history does matter of factly, is a mission for the poet. To rise to this mission, the poet must refuse service to the truths known beforehand, truths already 'obvious' because floating on the surface. It does not matter whether such 'assumed in advance' truths are classified as revolutionary or dissident, Christian or atheist – or how just they are or are proclaimed to be. Whatever their nature and denomination, those 'truths' are not this 'something hidden' which the poet is called to uncover; they are, rather, parts of the wall which the poet's mission is to crush. Spokesmen for the obvious, self-evident and 'what we all believe, don't we' *are false poets*, says Kundera.

These are bold and insightful words, no doubt; they say a lot about the poets' quandary and set them a hard task. But what has the poet's vocation to do with the sociologist's calling? We, the sociologists, do not write poems – and some of us who occasionally do, take for the time of writing a leave of absence from our professional pursuits. And yet, if we do not wish to share the fate of 'false poets' and resent being 'false sociologists', we ought to come as close as the true poets do to the yet-hidden human possibilities; and for that reason we must need to crush the walls of the obvious and self-evident, of that prevailing ideological fashion of the day whose commonality is taken for the proof of its sense. Demolishing such walls is as much

---

1 This chapter has previously been published in a number of almost identical versions in, for example, Zygmunt Bauman's book *Liquid Modernity* (Cambridge; Polity Press, 2000). Slightly revised versions have appeared in: *Theory, Culture & Society*, 2000, 17(1): 79-90, *Cultural Studies ↔ Critical Methodologies*, 2002, 2: 359-70, and in Norman K. Denzin and Yvonna S. Lincoln (eds): *The Sage Handbook of Qualitative Research*, 3rd edition. London: Sage Publications, 2005. The piece here reprinted is from *Theory, Culture & Society* (2000) and is published with kind permission from Sage Publications.

the sociologist's as it is the poet's calling, and for the same reason: they lie about human potential while barring the disclosure of their own bluff.

Perhaps the verses which the poet seeks 'were always there'. One cannot be so sure, though, about the human potential discovered by history. Do indeed humans – the makers and the made, the heroes and the victims of history – carry forever the same volume of possibilities waiting for the right time to be disclosed? Or is it rather that – as human history goes – the opposition between discovery and creation is null and void and makes no sense? Since history is the endless process of human creation, is it not for the same reason (and by the same token) the unending process of human self-discovery? Is not the propensity to disclose/create ever new possibilities, to relentlessly expand the inventory of possibilities already discovered and made real, the sole human potential which always has been, and always is, 'already there'? The question whether the new possibility has been created or 'merely' uncovered by history is no doubt a welcome nourishment to many a scholastic mind; as for history itself, it does not wait for an answer and can do quite well without one.

Niklas Luhmann's most seminal and precious legacy to fellow sociologists has been the notion of *autopoiesis* – self-creation (from Greek ποιειυ: do, create, give form, be effective) – meant to grasp and encapsulate the gist of the human condition. The choice of term was itself a creation/discovery of the link (inherited kinship rather than chosen affinity) between history and poetry. Poetry and history are two parallel currents ('parallel' in the sense of a non-Euclidean universe ruled by Boylai/Lobachevski's geometry) of that autopoiesis of human potentialities, in which creation is the sole form discovery can take while self-discovery is the principal act of creation. Sociology, one is tempted to say, is a third current, running in parallel with those two. Or at least this is what it should be if it is to stay inside that human condition which it tries to grasp and make intelligible – and what it has tried to become since its inception, though it has been repeatedly diverted from trying by mistaking the seemingly impenetrable and not-yet-decomposed walls for the ultimate limits of human potential and going out of its way to reassure the garrison commanders and the troops they commanded that the line they have drawn will be never crossed.

Alfred de Musset suggested almost two centuries ago that 'great artists have no country'. Two centuries ago, these were militant words, a war-cry of sorts. They were written down amid deafening fanfares of youthful and credulous, and for that reason boisterous and pugnacious, patriotism. Politicians were discovering their vocation in building the nation-states of one law, one language, one world-view, one history and one future. Many poets and painters were discovering their mission: nourishing the tender sprouts of national spirit, resurrecting long-dead national traditions or conceiving of brand new ones that had never lived before, giving to the nation as yet not-fully-enough-aware-of-being-a-nation the stories, the tunes, the images and the names of heroic ancestors – something to share, love and cherish, and so to lift the mere living together to the rank of belonging together: opening the eyes of the living to the beauty and sweetness of belonging by enthusing them to remember and venerate their dead and rejoice in guarding their legacy. Against that background, Musset's blunt verdict bore all the marks of a rebellion and a call to arms: it summoned fellow writers to refuse cooperation with the enterprise of the politicians, the prophets and the preachers of closely guarded borders and gun-bristling trenches. I do not know whether Musset intuited the fratricidal capacities of the kind of fraternities which the nationalist politicians and ideologist-laureates were determined to build; or whether his words were but an expression of the intellectual's disgust and resentment of narrow horizons, backwaters and a parochial mentality. Whatever was the case then, when read now, with the benefit of hindsight, through the magnifying glass of experience stained with ethnic cleansings, genocides and mass graves, Musset's words seem to have lost nothing of their topicality, challenge and urgency; nor have they lost any of their original controversiality. Now as then, they aim at the heart of the writers' mission and challenge their consciences with the question decisive for any writer's raison d'être.

A century and a half later Juan Goytisolo, probably the greatest among living Spanish writers, takes up the issue once more. In a recent interview ('Les Batailles de Juan Goytisolo' in *Le Monde* of 12 February 1999), he points out that once Spain had accepted, in the name of Catholic piety and under the influence of the Inquisition, a highly restrictive notion of national identity, the country became, towards the end of the 16th century, a 'cultural desert'. Let us note that Goytisolo writes in Spanish, but for many years lived in Paris and in the USA, to settle in the end in Morocco. And let us note that no other Spanish writer has had so many of his works translated into Arabic. Why? Goytisolo has no doubt about the reason. He explains: 'intimacy and distance create a privileged situation. Both are necessary'. Though each for different reasons, both these qualities make their presence felt in his relations to his native Spanish and to his acquired Arabic, French and English – the languages of countries which in succession became his chosen substitute homes. Since he spent a large part of his life away from Spain, the Spanish language ceased to be for him the all-too-familiar, always at hand and calling for no reflection, tool of daily, mundane and ordinary communication. His intimacy with his childhood's language was not – could not be – affected, but now it has been supplemented with distance. The Spanish language became the 'authentic homeland in his exile', a territory known and felt and lived through from the inside and yet – since it became also remote-full of surprises and exciting discoveries. That intimate/distant territory lent itself to the cool and detached scrutiny *sine ira et studio*, disclosing pitfalls and possibilities invisible in vernacular uses, showing previously unsuspected plasticity, admitting and inviting creative intervention. It is the combination of intimacy and distance which allowed Goytisolo to realize that the unreflexive immersion in a language – just the kind of immersion which exile makes all but impossible – is fraught with dangers: 'If one lives only in the present, one risks disappearing together with the present'. It was the 'outside', detached look at the native language, which allowed Goytisolo to step beyond the constantly vanishing present and so enrich his Spanish in a way otherwise unlikely, perhaps altogether inconceivable. He brought back into his prose and poetry ancient terms, long fallen into disuse, and by doing so he has blown off the store-room dust which has covered them, wiped out the patina of time and offered the words new and heretofore unsuspected (or long forgotten) vitality.

In *Contre-allée*, a book published recently in cooperation with Catherine Malabou, Jacques Derrida invites his readers to think *in travel* – or, more exactly, to 'think travel'. That means – to think that unique activity of departing, going away from *chez soi*, going far, towards the unknown, risking all the risks, pleasures and dangers that the 'unknown' has in store (even the risk of *not returning*). Derrida is obsessed with 'being away'. As Christian Delacampagne (in *Le Monde*, 12 March 1999) points out, there is reason to surmise that the obsession was born when the 12-year-old Jacques was, in 1942, sent down from the school which by the decree of the Vichy administration of North Africa was ordered to 'purify' itself of Jewish pupils. This is how the 'perpetual exile' of Jacques Derrida started. Since then, Derrida has divided his life between France and the USA. In the USA he was a Frenchman; in France, however hard he tried, the Algerian accent of his childhood kept breaking time and again through his exquisite French *parole*, betraying a *pied noir* hidden under the thin skin of the Sorbonne professor (this is, some people think, why Derrida came to extol the superiority of writing and composed the aetiological myth of priority to support the axiological assertion). Culturally, Derrida was to remain 'stateless'. This did not mean, though, having no cultural homeland. Quite the contrary: being 'culturally stateless' meant having more than one homeland, building a home of one's own on the crossroads between cultures. Derrida became and remained a *meteque*, a cultural hybrid. His 'home on the crossroads' was built of language. And building a home on a cultural crossroads proved to be the best conceivable occasion to put language to the tests it seldom passes elsewhere, to see through its otherwise unnoticed qualities, to find out what language is capable of and on what promises which it makes it can never deliver. From that home on crossroads came the exciting and eye-opening news about the inherent plurality and undecidability of sense (in *L'Ecriture et la différence*), about endemic impurity of origins (in *De la grammatologie*), and the perpetual unfulfilment of communication (in *La Carte postale*).

Goytisolo's and Derrida's messages are different from that of Musset: it is not true, the novelist and the philosopher suggest in unison, that great art has no homeland – on the contrary, art, like the artists, may have many homelands, and most certainly has more than one. The trick is to be inside and outside at the same time, to combine intimacy with the critical look of an outsider, involvement with detachment; a trick which sedentary people are unlikely to learn. Learning the trick is the chance of the exile: *technically* an exile – one that is *in,* but not *of* the place. Unconfinedness that results from this condition (that *is* this condition) reveals homely truths to be man-made and un-made, and the mother tongue to be an endless stream of communication between generations and a treasury of messages always richer than any of their readings and forever waiting to be unpacked anew.

George Steiner has named Samuel Beckett, Jorge Luis Borges and Vladimir Nabokov the greatest among contemporary writers. What united them, he said, and what made them all great, was that each of the three moved with equal ease – was equally 'at home' – in several linguistic universes, not one. (A reminder is in order: 'linguistic universe' is a pleonastic phrase: the universe in which each one of us lives is and cannot but be 'linguistic' – made of words. Words light the islands of visible forms in the dark sea of the invisible and mark the scattered spots of relevance in the formless mass of the insignificant. It is words that slice the world into the classes of nameable objects and bring out their kinship or enmity, closeness or distance, affinity or mutual estrangement – and as long as they stay alone in the field they raise all such artefacts to the rank of reality – the only reality there is.) One needs to live, to visit, to know intimately more than one such universe to spy out human invention behind any universe's imposing and indomitable structure and to discover just how much of human cultural effort is needed to divine the idea of nature with its laws and necessities; all that in order to muster, in the end, the audacity and the determination to join in that cultural effort *knowingly,* aware of its risks and pitfalls, but also of the boundlessness of its horizons.

To create (and so also to discover) always means breaking a rule; following a rule is but routine, more of the same – not an act of creation. For the exile, breaking rules is not a matter of free choice, but an eventuality that cannot be avoided. The exiles do not know enough of the rules reigning in the country of arrival, nor do they treat them unctuously enough, for their efforts to observe them and conform to be approved as genuine. As to their country of origin, going into exile has been recorded there as their original sin, in the light of which all that the sinners later may do would be taken down and used against them as the evidence of rule-breaking. By commission or by omission, rule-breaking becomes a trademark of the exiles. This is unlikely to endear them to the natives of any of the countries between which their life itineraries are plotted. But, paradoxically, it also allows them to bring to all the countries involved gifts which they need badly even without knowing it, and which they could hardly expect to receive from any other source.

Let me make myself clear. The 'exile' under discussion here is not necessarily a case of physical, bodily mobility. It may involve leaving one country for another, but it need not. As Christine Brooke-Rose put it (in her essay 'Exsul'), the distinguishing mark of all exile, and particularly the writer's exile (that is, the exile articulated in words and thus made a communicable *experience*) *is the refusal to be integrated:* the determination to stand out from the physical space, to conjure up a place of one's own, different from the place in which those around are settled, a place unlike the pieces left behind and unlike the place of arrival. Exile is defined not in relation to any particular physical space or to the oppositions between a number of physical spaces, but through the autonomous stand taken towards space as such. 'Ultimately', asks Brooke-Rose:

> ... is not every poet or 'poetic' (exploring, rigorous) novelist an exile of sorts, looking in from outside into a bright, desirable image in the mind's eye, of the little world created, for the space of the writing effort and the shorter space of the reading? This kind or writing, often at odds with publisher and public, is the last solitary, nonsocialized creative art.

A resolute determination to stay 'nonsocialized'; consent solely to integrate with the condition of non-integration; resistance – often painful and agonizing, yet ultimately victorious – against the overwhelming pressure of the place, old or new; rugged defence of the right to pass judgement and choose; an embracing of ambivalence or calling ambivalence into being – these are, we may say, the constitutive features of 'exile'. All of them – please note – refer to the attitude and life strategy, to spiritual rather than physical mobility.

Michel Maffesoli (in *Du nomadisme: vagabondages initiatiques*, 1997) writes of the world we *all* inhabit nowadays as of the 'floating territory' in which a 'fragile individual' meets 'porous reality'. In this territory, only such things or persons may fit as are fluid, ambiguous, in a state of perpetual becoming, in a constant state of self-transgression.

'Rootedness', if there is any, can only be dynamic: it needs to be re-stated and re-constituted daily – precisely through the repeated act of 'self-distantiation', that foundational, initiating act of 'being in travel', on the road. Having compared all of us – the inhabitants of the present-day world – to nomads, Jacques Attali (in *Chemins de sagesse*, 1996) suggests that apart from travelling light and being kind, friendly and hospitable to strangers whom they meet on their way, nomads must constantly be on watch – remembering that their camps are vulnerable, having no walls nor trenches to stop the intruders. Above all, nomads, struggling to survive in a world of nomads, need to grow used to a state of continuous disorientation, to travelling along roads of unknown direction, for an unknown duration, seldom looking beyond the next turn or crossing; they need to concentrate all their attention on that small stretch of the road which they need to negotiate before dusk.

'Fragile individuals', doomed to conduct their lives in a 'porous reality', feel they are skating on thin ice; and 'in skating over thin ice', Ralph Waldo Emerson remarked in his essay on *Prudence,* 'our safety is in our speed'. Individuals, fragile or not, need safety, crave safety, seek safety. And so they try, to the best of their ability, to keep up a high speed whatever they do. When running among fast runners, to slow down means to be left behind; when running on thin ice, slowing down also means the real threat of being drowned. Speed, therefore, climbs to the top of the list of survival values.

Speed, however, is not conducive to thinking; not to thinking far ahead, or to long-term thinking at any rate. Thought calls for pause and rest, for 'taking one's time', recapitulating the steps already taken, looking closely at the place reached and the wisdom (or imprudence, as the case may be) of reaching it. Thinking takes one's mind away from the task at hand, which is always running and keeping up speed, whatever else it may be. And in the absence of thought, the skating on thin ice which is *the fate* of fragile individuals in the porous world may well be mistaken for their *destiny*.

Taking one's fate for destiny, as Max Scheler insisted in his *Ordo Amoris*, is a grave mistake: 'the destiny of man is not his fate ... [T]he assumption that fate and destiny are the same deserves to be called fatalism'. Fatalism is an error of judgement, since in fact fate has 'a natural and basically comprehensible origin'. Moreover, though fate is not a matter of free choice, and particularly of individual free choice, it '*grows up* out of the life of a man or a people'. To see all that, to note the difference and the gap between fate and destiny, and to escape the trap of fatalism, one needs resources not easily attainable when running on thin ice: 'time off' to think, and distance allowing a long view. 'The image of our destiny', Scheler warns, 'is thrown into relief only in the recurrent traces left when we turn away from it'. Fatalism, though, is a self-corroborating attitude: it makes the 'turning away', that *conditio sine qua non* of thinking, look useless and not worth trying.

Taking distance, taking time in order to separate destiny and fate, to emancipate destiny from fate, to make destiny free to confront fate and challenge it: this is the calling of sociology. And this is what sociologists may do, if they consciously, deliberately and earnestly strive to reforge their calling – their fate – into their destiny.

'Sociology is the answer. But what was the question?', states, and asks, Ulrich Beck in *Politik in der Risikogesellschaft*. A few pages earlier Beck seems to articulate the question he seeks: the chance of a democracy that goes beyond 'expertocracy'; a kind of democracy which 'begins where debate and decision-making are opened about whether we *want* a life under the conditions that are being presented to us ...'. The chance is under question not because someone has deliberately and malevolently shut the door to such a debate and prohibited an informed decision-taking; hardly ever in the past has freedom to speak out and to come together to discuss matters of common interest been as complete and unconditional as it is now. The point is, though, that more than the formal freedom to talk and pass resolutions is needed for this kind of democracy, thought by Beck to be our imperative, to start in earnest. We also need to know what it is that we need to talk about and what the resolutions we pass ought to be concerned with. And this in our type of society, in which the authority to speak and resolve issues is the preserve of experts, who own the exclusive right to pronounce on the difference between reality and fantasy and to divide the possible from the impossible (experts, we may say, are almost by definition people who 'get the facts straight' – who take them as they come and think of the least risky way of living in their company), is not easy to achieve.

Why is this not easy and why it is unlikely to become easier unless something is done, Beck explains in his *Risikogesellschaft: Auf dem Weg in eine andere Moderne*. He writes: 'what food is for hunger, eliminating risks, *or interpreting them away,* is for the consciousness of risks'. In a society haunted primarily by material want, such a choice – between 'eliminating' misery and 'interpreting it away' – did not exist. Now it does exist – and is daily taken. Hunger cannot be assuaged by denial; in hunger, subjective suffering and its objective cause are indissolubly linked, and the link is self-evident and cannot be belied. But risks, unlike material want, are not subjectively experienced; at least are not 'lived' directly unless mediated by knowledge. They may never reach the realm of subjective experience – they may be trivialized or downright denied before they arrive there, and the chance that they will be indeed *stopped on their way grows*, together with the extent of the risks.

What follows is that *sociology is needed today more than ever before*. The job in which sociologists are the experts – the job of restoring to view the lost link between the objective affliction and subjective experience – has become more vital and indispensable than ever, while less than ever likely to be performed without the professional help of sociologists, since its performance by the spokesmen and practitioners of other fields of expertise has become utterly improbable. If all experts deal with practical problems and all expert knowledge is focused on their resolution, sociology is one branch of expert knowledge for which the practical problem it struggles to resolve is the *enlightenment aimed at human understanding*. Sociology is perhaps the sole field of expertise in which (as Pierre Bourdieu pointed out in *La Misère du monde*) Wilhelm Dilthey's famed distinction between *explanation* and *understanding* has been overcome and cancelled.

To understand one's fate means to be aware of its difference from one's destiny. And to understand one's fate is to know the complex network of causes that brought that fate about and its difference from destiny. To *work* in the world (as distinct from being 'worked out and about' by it) one needs to know how the world works.

The kind of enlightenment which sociology is capable of delivering is addressed to freely choosing individuals and aimed to enhance and reinforce their freedom of choice. Its immediate objective is to reopen the allegedly shut case of explanation and so to promote understanding. It is the self-formation and self-assertion of individual men and women, the preliminary condition of their ability to decide whether they want the kind of life that has been presented to them as their fate, which as a result of sociological enlightenment may gain in vigour, effectiveness and rationality. The cause of the autonomous society may profit together with the cause of the autonomous individual; they can only win or lose together. To quote from *Le Délabrement de l'Occident* of Cornelius Castoriadis:

> ... an autonomous society, a truly democratic society, is a society which questions everything that is pre-given and by the same token *liberates the creation of new meanings*. In such a society, all individuals are free to create for their lives the meanings they will (and can).

Society is truly autonomous once it 'knows, must know, that there are no 'assured' meanings, that it lives on the surface of chaos, that it itself is a chaos seeking a form, but a form that is never fixed once for all'. The absence of guaranteed meanings

–of absolute truths, of preordained norms of conduct, of pre-drawn and no-longer-needing-attention borderlines between right and wrong, of guaranteed rules of successful action – is the *conditio sine qua non* of, simultaneously, a truly autonomous society and truly free individuals; an autonomous society and the freedom of its members condition each other. Whatever safety democracy and individuality may muster depends not on fighting the endemic contingency and uncertainty of human condition, but on recognizing it and facing its consequences point blank.

If orthodox sociology, born and developed under the aegis of 'solid' modernity, was preoccupied with the conditions of human obedience and conformity, the prime concern of a sociology made to the measure of 'liquid' modernity needs to be the promotion of autonomy and freedom; such a sociology must therefore put individual self-awareness, understanding and *responsibility* in its focus. For the denizens of modem society in its solid and 'managed' phase, the major opposition was one between conformity and deviance; in modem society in its present-day 'liquefied' and 'decentred' phase, the major opposition which needs to be faced up to in order to pave the way to a truly autonomous society, is one between taking up responsibility or seeking a shelter where responsibility for one's own actions need not be taken by the actors.

The other side of the opposition, seeking shelter, is a seductive option and a realistic prospect. Already Alexis de Tocqueville (in the second volume of his *De la démocratie en Amérique*) noted that if selfishness, that bane haunting human kind in all periods of its history, 'desiccated the seeds of all virtues', individualism, a novel and typically modem affliction, only dries up 'the source of public virtues'; the affected individuals are busy 'cutting out small companies for their own use' while leaving the 'great society' to its own fate. The temptation to do so has grown considerably since de Tocqueville jotted down his observation.

Living among a multitude of competing values, norms and lifestyles, without a firm and reliable guarantee of being in the right, is hazardous and commands a high psychological price. No wonder that the attraction of the second response, of hiding from the requisites of responsible choice gathers in strength. As Julia Kristeva puts it (in *Nations without Nationalism*), 'it is a rare person who does not invoke a primal shelter to compensate for personal disarray'. And we all, to a greater or lesser extent, sometimes more and sometimes less, find ourselves in that state of 'personal disarray'. Time and again we dream therefore of a 'great simplification'; we engage on our own account, unprompted, in regressive fantasies of which the images of pre-natal womb and walled-up home are prime inspirations. The search for a primal shelter is the 'other' of responsibility, just as deviance and rebellion were the 'other' of conformity. The yearning for primal shelter has come these days to replace rebellion which has by now ceased to be a sensible option; as Pierre Rosanvallon points out (in a new preface to his classic *Le Capitalisme utopique*), there is no longer a 'commanding authority to depose and replace. There seems to be no room left for a revolt, as the social fatalism *vis-à-vis* the phenomenon of unemployment testifies'.

Signs of malaise are abundant and salient, yet, as Pierre Bourdieu repeatedly observes, they seek in vain a legitimate expression in the world of politics. Short of articulate expression, they need to be read out, obliquely, from the outbursts of xenophobic and racist frenzy – the most common manifestations of the 'primal shelter' nostalgia. The available and no less popular alternative to neotribal moods of scapegoating and militant intolerance – departure from politics and withdrawal behind the fortified walls of the private – is no more prepossessing and, above all, no more adequate to the genuine source of the ailment. And so it is at this point that sociology, with its potential of explanation that promotes understanding, comes into its own more than at any other time in its history.

According to the ancient but never bettered Hippocratic tradition, as Pierre Bourdieu reminds the readers of *La Misère du monde*, genuine medicine begins with the recognition of the invisible disease – 'facts of which the sick person does not speak or forgets to report'. What is needed in the case of sociology is the 'revelation of the structural causes which the apparent signs and talk disclose only through distorting them [*ne dévoilent qu'en les voilant*]'. One needs to see through – explain and understand – the sufferings characteristic of the social order which 'no doubt pushed back the great misery (though not so much as it is often said), while ... at the same time multiplying the social spaces ... offering favourable conditions to the unprecedented growth of all sorts of little miseries'.

To diagnose a disease does not mean to cure it – this general rule applies to sociological diagnoses as much as it does to medical verdicts. But let us note that the illness of society differs from bodily illnesses in one tremendously important respect: in the case of an ailing social order, the absence of an adequate diagnosis (elbowed out or silenced by the tendency to 'interpret away' the risks spotted by Ulrich Beck) is a crucial, perhaps the decisive, part of the disease. As Cornelius Castoriadis famously put it, society is ill if it stops questioning itself; and it cannot be otherwise, considering that – whether it knows it or not – society is autonomous (its institutions are nothing but human-made and so, potentially, human-unmade), and that suspension of self-questioning bars the aware ness of autonomy while promoting the illusion of heteronomy with its unavoidably fatalistic consequences. To re-start questioning means to take a long step towards a cure. If in the history of the human condition discovery equals creation, if in thinking about the human condition explanation and understanding are one – so, in the efforts to improve human condition, diagnosis and therapy merge.

Pierre Bourdieu expressed this perfectly in the conclusion of *La Misère du monde:* 'to become aware of the mechanisms which make life painful, even unlivable, does not mean to neutralize them; to bring to light the contradictions does not mean to resolve them'. And yet, sceptical as one can be about the social effectiveness of the sociological message, the effects of allowing those who suffer to discover the possibility of relating their sufferings to social causes cannot be denied; nor can the effects of the effects of becoming aware of the social origin of unhappiness 'in all its forms, including the most intimate and most secret of them', be dismissed.

Nothing is less innocent, Bourdieu reminds us, than laissez-faire. Watching human misery with equanimity while placating the pangs of conscience with ritual incantation of the TINA ('there is no alternative') creed, means complicity. Whoever willingly or by default partakes of the cover-up or, worse still, denial of the human-made, non-inevitable, contingent and alterable nature of social order, notably of the kind of order responsible for unhappiness, is guilty of immorality – of refusing help to a person in danger.

Doing sociology and writing sociology are aimed at disclosing the possibility of living together differently, with less misery or no misery: the possibility daily withheld, overlooked or unbelieved. Not-seeing, not-seeking and thereby suppressing this possibility is itself part of human misery and a major factor in its perpetuation. Its disclosure does not by itself predetermine its use; also, when known, possibilities may not be trusted enough to be put to the test of reality. Disclosure is the beginning, not the end of the war against human misery. But that war cannot be waged in earnest, let alone with a chance of at least partial success, unless the scale of human freedom is revealed and recognized so that freedom can be deployed fully in the fight against the social sources of all, even the most individual and private, unhappinesses.

There is no choice between an 'engaged' and 'neutral' way of doing sociology. A non-committal sociology is an impossibility. Seeking a morally neutral stance among the many brands of sociology practised today, stretching all the way from the outspokenly libertarian to the staunchly communitarian, would be a vain effort. Sociologists may deny or forget the 'world view' effects of their work, and the impact of that view on human singular or joint actions, only at the expense of forfeiting that responsibility of choice which every other human being faces daily. The job of sociology is to see to it that the choices are genuinely free, and that they remain so, increasingly so, for the duration of humanity.

Chapter 6
Alice in Computerland[1]

Laurel Richardson

Prelude

I was a published poet before I was a sociological ethnographer. For 30 years, I belonged to the "Women's Poetry Workshop", where I learned craft and critique. I still begin most days with either the reading or writing of poetry because I want the sense of the poetic in my mind before I begin my academic writing. My favourite poets – such as Robert Frost, Billy Collins, and Mary Oliver – all write poems that are understandable, literally and metaphorically. Their writing deploys standard poetic devices such as rhythm, assonance, alliteration, replication and variation, but does not call attention to these devices because they write using a 'natural-sounding' voice. It is that 'natural-sounding voice' that I also seek in my ethnographies – my voice as narrator and the exact speech of my ethnographic hosts. Because 'voice' is central to both my poetry and my ethnographic practices, I read my prose writing aloud, listening for awkward phrases and ungainly rhythms, and listening for places where a poetic device (such as doubling or alliteration) might intensify the text, snap it up, or evoke in the reader a sigh or a laugh. Poetry loosens my claim to 'knowing-it-all'; it is my good and dependable partner in discovering what I didn't know. When I pay attention, it can lead me past description to theory.

Computerland

'What have I been talking about this past week?', I say somewhat accusingly to my husband, Ernest. It's Wednesday, and we're having our lunch of Monday's leftover sausage and wild rice soup.
    'Hmm, hmm, good'.
    'What?'
    'Soup's still good'
    'Soup's not what I'm referring to', I say, my voice rising in exasperation. Not at him, actually, but at the situation.

---

1 This piece is part of a larger work-in-progress called "Seven Minutes from Home". I thank Ernest Lockridge for his reading of this piece and Michael Hviid Jacobsen for his encouragement that I clarify how my writing of poetry informs my ethnographic writing.

'Oh', he says. 'Computer troubles?'. He recognizes the particular tone of vexation that overcomes me when my computer fails me. In 1980, I had a near psychotic break over the Kaypro. After many agonizing nights when I kicked-out at unseen demons, I had a nightmare about a world where everything was backward. Upon awakening, I figured out the problem with the Kaypro – the 'delete' and 'save' keys had been reversed. Later, switching from an Apple to a PC, because my department had done so, nearly undid me. Trying to switch to a Mac, after a bad experience with an IBM, was hopeless. There were seven other computer traumas that sent me down the rabbit hole. Ernest has lived through each and every one of them.

'Yes! Damnit! Damn Computer!'

My Dell computer is a wheezing five-year-old and this past year has shown signs of electronic apnoea. 'It's going to crash, soon', my son Ben, the computer-guy says. 'You've got lots of time', my son Josh, the other computer-guy says. It's like getting consultations from two different surgeons. A college friend had two psychiatrists. One always said 'yes'. One always said 'no'. She only had to decide which one to call.

'I keep getting a warning signal that I have a Trojan – a horse? A condom?', I say to Ernest. 'It tells me to download some program to protect myself. Virtual condom for a virtual horse? But no matter what I do the program will neither download nor go away. It keeps popping up, like … Oh, never mind'. I stomp out of the kitchen into my study.

'Josh', I say on the phone. He's gone cellular which I like because I can reach him most any time. I tell him my problem. 'It's nothing', he says. 'Ignore it'. Long silence on my part. 'Okay, if you're freaked out, I'll come by this weekend and check it out, Mom'. That's three days away.

'Ben', I say on the phone. He's gone cellular, too, and he's actually turned his phone on. I explain the problem. 'It's serious', he says. 'What's your security system?'. 'McAfee', I say. I have McAfee because it keeps renewing itself automatically. 'No wonder', he says. I can see him raising his eyebrows in disbelief that *his* mother has McAfee. 'Download anti-Virus Malware', he says.

My choice is simple! I call 688-HELP, the Ohio State University's computer desk and tell my problem to the $8.00 an hour work-study freshman, Jason. Everyone at the Help-Desk is named 'Jason', except for the managers. They're Kevins. 'Download Malware', Jason says. Okay, that's two against one. Jason talks me through the process of downloading, running, and scanning. An hour later I call him back because the Malware refuses to scan. 'Too late', Jason says, in a flat voice. He's not emotionally involved with *my* computer. 'Turn it off, and bring it to a computer repair shop'.

'Someone in Microcenter will help you carry the computer into the store', Ernest says as he carries the Dell into my Chrysler 300M. I'm not allowed to lift heavy things as my left shoulder, elbow, wrist, hand and fingers, too, are in a sorry state from, hopefully, only a pinched nerve, probably from a long ago car accident but discovered this week through an x-ray of my neck: two totally fused cortical vertebrae. Maybe the universe is telling me something?

'Can you help?', I ask Associate Bill. Bill looks official with his name-tag pinned on the left-side pocket of a light blue long-sleeved poplin shirt. My sister-in-law, who teaches etiquette classes, says the 'left side is the right side' for name tags because it can be seen while shaking hands. The shaking hand ritual proves you're not holding a weapon. Bill's hand is only pushing a cart of computer ware onto the sidewalk in front of Micro Center. My 300m is in the fire lane in front of the cart. He doesn't attack it, he veers around it.

'As soon as I finish here', Bill says. I watch him transfer the computer ware from the cart to an elderly woman's grey SUV. She's bent over as if she has spent her life at a keyboard. 'I'll leave the car door open and meet you at the repair desk', I say. 'Thanks'.

'Can I help you?', Ashley asks, flipping her pony tail. She looks fresh-faced, like a devotee of Neutrogena. She pats the Dell on its back as if burping it. I explain the problem. Ashley explains that it will cost $200 to check out the computer, reconfigure it, saving whatever files they can – but they are not promising anything about saving the files. They do promise, though, that all of my 'licensed' programs will be obliterated.

'Even Windows?', I ask, incredulous.

Ashley nods.

'I'm not sure I even have the discs', I say. My voice is hoarse.

Ashley nods again.

'What will a new computer cost?', I ask.

'About $400', she says. 'And you'll have Windows 7 op, 500 GB hard drive, dual core processor, 2 GB ram, and …'

But, since she was talking in computer language, I'm not really sure what she said.

'Ernest', I call his cellular phone from my cellular phone to explain the situation.

'Get a new one', he says, without hesitation. 'And while you're there get me two 4 gigabyte flash drives'.

'I'll be back in a *bit*', I say to Ashley. I laugh at my little joke. She doesn't. I leave my Dell in her hands and enter the bowels of the 'new' Micro Center.

In 1979, when Micro Center opened its doors in a 900 square-foot storefront, I shook my head in wonderment: How could a whole store be devoted to computers? It'll be defunct, I thought, within the year. About computers, I am always wrong. That little store survived, invented the 'technical department store', generated 21 other stores, a billion dollar a year business and its own brand of computer stuff. Some few years ago they moved the landmark store into 44,000 square feet of retail space. Like a supermarket, each of its central 22 aisles have titles – surge protectors, AN cables, peripheral cables, printer ink, office supplies, media storage, games and toys, handsets, security, tools, keyboards, mice, cameras, networking-routers, networking-cards, speakers, notebook cases, mobile, cleaning, and, yes, even, software and HOT OFFERS. Everything else, I guess, is cool. Metal bins between the aisles overflow with older software programs, tools, opened packages of cables and stuff that I have no idea what is. At the front of the store are six check-out stations. On one side are the 'Repair and Service' and 'Returns and Exchanges' desks; on the other side is the 'Pick-up Express' – with a guarantee of only 18 minutes wait, if you've texted in your order. I'm not sure what you get if it takes 19 minutes. That's not on the sign.

Around the walls, piled high with boxes, are the departments – Technical Support, Peripherals, Portable Devices, Name Brand Systems (including their own brand, PowerSpec), Apple (I guess Mac's not a name brand), Books, and Gaming Department where a 60 inch LCD is on showing two cartoonish men boxing. Each of these departments is behind a windowed wood-panelled wall and a large doorway, as if to suggest you will enter a special room in the High-Tech Castle. As I bump into bins, I shake my head. My God, they've outgrown this space, too!

I make my way through the makeshift roundabouts in the aisles to the Named Brand Systems Department. Several customers are waiting for a sales associate. Everyone here is male, except me, and all the machines (are computers machines?) are sleek – silver and black – very yuppie masculine looking. The customers are looking at, reading about, and touching the equipment. It's like being in a hardware store or gun store where waiting for service is de rigueur. Men don't seem to mind waiting in any of these places.

'I think I'm next', I say to the Manager Alex. He has steered the newly freed-up Associate Mike to a young guy who came in after I did. I feel like an invisible interloper, if that oxymoron is possible.

'Mike just has to get a USB cable', Manager Alex says. 'Then he'll be with you'.

'Of course, men are served first', I say to the young guy customer.

He smiles.

'I'm not surprised or angry', I say.

He's still smiling.

'I expect it'. I deploy my credentials. 'I'm a professor of sociology at Ohio State University. I taught sociology of gender'.

'That was my favourite course', young guy says. His smile looks genuine now. 'Inequality by race, class and gender. I use it in my law practice'.

Now, I'm smiling.

'How can I help you', Mike asks me.

I explain my computer situation and my plan to purchase a new one.

'Are you a gamer?', Mike asks.

'No', I say. *Whatever I am, I am not that – whatever it is!*

'Download music?'

'No. Never'. *I'm too picky about sound quality.*

'Watch videos on your screen?'

'No'. *Absolutely not!* Unsure what the next set of questions might be, I assert my computer practices. 'I download my camera photos, do email and write'. *And if you're not careful, I'll write about you.*

'Do you have anyone to help you set up the system?', Mike asks.

'I have two sons – both computer experts. But both are busy and I don't like taking advantage of them'.

'Mothers are the worst', Mike says.

I look wide-eyed at him.

'Grandmothers are even worse', he says.

'I'm both of those', I say.

'Well, then', Mike says, 'you have two choices – a Dell or a PowerSpec. They're both easy to set up and the price and components are pretty much the same"' Mike points to two computers. Tweedledee and Tweedledum. PowerSpec, though, does have an upgraded model.

'Excuse me a moment', he says, 'while I help Mr. Armstrong at the sales desk'. I nod my acceptance acting as if I know who it is he's talking about, and call Josh. 'Which computer should I get?', I ask. 'The PowerSpec', he says, 'because Micro Center can repair it right there or give you a new one. Get 4 MB of ram though. And a quad core'. Still waiting for Mike, I call Ben. 'Get the PowerSpec', he says, 'because Micro Center can repair it right there or give you a new one. Get 4 MB of ram, though. And a quad core'. Bingo!

'I'll take an upgraded PowerSpec', I say to Mike when he returns, as if I am ordering a latte grande. He smells of tobacco. 'Ready for a new LCD too?', Mike says, nodding at the shelf of monitors. The 21 inch Dell sports a turquoise screen, a splash of ocean in this heavy metal land. 'I like this Dell monitor', I say, basking in its light. I am choosing a monitor based on its screen colour. It's how I buy my cars, too. The Chrysler dealer searched the nation to find the 300M car colours I wanted – cream on the outside, black leather on the inside, mahogany on the dash with retro-dials that glow turquoise at sunset. In my car, I feel simultaneously like a little girl riding in my father's fancy car and a grown-up capable woman. I wish I felt that way now.

'It's a very good monitor', Mike says, 'it's the one I have'.

I wonder if he says that to all the girls.

'What about a printer/scanner?', I say. 'Mine's a five-year old HP'.

'I think it's smart to upgrade everything at once', Mike says, soothingly, as he steers me toward the Peripherals Department. 'That's what I do about every 18 months or so. But I …'

I stop listening and start looking at the printers. They're all black and silver, too, like bad cowboys and AR15's. No women here, either – shopping or selling. Mike recommends an HP 6550. It looks like an aircraft carrier with levels and decks. It can print/scan like a Xerox, singles and multiples, fax and shoot down enemy missives. It takes a more expensive ink cartridge, but Mike assures me, I'll get twice as much printing from it. Micro Center is offering a no-interest one year purchase plan on computers, plus, I'll get a $60.00 mail-in rebate from HP. Here's an offer I can't refuse.

Mike carts my choices to the Pick-Up Express desk, where Associate Chong hands me the paperwork and asks for my driver's license. I start filling it in and start laughing.

'Why's funny?', he asks.

'*Physical* address', I say. 'Like I would use my virtual address?'

'Why's funny?', he asks again.

'Jus' is', I say.

I complete the form and hand it back. Chong's eyes narrow.

'You wrote diffren' numbers on the side', he says, pointing to the right margin, 'than you did in the blank'.

'I couldn't quite remember my social security number. I use it so seldom'.

'Ah, so', he says, as he checks out my driver's license.

Do I not look like myself? (I wonder)

'Your license expire', he says.

Earlier this week when a fit of orderliness overcame me, I cleaned out my wallet and tossed away extraneous cards. I must have tossed out my new driver's license.

'Here's credit cards', I say.

'No. Mus' have picture'.

'My Buckeye card?'

'No. Mus' be state issue'.

'Passport, okay?', I say, searching for my Xerox copy.

'Mus' be original'.

'Okay. I'll go home and get my passport. I live less than seven minutes away'.

'Take your fill-in paper', Chong says.

'All set?', Mike asks, reappearing at the just the right moment.

I explain what happened and head towards the automatic exit-door.

'Oh my God!', I blurt out to Mike. 'I left my car in the fire lane'.

'All the while you were here?', Mike asks, shaking his head. Was he thinking of his mother? Grandmother?

'I'm lucky I wasn't towed'.

'Nah', Mike says. 'We announce the car before towing. The last thing we want is an unhappy customer. We aim to please'.

Fifteen minutes later, I am back in Chong's line. Chong approves of my passport and disappears into the crevice behind his work station. I notice flash drives on the counter and choose two for Ernest. I feel gratified that that part of my memory is still intact. Twelve minutes later Chong reappears. 'Congratlation', he says. 'You approve for twenty-one hundred dollar credit'. That's twice the cost of my new computer ware. Maybe they know something about maintenance that I don't?

Associate Bill pushes my cart to the check-out line which snakes around, like the airplane security lines. The edges of the line are overflowing with big-boy toys – little screw-driver sets, wrench sets, drill bits, laser lights, laser pointers, flashlights, and XXL T-shirts emblazoned with 'Trust Me! I'm an Engineer' and

'Fix your own #%@# computer!' (I'm glad my sons haven't purchased those). Where the line makes its final curve, there are ''kids' toys' – potato guns, spit balls, rattlesnake eggs, and Rapid Fire Power Poppers. Little boy toys. For their dads, who might be thirsty by now, the glass-faced cooler holds Red Bull and three kinds of the power drink, Bawls. Where are the Hershey bars I find along the way to the check-out at JoAnne's Fabrics?

'Hi, Ashley', I say. 'So, why are you at the check-out counter now?'. It feels to me that she's been demoted.

She shrugs, and says: 'Just helping out'.

'We're the only two women in this whole store, Ashley', I say.

She nods.

'Find everything you were looking for?', she asks.

'*More* than', I say.

I phone Josh and ask if he can help. Josh is a single-father and a full-time math major and a certified Microsoft engineer. He has very little free-time. 'Sure, Mom. I'll come on Friday evening after supper and bring Akiva. We'll bring the system in and set it up before we go the movies'. Akiva's my 15 year-old grandson, he and his father always go to the movies on Friday night. 'Good', I say. 'Akiva can learn about computer systems'. 'Mom', Josh says with a hint of exasperation, 'Akiva's already put together two systems'.

'So you got a laser printer, huh, Mom', Josh says carrying in the gigantic carton from my 300M. It is Friday evening at 7:00 p.m.

'No', I say. 'It's an ink-jet'.

'Akiva, you set up the printer', Josh says.

Ernest comes into my study to see the sleek new machinery. Josh is setting up the computer, monitor and keyboard. Akiva is loosening the printer from its mooring, and Ernest is doing a little sailor jig. 'Terrific!', he says, 'looks like an aircraft carrier'. 'Or an alien space ship', adds Akiva. He opens and closes different portals and attaches the printer to an energy source. Josh inserts the ink cartridges. Lieutenant Ernest is standing by. Josh explains that in this printer the jet-spray heads have to be periodically cleansed.

'Terrific!', Ernest repeats, as he pats the printer's top side 'missile launcher'. I think he's imagining preparing its 'jets' for take-off.

'Everything's set now', Josh says, 'except loading the drivers for the printer'. It's 8:00 o'clock. Josh tries to install the right 'drivers'. The computer system I have purchased – Windows 7 – will not accept the HP printer. It is 10:00.

'Go on to your movie', I say. 'Maybe Ben can do it tomorrow'.

I phone Ben. He has a Bachelor of Science degree in computer hardware and software. He works long hours as a software designer and trouble-shooter, takes advanced classes, and remodels his home. Like his younger brother, he has little free-time. I explain the HP 4550 printer problem and ask him if he can help me over the week-end.

'Sure, Mom', he says. 'I'll come Saturday afternoon. Tami will come, too'. Tami is Ben's wife, and she is about as computer savvy as I am.

Ben and Tami arrive about 1:00 on Saturday. Ben has brought cd's upon which he has downloaded drivers. 'Would you mind if Tami and I went shopping while you fix the problem?', I ask. 'That's a good idea', Ben says. He won't have to hear my grating computer-anxiety voice. Tami and I return at 5:00, after a lovely girls-day-out-at-the-mall. Ben and Ernest are sitting at the kitchen table, talking about rams, gigabytes and insurgencies.

'It's working', Ben says, showing me the 'test-sheet'.

'Great', I say. 'Let's see how it does with my writing'.

Ben finds my VITA on my external drive, opens it and requests the HP to print it. 'Oh, NO!', I say. 'It isn't printing the italics!'.

Ben has two special gifts – patience and persistence. When the printer didn't do as it should, he tried six other ways to make it print correctly, while I was bouncing off the walls in the kitchen. Ben comes in shaking his head in defeat.

'Let's go to the Greek place for supper', I say. 'And Ben, could you help me pick out a different printer tomorrow?'.

'I really like my Canon', he says.

Sunday afternoon, Ben comes by and packs up the HP. We drive to Micro Center and Ben carries the printer into the 'Returns and Exchanges section'.

'Hi Ashley', I say. 'Helping out over here now, too?'

She nods.

I leave the printer, and enter the 'Peripherals Department' with Ben. A lot of men are looking at machinery. There is no 'next number' system like at the meat departments and Joanne's Fabrics, where I feel a sense of fairness. But, I don't need a sales associate. I have Ben. He looks, reads the information – checks out the driver's situation – and chooses a compact (silver and black) Canon that he carries back to Ashley. She does the exchange, smiles and says, 'The Canon costs less than the HP. I've credited you're account with the difference of $100'.

Ben sets it up and prints a sheet of so-reassuringly womanly *italics*.

'Thanks, Ben', I say, and then ask: 'Would you like a cup of soup?'

Postscript 1

I did not come to 'Computerland' with the intention of doing a study in gender. But when I found, there an extreme male-centric world, I was concerned. Whether I considered the demographic, interactional or cultural characteristics of 'Computerland', I was overwhelmed by 'maleness'. I wondered how any girl or woman could prosper in this environment. I was troubled that this tech world upon which my livelihood depends is overtly and covertly one that excludes women. The exclusion of women is an old story – a ho-hum story when framed in the exhausted blame-laying of an abstraction, patriarchy.

We see through frames, and if 'Computerland' was going to be seen afresh, so that its practices might be changed, I needed a fresh frame. I chose *Alice's*

Adventures in Wonderland for that frame: It is iconic for the 'literary nonsense' genre and iconic for the 'little girl in danger' trope. As such, *Alice* offers an appropriate frame (metaphor) for the writing about ethnographic experiences in 'Computerland', a real world for the 'virtual' community.

Postscript 2

This chapter is replete with poetic devices. In revision after revision I increased my writing dependence on them, thereby heightening the ethnographic story and deepening its analytical relevance to the sociological. There are four devices I have used liberally in this piece. First, there is repetition and variation. For example, the word 'soup' is used four times, and my conversations with my sons, husband, and sales-associates are repetitions of each other. Second, there is assonance, such as starting the article with a plethora of 's' sounds, hissing my 'exasperation' with computers. Third, I reworked sentences so that their rhythms matched the 'sense' of the sentences. When I describe the computer-store's objects, the sentences are short, and piled one after the other like the 'rat-a-tat-tat' of a machine gun. The sub-textual 'guys at war' image is repeated when the 'aircraft carrier' – err, printer – is oohed and aahed about when it is opened by the guys at home. Fourth, I use the 'natural language' (diction and pronunciation) of the speakers. There are other poetic tropes in the chapter, too. You might re-read for them, or not.

PART III
Exploring

Chapter 7

Getting in Touch with the World: Meaning and Presence in Social Science

Svend Brinkmann

It don't mean a thing, if it ain't got that swing.
Doo-ah, doo-ah, doo-ah, doo-ah, doo-ah, doo-ah, doo-ah, doo-ah
It don't mean a thing, all you got to do is sing.
Doo-ah, doo-ah, doo-ah, doo-ah, doo-ah, doo-ah, doo-ah, doo-ah.

Duke Ellington (1922)

Introduction

Our individual and collective lives incorporate a dimension of meaning. This dimension is usually the centre of attention in what has come to be known, roughly since the early 1970s, as qualitative research. Meaning is central to human lives on individual as well as on collective levels. In relation to the individual level, Paul Ricoeur once argued that a life 'is no more than a biological phenomenon as long as it has not been interpreted' (Ricoeur 1991: 28). It is the interpretation of meaning that elevates human life from a biological, animalistic state to something like a state of spirit and self-consciousness. Stripped of meaning and interpretation, a human life is pure biology. In the human and social sciences, we should therefore, Ricoeur argues elsewhere, approach human action as if it were a text (Ricoeur 1971). The meanings of the actions that comprise a human life should be interpreted more or less in the same way as when we interpret a novel and consider how the text obtains meaning through contextual and intertextual relations.

If we move from an individual life to the collective life of a culture, Clifford Geertz' (1973) famous definition of culture – as a historically transmitted pattern of meanings – points in the same direction. Meanings (materialized in symbols, rituals and works of art, for example) are at the core of human social life, and understanding a culture through interpreting its meanings becomes a key method in the social sciences, again closely related to the process of understanding a text through textual interpretation.

This insistence on meaning – and the associated insistence on using interpretation to convey meanings – has been highly successful in establishing the qualitative corners of the social sciences on a firm hermeneutic footing. It has brought us the linguistic, discursive, literary, postmodern and other similar turns in qualitative inquiry and has created a vibrant, critical and fruitful field of research (for a recent overview, see Denzin and Lincoln 2011), which, alas, still strives to become respected in some disciplines such as psychology.

In this chapter, however, I shall question the almost exclusive focus on meaning and interpretation in qualitative social science. I will contrast a meaning-centred approach with what I shall call a presence-centred approach to (qualitative) social science. In the first part, I will do so theoretically, before going on in the second part to show how various researchers have worked with the latter approach. I am not alone in taking an interest in presence. In recent years, a number of scholars from many different disciplines that are otherwise positive towards qualitative research, ranging from science studies to literature, have begun to question meaning centred-approaches. What do we leave out, some ask, if we are only doing meaning interpretation, either in the form of extracting meanings from cultural phenomena (if we are realists) or attributing meanings to them (if we are anti-realists)? Is human life really exhaustively understood – from the point of view of qualitative inquiry – when meaning interpretation has been done? What about the aspects of human lives that are little, if at all, connected to meanings, such as the *eating* and *digesting* of foods (Mol 2008) the *rhythms* of collective performances, such as rowing a competitive racing boat (King and de Rond 2011), or the sheer *joy* felt in our bodies when we experience aesthetic moments, to name but a few examples that I will return to in this text. Such aspects are – in one sense – meaningless, and may only be understood and expressed poetically and metaphorically, as when literary theorist Hans Ulrich Gumbrecht talks about 'the almost excessive, exuberant sweetness that sometimes overcomes me when a Mozart aria grows into polyphonic complexity and when I indeed believe that I can hear the tones of the oboe on my skin' (Gumbrecht 2004: 97). Hearing the tones of the oboe on one's skin is not necessarily a meaningful experience, but it is, indeed, something *felt*, and it is hard to deny that such experiences are of prime importance to living human beings.

Somatic experiences of eating and digesting foods, the rhythmic patterns of people doing something together, and the joy that aesthetics can bring to our bodies are well known aspects of our lives. They are all valuable and important in individual and also collective activities, but, like the paper on which a novel is written, they appear to have little to do with meaning, intentionality and representation. It seems at least somewhat artificial to talk about such things in the idiom of hermeneutics. Such aspects are more properly thought of as material, biological, physiological, haptic and acoustic, for example, since they are about tempo, pulse, intensity, pitch, warmth, volume and other similar material factors rather than representation. But still, they are cultural phenomena that we should not want to leave out from qualitative analyses of our lives. In short, they are about what Gumbrecht calls *presence*. The word presence comes from the Latin *prae-esse*, which literally means 'to be in front of' and it signals something that is *within reach*, something that we can touch and have immediate perceptions of. In that way, presence 'always binds time to a particular place' (Gumbrecht 2006: 61).

Narrative, Plot and Poetry

This chapter introduces the notion of presence in Gumbrecht's sense and seeks to make it useful in relation to the poetic imagination in social science. Presence is deeply and primarily (but not exclusively) connected to the poetic – in the same was as meanings are primarily (but again not exclusively) connected to narrative. To explain this point we may recall the famous example of narrative and plot given by E.M. Forster (1927): If we say 'the king died, and then the queen died', we may have a primitive kind of story, but, in a deeper sense, we have no narrative, because there is no plot – and thus no meaning. We have two separate events that follow each other in time. However, if we say 'the king died, and then the queen died *of grief*', we have a plot that connects the two events, which creates a narrative. As such, we rise above the pure material events, conceiving – as Ricoeur said – of human life as more than a biological phenomenon, viz. as involving meanings that connect the episodes, which call for interpretation.

Still, even if we have a narrative in the latter case, it does not really enable one to feel or understand what happened. It says nothing about what dying is, or what 'dying *of grief*' implies. Although we have meaning in this case, because we have a plot, we have very little presence. This becomes evident when we draw a contrast to a famous passage on the death of a queen, taken from another source entirely: I have in mind the soliloquy of Shakespeare's Macbeth upon hearing that his wife, the queen, has died. Macbeth hears a cry and his officer, Seyton enters:

> Seyton: The queen, my lord, is dead.
>
> Macbeth: She should have died hereafter;
> There would have been a time for such a word.
> To-morrow, and to-morrow, and to-morrow,
> Creeps in this petty pace from day to day,
> To the last syllable of recorded time,
> And all our yesterdays have lighted fools
> The way to dusty death. Out, out, brief candle!
> Life's but a walking shadow, a poor player
> That struts and frets his hour upon the stage
> And then is heard no more: it is a tale
> Told by an idiot, full of sound and fury,
> Signifying nothing (Shakespeare 1972: 843).

In Macbeth's soliloquy we have no narrative, but we have full presence. In fact, we are never told *why* the queen dies in the play. The meaning of her death is ignored. It is natural to think that she committed suicide (suffering from guilt because of the crimes she had committed with her husband), but there is no certain proof of this. What we get instead of narrative integration, plot and explanation is a sense of life's ultimate mystery and meaninglessness. Macbeth's soliloquy is poetic and articulates a sense of death and the insignificance of life by talking about dusty death and life as a walking shadow, which signifies nothing. Obviously, this is not the last word on the human experience of loss and death, but it certainly is one possible experience, which arguably has a form of universality that makes *Macbeth* appealing even to readers and viewers of the play now more than 400 years after it was written.

The point is that what moves us in *Macbeth*, and in particular in the celebrated soliloquy, is not only meaning, plot or narrative, but also aesthetics, the poetic and the sheer intensity of the tragedy – all of which Gumbrecht refers to as *presence*. We can thus summarize three layers that we may study as social scientists in human affairs:

- *Meaning* (typically articulated as narrative). Example: 'The king died, and then the queen died of grief' (researchers will here interpret the plotlines that connect actions and events and render them meaningful in our lives).
- *Presence* (typically articulated as poetry). Example: Macbeth's soliloquy (researchers will here seek to recognize the intensity and nature of human experience).
- *Brute events* (typically articulated as discrete episodes, which can be studied statistically). Example: 'The king died, and then the queen died' (researchers can here investigate the probability that some event B follows some other event A).

Normally, the top layer of meaning is brought forth as the qualitative contrast to the quantitative focus on causality and probability (the bottom layer of brute events). However, there is also the "middle" layer of presence, which has been given the most focused discussion by Gumbrecht in his book *Production of Presence: What Meaning Cannot Convey*, published in 2004. I shall here follow him in first asking what it is that meaning cannot convey in qualitative social science, and second how we may engage in the production of presence in qualitative inquiry (and why this is a significant thing to do). Along the way, we might come to swim in deep philosophical waters, but I hope that some of the examples to be included can serve as life vests that will bring us safely to the shore. Crawling up on the shore will not mean that we abandon meaning and interpretation, but it might mean that we come to appreciate those aspects of human and social life that cannot be framed hermeneutically, but are no less important for that. It may mean – to explain the title of the chapter – that we become better able to get *in touch* with the things and processes of this world. For the interpretation of meaning, as practiced in much qualitative social science, has a tendency to *distance* the interpreter from the world, since she must find a proper *perspective* from which to interpret something (a perspective that is sometimes conceived metaphorically, especially when teaching undergraduates, as a pair of spectacles, or – on a misguided reading of Thomas S. Kuhn, as a paradigm), thus privileging the *eye* as the organ of experience.

Getting in Touch with the World: Meaning and Presence in Social Science 137

In advocating a *presence* approach, we should instead revitalize the *hand* as a prime organ – both metaphorically and literally – that we use to know the world. Thus, the emphasis on presence goes hand in hand (pardon the pun) with what I have elsewhere called an epistemology of the hand (Brinkmann and Tanggaard 2010). The difference between the distant, perspectival eye and the closeness of the touching hand may initially be captured with a quote from the architect and phenomenologist Juhani Pallasmaa, who invokes the relevant difference in his book, *The Eyes of the Skin* as follows: 'The eye is the organ of distance and separation, whereas touch is the sense of nearness, intimacy and affection. The eye surveys, controls and investigates, whereas touch approaches and caresses' (Pallasmaa 2005: 46). Or, as I will put it in this context, the eye is the organ of meaning, whereas the hand is the organ of presence as that which enables us to get *in touch* with the world.[1]

The Layer of Presence in Human Life

Gumbrecht's (2004) argument revolves around a contrast between meaning and presence. Although he has a background in literary theory, he plays out this contrast in relation to many different phenomena including subjectivity, aesthetics and even culture as such (introducing an original distinction between meaning cultures and presence cultures). His overarching ambition is to go against what he sees as the current tendency, both in our culture at large and in the human and social science more specifically, to forget the possibility of a presence-based relationship to the world.

Gumbrecht begins by telling the story of how his interest in presence emerged in the 1980s when he, as a young literary theorist, became interested in 'materialities of communication'. These are all the technological devices that we employ to be able to communicate (ranging from the paper of written books to technologies of modern electronic communication and perhaps also human speech as a bodily performance). In agreement with another contemporary spokesperson for things and materialities, Bruno Latour (but without making the reference), Gumbrecht argues that such materialities of communication are not simply *means* of communication that transmit meanings and messages unaltered. Rather, they are *mediators* that have an impact on the meanings they are carrying (Gumbrecht 2004: 16). Or, as Latour would say, mediators are always 'actors endowed with the capacity to translate what they transport' (Latour 1993: 54).[2] Meanings do not float freely in some hermeneutic

---

[1] This should be taken with a pinch of salt. We may certainly experience presence effects (to be explained) by using our eyes, and also meaning effects (to be explained) by using our hands, but the point is that the former effects are more readily connected to the hands, because of the necessity of physical nearness to the world when using the hands, while the latter effects are more readily associated with vision.

[2] There are interesting parallels between Latour, the anthropologist of science, and Gumbrecht, the literary theorist, but it is significant that they employ different strategies.

ether, but depend on their material constitutions. To quote Duke Ellington, one of the great communicators of presence, whom I also used in my epigram for this chapter: 'It don't mean a thing, if it ain't got that swing'. The words themselves sung by Ella Fitzgerald, when performing Ellington's famous jazz standard, don't mean a thing, if they don't make the listener want to move the feet; if the rhythm, pulse and intensity of the performance don't have an impact on the bodies of the audience. And the 'Doo-ahs' are just as effective in conveying presence in the song as the (other) lyrics, although they do not have semantic meaning.

There is, as Gumbrecht says, 'a layer in cultural objects and in our relation to them that is not the layer of meaning' (Gumbrecht 2004: 54), and it is this layer that he seeks to capture when talking about presence. To avoid being misunderstood, I should perhaps repeat once more that the point is not to say that meanings are irrelevant or that hermeneutics should be disqualified in the human and social sciences. For when our practices of speaking, musicking or working do have 'that swing', they may certainly '*mean* a thing', and hermeneutic interpretation is thus demanded. Hans-Georg Gadamer, arguably the most important hermeneutic philosopher, pointed to this in his own way, when arguing for greater acknowledgement of the nonsemantic. As Gumbrecht reports, when Gadamer was asked by an interlocutor if the function of the nonsemantic features of poetry (for example, rhyme, rhythm etc.) was to challenge the 'hermeneutic identity' of the text, Gadamer answered (in Gumbrecht's translation from the German):

> But – can we really assume that the reading of such texts is a reading exclusively concentrated on meaning? Do we not *sing* these texts? Should the process in which a poem speaks only be carried by a meaning intention? Is there not, at the same time, a truth that lies in its performance? This, I think, is the task with which the poem confronts us. (Gadamer quoted in Gumbrecht 2004: 64; my italics)

Gadamer's answer is interesting, because it emphasizes the material factors of poetry (without, of course, forgetting about meaning and interpretation). Poems are supposed to be 'sung' (not necessarily, of course, in a literal sense), as Gadamer says, and there are vital aspects of singing and performing poetry that have little to do with meaning, but which are nonetheless central to the aesthetic experience of poetry.

Both are interested in the importance of material factors for social life, but whereas Gumbrecht wishes to uncover a pervasive but forgotten nonhermeneutic dimension of experience, thus showing us the limit of meaning and interpretation, Latour (on my reading) tries to completely empty hermeneutics of meaning (sic!) by stretching it to encompass the whole sphere of reality, for, as he says: 'Hermeneutics is not a privilege of humans but, so to speak, a property of the world itself. The world is not a solid continent of facts sprinkled by a few lakes of uncertainties, but a vast ocean of uncertainties sprinkled by a few islands of calibrated and stabilized forms' (Latour 2005: 245). When *all* relations in the world, not just those between persons and things, but also between things themselves, become hermeneutic, hermeneutics and Verstehen is no longer an alternative to *Erklären*.

The prime reason that we have poetry in the first place may have to do with all these effects that meanings themselves cannot capture, but which are generated by rhyme, rhythm, prosody, intensity etc. We need poetry – also in the broader sense that includes some of the things that go on in qualitative social science – when we wish to produce *presence effects* rather than *meaning effects*. And Gadamer emphasizes in the quote that this is not at the expense of truth. On the contrary: There is a kind of truth that lies in the *performance* itself (for example, when Ella Fitzgerald sings Ellington or when Macbeth delivers his soliloquy).

Contrasting Meaning and Presence

Now, all this may still sound very odd, even for insiders to qualitative inquiry in the social sciences who are used to think in terms of meaning and interpretation, so, in order to try a more schematic approach for pedagogical purposes, I have constructed the table below based on my reading of Gumbrecht. This table highlights some of the points of contrast between meaning and presence, and I shall try to say a little bit about each of the concepts.

Table 7.1   Meaning Effects and Presence Effects

Meaning effects	Presence effects
Meaning cultures	Presence cultures
Hermeneutics	Materiality
Mind	Body
Time	Space
Depth	Surface
Subjectivity as eccentric to the world (interpretative relationship to the world)	Subjectivity as being-in-the-world (non-interpretative relationship to the world)
Humans seeking to transform the world (mastering reality)	Humans seeking to inscribe themselves into the rhythms of the world (becoming *in sync*)
Knowledge as interpretation of meaning (either extracting or attributing meaning to reality)	Knowledge as revelation ('the happening of truth')

Martin Heidegger's phenomenology is arguably the most important source of inspiration for Gumbrecht, and the keyword itself – *presence* – refers first and foremost to a *spatial* and bodily relationship we have to the world and its objects. Things, events and episodes may literally be 'at hand' for us, or, as Heidegger famously said, 'ready-to-hand' (Heidegger 1927/1962). This means that things primordially appear to us in a practical context of use, prior to any theorizations we may engage in about the world, and prior to any representations we may form of it. This was for Heidegger a relationship that is non-conceptual and involves the body rather than an observing or reflective mind. We know the world already with the body before we know it reflectively with the mind.

Maurice Merleau-Ponty followed suit and emphasized even more the role of the body in our being-in-the-world. He argued that it is our motility – the capacity of the body to move actively in space – which is the basic form of intentionality, prior to representational or interpretational skills (Merleau-Ponty 1945). Intentionality is here something operational that signifies an 'I *can*' rather than the Cartesian 'I *think*'. The body, on the presence side of Table 7.1, should not be taken as an object, like, for example, in the medical sciences, but should be conceived as a phenomenological body, which is 'the living, moving, feeling, pulsing body of our being-in-the-world' (Johnson 2007: 276). It is the body as ground for experience of the world, prior to meaning and explicit interpretation.

When we are engaged with our bodies in the processes of the world, we may witness what Gumbrecht calls 'the production of presence', by which he refers to all those events and processes where 'the impact that 'present' objects have on human bodies is being initiated or intensified' (Gumbrecht 2004: xiii). Interpretation, on the other hand, is not mainly spatial or 'intense', but is a temporal relationship of trying out different framings of situations. Gumbrecht makes clear, however, that 'every human contact with the things of the world contains both a meaning- and a presence-component' (Gumbrecht 2004: 109). The point, again, is not to get rid of meaning, but to understand the layer of presence that we too often gloss over (in particular as social scientists) in our attempts to go behind the present and interpret it.

This also explains why meaning is typically associated with *depth* while presence is associated with *surface*. Interpreting the meaning of something often involves going *beyond* what is available to the sensing human body, whereas production of presence is about intensity and nearness in a spatial and physical way. To return to the example of poetry, so many high school students have been taught to employ different versions of psychoanalysis or Marxism to interpret the meaning of the words in a poem, while missing out entirely on the presence effects, that is,, on the sheer pleasure of reading or listening to the sounds and words. Poetry, as Gumbrecht says, 'is perhaps the most powerful example of the simultaneity of presence effects and meaning effects – for even the most overpowering institutional dominance of the hermeneutic dimension could never fully repress the presence effects of rhyme and alliteration, of verse and stanza' (Gumbrecht 2004: 18). Here we find an emphasis on the *simultaneity* of presence effects and meaning effects, which lies at the core of Gumbrecht's theory of aesthetic experience, which, he argues, is an oscillation between the two kinds of effect.

The simultaneity or oscillation between meaning and presence is also found at the macro level of culture, the analysis of which may be the most original part of Gumbrecht's contribution. Gumbrecht himself is an expert on the European literatures of the Middle Ages, and he provides an analysis of medieval culture as paradigmatically focused on presence. All cultures, he says, 'can be analysed as complex configurations whose levels of self-reference bring together components of meaning culture and presence culture' (Gumbrecht 2004: 79). So there are no pure meaning or presence cultures, not even medieval ones, but cultures tend to be focused on one kind of relationship to the world rather than another (contemporary Afro-Brazilian cults and also Japanese Kabuki and No theatres thus exemplify typical presence focused cultural practices). And today, so the argument goes, the culture of the so-called Western world is extremely focused on meaning effects, which includes the culture's investigations of itself (institutionalized in the social sciences).

Meaning cultures tend to cultivate people who understand themselves as subjects detached from, or eccentric to, the world in which they live. They are intent to transform the world through the interpretations they make of it (here, once again, we find the primacy of temporality in relation to meanings). In contrast, presence cultures have a tendency to cultivate people who aim to become *in sync* with the rhythms of the world and the things around them. This means first and foremost inscribing oneself into something (the rhythms of the cosmology, to use Gumbrecht's expression) rather than seeking to transform it. The subject of presence cultures, living a life that revolves around non-interpretative relationships to the world, will often devote particular attention to bodily actions and practices that are non-representational, such as the Japanese tea ceremony in which the question of meaning is secondary to presence questions of movement, tactility and taste.[3]

This brings us to the final contrast between meaning and presence, viz. concerning knowledge and truth. From the perspective of meaning, knowledge is a product of our interpretations of the world that are tried out temporally. This was of course emphasized by the pragmatists, who believed that knowledge is not about correspondence between theory and world (between representation and what is represented), but is a matter of what our theories enable us to *do* to transform the world to better human lives. Once again, there is no reason to reject this mode of knowing, without which human lives would be very different from what they are. But Gumbrecht says that we should not reserve our epistemic words (like knowledge and truth) to these kinds of relationships to the world, for there is also what Heidegger called truth as unconcealment (*aletheia* in Greek), as a kind of revelation that does not rest on interpretation, but instead on presence.

According to Heidegger, this kind of revelation is typically found in poetic practices and in great works of art (again, we may have Macbeth's soliloquy in mind). Thus, for Heidegger, the work of art is a privileged site for the happening of truth in the sense of unconcealment (Gumbrecht 2004: 72). What Heidegger argues in his essay on the origin of the work of art is that for a work of art to be great, it has to be *true* (Heidegger 1993). As he says: 'In the artwork, the truth of beings has set itself to work. Art is truth setting itself to work' (Heidegger 1993: 165). For Heidegger, truth is not confined to science or logic, for a great

---

3 Sports represent another range of practices that are centrally concerned with presence effects, and while questions such as 'what is the meaning of football?' sound curious, it is more helpful to ask about what presence effects such practices produce (see Gumbrecht 2006 for an analysis of the aesthetics and *beauty* of sports).

work of art can convey an experience of the truth of Being. Truth in Heidegger's sense means that beings are brought into unconcealedness, which is not truth as correct representation of the world, but truth as an *occurrence*, as something that happens (for example *as* a work of art). A work of art, therefore, 'is not the reproduction of some particular entity that happens to be at hand at any given time; it is, on the contrary, the reproduction of things' general essence' (Heidegger 1993: 162). Heidegger illustrates his point with a detailed analysis of Vincent van Gogh's famous painting of the peasant shoes that point to the truth that 'this equipment belongs to the *earth*' (Heidegger 1993: 159) in Heidegger's special terminology.

With our modern notion of truth, so firmly tied to 'correctness' and even science, it may be very difficult to grasp what Heidegger is getting at here. How on earth can poetry and paintings be *true*? A poetical answer it given by Ron Pelias, who, in his *Methodology of the Heart*, states the following: 'Science is the act of looking at a tree and seeing lumber. Poetry is the act of looking at a tree and seeing a tree' (Pelias 2004: 9). The act of looking at a tree and seeing lumber is actually a hermeneutic act of interpretation that goes beyond the presence and the 'surface' of the tree to interpret its possibilities (here in quite an instrumental sense). The act of looking at it, in all its presence and thisness (in Scholastic terms, as taken up by the ethnomethodologists, its *haecceity*), is too experience it truly, as a concrete, material entity.

The Conservatism of Presence?

Before moving on, I shall concern myself with a legitimate objection to the emphasis on presence. The objection runs something like this: Is it not deeply conservative to want to inscribe oneself into the 'rhythms of the cosmology', to accept things and resist the temptation to transform them through interpretation? Doesn't this go against what we admire most about the social sciences, their capacities to change and improve the social world that they study?

However fascinated we may become by presence effects, I believe that this question should continually be raised, but I also believe that there are at least two valid ways of answering it. The first way repeats that *of course* we should interpret – and through our acts of interpretation – transform the world. We could not imagine human life without our arrays of transformational practices in science, education and also the arts. The point is not that we should stop interpreting, criticizing or transforming, but simply that we *also* need to be aware of presence if we want to appreciate the phenomena on the right hand side of Table 7.1 above. We should not choose presence over meaning, but study how the two are related and oscillate, and sometimes appreciate the fact that meanings *depend* on presence as something deeper and more fundamental (and sometimes not): That representation is possible only on a background of the non-representational (Dreyfus 1991), that conscious intentionality is possible only on a background of 'motor intentionality' (Merleau-Ponty 1945) and that reflective knowledge is possible only because we can meet the world unreflectively, as ready-to-hand (Heidegger 1927/1962).

The other way of answering the objection is less philosophical and points out, more pragmatically, that meaning and interpretation no longer liberates us (if they ever did) in an unproblematic way. Interpretation of meaning may favour the status quo at least as much as an emphasis on presence. Why so? Because the contemporary 'culture of communication' of the West (Briggs 2007) is already completely saturated with meanings, interpretations and different perspectives to an extent that nothing today is more tiresome than 'the production of yet another nuance of meaning' (Gumbrecht 2004: 105). What we miss today may precisely be impressions of presence, and it may actually be here that we can find ways to change what needs to be changed. A democratization of interpretation has occurred, with the risk that there is no longer transformational fuel left in the engine of meaning. We may refer to Slavoj Žižek's (2000) well-known example from *The Ticklish Subject* of the skinhead who has been beating up foreigners. When pressed to articulate the reasons for his violence, Žižek reports that he

> ... will suddenly start to talk like social workers, sociologists and social psychologists, quoting diminished social mobility, rising insecurity, the disintegration of paternal authority, the lack of maternal love in his early childhood ... In short, he will provide the more or less precise psychosociological account of his acts so dear to enlightened liberals eager to 'understand' violent youth as tragic victims of their social and familial conditions. (Žižek 2000: 202)

The skinhead can, in Žižek's rendition, interpret himself and his own acts from now on and forever – and his interpretations may even be correct and uncover the 'true meaning' of his violence – but the interpretations do not have any kind of *impact* on him, as they are just spinning hermeneutically in the void. I am tempted to say that what is lacking is exactly *presence*. Perhaps, if I may be allowed to speculate a little bit, what the violent young man needs is not one more turn of interpretation, but rather some 'unconcealment' of the lives of his victims?

Now, having drawn up these contrasts between two ways of relating to the world, which, I hope, have helped articulate the often forgotten dimension of presence, I will move on to describe all too briefly how qualitative social science may work with presence effects by giving a couple of examples. I shall first show how presence may (and should) be an *object* in qualitative inquiry, and then go on to discuss if and how qualitative research itself may *produce* presence effects. Unsurprisingly, we shall see that the two are intimately connected.

Analysing the Layer of Presence in Cultural Phenomena

How can we discover, appreciate and analyse what Gumbrecht calls the layer of presence in cultural phenomena? The layer, which, as I have argued, lies between causality and meaning? How can we, as social scientists, develop an eye, ear and hand for the material and spatial features of reality and convey a sense of presence?

First, there is little doubt that we need to work philosophically with the dimension of presence. We have so many concepts about the semantic, the intentional, the representational and the normative, all of which are connected to the interpretation of meaning. We have fewer concepts about presence, and those we do in fact have (in this text I have used words such as intensity, rhythm and tempo) may sit uneasily with the human and social sciences due to their almost physicalistic overtones. The point of working with the layer of presence is not to be reductionistic in a physicalistic way (that is, reducing human life to what can be addressed in the language of the physical sciences), but exactly the opposite: Avoiding reducing human life to one dimension only (in this case to meaning effects).

It may be preferable to discuss these matters in relation to a concrete example. I shall use a recent article by Anthony King and Mark de Rond on boat race, because their article demonstrates how it is possible to do a very thorough in-depth study of a tiny fragment of social life, which nonetheless has wide ramifications for social theory in general (King and de Rond 2011). The authors are interested in a phenomenon that is at once quite specific – rhythms or synchronized bodily movements – but which are at the same time extremely general. They note that rhythms are essential to group life; most obviously, perhaps, in the military where marching together often for days is an age-old practice to build togetherness and group cohesion. To make a long story short, King and de Rond argue that rhythm is central to concerto performance in a number of social practices, and rhythm thus gives one important clue to what is arguably *the* fundamental question of sociology: How is collective action possible? (King and de Rond 2011: 567). To put empirical flesh to the theoretical bone, they analyse minutely an intense sporting episode in which a social group (a rowing team) generated rhythm and coordinated their social practice in such a way that they won the annual prestigious boat race between Cambridge and Oxford Universities, dating back to 1829 – so famous that it is now simply referred to as The Boat Race. In the paper, we follow the Cambridge crew, and learn about how they have prepared and gone through a number of difficulties before the day of the race. They start off, rather unimpressively, before ultimately getting in sync and overtaking the Oxford boat and finally winning the race. The paper has detailed analyses of the communication of the crew and the calls of the different members of the crew, in particular the 'cox', who is the non-rowing person in the boat, issuing calls and steering the vessel.

The analysis is interesting not least because it succeeds in showing us the insights that may come from descriptions of a very concrete phenomenon of rhythm. In a conventional sense, there are no interpretations in the text – that is,, no reflections on what the phenomena under scrutiny may 'mean', 'represent' or 'signify' – but the reader first and foremost gets a sense of being there, *in* the boat. The analysis is not hermeneutic, for it does not uncover relations of meaning, but it is also not causal, for there are no causal laws or variables in the text. In the terminology of this chapter, the text shows us the layer of presence in social life without reducing it, either 'upwards' to meaning or 'downwards' to causality, and the reader secondarily comes to appreciate the importance of rhythm to a wide range of collective activities in human life. This illustrates the idea that getting in touch with the world can be achieved through careful descriptions of bodily movements.

Needless to say, this is relevant not only in relation to ethnographic work, but also, for example, in relation to interviewing. Here, a focus on presence will minimally involve an awareness of the fact that the meaning of what we say is not independent of *how* we say it, that is, of the material factors of the voice (loudness, pitch, prosody etc.), so restricting one's analysis to a transcript when doing a qualitative interview study is to leave out so much of the *materiality* of what makes speaking significant.[4] Today there is, as Maggie MacLure has recently argued, a widespread suppression of materiality in qualitative research, which is ironic since the *spoken* voice remains central to so many research endeavours (MacLure 2010). What people say is indeed meaningful (much of the time), but alongside the level of meaning runs this level of something else that does not necessarily signify, represent or mean anything, but which nonetheless is greatly important to how we experience people and things. Once more, we lack words and concepts with which to grasp this dimension, and Gumbrecht refers to Paul Zumthor's ambition of developing a 'phenomenology of the voice' and also of the activity of writing 'as body-centered modes of communication' as pointing in the right direction (Gumbrecht 2004: 9).

Poetics of Presence

Whereas the social sciences, as I have alluded to above, may be quite mute in relation to the dimension of presence in human life, the arts, in contrast, specialize in presence. This may partly explain the contemporary fascination with 'arts based research' (Barone and Eisner 2012), but here I shall look directly at one specific artist, who is not only famous for his art works, but also for his poetics (that is, more theoretical writings on poetry, film and other art forms in which he excels). The person is the Danish poet, filmmaker and commentator of international cycling events, Jørgen Leth (b. 1939). Leth is a multi-talented artist, who has been part of the Danish avant-garde scene since the early sixties. He mainly works as a poet and film director, but he has also made music and recently authored a couple of quasi-autobiographical novels. He has also been involved in public scandals. In 2005 he was attacked in Denmark, because of explicit descriptions of sex with a young woman from Haiti, where he resided at the time. I shall include an intermezzo on his poetics here, because of the way he goes against meaning and narrative in his work and works explicitly to create presence effects.

---

4   I am not arguing against the use of transcripts in qualitative research, but I am arguing for more reflection on what is 'lost in transcription', to borrow a phrase from Pierre Bourdieu et al. (1999: 622). Unfortunately, this kind of reflection is most often completely absent in interview studies that follow 'standard practice'.

Leth's simple and naïve credo, which he has repeated many times in books, poems and interviews (for him these appear to melt into each other), is: 'Life is interesting. We shall examine it' (Leth in Wichmann 2007: 46). These words express why most of us are in the business of social science. We believe that life is interesting. We wish to examine it. Leth, who also studied anthropology as a young man, consistently talks about the arts as practices of investigating the world (and one of his heroes is Bronislaw Malinowski, who founded modern social anthropology). Art is not just irrational bursts of expression, but a way of studying phenomena. To use Leth's words again: 'My basic idea is: I don't know anything, but I would like to know something' (Leth 2006: 4).

Leth has articulated his 'method' as follows: 'I am more or less consciously against narrative, against a leitmotif ... I am not interested in syntheses. I am more interested in the fragmented. I am interested in freezing the fragmented and then see what it may provide of utterances, or how it may be read' (Leth in Wichmann 2007: 79). This is a clear expression of an attempt to understand the world that does not seek meaningful, connecting threads, but instead focuses on fragments. But although Leth is interested in the fragmented, and does not care for narratives, he is not methodologically sloppy. On the contrary, in order to capture the fragmented, he argues that we need quite strict 'rules of the game'. Such rules always structure his work as an artist. The artist — just as any other researcher — necessarily needs a way to systematize chaos (Leth in Wichmann 2007: 24). There is no doubt in Leth's mind that the world as such is chaotic, and there are no larger contexts of meaning in his work, no metaphysics. Instead, there is a focus on presence in his awareness of the discrete, fragmented parts of the world. He is not looking for meaning as *coherence* between different parts (compare 'the king dies, and then the queen died of grief' example), but is rather interested in the *intensity* of the parts themselves, as he says (Leth in Wichmann 2007: 41). Although the world is chaotic and fragmented, Leth wants to write it down and categorize it, which demands an explicit non-narrative way of working (Leth in Wichmann 2007: 54). As he said in an interview: 'it's about survival. I simply feel that the world and my life are full of chaos, that is, disorder' (Leth in Wichmann 2007: 69). Writing and categorizing are artistic ways of survival. In general, Leth does not consider art and life as opposites, but as two sides of the same coin, and he states that he lives his own life as a work of art (Leth in Wichmann 2007: 31, 36).

From watching his films, reading his books and interviews, attending lectures held by him, and from following his career as a sports reporter in the field of professional cycling (on cycling, see Brinkmann 2010), it is possible to distil the method by which Leth works. In his own words, what he does is this: 'Find an area, delimit it, examine it, write it down' (Leth 2006: 7). Let us unpack this bit by bit, since it arguably represents a way of nourishing the poetic imagination:

1. Find an area. An 'area' is some dimension of human experience. Leth has found such dimensions as play (for example, in his film on "The Playing Human Being"), the erotic (for example, in his new film on "The Erotic Human Being"), and the phenomenology of simple human movements and sounds (for example, in his breakthrough film from 1967 "The Perfect Human Being" or in "66 Scenes from America", which has a long scene featuring Andy Warhol eating a hamburger, then waiting, and finally saying: 'My name is Andy Warhol, I've just finished eating a hamburger'). An important part of finding an area is boredom. Boredom is used consciously, constructively, and methodologically by Leth. As he says: 'Boredom is not a problem, but a potential creative power in our existence' (Leth in Wichmann 2007: 8) – 'Boredom is definitely the starting point for my work' (Leth in Wichmann 2007: 20). Boredom is a necessary first step in the poetic process. One must wait and observe with patience, and then something happens. Using the terminology of this chapter, the point is not to jump into interpretation too soon, but allowing the world to show itself in presence, which demands patience and luck. 'Chance is my good friend', says Leth (2006: 3).

2. Delimit it. Since the world is chaotic, we must introduce limits and rules in order to be able to get in touch with it. According to Leth, 'art should be an exercise in framing life so that it can be seen' (Leth in Wichmann 2007: 51). He delimits or frames the world by using methodological 'rules of the game'. He imposes these rules on himself and then observes how the world performs within the delimitation specified by the rules: 'That is the key sentence: To see what happens' (Leth 2006: 7). To obtain presence, it is necessary to invite it in by means of rules. Some examples of his strict rules include: Not allowing the camera to move when shooting films, only use naturally occurring sounds, or only shoot scenes that last for a specific number of seconds (Leth 2006: 7). Such rules resemble those of the Danish dogma film movement led by Lars von Trier and Thomas Vinterberg, and von Trier himself is heavily inspired by Leth's philosophy, and they have also made a movie together – "The Five Obstructions" – in which von Trier challenges Leth five times to shoot a movie with five different, and increasingly challenging, sets of rules. Anyone who has watched this film will recognize the lack of meaning, but likely appreciate the presence effects it generates. In talking about his new film on "The Erotic Human Being", Leth introduced the rule that all scenes must be shot in hotel rooms. People are placed in various situations, and then something interesting or moving often happens *in* the situations: 'My films do not tell stories', he says, 'the contents are in the individual scenes' (from a public lecture at the University of Aarhus, Denmark, June 4, 2008).

3. Examine it. We examine the world through our engagement and involvement with it. We must *be there* with our bodies, in a direct and spatial relationship to what we are trying to know about. Leth therefore uses his own person as an instrument of examination. There is here explicit inspiration from Malinowski, and Leth wants to break 'with the anthropology of the porch. One needs to become a part of what one investigates' (Leth in Wichmann 2007: 25). For example, in his film on the erotic, Leth himself appears in erotic scenes with a woman while holding the camera himself during the act. But Leth insists that he is no pornographer, and that pornography is completely uninteresting and even the opposite of the erotic. What interests him is presence and beauty.

4. Write it down. As a tool of examination, Leth uses notes and notebooks, for which he has an almost religious veneration. 'For me', he says, 'the notebook is the most important tool' (Leth 2006: 4). Often, when writing his poems, he simply copies the fragments from his notebooks without further editing. The notes represent immediate impressions in moments of presence. He believes in the power of chance, in the raw, unedited experience of the world. 'I collect material like an anthropologist', Leth explains. And working with the notebooks is not just a technical aspect of having to 'write it down'. As he says on one of his (improvised) spoken word albums in a song simply entitled "The Notebook": 'It's a philosophy', it is a way of life, a way of surviving in a world in fragments.

In concluding on Jørgen Leth, we may return to his simple credo: 'Life is interesting. We shall examine it'. Since the world is chaotic and fragmented, but also interesting, we need to examine it in ways that respect its patchy nature, and yet are rigorous. Thus, a piece of art from Leth, whether a poem or a film, is, in his own words, 'not a story with a conclusion. It is a (fictitious) investigation' (Leth 2006: 3). And further: 'One can say that there is a game in saying that life is interesting. It is something one says in order to make it interesting in the first place' (Leth in Wichmann 2007: 77).

I have here devoted considerable space to the poetics of Jørgen Leth, because it connects so elegantlæy with Gumbrecht and his focus on presence and is an attempt to develop it into a workable methodology (resembling those of arts based research, see Barone and Eisner 2012). It demonstrates that a focus on presence does not equal an 'anything goes!' but is something one can hope to achieve when arranging social situations carefully and methodologically. In order to unveil the dimension of presence, the social scientist may thus occupy herself with mundane patterns of rhythm and movement (as in the example of boat race), but can also find inspiration in those parts of the art world (represented by Leth) where practices of presence rather than meaning are cultivated. But this is on the side of *studying* presence. What about using presence in *communicating* one's research? This is what I will turn to now.

Presence Effects in the Social Sciences

One sociologist who has engaged in an exploration of qualitative alternatives to 'meaning' and 'narrative' is Andrew Abbott (2007). He does not talk about presence or the poetic, but articulates his approach under the banner of 'lyricism' (I have analysed lyrical sociology in Brinkmann 2009 from which the following is based). In advocating 'lyrical sociology', Abbott positions himself (somewhat one-sidedly) 'against narrative'. He argues that mainstream 'analytic social science and the new narratives of the 1990s are simply different versions of the same thing: stories in the one case of variables and in the other of actors' (Abbott 2007: 70). According to Abbott, a lyrical approach is in a profound sense *not* narrative. For unlike a narrative that reports a *happening* (think again of 'the kind died, and then the queen died of grief'), lyrical writings express a *state of affairs* (Abbott 2007: 69). Abbott opens his piece with Harvey Zorbaugh's (1929) sociological paean to the city of Chicago, a lyrical description of how the city struck this classical sociologist. It is worth quoting at length to get a feel for lyricism:

> The Chicago River, its waters stained by industry, flows back upon itself, branching to divide the city into the South Side, the North Side, and 'the great West Side'. In the river's southward bend lies the Loop, its skyline looming towards Lake Michigan. The Loop is the heart of Chicago, the knot in the steel arteries of elevated structure which pump in a ceaseless stream the three millions of population of the city into and out of its central business district. The canyon-like streets of the Loop rumble with the traffic of commerce. On its sidewalks throng people of every nation, pushing unseeingly past one another, into and out of office buildings, shops, theaters, hotels, and ultimately back to the north, south, and west 'sides' from which they came. For miles over what once was prairie now sprawls in endless blocks the city. (Zorbaugh 1929: 1)

However much Zorbaugh's paean differs from Macbeth's soliloquy, they are united in the way they produce a presence effect. Zorbaugh focuses directly on the spatial arrangement of the city, on its surfaces and materiality. As we see, there are no stories (in a conventional, narrative sense) in lyric, no 'recounting, explaining, comprehending – but rather the use of a single image to communicate a mood, an emotional sense of social reality' (Abbott 2007: 73). Unlike a narrative writer, who tries to tell us and explain what happened, a lyrical writer 'aims to tell us of his or her intense reaction to some portion of the social process' (Abbott 2007: 76). This corresponds closely to Gumbrecht's analysis of the production of presence. A lyrical writer does not seek connecting threads, but 'looks at a social situation, feels its overpowering excitement and its deeply affecting human complexity, and then writes a book trying to awaken those feelings in the minds – and even more the hearts – of his readers' (Abbott 2007: 70). It is easy to see what connects Abbott's lyricism with Leth's poetics, for, according to Abbott, it is a mark of lyricism to get *in touch* with the phenomena one studies: 'the lyrical writer does not place himself or herself outside the situation but in it' (Abbott 2007: 74).

The Presence Effects of Eating an Apple

To convey a sense of lyricism and possible presence effects in social science writings, I will now refer to a final example (this section builds on Brinkmann 2012). In just a little more than six printed pages of text, the ethnographer and philosopher Annemarie Mol uses the mundane process of eating an apple as a basis for theorizing subjectivity (Mol 2008). And she does not just theorize subjectivity – the *I* who eats an apple – she also suggests explicitly in her conclusion that if we draw upon exemplary situations to do with eating as we engage in philosophy, many things, including subjectivity, may change (Mol 2008: 34). Without using the term herself, I propose that she is using her lyrical description of apple eating to generate presence and thereby deconstruct our traditional notion of the subject as a discrete, bounded self with agency. 'The eating self', as she says, 'does not control 'its' body at all' (Abbott 2008: 30); it does not *interpret* the world, but *consume* it. And it is worth continuing the quote:

> Take: *I eat an apple.* Is the agency in the *I* or in the *apple*? I eat, for sure, but without apples before long there would be no 'I' left. And it is even more complicated. For how to separate us out to begin with, the apple and me? One moment this may be possible: here is the apple, there I am. But a little later (bite, chew, swallow) I have become (made out of) apple; while the apple is (a part of) me. *Transsubstantiation.* What about that for a model to think with? (Mol 2008: 30)

By describing the everyday occurrence of eating an apple in a way that generates presence effects, Mol wants to make us think about how to remodel the subject. The subject emerges in her text as much more embedded in the world, or saturated with the world, so to speak (Gumbrecht would say *inscribed* into the cosmology), than on traditional accounts. The subject emerges in her analysis as something with semi-permeable boundaries (Mol 2008: 30). Mol takes the 'thin' situation of apple eating as her starting point, but she goes on to provide much more 'thick' history around it. Thus, she tells us the cultural history of apples, how the apple has biblical connotations, how apples came to the Netherlands (her home country), and how there is a politics of apples (Mol dislikes Granny Smiths, because they used to be imported from Chile during the Pinochet dictatorship). Eating apples is an everyday phenomenon that is radically situated, and which is made possible because of complex webs of relationships (agricultural, religious, geographical, political etc.) that it is possible and interesting to study.

Instead of confining action, activity, uniquely to human subjects, Mol deconstructs the whole subject-object split and posits an image of *inter-activity* – 'shared activity all round' (Mol 2008: 31). And her deconstructive tools are deeply poetical. Consider the following statement:

> In the orchard, the apples. The trees carefully grafted. The colours and textures and tastes and cellar life attended to and the best fruit selected. And again. Without the work of ever so many generations of cultivators my apple would not have been. The cultivators, meanwhile, owed their lives to their apples. When and where in all these flows does subjectivity emerge? Where to stop the flow and point at it? (Mol 2008: 31)

Should we consider this as poetry, philosophy or as an ethnography of apple eating in everyday life? In my view, it qualifies as all three things, and the result is a beautiful presence-generating account of subjectivity as always already in transaction with its surroundings.

Mol's text illustrates that it is possible to do provocative and interesting deconstructive work simply by taking an everyday occurrence as a starting point and making it impress us through presence. She questions our standard preconceptions of subjectivity by showing us other possible ways of thinking that are immanent in eating practices (indeed a spatial, bodily and material relationship to the world, as emphasized by Gumbrecht). In the process, the world itself appears as re-enchanted; the world is no longer a collection of lifeless objects in Newtonian space, but an active process of change and becoming. This re-enchantment is achieved by a movement similar to Richard Rorty's claim that 'the way to re-enchant the world, to bring back what religion gave our forefathers, is to stick to the concrete' (Rorty 1991: 175). Presence is all about sticking to the concrete.

There is no easy recipe of how to communicate research with presence effects. But it seems certain that researchers interested in the task can learn as much from poets as narratologists have learned from novelists. I can recommend the work of Laurel Richardson (see her chapter in this volume) for those who are interested in learning how to write in ways that show rather than tell, evoke a response rather than explain, and put poetics and aesthetics on an equal footing with epistemics (see also Richardson and St. Pierre 2005).

Conclusions

I ended with Richard Rorty's defence of the concrete above. Rorty, the neo-pragmatist, followed Hans-Georg Gadamer in emphasizing the hermeneutic, but unlike Gadamer he would stretch hermeneutics to cover not just the human and social sciences, but also the natural sciences. Even natural science, for Rorty, is an interpretative tool. But just like Gadamer, Rorty also, in his own way, sought the presence effects that come from the poetic and the non-interpretative. In what was his last published essay before his death in 2007 – entitled "The Fire of Life" – from *Poetry Magazine*, Rorty tells us of his relationship to poetry. After being diagnosed with pancreatic cancer, Rorty explains that he could find no comfort in religion or philosophy, but he quotes the 19th century poets Algeron Swinburne and Walter Landor and says: 'I found comfort in those slow meanders and those stuttering embers. I suspect that no comparable effect could have been produced by prose. Not just imagery, but also rhyme and rhythm were needed to do the job' (Rorty 2007). The presence effects of rhyme and rhythm are emphasized as providing some kind of consolation. He ends by articulating a single regret he has in his life:

> I now wish that I had spent somewhat more of my life with verse. This is not because I fear having missed out on truths that are incapable of statement in prose. There are no such truths; there is nothing about death that Swinburne and Landor knew but Epicurus and Heidegger failed to grasp. Rather, it is because I would have lived more fully if I had been able to rattle off more old chestnuts

– just as I would have if I had made more close friends. Cultures with richer vocabularies are more fully human – farther removed from the beasts – than those with poorer ones; individual men and women are more fully human when their memories are amply stocked with verses (Rorty 2007)

This, it seems to me, is as beautiful and evocative a defence of presence as one can find. It emphasizes what is on the right hand side of Table 7.1 as discussed above. It emphasizes that the rhymes of verse have a value in our lives that is beyond meaning, connecting us through our bodies with the world, in a way similar to the rhythmicity of collective activities and the sensations of eating. Meaning and interpretation are no doubt important in our lives, but without the presence that poetry can give us, we risk becoming less than fully human. I have used boat race, eating and poetry as examples to illustrate the presence dimension in human life that runs through anything we do and experience. But many other examples could be used as well. Whether we think in terms of presence, lyricism, or Jørgen Leth's investigative and fragmented art, we are looking in the direction of the non-hermeneutic, that which is neither interpretation nor brutely causal. Meanings may enable us to understand the world, but presence makes possible getting in touch with the world. Both ought to be laudable aims for the human and social sciences. There is no doubt that presence – like other existential dimensions – can be perverted, which is seen in some current cultural and quasi-spiritual discourses (for example, emphasizing 'the power of now', 'just do it!' and a focus on the intensity of the here-and-now), but such discourses, I believe, represent an expression of a cultural lack of the kind of presence addressed by Hans Ulrich Gumbrecht. The continuing discussion of presence in the social sciences should thematize how presence relates to the general 'cult of the now', but this remains outside the scope of the present chapter.

References

Abbott, A. (2007): "Against Narrative: A Preface to Lyrical Sociology". *Sociological Theory*, 25: 67-99.
Barone, T. and E.W. Eisner (2012): *Arts Based Research*. Thousand Oaks, CA: Sage Publications.
Bourdieu, P. et al. (1999): *The Weight of the World: Social Suffering in Contemporary Society*. Palo Alto, CA: Stanford University Press.
Briggs, C. (2007): "Anthropology, Interviewing and Communicability in Contemporary Society". *Current Anthropology*, 48: 551-67.
Brinkmann, S. (2009): "Literature as Qualitative Inquiry: The Novelist as Researcher". *Qualitative Inquiry*, 15(8): 1376-94.
Brinkmann, S. (2010): "Guilt in a Fluid Culture: A View from Positioning Theory". *Culture & Psychology*, 16(2): 253-66.

Brinkmann, S. (2012): *Qualitative Inquiry in Everyday Life: Working with Everyday Life Materials.* London: Sage Publications.
Brinkmann, S. and L. Tanggaard (2010): "Toward an Epistemology of the Hand". *Studies in Philosophy and Education*, 29: 243-57.
Denzin, N.K. and Y.S. Lincoln (2011): "Introduction: The Discipline and Practice of Qualitative Research", in *The Sage Handbook of Qualitative Research* (4th Edition), edited by N.K. Denzin and Y.S. Lincoln. Thousand Oaks, CA: Sage Publications.
Dreyfus, H. (1991): *Being-in-the-World: A Commentary on Heidegger's Being and Time, Division I.* Cambridge, MA: MIT Press.
Forster, E.M. (1927): *Aspects of the Novel.* London: Edward Arnold.
Geertz, C. (1973): *The Interpretation of Cultures.* New York: Basic Books.
Gumbrecht, H.U. (2004): *Production of Presence: What Meaning Cannot Convey.* Stanford, CA: Stanford University Press.
Gumbrecht, H.U. (2006): *In Praise of Athletic Beauty.* Cambridge, MA: Harvard University Press.
Heidegger, M. (1927/1962): *Being and Time.* New York: HarperCollins Publishers.
Heidegger, M. (1993): "The Origin of the Work of Art", in *Martin Heidegger: Basic Writings,* edited by D.F. Krell. London: Routledge.
Johnson, M. (2007): *The Meaning of the Body: Aesthetics of Human Understanding.* Chicago, IL: University of Chicago Press.
King, A. and M. de Rond (2011): "Boat Race: Rhythm and the Possibility of Collective Performance". *British Journal of Sociology*, 62: 565-85.
Latour, B. (1993): *We Have Never Been Modern.* Cambridge, MA: Harvard University Press.
Latour, B. (2005): *Reassembling the Social.* Oxford: Oxford University Press.
Leth, J. (2006): "Tilfældets gaver: En filmisk poetic" ["The Gifts of the Present: A Poetics of Film"]. *Kritik,* 2-10.
MacLure, M. (2010): "Qualitative Inquiry: Where are the Ruins?". Keynote presentation at the New Zealand Association for Research in Education Conference, University of Auckland, 6-9 December.
Merleau-Ponty, M. (1945/2002): *Phenomenology of Perception.* London: Routledge.
Mol, A. (2008): "I Eat an Apple: On Theorizing Subjectivity". *Subjectivity,* 22: 28-37.
Pallasmaa, J. (2005): *The Eyes of the Skin: Architecture and the Senses.* Chichester: Wiley-Academy.
Pelias, R. (2004): *A Methodology of the Heart: Evoking Academic and Daily Life.* Walnut Creek, CA: AltaMira Press.
Richardson, L. and E.A. St. Pierre (2005): "Writing: A Method of Inquiry", in *Handbook of Qualitative Research* (3rd Edition), edited by N.K. Denzin and Y.S. Lincoln. Thousand Oaks, CA: Sage Publications.
Ricoeur, P. (1971): "The Model of the Text: Meaningful Action Considered as a Text". *Social Research,* 38: 529-62.

Ricoeur, P. (1991): "Life in Quest of Narrative", in *On Paul Ricoeur: Narrative and Interpretation*, edited by D. Wood. London: Routledge.

Rorty, R. (1991): "Habermas and Lyotard on Postmodernity", in *Essays on Heidegger and Others: Philosophical Papers, Volume 2*, edited by R. Rorty. Cambridge: Cambridge University Press.

Rorty, R. (2007): "The Fire of Life". *Poetry Magazine* (November).

Shakespeare, W. (1972): *The Complete Works of William Shakespeare*. London: Abbey Library.

Wichmann, J. (2007): *Leth og kedsomheden [Leth and Boredom]*. Copenhagen: Informations Forlag.

Zorbaugh, H. (1929): *The Gold Coast and the Slum*. Chicago, IL: University of Chicago Press.

Žižek, S. (2000): *The Ticklish Subject: The Absent Centre of Political Ontology*. London: Verso.

Chapter 8

Theatricalized Reality and Novels of Truth: Respecting Tradition and Promoting Imagination in Social Research

Arpad Szakolczai

Introduction

Are the social sciences in need of new, innovative and especially imaginative methods, in research just as in teaching? The answer, evidently, is so obvious that the question seems purely rhetorical. And, indeed, there is need for innovation, and even imaginativeness, today in social science methods, perhaps more than ever. The reason why the starting question is not meaningless is that *this is exactly the problem*.

But what can be problematic with the need to be innovative, creative, experimental and imaginative? The answer, talking about rhetoric, is partly that such terms have become, in a by now imperceptible manner, parts of the 'modernistic' rhetoric, seemingly beyond reproach, like other similar catchwords of the day, be it modernization, democratization, transparency, or autonomy. Yet and furthermore, it is not at all a trivial matter that one must be innovative and especially imaginative in scholarly research methods. This is due to the significance, indeed weight, of two basic words: *reality* and *tradition*. Reality, following the lines (or the tradition) of Parmenides, Plato, Martin Heidegger and Eric Voegelin, first of all *is*, it is Being, and in a very fundamental way this does not change. In a particularly important passage of the *Philebus* Plato requires a 'solemn declaration' from his interlocutors: 'that fixed and pure and true and what we call unalloyed knowledge has to do with the things which are eternally the same without change or mixture' (59C). The social and human sciences, in so far as they are dealing with the fundamental truths related to the most important realities of existence, like birth, life and death, love, friendship and hatred, health, sanity/ integrity and illness, happiness, fear and despair, are certainly in need for deepening understanding, but not necessarily innovation, and particular problems emerge with imagination. In his famous eighth fragment Parmenides stated that understanding must deal with whatever exists, and should ignore non-being; and Plato in his related dialogues, especially the *Sophist*, declared image-making and fantasy as aspects of non-being. One must be careful here: Plato was not definitely against imagination or the arts; rather, he claimed that they do not belong to the realm of understanding; and that one must beware concerning the interference of fantasizing and especially the arts with the process of understanding, and even with reality.

We thus need a sound tradition that helps to place understanding on a stable footing, especially concerning the ways (or approaches) of proceeding, or 'methods' (*meta hodos*, thus *met'hodos*, 'according to the way'; the term 'way' (*hodos*) was in the title of Parmenides's work), which guide us into reality. Today, however, we indeed first of all need innovation and imagination because there are problems with the conventional methods of the social sciences, and even more with the very nature of the 'reality' in which we are living.

As far as methods in the social sciences are concerned, the problem is partly due to the limitless search of novelty *in the past*. Since their birth in the 19th century the social sciences are permanently in need of new and innovative methods, desperately trying to discover the magic wand that would make their efforts truly scientific. The question of the proper, rightful approach to gaining knowledge about social reality is indeed a most serious issue, but in order to respect seriousness this should be combined with respect for traditions. Problems of method, going back a long way, are created by a reckless pursuit of innovativeness and creativity at any price, combined with ideologies of progress and the self-flattering belief, repeated generation after generation, that finally the time has come for truly scientific or innovative methods, triumphantly throwing into the wastebasket the wisdom of previous ages. As a result, just as in other areas of the modern world, conventional wisdom, the 'canon' or the 'tradition' has very little traditional or even wise about it, being rather the ossified, dogmatic remains of the 'revolutions' accomplished in the previous generations. The cumulative outcome of such revolutions, apart from a genuine increase in technical know-how, is rather a sad state of confusion concerning the basic aims of intellectual endeavour, breeding an increasingly pervasive cynicism. Innovativeness is indeed needed today; but, while this must challenge and question assumptions of the past centuries, it should be combined with a return to and restoration of the genuine traditions of knowledge, going back to the Presocratics and especially Plato.

Such a perspective is particularly helpful as it offers clarity about the basic, 'meta-methodological' assumptions concerning the very nature of reality, helping to tackle the problem, fundamental for understanding the modern world, of what happens when the nature of reality is altered – or, in the terms of classical philosophy, when non-Being becomes real (Plato *Sophist* 236E-237A, 251A). Such 'falsified' reality must be tackled in its own terms, and thus social understanding today requires imaginative methods.

The Character of Reality

The primary question to address by any methodology is basic assumptions concerning the very character of the reality one is supposed to study. In the words of Michel Foucault, we need both 'a historical awareness of our present circumstance', and also must be clear about 'the type of reality with which we are dealing' (Foucault 1982: 227). The central assumption of positivism is that social reality is 'objective', or external to the observer, who can thus proceed to investigate this body of facts. For proponents of social constructivism, reality is much less solid, rather a 'construct' of human efforts, including thought and language, so the investigator is given the freedom to 'construct' and test his own theoretical categories, assuming a pseudo-divine omnipotence in face of the world. Deconstructivists thus take the liberty of simply dismantling such constructs. These approaches are part of a circle, and a quite vicious one.

While the presentation of these positions was obviously quite sketchy, hopefully this is sufficient to indicate that a very different, much more nuanced and interactive approach is necessary concerning the very character of the 'real'. The 'natural' sciences, after their unnaturalization through the Newtonian revolution, offer us a particularly misleading image in this regard, far from a model to copy, as the basic characteristics of our social reality are very different from the 'ultimate' reality of indivisible particles moving in the void, reference point of Newtonian physics.[1] We need very different assumptions concerning 'different modes of existence' (Latour 2011).

A piece of social reality can be in a normal, ordinary or in an out-of-ordinary state, much as a living organism can either be healthy or sick; or a sea can be calm or stormy. This feature was well known to Max Weber or John Maynard Keynes.[2] The distinction between the sacred and the profane, central for Émile Durkheim or Mircea Eliade, is also quite similar, though by no means identical, as the sacred is a highly special kind of out-of-ordinary situation.

However, even ordinary social reality is not simply a solid block of facts, or an interconnected system, but consists of a series of accumulated *layers*, forming altogether a meaningful unity. Furthermore, this is not only a characteristic of social reality, but of life in general, even of physical nature. Here we arrive at a basic shortcoming of the Newtonian perspective. We now 'know' that the Earth, just as any other planets, and indeed any object, consists of a practically infinite number of minuscule particles that move in a void, but this knowledge has only remote, partial and dubious relevance to the kind of life we are leading, and especially the one that we should be leading, on this planet. 'Ultimate truths' have little to do with concrete beings, animate or inanimate, that exist around us, and that have very different, non-Newtonian kind of characteristics: they can be useful or fine, threatening or dangerous, or – most importantly – can be beautiful and be loved; terms without any meaning in a reductive, Newtonian universe.[3] This shortcoming has been identified in a well-known quip by Keynes, according to which neoclassical economic theory is only interested in the 'long run', but 'in the long run' we are all dead.

---

1 Here, as throughout the chapter, I am making much use of Horvath (2013).
2 For details, see Szakolczai (2013b).
3 Concerning the centrality of beauty for the Platonic universe, see the *Timaeus*.

The idea that reality consists of a huge number of layers that were formed during an immense amount of time is argued most forcibly by geology, a science that had an immense influence on Darwin, being a major source of inspiration for the theory of evolution. It was also the direct model for Friedrich Nietzsche's genealogy (Treiber 1993), and played a decisive role in the by far most important discovery concerning human life and culture over the past century or so: Palaeolithic cave art. It is well known that geology overcame the time-horizon based on the Old Testament; however, it was much less realized, if at all, that it also rendered inacceptable the Newton-based, technological-engineering vision of the world, which appropriates the role of a secular god, 'constructing' objects at its own will, by decomposing or de-fusing existing things into components, and then re-composing or re-fusing them into new objects. This amounts to an irresponsible interference with many millions of years of 'history' or 'evolution', during which not only animals but plants and landscapes evolved as well, creating a *nature* that is singular, unique, and – most importantly of all – is extremely beautiful. The foolish pretence to meddle with it is a *very* risky business.

By analogy, human cultures are also best considered as accumulated layers of vast amounts of past experiences. It helps to realize that, after all, Plato offered us a truer vision of this *our* world than Newton. In the *Philebus* Plato argued that whatever exist are from the one and the many, and have inherent in them the limit and the unlimited (16C), and his central question concerned the right mixing of the limit and the unlimited. This is an issue more of *recognition* than cognition: one must recognise the rightful, harmonious mixture, preserving and promoting it, rather than searching for a kind of 'cognitive' knowledge which can then be mechanically imposed on existing beings, by decomposing them into elements to be recomposed according to a master plan – though this does not imply that every existing being contains a right mixing.

Here we already move from assumptions about the nature of reality to knowledge; so we must be very careful about how to proceed. The two are of course connected; but the right attention to such connectedness assumes that one does not 'jump' between extremes, rather pays attention to in-between stages, or the concrete, layered structure of reality. It is against such 'jumps' that Plato warns again in the *Philebus*, using the term '*metaxy*' that would become so important for Eric Voegelin (1974, 1978), and charges the Sophists that they 'make the one and the many too quickly or too slowly, in haphazard fashion, and they put infinity immediately after unity; they disregard all that lies between them' (*Philebus* 17A). The stunning, and extremely important inference is that Newtonian science, with its reckless decomposition of meaningful objects into their ultimate composing elements, with no attention to meaning, connectedness, tradition and context, is technically identified by Plato's 'method' as Sophistic.

The layers of reality are not immediately visible as the reality of the present is a concrete, given presence: a single, interconnected entity: a mountain or a lake, a family or a city. Thus, the acquisition of genuine, meaningful knowledge, attuned to the reality of human existence on planet Earth, as part of nature, outcome of many hundred million years of evolution, implies a careful and disciplined immersion into the manifold layers of this reality. Such immersion implies a long life of experience and the coherent use of reasoning, at the end of which one might gain some glimpse concerning the first principles, or the ideas, which guide such mixing, while respecting the infinite variety of concrete mixtures. However – and here comes the complication, the *real* complication – suddenly a shortcut might appear. The constitutive layers might become visible due to a sudden event, comparable to an earthquake, provoking a crisis, where the entity is threatened to fracture into its components.

Knowledge of the Out-of-Ordinary

A unique feature of the human world is a knowledge that is derived from out-of-ordinary (liminal, crisis) situations; a knowledge that, beyond the basic wisdom of human life about death and new birth, implies a specific, technical knowledge about the procedures to follow under emergency conditions; about certain 'tricks' that can be made to function, even turning such an emergency to one's advantage. Here we move from general assumptions about the nature of reality to the gaining of knowledge about reality; however, only from a specific angle, given by a shift at the very level of reality, thus an angle that, from the perspective of life, implies not simply rare but most negative, threatening situations, while from the perspective of knowledge something deeply problematic, associated with a reverse or perverted angle.

Let me try to be more specific. Knowledge is about reality, the actual features of the world, offering an orientation that is necessary for the conduct of human life. The reality we face has a degree of coherence, for many reasons, but is composed of an intricate web of innumerable layers, that must be respected and handled with extreme care so as not to mess up the delicate balance between its various elements that altogether produce an experience of beauty, love and pleasantness. Knowledge primarily consists of an immersion in the manifold layers of this reality. However, the situations that threaten the very existence and survival of a community also seem to offer a special shortcut to knowledge, as the collapsing order of things literally reveals its layers.

This, however, requires a very special condition, explored by Norbert Elias (1987), suggested by such a peculiar observer of the human condition as Edgar Allan Poe: the ability to detach oneself from one's all-encompassing existential situation. Such ability is not only extremely rare, difficult to acquire, but also – and here Elias no longer helps – highly problematic.

The point can be illustrated through the metaphor of an earthquake. Those witnessing it can hardly be expected to stop and watch the manner in which the various layers of the ground reveal the composition of the Earth. The enormous impact natural disasters left on human culture can be followed through the various mythologies, with the importance of mountain gods and their thunders, like Yahweh,

Zeus or Thor. Such memories can be traced to the experiences of witnesses, frightened out of their wits, so far from the 'supermen' managing to keep their cool.

Yet, somehow, such kind of knowledge, produced out of a cool, external observation of extreme crisis situations did emerge, and eventually even had a profound impact on reality itself.

Exterior Trickster Knowledge or the Two Paradigms of Rationality

For modern scholars, as evidenced even by Norbert Elias, an exterior, neutral, emotion-free, pure-spectator observing status is taken in a matter of fact way as ideal. Furthermore, at least since Adam Smith, and given a huge boost by Immanuel Kant, such position is even considered as a necessary precondition for morality. However, the idea of such exteriority is quite recent and extremely problematic. If a disaster or a crisis hits a human community, nobody can, or should, take up the position of a purely neutral observer, and not even due to the need to save one's life, but of their beloved. This by no means implies irrationality, though certainly excludes cool, lucid, 'rational' thinking. By considering carefully the example above one can realize that Elias's reasoning is highly problematic on several counts. First, it can easily be admitted that the most effective human behaviour in an emergency situation does not follow the Eliasian steps. Whether this happens when guiding a car or when a child is about to fall down from a height, we cannot observe coolly, from the outside, what is going on, carefully considering the alternatives, testing them and finally finding the best solution, but we must trust our 'instinctive' reactions, where such instincts represent a delicate combination of in-born abilities and learning experiences. Second, in a similarly instinctive way, a parent looks first for the welfare of his or her child, and not one's own – this is why airplanes advise their passengers before every take-off that in this extremely singular situation, so far from the experiences under which human beings 'evolved', they should exceptionally inflate first their *own* life jackets; just as drivers instinctively turn away the wheel if their car is about to hit a passer-by, thus risking their own lives. The exterior position assumed in a taken for granted manner by modern science, far from being normative, was extremely rare. *And yet it existed.*

The first point to notice is that this indeed assumes existential exteriority. For a natural disaster, this means a lack of care about one's own survival; for a social crisis, a lack of involvement with the community. The first seems to imply feeble-mindedness, thus the opposite of the super-human rationality assumed by Elias; while the second a practical impossibility, as life outside a community, especially in earlier times, hardly seemed possible. Still, the two can be combined in the singular figure of the *outsider*.

The outsider is the special case of the stranger – in the words of Roland Barthes, it could be considered as its 'zero degree'. The stranger is the outsider to a particular community, belonging to another. The outsider, however, is a stranger to every community. This can happen in various ways, and mythological and folk-tale stories about the Trickster – this par excellence outsider – offer abundant examples for such a possibility. Similarly important sources are the analysis of the ban by Giorgio Agamben (1988), and of hubris by Louis Gernet (1917/2001). This suggests that, at least in pre-historical European communities, the most serious punishment was not death, rather exile; and that such punishment was not given to those who transgressed the law, but who were judged as being incapable of living in a community. A third such example is offered in prehistoric cave art, by the 'shaft scene' (Horvath 2013).

The Trickster cannot love, thus cannot offer any emotional commitment – he has no family, no parents and no children, and so he simply does not care; even further, he does not even much care about his own life. All he cares about is the immediate satisfaction of his bodily functions. Here Alessandro Pizzorno's theory of identity and recognition is particularly helpful in moving beyond the Hobbesian paradigm of self-preservation. Pizzorno (1991) argues that the self one is trying to preserve is not simply one's naked life, rather one's identity as it is assigned by those who are part of one's 'circle of recognition'. This explains that one can be much more willing to give up one's life than to continue living in a way that involves the loss of respect by those from whom one expects recognition. Given that the Trickster does not receive recognition, does not have loved ones who would miss him, he can risk his life, generating a semblance of courage, thus could even observe a volcano in eruption; just as he preserves his calm in the case of an emergency, simply observing how others behave, and thus *obtains a kind of knowledge that could be turned to his own advantage just when others are at a loss.*

Having identified the position of the outsider, we need to specify what is the kind of knowledge that we can attribute to him. The example of Elias seems to suggest that this is 'rational' knowledge; however, the term has two quite different meanings. Today it is indeed identified with an external, neutral position, whether characteristics of modern science or economic choice; but this is the polar opposite of the etymological meaning of the term, still shared by classical thought. In this sense 'rational' is something that possesses 'ratio', or rightful proportionality, which can only be understood by those who share and participate in the order of things, thus it *excludes* the outsider. The outsider has no knowledge about the nature of reality, only a technical know-how concerning the manipulative use of decomposition and dissolution.

The dilemma is captured in the figure of the 'trickster' as a 'culture hero', analysed so well by Paul Radin (1972): the trickster is unreliable, as trick-ful, cunning, cruel and viciously egoistic; and yet, this same figure is also a 'culture hero', associated with the 'second foundation' of the world, a title clearly indicating a *re*-foundation, after the collapse of the original one. Such advices thus have two problems: they are mechanical, technical; and they are suspect, due to the trickster's lack of involvement in the community.

The argument must be resumed with two points. The first concerns the connection of this timeless, anthropological-mythological figure to concrete historical processes. This can be done by alluding to the similarity between such de-composition and re-fusion with metallurgical processes and their theorization in alchemy; with rites of passage that simulate such procedures, with the prior rites of separation and the stamping of a new shape, or identity, in the performative centre of the ritual, though rendering such violence tolerable through the re-socialization offered in the rites of re-aggregation – rituals that according to Victor W. Turner, the main theorist of liminality, were particularly close to theatre (Turner 1974); and with the thinking characteristic of the Sophists, who are repeatedly accused by Plato of systematically setting things apart, without having an understanding of how to put them harmoniously together, and also of manipulating images and being 'theatrical'. Second, and moving towards the present, it is this obsession of taking everything apart, generating a *tabula rasa*, and then putting them back together without respecting the delicacy of life and history (whether human, social or ecological), rather following some technological, utilitarian, monetary or political 'rationality', that marks the modern 'scientific method' in its various guises (positivism, neo-Kantianism, critical theory, rational choice theory, etc.).

Schismogenesis or Being Stuck in a Pathological Situation

Crises are solved by restoring and thus renewing normality and tradition, or in some kind of artificial, technological, quasi-alchemical manner. Otherwise, if they don't manage to restore order, human societies face extinction and disappearance. However, at the level of human culture, there also exists the paradoxical possibility of the survival of a schismatic entity. This is a strange, liminal, in-between case, between the successful solution of a crisis and return to healthy normality, and the wholesale collapse and disappearance of the entity. The discovery of such a possibility, and its analysis, is due to Gregory Bateson, who coined the term 'schismogenesis'.

There are a number of methodologically most important features of this term and the conditions of its discovery. First of all, Bateson was an anthropologist, who discovered the concept during his fieldwork, due to the patent inability of the conceptual framework he acquired in Cambridge University to illuminate the actual situation. He repeatedly witnessed acts of extreme violence, both in real life and in ritual performances, which could not be attributed either of social function, structure, power relations, or the necessities of making a living. Thus, working backwards from the present, he deduced that in a remote, unrecorded past the unity of that particular society, and indeed of the social world of the entire island, must have been fractured, entrapping human beings in a violent, hardly tolerable mode of existence. Bateson was therefore besotted with what Friedrich Nietzsche called historical 'sense' or the capacity for 'backward inference' (Nietzsche 1974, no. 370). Second, no doubt sparked by such experiences, Bateson became one of the most important innovative figures in the epistemology of the social sciences (Bateson 1972, 1979/2002; Bateson and Bateson 1988). Third, this epistemology eventually extended to the most important traditions, the thinking of Plato and the epistemology of the sacred, focusing in particular on the concern with beauty, in search for a 'science that connects'. Finally, a central aspect of the social reality that led Bateson coining the term schismogenesis were the highly violent and mocking, non-participatory thus theatrical *naven* rituals.

This is now the second time that a vital link comes to be perceived between a position of exteriority, central for certain kind of knowledge, and the theatre, alluding to a peculiar affinity between a position of exteriority to social life, the in-depth transformation of social existence through a permanentization of the out-of-ordinary, and theatrical rituals. The reason for such affinity is a complex question, and has much to do with imitation; however, details cannot be discussed here.[4] I can only allude to the eminently plausible point that somebody in a position of exteriority to one's social existence – out of a figure of remote distance and irrelevance – can easily and suddenly become a model to be imitated. The central issue is that through a peculiar alternation between theatrical and everyday modes of existence social reality can be altered, resulting in a new, highly theatrical type of social reality. The concern with capturing the nature of such a theatricalized reality was central for Plato, who considered the Sophists as not simply rhetoricians and flatterers, but conjurers of image-magic, managing to transform Athenian culture into a 'kind of base theatrocracy' (Plato *Laws*: 701A). The point also has a crucial relevance for modern Europe, as the re-birth of theatre, at the end of the Renaissance, under Byzantine influence, changed the very fabric of European culture, thus altering reality.

Conventional methods of modern inquiry, having foolishly dismantled the classical philosophy of Plato and Aristotle, declared as obsolete,[5] are simply incapable of getting a handle on this process. The analysis of this altered reality, invested with 'non-Being' like fantasy, imagination and image-magic, requires innovative methods that *as* methods must literally be imaginative, as they must be able to capture the way in fact figments of the imagination gain real life and become part of everyday reality.

One such possibility is genealogical, following not just the spirit but literally the word of Nietzsche, as it was certainly not accident, though little reflected upon, that the genealogist of modern nihilism devoted his first work to theatre. This is the approach I followed in a recently published book, which offers a genealogy of the re-birth of theatre and its wider effect, amounting to a 'theatricalization' of Europe (Szakolczai 2013a). The other possibility is to identify a way in which the theatricalized nature of the everyday life of the modern world can be captured,

---

4 For a particularly important analysis, see Agnew (1986).

5 This also has to do with the fact that the reception of Plato and Aristotle in Europe was much influenced by the Byzantine world.

separating genuine from fake reality. This can be done through the analysis of modern novels.

An Imaginative Method for Understanding the Real: Novels of Truth and the Novelist as Social Theorist

As examples for a highly innovative approach concerning the significance of works of arts for philosophical, anthropological and sociological understanding, with great potential for the sociology of culture, the chapter will shortly present the strikingly concordant ideas of René Girard, French literary historian and comparative anthropologist, and the Hungarian philosophical essayist and historian of religion Béla Hamvas.[6]

René Girard

In his 1961 classic *Mensonge romantique et vérité romanesque*[7] René Girard argues that 19th-century novels offer a unique insight not simply into the character of their times but the very heart of modern society; that these novels contain truths superior to the presumed 'truths' of sociological or philosophical analyses. Girard was not a social scientist, but a literary scholar, with a background in history, and would later substantiate his ideas with an anthropological theory, focusing on the role of imitation, scapegoating and the sacrifice. These works are now having a considerable impact on social theory; this is much less true of his first work about novels. Yet, it throws a challenge to social scientists that they cannot ignore, especially given its potential usefulness for the sociology of culture.

Girard's work has definite affinities with the new sociology of literature. This field for long was dominated by attempts to reduce works of art to reflections of social processes, structure, or simply 'power'. This meant that their analytic potential was ignored in a matter of fact way. Recent work by David Inglis, editor of *Cultural Sociology*, represents an important corrective (Inglis and Hughson 2005). Inglis argues that the critical approach in the sociology of culture as represented by Pierre Bourdieu or Janet Wolff, according to which works of art are part of structures of power, being nothing but a bourgeois ritual for showing off, is both reductivist and misleading, calling for a renewal in the sociology of art.[8]

In line with the analysis presented so far, the central question concerns the nature of the reality to be investigated. The theme of Girard's book is desire; and through a preliminary study of these novels Girard (1961: 99) gained a striking idea: there is no realism of desire.

---

6   About Hamvas, see Szakolczai (2005), and Szakolczai and Wydra (2006).

7   Due to the difficulties of its translation the English title became the somewhat deceptive 'Deceit, desire and the novel'. The title literally means 'Romantic lie and novel-like truth'.

8   For similar ideas, see Ferguson (2004, 2010), Müller (2011), and Tester (in this volume).

The 'realistic' perspective argues that desire is evoked in the subject due to qualities in the object; thus, in the case of sexual desire, these are certain characteristics of other human beings, like beauty or attractiveness, that elicit a desire in someone. However, Girard came to perceive that some of the most important novelist of the 19th century, like Stendhal, Gustave Flaubert, Fyodor Dostoevsky or Marcel Proust, presented a quite different scenario for the genesis of desire: the protagonists fell in love rather by following the example of somebody they took as a model to follow; or their desire was 'mediated'. Instead of a dualism and dialectic between an object and a subject, desire is triangular; and the central moving force, instead of autonomy, freedom of choice, and other rational considerations, was imitation. This enabled Girard to develop an entire conceptual arsenal analysing the phenomenon captured by the 'novelists of truth', like 'metaphysical desire' (Girard 1961: 84), 'internal mediation' (Girard 1961: 22-3), or the 'divinization of the mediator' (Girard 1961: 95).

'Realist' approaches, which focus on the object and subject of desire and ignore its mediator are simply defective; they can be compared to someone who looks at a triangle from one of its edges, and mistakes it for a ruler. A genuine, social realism (arguably close to the 'social psychology' of Gabriel Tarde, also emphasizing imitation) rather takes seriously the interior life of human beings, as this is where the socially effective 'metaphysics of desire' is generated, through 'internal mediation'. The emergence of such desires represents a triumph of the imagination and a progressive decline of the sense of reality (Girard 1961: 103-5). Such mediated desires, nurtured by the imagination, become effective social forces through contagious imitation (Girard 1961: 57, 115), which spreads, spiralling, like a whirlwind (*tourbillon*) (Girard 1961: 124, 280).

At this point we must return to our fundamental question of method. Why is it that the identification of this process had to be attributed to novelists? Part of the answer was already given by the major shortcoming of objectivist, positivist approaches, that simply accept mediated desire as real, thus authentic. The other aspect concerns the illusion of autonomy. Such romantic illusion, on the back of a titanic self-glorification, even self-divinization, assumes that whatever wish, inclination or desire is formulated by a – supposedly – autonomous and rational self is his or her own, as if an alienable property, flattering such individuals about the need to satisfy such desires in order to 'realize' themselves. Such illusion of the autonomous self is not restricted to romantics, but is shared by critical theorists, idealist philosophies, political or cultural revolutionary movements, or rational choice theorists; as many branches of progressive modernism. As the illusion is thus almost universally shared, being part of the modern episteme, it thus – together with the positivist-objectivist illusion about the nature of desire – hardly leaves a possibility for the recognition and proper analysis of mediated desire.

This is where we come to the methodological core of what it takes to become a novelist of truth. Such novelists, like practically every main figure of modern culture, also shared the romantic illusion of autonomy at an early stage in their life, just as Proust was also a snob once. The difference is that they managed to go beyond such an illusion; had the force for self-overcoming (Girard 1961: 248), a characteristic that Nietzsche also placed at the centre of his philosophy. The recognition that spontaneous desire is a lie, or the identification of the problem of mediation, cannot be made through sociological or philosophical studies of others, but much be experienced at the heart of one's being. It is only in this way that one can 'penetrate to the source of spiritual poison' (Girard 1961: 29). Thus, 'only the novelists restore to the mediator the role usurped by the object; only the novelists reverse the commonly accepted hierarchy of desire' (Girard 1961: 28). Doing so, they were immediately placed beyond the meaningless sides of their contemporary social, political and cultural dividing lines and debates, part of the schismatic nature of modern society, and managed to capture the source of the problem, considering social reality as an immense laboratory (Girard 1961: 137), where figures of the novel impersonated stages of the process by which mediation takes place, just as the stages through which the author managed to overcome his own romantic illusions and obsessions. At the same time, such novelists of truth also managed to identify the sources of the invading metaphysics of desire in the values and orientations of the new, post-revolutionary social order. In particular, they came to the recognition that the contagious spread of such internal mediation is due to the destruction of the entire traditional universe, and the replacement of its values by the central modern concerns of vanity and envy (Girard 1961: 83), consequences of modern egalitarianism which generates 'undifferentiation' (using a term Girard only introduced later) by destroying the limits, or the distinction between 'what to say and what not to say; what to do and what not to do' (Girard 1961: 141).

The consequences of succumbing to the romantic illusion are extremely grave. They represent a radical reversal of the meaning of words; eventually a corruption of language. Those taken in by the illusion of a spontaneous desire think to free themselves from the chains of tradition and realize their true self when in fact they are only enslaving themselves to the desires implanted in them by their 'liberator' mediators. The Enlightenment and the Revolutions promised to render individuals not only free but happy; and yet, Stendhal's entire work came to be motivated by a question he had to pose himself in the years around 1820: why are people around so desperately unhappy? (Girard 1961: 137). Not surprisingly, suicide was becoming a major social phenomenon (Girard 1961: 313). Similarly, at the political level, the yearning for the full realization of freedom and equality only ended up producing totalitarian rule. In one of the most striking passages of the book Girard argues that what Alexis de Tocqueville called democracy is identical to what we now call totalitarianism (Girard 1961: 160). By pursuing such a line of analysis novelists gain an understanding far superior to the main sociologists and philosophers of the period, visible in the fact that their predictions turned out to be strikingly correct – it is enough to compare the vision of Dostoevsky on anarchism and socialism with Karl Marx's.

The ultimate consequences, however, move beyond matters of individual freedom and social dictatorship, touching upon the depths of existence. The tyranny of mediation or – using a different terminology – trickster initiation yields as its ultimate result emptiness or void. In fact, Girard offers a highly unusual definition of totalitarianism: it is 'when one arrives, from one desire to another, to a general and permanent mobilization in the service of nothingness (*néant*)' (Girard 1961: 161). The absurd will to self-divinization thus results in the opposite: a not simply animal- but outright insect-like existence, haunted by dreams of spiders and reptiles, and even ending up in the 'driest of deserts, the "metal-like kingdoms of the absurd" ' (Girard 1961: 320-1). Thus, 'the individual, always more disoriented (égaré), always more unbalanced (*désaxé*) by a desire that nothing can satisfy, ends up by searching for the divine in what radically denies his own existence, in the inanimate' (Girard 1961: 320).

Béla Hamvas

Hamvas wrote his 'Fragments for a theory of the novel' in 1948 (Hamvas 1994), just before he started *Carnival*, his literary *magnum opus*, a novel of well over 1,000 pages, covering a century of Hungarian history through three generations (Hamvas 1997). Most appropriately, it starts with an assessment concerning the nature of contemporary reality, since the Thirty Years' War, but going back at least to the contemporaneity of Miguel de Cervantes and William Shakespeare, or *Don Quixote* and *Hamlet* (which, for Hamvas, in contrast to *King Lear* and *Othello*, is not a play, but a novel; see Hamvas 1994: 287), marked by time being 'out of joint' and Jakob Böhme's concern with the Fall (Hamvas 1994: 268).[9] In such a world turned upside down, where base crookedness and perfidious corruption rule, the carriers of truth and their relationship to the real is also altered: when reality becomes a lie, where the 'truth' of reality is defined by the police, banks, the 'Great Inquisitor' of Fyodor Dostoevsky, or, putting it more mildly, by William M. Thackeray's *Bonfair of Vanities*, outsiders will rule and the real human being will become an *outsider* (*sic* in the original). Thus, referring to the face-value of reality becomes false and simply comical, and the *real* truth will be contained in novels, with its carriers being fools – *sacred* fools – like Don Quixote or Hamlet (Hamvas 1994: 271-5).[10]

The question now concerns the exact character of the out-of-order times; the paradoxical contribution of the novel in bringing about of this situation; and the reasons why and the manners in which the novel can become a genuine carrier of truth.

---

9 In a companion piece, 'Arlequin', the Hamletian expression 'time is out of joint' is cited several times (Hamvas 2000).
10 Hamvas's Russian alter ego, Mikhail Bulgakov had a similarly great respect for Don Quixote.

Concerning the first, the central issue and the ontological basis of claims made about the novel is the destruction of communities. The moment this happens any blank reference to 'the social' becomes shallow, a mere justification for personal cowardice. For Hamvas, the central concern is not the individual, a simple consequence of social fragmentation, rather the *person* who takes a stance with respect to that process, overcoming resignation, and becomes concerned with his own spiritual status. Moving further, Hamvas defines the process leading to this unreal reality as *elregényesedés*, which can be translated as 'fictionalization' or novelization', but in French could be called *romancisation*, which brings out better its inherent connection to Romanticism, and also to what I called 'theatricalization'.[11] This refers to the fact that through a series of stages reality was transformed into the likeness of the novel: it is not the individual that has become 'historical', rather history became 'fictional' (Hamvas 1994: 321). As a result 'mankind has become fictionalized in a way that was never before imaginable' (Hamvas 1994: 323). The main agents of this 'fictionalization' are the novel and the film, and also the media, which 'represent the ultimate victory of the novel over history' (Hamvas 1994: 326). As a result, 'all of us today no longer live in history, but in the novel' (Hamvas 1994: 339).

Given that history has become fictional, with the most absurd utopias turning into actual nightmares (similar to the manner in which Franz Kafka's *Trial* and *Castle* hauntingly capture the dawn-time arrests and night-time interrogations of Communist terror, as if Josef Stalin used Kafka's novels as models for directing the secret police, one could add), it is the task of the novel to capture the truth of this process. Novels have two main ways of doing so; thus, there are two main types of 'novels of truth'. The first is the historical novel, which can recuperate the process of 'fictionalization' (Hamvas 1994: 317-19). The source of this form are the great memoires of the 17th century, according to Hamvas, but they can be taken back to the decades around 1500 in Venice and the Burgundy court, or the time when the theatre was re-born. These memoires, and the great historical novels of Honoré de Balzac, Émile Zola, Marcel Proust, Martin du Gard and others capture this 'pullulation, this comedy and fair, this insect collection, this carnival of manias and passions, puppets and madmen, saints and criminals' (Hamvas 1994: 317), or the genealogy of the fairground capitalism as 'fictionalization', culminating in the French Revolution, one of its main consequences (Hamvas 1994: 318). The second form is the novel of confession, testimony, or examination of conscience.[12] Far from being 'socially irrelevant', such novels are utmost expressions of existential truths in a world where communities have disappeared. Such a concern

---

11 The reasons for the differences in the terminology of Hamvas and mine cannot be discussed here, but are concerned with the connotations of the Hungarian word *regényes*, literally meaning novel-like, but evoking both 'Romantic' and 'theatrical'.

12 One should note that 'religion' in Hungarian is *vallás*, linked not to 're-connecting', as in Latin, according to a somewhat controversial etymology, rather to 'confessing' or 'admitting' (*vall*).

is also present in philosophy, with Schopenhauer, Nietzsche, and especially Søren Kierkegaard, whose philosophy acquired a new depth exactly because he wrote not philosophical works but pseudo-novels (Hamvas 1994: 304-6), and which became a major source for a streak of important Scandinavian novels, including Henrik Ibsen (who 'conclusively fictionalized theatre'), August Strindberg, Knut Hamsun, and others (Hamvas 1994: 312-13). The main figures of such confession-like or psychological novels, however, are Stendhal, its ultimate source, and also Dostoevsky and Proust (Hamvas 1994: 328-9).

While parallels with Girard's work were already visible, here they become striking. There can be no question of direct influence, as Hamvas wrote this piece in 1948, way before Girard even started his work, but it was only published in 1994. One can list a series of further, fundamental and direct parallels: just as for Girard, the main opposite of novels of truth is Romanticism, with its mythologized heroism and sentimentalism, its excessive demands and sensitivities, further wedging the gap between the individual and the collective, thus evoking the void (Hamvas 1994: 316-17). Similarly to Girard, Hamvas (1994: 332) also defined towards the end of his essay the nature of the times as apocalyptic, where a central means for tolerating the terrors of 'reality' is humour (Hamvas 1994: 334); and, following Nietzsche, considers self-overcoming as a main technique of novels of truth (Hamvas 1994: 337).

In such out-of-joint times, in a world turned upside down, for Hamvas, just as for Girard, novels not only provide a way for analyzing the unreality of the real, but also return, in a truly Platonic manner, to the very meaning of existence: 'Form is nothing but the creation of [the possibility of] a meaningful life.' Under the conditions in which she has lived for centuries, 'for Europe the meaning of life is exclusively provided by novels' (Hamvas 1994: 319-20).

An Example: Goethe or *Bildungsroman* as Theatricalization

Johann Wolfgang von Goethe is only sparingly mentioned by Hamvas and, as Hans-Peter Müller perceptively and convincingly argues, he can even be considered as an anti-sociologist – though one who yet had a sociology (Müller 2011: 170-1). Still, he occupies a crucial position, as if on a saddle, between a novelist of truth and a witness to historical transformation processes – helping to understand why Wilhelm Dilthey would take his term *Erlebnis* from him. Goethe's liminal status, and its significance, can be indicated by his death and birth dates being almost identical to Jeremy Bentham's. This is much more than mere coincidence, as the parallels between Bentham's *Panopticon* and Goethe's *Wilhelm Meister* are particularly tight and significant, connecting the two main techniques of modern political alchemy, the disciplinary mechanism, as embodied in the Panopticon, and the entertainment industry, as embodied in the theatre and the circus, central concerns for Goethe's *Wilhelm Meister*.

The type of novel called *Bildungsroman*, dealing with a person's formation, is widely recognized as having played a major role in the kind of humanist education pioneered by Germany in the decades before and after 1800, together with romantic and classicizing poetry, the university education that followed the model of Wilhelm von Humboldt, and the major systems of idealist philosophies, especially Immanuel Kant, Johann Gottlieb Fichte and G.W.F. Hegel. It is also well known that Goethe's *Wilhelm Meister* novels are among its primary examples. However, in discussing the *Bildungsroman*, or the broader issues of humanist education, hardly any reference is made to the theatre as an important contributor to this educational project, in spite of the fact that the first version of Goethe's novel project, written during the first decade of his life-long stay in Weimar, was entitled *Wilhelm Meister's Theatrical Mission*. This fact, just as the important theatrical dimension of the published versions, is not mentioned in Harvey Goldman's otherwise informed discussion of Goethe and *Bildung* (Goldman 1988: 128-30, 242-3, 1992: 2-3, 286), which incorporates Weber's relevant remarks in the *Protestant Ethic* (Goldman 1988: 129), though the term 'mission' (*Sendung*) is a major component of Protestant, even Puritan religiosity, comparable to 'vocation' (*Beruf*). It is therefore well worth investigating, following René Girard's hints, the reasons for Goethe's original choice of title, and the manner in which its abandoning is reflected upon, directly or indirectly, in the work.

We must start by reviewing the facts, though with due attention, from the very start, to what they try to hide and thus forcibly reveal. The fact that Goethe wrote a first version of *Wilhelm Meister* by that strange title was not known until December 1909, when the manuscript, which in the analogy of the *Ur-Faust* could be called the *Ur-Wilhelm Meister*, was accidentally discovered in Zürich.[13] While the discovery was accidental, the long latency of the manuscript was certainly not. The writing was not by Goethe but by Barbara Schulthess, one of his female correspondent friends; so it is reasonable to assume that Goethe must have purposefully destroyed all the copies he could lay a hand to. However, as we know from Mikhail Bulgakov, manuscripts don't burn.[14]

The two *Wilhelm Meister* novels, especially *Wilhelm Meister's Apprenticeship* (*Lehrjahre*), but also *Wilhelm Meister's Journeyman Years* (*Wanderjahre*), are stunning documents of the theatricalization of modern Europe and its tight connections with education, while also illustrating the thesis that the best artists are also most perceptive reflexive social theorists.

The writing of the *Wilhelm Meister* accompanied Goethe practically throughout his life, in a manner comparable to the *Faust*. Goethe started to work on it in

---

13 The work was thus found and published well after Max Weber wrote the original version of the *Protestant Ethic* essays; and the extremely busy period of the 1910s was not the time for him to update his reading of Goethe. Social scientists, as always, following more Weber's words than the spirit of his research, evidently never bothered to consult this work.

14 This is the most famous sentence of the *Master and Margarita*; it became an adage in Russia, and the title of a Mikhail Bulgakov biography.

February 1777, at the age of 27, little more than a year after he arrived in Weimar; and finished the second volume in January 1829, so well over half a century later. Still similarly to the *Faust*, the *Wilhelm Meister* also tested the limits of the genre in a most extreme manner. As it is known, the *Faust* is not really a tragedy, as it has a happy ending – which Goethe explicitly forbade to publish in his life-time – and is not even a theatrical play at all, as it is impossible to stage it in its integrity. The *Wilhelm Meister* is also not really a novel, as it has considerable gaps, just as insertions that are unconnected to the storyline; it promises developments that would not take place, has protagonists that disappear without explanation, or links between them that are simply not explained or developed. It is also not only very long but practically illegible by contemporary standards, as – helped by the extremely long period of gestation and numerous re-writings – it is also its own ironic commentary.

The manner in which the novel deals with coordinates of time and place is extremely peculiar and most significant. On the one hand, the novel is situated in the here and now of Goethe, and is full of autobiographical allusions. The events take place in Germany, and the novel is not historical. It also takes up, and prominently, some of the most important events of Goethe's life, elaborated in detail in his autobiography, *Poetry and Truth*, whose writing also accompanied Goethe for decades, and on which he worked often almost contemporaneously. Autobiographical aspects include his lasting fascination with theatre after getting a puppet theatre from his grandmother as a Christmas gift at the age of four; the long period of sulking and self-pity that followed his distancing from Gretchen, at the age of 15–16, who would also inspire the Gretchen of *Faust*; or the similarly life-long attraction to Shakespeare, especially *Hamlet*. Yet, the correspondence is by no means narrow. The time and place of the events is never specified, no major German towns are named, and the time that expired between sections is often difficult to specify. The only historical allusion is to the imminent coming of the French Revolution; an event that increasingly gained a most negative meaning to Goethe: part of the 'spiralling movement' that takes mankind to unknown directions, but where sometimes 'supreme evil' takes the upper hand, by 'imitating the semblances and language of the supreme good. The French Revolution resembled the kingdom of God as its reversed image, as its bleak infernal falsification' (Citati 1990: 52). Furthermore, in the novel Wilhelm Meister painfully realizes that he has no talent for poetry, and mercilessly burns all his poems. It also does not contain any sustained description of daily activities, as if Goethe wanted to dissolve all connections to the mundane realities of everyday existence, which often renders the scenes depicted particularly picturesque and theatrical in a manifold way (Citati 1990: 181). Such facts imply that with the novel Goethe simply wanted to build a world of his own; but at the same time this world is not simply a figment of his imagination, rather it captures the distilled essence of his times, amounting to a clear vision of the ongoing theatricalization of Europe (Citati 1990).

This is reinforced by the manner in which Goethe reflected upon and further developed the novel through the long decades of its composition. According to

Pietro Citati (1990: 182-3), when Goethe returned to the novel in 1794, having abandoned its writing almost a decade ago, shortly before his trip to Italy in 1786, as part of the general malaise that overtook him, forcing him to radically change his mode of living, he was evidently disturbed by the state of the manuscript, its lack of unity. He thus decided to take it apart, into its constitutive elements, and in a second stage interwove all the motifs into a systematic texture. As a result, and probably for the first time in history, Goethe liberated the novel from the caprices of chance, giving it a Law and a Form, 'transforming it into a systematic construction like a work of philosophy, tied together and continuous like a theorem' (Citati 1990: 186), giving the *Lehrjahre* a granite-like perfection (Citati 1990: 189-90).

In the novel matters of education (*Bildung*) and theatrical 'mission' (*Sendung*) are tightly articulated upon each other, occasionally all but coinciding. This is especially true for the first version, where such a mission is presented from the inside, in full seriousness. In the book, however, Goethe came to mark his difference, in both very subtle and most direct ways. The former is particularly visible in the exaggerated sentimentalism of the novel. Sentimentalism, of course, is a prime consequence of a theatricalized life, and it was the highly sentimental novel *The Sufferings of Young Werther*, culminating in the pathetic suicide of the hero, that brought fame to Goethe, becoming a flag and battle cry for the *Sturm und Drang* (storm and stress) movement, one of the direct historical consequences of the relatively sudden theatricalization of German society in the mid-18th century, resulting in his invitation to Weimar. He started to write *Wilhelm Meister* as a follow up to *Werther*, thus in a highly sentimental key, but in the final version, while leaving much of the text intact, he marks his difference – for example, by the punishing fate of those who live according to such theatrical ideals. Goethe was facing the same problem here as Catherine Deneuve in François Truffaut's masterly, and – as usual – highly Goethean *Mississippi Mermaid*, as she, acting in a film, had to enact somebody who was faking a role, intimating to the audience that she was merely acting, though differently from a bad actor who simply cannot play a role in a convincing manner.

Another clearly marked problem concerns the manner in which theatre can be, and was then, used to elicit nationalistic feelings. This was a particularly German problem, as – of all countries of Europe – 'it was in Germany that the theatre proved to be the strongest focus for national sentiment in the eighteenth century' (Brown 1995: 289). In a scene of Book II, Chapter 10, Goethe shows how the presentation of a play, written in order to elevate feelings of patriotism, succeeds so well that in a completely innocuous situation the normal everyday audience, out of their sheer happiness of being Germans, proceed to break the glasses, damage the furniture, and end in a drunken brawl, leading Wilhelm Meister to reflect upon how 'bad effects can a well-intentioned poetic work produce' (Goethe 1869, XVIII: 79). The analytical power and socio-historical significance of Goethe's work becomes all the clearer if we compare these events to the itinerant circus show and its effects, taking place shortly before (Chapter 4). There Goethe analyses in minute details the trick-ful effect mechanism of such shows, starting with the clown and the female soubrette, behaving in a manner that members of the public want to become acquainted with them; continuing with provoking the most different but equally intensive emotions through showing excesses like a deformed child, in order to evoke pity, or acrobats and tight-rope walkers, to evoke admiration and fear; and then ending with the entry of the main stars who enact a love story through tricks of seduction, spinning further the incited desires of the audience, so that the enthusiasm of the public would spread contagiously, with all men lustfully watching the female actor, and all women the male (Goethe 1869, XVIII: 60).[15] The stunning, and highly Platonic, conclusion is that the most high-minded presentation of a national theatre uses the same technique, having identical aims, as an ambulant circus show: to incite emotions in the spectators. Thus, considering the importance that the issue of 'national theatre' assumed in Germany, largely due to the works of Lessing, singular fountainhead of the German obsession with 'critique' as well, one can argue that the excessive emotionality and violence of German nationalism has less to do with some presumed German 'historical national character', and more with the particularly sudden and strong theatricalization of German society in the direction of 'national theatre'; a direction that could exert such an overwhelming effect due to the previous, excessively Puritanical religiosity which – through its inhuman rejection of normal human emotions and pleasures – rendered the populace incapable of resisting the sudden and contagious spread of fake emotionality. The parallel is particularly strong with the US today, where an originally even more markedly Puritanical society has become, over long decades, thoroughly and haplessly theatricalized through Hollywood, television, video and the internet.

In the same spirit, the novel also contains a series of explicit negative judgments on theatre and a theatricalized society. These start with the initial love-story, of the most trivial kind, as Wilhelm Meister falls in love with an actress, herself torn, as an almost inescapable professional destiny, between her true love and the man who is paying her bills; and continues through the tragic story of Therese who – as a stunning condemnation of her own mother – flares up against those who searched for an escape in books, and thus transform 'their lives into theatre and novel', wondering 'how people could have believed that God talks to them through books and stories' (Goethe 1869, XIX: 120). The most important and direct, truly stunning and resolutely Platonic condemnation of theatre, however, comes from representatives of a supposedly model educational institution. Of all the arts theatre or drama – the two words are used interchangeably – is the only one that the institution does not support, as 'it assumes an idle crowd, even a mob', set on provoking artificial feelings through 'deceitful fun or fake pain' (Goethe

---

15 In order to indicate the void disseminated by theatre, with his usual, careful capacity for observation Goethe intimated that actors often do not even have after an interest in their own successful performance; after all, they know it only too well that their success is the mechanical result of well prepared and much practiced tricks, repeated to boredom (Goethe 1869, XVIII: 64).

1869, XX: 168). While all the arts are brothers, theatre is the single exception and prodigal son, which 'would appropriate the goods of the entire family for itself, and would even waste this', given that it is parasitical on them, and is their corruptor (Ibid.); even its origins are ambiguous (*zweideutige Ursprung*) (Goethe 1869, XX: 169) – an expression that identifies the theatre as having a schismatic origin, or being literally *schismogenic*. These passages are followed by a rare explicit comment by Goethe, as if falling out of his role, presenting himself as the editor of these writings, and admitting that he was deeply disturbed by this strange passage, as he himself spent much more time on theatre than should have been proper, and that it was therefore difficult to convince him that all his related efforts were in vain: 'unpardonable errors'; 'fruitless fatigues' (Goethe 1869, XX: 169).

These comments can be further supported by a passage from his conversation with Johann Peter Eckermann, of 22 March 1825. His young interlocutor confides to him that in his youth he not only could not miss a spectacle, but attended the rehearsals as well, and even visited the empty stage. Goethe offers some reasons why all young people love the theatre so much: '[n]o one asks you any questions; you need not open your mouth unless you choose; on the contrary, you sit quite at your ease like a king, and let everything pass before you, and recreate your mind and senses to your heart's content' (Goethe 1850: 214-15). Goethe shows understanding about the youth, but he is pitiless concerning the lasting effects of an infatuation with theatre.

Those still not convinced about the metaphorical and real void generated through theatricalization, a genuine source of nihilism, should read carefully one of the most significant and direct reflections by Goethe, through Wilhelm Meister, on the lasting effect of a preoccupation with the theatre – which is the nothing, or the *nulla* (see Horvath 2010). Reflecting back on his years spent in pursuit of his 'theatrical mission', at the start of Book VII, thus the first chapter added to the book in 1795–1796, Wilhelm Meister melancholically states that 'when thinking back on the times that I spent with the theatre, I think I only see an infinite void; nothing remained of the whole thing' (Goethe 1869, XIX: 95).

Conclusion

According to conventional standards, the term 'imagination' is highly problematic in social research, which is supposed to deal with the social world as it is, and not bring 'imagination' into the study of this reality. However, the modern life we all lead has become largely shaped through figments of imagination, invested in social life by centuries of theatrical techniques, the theatre – in various guises and 'modernized' forms – being a main 'sorcerer's apprentice' of modernity since the time of late-Renaissance charlatans. The analysis of this process, and its pervasive impact on human lives, needs methods that are up to it, being able to distinguish between genuine and false in reality. This chapter offers some such methods, by introducing 'novels of truth', focusing in particular on Goethe's *Wilhelm Meister*, with the help of René Girard and Béla Hamvas.

References

Agamben, G. (1998): *Homo Sacer*. Stanford, CA: Stanford University Press.
Agnew, J-C. (1986): *Worlds Apart: The Market and the Theater in Anglo-American Thought, 1550-1750*. Cambridge: Cambridge University Press.
Bateson, G. (1958): *Naven*. Stanford, CA: Stanford University Press.
Bateson, G. (1972): *Steps to an Ecology of Mind*. New York: Ballantine.
Bateson, G. (1979/2002): *Mind and Nature: A Necessary Unity*. Cresshill, NJ: Hampton Press.
Bateson, G. and M.C. Bateson (1988): *Angels Fear: Towards an Epistemology of the Sacred*. Chicago, IL: University of Chicago Press
Brown, J.R. (1995): *The Oxford Illustrated History of Theatre*. Oxford: Oxford University Press.
Citati, P. (1990): *Goethe*. Milan: Adelphi.
Elias, N. (1987): *Involvement and Detachment*. Oxford: Blackwell.
Ferguson, H. (2004): "The Sublime and the Subliminal: Modern Identities and the Aesthetics of Combat". *Theory Culture Society*, 21(1): 1-33.
Ferguson, H. (2010): "Comparing (Sick)-notes: Intercultural Reflections on Modernity and Disease in the Writings of Thomas Mann and Jun'ichiro Tanizaki". *International Political Anthropology*, 3(1): 29-53.
Foucault, Michel (1982): 'The Subject and Power', in H. Dreyfus and P. Rabinow, *Michel Foucault: Beyond Structuralism and Hermeneutics*. Chicago, IL: University of Chicago Press.
Gernet, L. (1917/2001): *Recherches sur le développement de la pensée juridique et morale en Grèce*. Paris: Albin Michel.
Girard, R. (1961): *Mensonge romantique et vérité romanesque*. Paris: Grasset.
Goethe (1850): *Conversations of Goethe with Eckermann and Soret*. London: Smith, Elder & CO.
Goethe, J.W. (1869): *Goethes sämmtliche Werke* (40 volumes). Stuttgart: J.G. Cotta.
Goldman, H. (1988): *Max Weber and Thomas Mann: Calling and the Shaping of the Self*. Berkeley, CA: University of California Press.
Goldman, H. (1992): *Politics, Death and the Devil: Self and Power in Max Weber and Thomas Mann*. Berkeley, CA: University of California Press.
Hamvas, B. (1994): "Regényelméleti fragmentum (Fragment for a Theory of the Novel)", in *Arkhai*. Szentendre: Medio.
Hamvas, B. (1997): *Karnevál I-III*. Szentendre: Medio.
Hamvas, B. (2000): "Arlequin", in *Silentium/ Titkos jegyzőkönyv/ Unicornis*. Szentendre: Medio.

Horvath, A. (2010): "Pulcinella, or the Metaphysics of the *Nulla*: In Between Politics and Theatre". *History of the Human Sciences*, 23(2): 1-21.

Horvath, A. (2013): *Modernism and Charisma*, London: Palgrave/Macmillan.

Inglis, D. and J. Hughson (eds) (2005): *The Sociology of Art: Ways of Seeing*. Basingstoke: Palgrave.

Latour, B. (2011): "Reflections on Étienne Souriau's *Les différents modes d'existence*", in *The Speculative Turn: Continental Materialism and Realism*, edited by G. Harman, L. Bryant and N. Srnicek. Melbourne: re.press.

Müller, H-P. (2011): "Goethe: The ambivalence of modernity and the Faustian Ethos of Personality", in *Sociological Insights of Great Thinkers*, edited by C. Edling and J. Rydgren. Oxford: Praeger.

Nietzsche, F. (1974): *The Gay Science*. New York: Vintage Books.

Pizzorno, A. (1991): "On the Individualistic Theory of Social Order", in *Social Theory for a Changing Society*, edited by P. Bourdieu and J.S. Coleman. Boulder, CO: Westview Press.

Radin, P. (1972): *The Trickster: A Study in American Mythology*. New York: Schocken.

Szakolczai, A. (2005): "In Between Tradition and Christianity: The Axial Age in the Perspective of Béla Hamvas", in *Axial Civilisations and World History*, edited by J. Arnason, S.N. Eisenstadt and B. Wittrock. Leiden: Brill.

Szakolczai, A. (2013a): *Comedy and the Public Sphere: The Re-birth of Theatre as Comedy and the Genealogy of the Modern Public Arena*. London: Routledge.

Szakolczai, A. (2013b): "The Social Pathologies of Contemporary Civilization: Meaning-Giving Experiences and Pathological Expectations Concerning Health and Suffering", in *Social Pathologies of Contemporary Civilization*, edited by K. Keohane and A. Pedersen. Farnham: Ashgate.

Szakolczai, A. and H. Wydra (2006): "Contemporary East Central European Social Theory", in *Handbook of Contemporary European Social Theory*, edited by G. Delanty. London: Routledge.

Treiber, H. (1993): "Nietzsche's Monastery for Freer Spirits and Weber's Sect", in *Weber's Protestant Ethic: Origins, Evidence, Contexts*, edited by H. Lehmann and G. Roth. Cambridge: Cambridge University Press.

Turner, V.W. (1969): *The Ritual Process*. Chicago, IL: Aldine.

Turner, V.W. (1974): *Dramas, Fields and Metaphors: Symbolic Action in Human Society*. London: Cornell UP.

Chapter 9

Creative Methods: Oracles, *Poiesis* and Epiphanies as Metaphors of Theorizing

Kieran Keohane

Methods of Theorizing

Social theory and method are inextricably bound up with one another, despite the convention of their separation and a recent tendency to differentiate them entirely, emphasizing technical training in particular methods over general education in culture and thinking. But to theorize, whether in Sociology, Philosophy, Politics, Anthropology, or in any cognate field in the Arts, Humanities and Social sciences means not simply to arrange empirical evidence, but also to seek to clarify ideals by virtue of a way of inquiry that is sustained and methodically pursued, so much so that we may speak of method(s) of theorizing.

Questions of method, or searches for the 'way' cannot be reduced to a search for means to satisfy given ends, but must incorporate a discussion of the very ends of social and human life, including the question of meaning. Methods of theorizing are thus ways of attending to the world so as to bring into view, contemplate and articulate radiant ideals of beauty, truth and the good life; ideals that illuminate and make possible an understanding and interpretation of our present practices and institutions, thereby enabling our education and self-transformation in light of such ideals.

Émile Durkheim says that 'the value of a thing cannot be, and never has been, estimated except in relation to some conception of the ideal' (Durkheim 1974: 90) and Max Weber concludes in "Politics as a Vocation" that 'it is perfectly true, and confirmed by all historical experience, that the possible cannot be achieved without continually reaching out towards that which is impossible in this world' (Weber 1978b: 225). Theorizing can thus be conceived of as the methodical reaching out for impossible ideals by which we can take the measure our civilization. But as *theoria* and *methodus* have become differentiated we lose sight of the ways towards recovering our ideals just at a time when economic crisis, ecological catastrophe and political turmoil threaten to overwhelm us.

In this chapter, I revisit the origins, the etymology and usages of 'method' and 'theory' in Ancient Greece in the practices of making pilgrimages to Oracles, paradigmatically the Oracle of Apollo at Delphi. From these primordial wellsprings I will draw a red thread linking Classical and contemporary methodic practices in modern social theory (Durkheim and Weber) and literature (James Joyce). By so doing, I hope to show the perennial and perpetually recurring sources of creative methods in terms of our attempts to grasp transcendental meaningful ideas from enigmatic and epiphanic phenomena and to and express these ideas in poetic form.

Methods of Theory: The Way to the Oracle

The centre of the world in Greek antiquity was at Delphi, the point where two eagles released by Zeus met after circling the world.[1] Delphi was the navel, where the interior of the world was open to the sky. Here was Apollo's Oracle, and delegates sent to consult the Oracle were called *Theorai*. Delphi was not always or exclusively Apollo's. It had been the Python's lair, the serpent embodiment of carnal and chthonic powers. Subdued by Apollo but never defeated, Python lay beneath the surface and wrestled with Apollo, so that when the *Pythia* uttered prophesy she expressed not simply Apollo's voice of reason, but Apollo's voice as he struggled with Python. Another etymology says that the *Pythia* was not alone Apollo's mouthpiece but his wife, as well as Python's object of lust. Python is gender ambiguous: in one obvious sense phallic, but as a representative aspect of *Gae*, feminine Earth Mother as phallic woman; Python represents the polymorphous ambivalence of desire and Pythia's union with Apollo was fraught with conflict and jealousy so that the Oracle's utterances were also the *Pythia's* own wilful distortions of Apollo's words as she showed her older, baser loyalties to Python and as she played one divine power off against the other. For half of the year the Oracle was silent and the temple was abandoned as the *Pythia* and her entourage participated in the orgiastic rites of Dionysus in the Corycian cave nearby.[2] The Delphic Oracle expressed the ambiguous and ambivalent manifestations of the struggles of the gods of the sky and the underworld, the forces of light and darkness, reason and animal passions intertwined with one another, alloyed together. It was the task of *Theorai* to make their way to Delphi, to interpret the enigmatic manifestations of conflicted divine powers and to carry that meaning back to the cities that sent them.[3] Oracles and the methods of consulting them are the most ancient human institutions, Giambattista Vico says,

---

1   My account of the Delphic Oracle is derived from several sources, including: Konstantinou (1957) Graves (1993) Eisler (1987) Broad (2007) Slater (1992) Harrison (1962) which in turn draw on Classical sources such as Plutarch and Strabo.

2   The Corycian where Dionysus was celebrated is located about 15km from Delphi further up Parnassus. The annual closing of Apollo's temple and the procession to the cave show the equivalence or perhaps even the higher status Dionysus held as the older and more fundamental divinity.

3   Ambiguity was politically amplified by the fact that the Greek city states were infamously conflicted and at odds with one another (hence the great rivalry represented by the competitive rituals of gifting at Delphi, manifest by conspicuous Treasuries), such that the Pythia was sometimes bribed, by rivals, to put people on the wrong track.

his *New Science* intended as a method of etymological recovery: 'From *nuo*, to make a sign by nodding, they derived *numen*, divine will, an idea that is utterly sublime and worthy to express divine majesty ... The science of this language the Greeks called theology, meaning the science of the gods' speech' (Vico 2000: 147). Through their oracles the gods give *theoremata*, 'things divine and sublime to contemplate' (Vico 2000: 153) and by virtue of reflection and contemplation on matters both human and divine, the method of theorizing means a deliberate and systematic way of reaching out for divine and sublime things to contemplate; ways by which 'to wonder, to venerate and to desire unity with the infinite wisdom of God' (Vico 2000: 491).

Divine and sublime *theoremata* are radiant ideas by the light of which the world is illuminated so that we may reflect on our current institutions and practices and desire to act more wisely. *Theorai* were ordinary members of their various city states elected for the occasion of consulting the Oracle,[4] like today's citizens selected for jury duty who temporarily but deliberately turn their minds towards ideals of truth and justice.[5] *Theorai* followed a [met]*hodus*, a road, a pathway between the agora and the temple, a way leading between an ideal world represented by the temples on the Acropolis where ideal man (the gods) resided (no humans could live there, an early Oracle had decreed) and the real world represented by the agora, where men met as men.[6] The journey to Delphi was

---

4   *Theorea* also meant a spectator at games, but this does not refer to the mob dumbly looking on at sports as it does now, but derives instead from the intimate relationship between games and the sacred for the Greeks; the Olympic and Delphic contests were occasions when mortals displayed the qualities of strength, speed, intellect, artistry, wit (the original games featured contests in music, poetry, sculpture, architecture, drama, as centrally as athleticism) that they owed, and had in common with the Gods. In this context *theoria* referred to the envoy sent to consult an Oracle, and more widely was the title of the collection of state ambassadors that a city state delegated to the sacral festivals of another city state. Since these festivals were usually connected with games, theory came to mean spectator, and more particularly, a traveller who visits foreign places to learn something of their customs and laws. "Because the witnessed events were usually connected with divine things, theory came to be seen as a particularly sublime way of life. If we begin with the Greeks in order to locate the primordial deep grammar of the usage, we find that theorizing was a more inclusive and powerful notion than science and that it encapsulated as parameters the ideas of spectator, search, and self, with the process originating in wonder and culminating in a transcendental realisation" (Blum, 1979, 303).

5   By the Classical era theory had a more diffused usage. Aristotle used *theorea* to describe that kind of contemplative mental activity in which we engage for its own sake: to theorize meant to inspect or to keep one's gaze fixed on. To theorize was to turn one's mind in a certain direction, or to look at the world under the auspices of a certain interest. Husserl's notion of reflexiveness and Heidegger's idea of astonishment are articulations of such a look (Blum, 1973).

6   In Athens an ancient street from the agora, by the Acropolis, leading towards Thebes and on to Delphi is still called 'Theorias'.

arduous, taking a week or so to walk from Athens, passing through the crossroads at Thebes where 'the Sphinx poses enigmas to travellers and kills them when they find no solution' (Vico 2000: 291). More mundane risks were bandits and wolves, so for safety and companionship (as is the practice amongst pilgrims of all civilizations) *theorai* fell in to company with others on the way to the Oracle and on the way home again, sharing their conversations, discussing their questions, so that the answer sought from the Oracle was already in the process of being worked out on the way to its being asked, so that the truth coincides with the path towards truth as G.W.F. Hegel says.

Arriving at Delphi *theorai* ritually washed in the Castilian spring, preparing to ask their questions afresh. Then they followed the 'sacred pathway', a ceremonial royal road winding its way past the treasuries of other cities, their sometimes allies and at other times enemies, upwards towards the seat of the Oracle. Waiting at the forecourt, 'in sober readiness to be astounded before the coming of the dawn' (Heidegger 1977: 327) *theorai* read three inscriptions: 'Know thyself,' 'Nothing in excess,' and 'Guarantee, and you will be destroyed'. These mottos are to guard against hubris by counselling self-reflection and moderation and the third, the least well known, warns *theorai* that having heard from the Oracle, they should not guarantee to others that they know the meaning (or, for that matter, that they are certain of knowing anything at all) for while theory desires unity with the wisdom of God humans cannot have absolute knowledge. Ascending a ramp, through a great colonnade of Doric columns, behind huge doors, inside the magnificent temple an awesome scene unfolded. The approach to the Oracle led downwards to a chamber below the level of the temple floor, where *theorai* encountered a gold statue of Apollo and the *omphalos* marking the sacred spot, the navel of the Earth. In an inner sanctum, the *Adytum* (meaning 'not to be entered') the *Pythia*, seated on a tripod spanning a chasm, inhaled vapours emanating from the earth – *pneuma* – the breath of the gods. Asking their question from outside the sanctum *theorai* gazed in astonishment and listened in wonder at the enigmatic phenomenal signs from the conflicted powers that animate the world.

The question that *theorai* asked (as theory still asks today) is 'what can these enigmatic signs mean?'. To help *theorai* make meaning from these phenomena there were the Priests and the Priestesses of the Temple – *prophetes* – who served as translators and interpreters, and *hosai,* poets*,* for poetry was the appropriate medium in which the meeting of minds between human and divine, moments of immanent transcendence, should be correctly represented. In Giambattista Vico's etymology poetry (from *poiein* 'to make', *poi sis* 'to create') is the creation of meaningful ideas out of enigmatic phenomena. Verse was also a mnemonic that enabled *theorai* to recollect and to communicate the beautiful and sublime *theoremata* when they returned to their respective cities. Transcendent powers manifest as immanent but enigmatic phenomena are reconciled, harmonized and rendered beautiful by the hermeneutical interpretive poetic work of *theorai,* working together with *prophetes, and hosai*; in dialogue between *theorai* on their way to Delphi and back, and through conversations amongst *theorai* and their fellow citizens on their return. This method, approaching and attuning with agencies both human and divine under the auspices of the conversation of mankind's making sense together (O'Neill 1975: 14) by interpreting, creating and representing meaning in the form of immanent-transcendent ideas that may be contemplated and reflected upon, may be called *poiesis*. 'What the Greeks called *aletheia*, revealing, the Romans translated as *veritas*, we translate as 'truth' and usually understand it as correctness of representation' (Heidegger 1977: 317).

Having created meaning by their collective interpretive work, *theorai* convey a correct representation of immanent transcendent ideas back to their cities. There, enlightened by reflecting and contemplating the beauty and truth of the correct representation of the radiant ideal, the city's course of action would become clearer, 'for once the mind is illuminated by a knowledge of what is highest, it will lead the spirit to choose what is best' (Vico 2000: 136) as 'true wisdom must teach us the knowledge of divine institutions in order to direct human institutions towards the highest good' (Vico 2000: 137). Methods of theorizing are ways by which we occasion moments of immanent transcendence, interpreting and correctly representing them as radiant ideals that are both unified and unifying, so that 'theorizing is the methodic search for the collective (the form of life) that it presupposes' (Blum 1973: 308).

The method of consulting the Oracle with its rituals of separation from the city; the *communitas* with fellow pilgrims; the liminality that pervades throughout and the apotheosis of liminality at the chasm between interior and exterior; the gulf between human beings and the immortal gods bridged by an ecstatic medium in entranced state; guidance by a priesthood of masters of ceremonies; translation and transmission of spirit wisdom by poetic incantation; returning to the city and reintegration with the community: these methodic steps correspond precisely to the classical anthropological pattern of the *rite de passage* as formulated by Arnold van Gennep (1961) and Victor W. Turner (1969). And, as is the case in all *rites de passage*, both individual *theorai* and the communities of which they are members are transformed and transform one another reciprocally and recursively through the experience, and they develop morally and politically by this method of individual and collective self-reflexion. As such, interpretive reflective methods of theorizing constitute the normative heartbeat of the social and bodies politic, the method by which we reach out towards grasping and representing the sublime and the beautiful as unified moments of immanent transcendence, seeking a fusion of horizons between human and divine powers; creating radiant ideals against which we may estimate prevailing values (Émile Durkheim); seeking an absolute knowledge, that, knowing that it is impossible and prohibited from the outset still 'reaches out for the impossible' (Max Weber). Let us see how this reaching out for the impossible ideal, a principle evident in the primordial grammar and in the political anthropology of methods of theorizing appears in the modern canon of social theory in the work of Weber and Durkheim.

Max Weber's Way of Beginning: *Poiesis* of the Spirit of Capitalism

So much has been written on Max Weber's method of theorizing that to try to say anything new risks redundancy or refutation by more specialized scholarship, but still, let us consider again how Weber begins. Theory begins *en medias res*; not from an *a priori* ground or from a transcendent objectivity but 'in the middle of things.' Socrates has his dialogues in the street. Friedrich Nietzsche's Zarathustra moves between the mountaintop and the marketplace. Weber too struggles in the middle, between his academic principle of value neutrality on the one hand and his responsibilities to his political historical situation on the other. What is shown in the tension in the 'vocations' essays is Weber's self-understanding of the ambivalent locatedness of the theorist as a member. *Theorai*, like Weber, must leave the city behind when they take the road to Delphi, but they necessarily bring the city along with them, as their inheritance, as the traditions and common understandings of the culture that has formed them and gives them their duties and responsibilities as citizens.

Even though membership – the inheritance of conventional wisdom and common sense (such as tradition and culture) – limits theorizing, it is also its limitless resource: it constitutes the 'materials', the 'evidence' and the 'data' that Weber works with. Weber as a theorist distinguishes himself from his membership by working methodically on the common inheritance. As knowledge begins in wonder (Aristotle) or with radical astonishment (Heidegger) Weber's approach begins by brushing against the grain, disrupting the tranquilized obviousness of the taken-for-granted, creating an occasion for contemplation and reflection. Weber opens the way for us with the astonishing statement that 'unlimited greed for gain is not in the least identical with capitalism, and is still less its spirit' (Weber 1978a: 17).

Having caught our attention, Weber now invites us to work with him. He draws our attention to the precise but quite intangible thing that he wants us to try to grasp together: 'the *spirit* of Capitalism'. 'What is to be understood by it?', he asks us. It cannot be easily defined: 'The attempt to give anything like a definition of it brings out certain difficulties which are in the very nature of this kind of investigation' (Weber 1978a: 47). The forms of speech in Weber's opening lines are not didactic or rhetorical. He does not instruct us or assert truth claims. On the contrary, his method is dialogical and inter-locutionary (Ricour 1976: 14). Weber invites us to become part of a discourse with him, a discourse oriented towards our collectively uncovering and formulating a meaning that we may come to share together. That we can come to agree on that meaning through our discourse is because we share that meaning already, though it is taken for granted and has become obscure to us.

The *spirit* of capitalism is an elusive, intangible thing, and yet it is essential that it be grasped and correctly represented, as it is the unifying, animating principle that gives the specific and peculiar form that is unique and particular to modern civilization. 'For the spirit of capitalism to have any kind of understandable meaning', Weber says, 'it can only be as an historical individual' – that is, a singular unified meaning, an individual meaning distilled from 'a complex of elements associated in historical reality which we unite into a conceptual whole from the standpoint of their cultural significance' (Weber 1978a: 47-8). Weber's method of theorizing is the work that we do together by which '*we* unite into a conceptual whole' diverse and enigmatic signs that may be meaningful 'from the point of view of their cultural significance' *to us*. The concept – the conception, creating and giving birth to meaningful ideas – is not inherent in an *a priori* form but is something of our own making. To form a concept it 'must be gradually put together out of the individual parts which are taken from historical reality to make it up'. Thus what the spirit of capitalism means for us, Weber says, 'cannot stand at the beginning of the investigation' ... but will rather emerge in the course of our discourse: 'We must ... work out in the course of our discussion ... the best conceptual formulation of what *we here understand* from the point of view that interests us here' (Weber 1978a: 47-8). And our point of view, our approach to the question 'is by no means the only possible one from which the historical phenomena we are investigating can be analysed'. The result is that 'it is by no means necessary to understand by the spirit of capitalism only what it will come to mean *for us* for the purposes of *our analysis*'. The conceptual whole that we, with Weber, are trying to grasp and correctly represent cannot be an absolute; 'it cannot be in the form of conceptual definition, but at least in the beginning only a provisional description' (Weber 1978a: 48).

Having engaged us as collaborators Weber proceeds by working methodically with the diverse materials that are at hand to us. The spirit of capitalism is something that we may come to see (and hear) if we attune to its phenomenal manifestations, Weber says. We can see (or rather hear) it if we listen to Benjamin Franklin's advice to young men of the lower middle classes (Weber reminds us that Franklin's words are addressed to tradesmen and clerks). But Franklin's is just one cadence, the spirit of capitalism with an American accent, as it were, so Weber draws in more interlocutors, articulating 'individual parts taken from historical reality', and we gradually attune to them: the sober habits, shrewd acumen and the dutiful vocations pursued by his own extended family and their acquaintances in the German business, professional, intellectual and political elites, materials gathered from dinnertime conversations in the Weber-Fallenstein-Souchay household from his childhood.[7] In Weber's text we meet shades and we hear echoes of his Calvinist ancestors, his pious mother and his publicly libertarian/privately authoritarian father and their extended kin, throwing themselves into restless activity to escape doubt of being the elect. As well as these familiar voices Weber's interlocutors include his contemporaries, the affluent scions of his university fraternity and military academy; fellow theorists and

---

7 For a comprehensive study of the Weber family see Lutz Kaelbe: "How Well Do We Know Max Weber After All? A New Look at Max Weber and His Anglo-German Family". *Connections: International Journal of Politics, Culture and Society*, Vol. 17, No. 2, *Winter 2003 and* Roth, Guenther. 2002. "Max Weber: Family History, Economic Policy, Exchange Reform." *International Journal of Politics, Culture and Society* 15: 509–20.

close friends like Georg Simmel. The ghost of Karl Marx haunts the conversation, and we hear ancient voices from Egypt, Rome, China and India called back to life by Weber's scholarship. Alongside Weber's passing acquaintance with hard-nosed, self-made English industrialists and leisurely country gentlemen, we see Weber's snapshots of pirates and buccaneers and we hear stereotypical snippets about Neapolitan cabdrivers, factory girls and peasants, and many others, esoteric and commonplace. From this wide range and variety of cultural sources, each offering an angle, a standpoint from which the object that he wants to formulate can be viewed or at least glimpsed, the spirit of capitalism that Weber gradually approaches and draws into our field of vision is as though seen through a prism, illuminated by light refracted and reflected through many facets, from numerous angles, in ways that are always partial, though sharing affinity with one another, together forming a reflective equilibrium in which we come to perceive 'a complex of elements associated in historical reality' as a single conceptual whole – the spirit of capitalism.

Even as he grasps and represents the spirit of capitalism and fixes it for our inspection, as Clifford Geertz would say, he does not allow us to hold it too tightly, to say 'that's it, precisely!'. Weber cautions us: 'every attempt at a final definition must be held in abeyance' (Weber 1978a: 59). Weber's method of theorizing correctly represents a unified idea as a form that cannot be represented with absolute clarity, because it discloses itself in phenomena that are historical contents that are emergent and in a state of becoming; perpetually being contested, undone, decomposed and reformulated. Theory tries to grasp and represent the *zeitgeist*, the spirit of the times, the unifying idea, as it emerges and becomes manifest in the fires of history, the flames of which we call the enigmatic 'signs of the times'. The best that Weber (or any theorist) can do is to catch glimpses of spirit as it flickers and dances in the fire. Weber does not experience this inability to grasp and correctly represent the spirit of capitalism with absolute clarity as a limit, a reason to stop theorizing, even though he was prone to despair as his method of theorizing led him to a bleak prognosis of modern civilization. Rather, Weber orients towards this impossibility as a horizon, as an incentive to go on.

Émile Durkheim's Approach to Representation

'The value of a thing cannot be, and never has been estimated except in relation to some conception of the ideal', Émile Durkheim (1974: 90) says, and his sociology is explicitly formulated as a method that we can we use to clarify ideals by attending to the common inheritance of society: collective representations are transcendental ideals that are immanent in individual representations. 'Society is ... a composition of ideas ... which realise themselves through individuals' (Durkheim 1974: 59):

> Because society exists there also exists beyond sensations and images a whole system of representations that possess marvellous properties. By means of them,

men understand one another, and minds gain access to one another. They have a kind of force and moral authority by virtue of which they impose themselves on individual minds. ... The individual realises, at least dimly, that above his private representations there is a world of type-ideas according to which he has to regulate his own. He glimpses a whole intellectual world in which he participates but which is greater than he. This is a first intuition of the realm of truth. (Durkheim 1995: 438)

Collective representations constitute the realm of truth, Durkheim says, because

collective representations are the product of an immense co-operation that extends not only through space but also through time; to make them a multitude of different minds have associated, intermixed and combined their feelings; long generations have accumulated their experience and knowledge. A very special intellectuality that is infinitely richer and more complex than that of the individual is distilled in them. (Durkheim 1995: 15)

They are 'ingenious instruments of thought, which human groups have painstakingly forged over centuries, and in which they have amassed the best of their intellectual capital' (Durkheim 1995: 18). Durkheim's social theory is a method of correctly representing the collective representations that unify individual representations.

Durkheim's approach to the relationship between individual and collective representations shows us the way to proceed. Durkheim says: 'Each civilisation has its own ordered system of concepts, which characterises it'. The individual strives to assimilate this system of ideas for

he needs them in order to deal with his fellow men, but this assimilation is always incomplete. Each of us sees them in his own way. Some escape us completely, remaining beyond our range of vision, while others are glimpsed in only some of their aspects. There are some, indeed many, that we distort by thinking them. Since they are by nature collective, they cannot become individualised without being added to, modified, and consequently distorted. This is why we have so much difficulty understanding one another, and why, indeed often, we lie to one another unintentionally. This happens because we all use the same words without giving them the same meaning. (Durkheim 1995: 437)

Because each individual moral conscience expresses the collective morality in its own way 'the diversity of individual moral consciences shows how impossible it is to make use of them in order to arrive at an understanding of morality itself' (Durkheim 1974: 40). The method of theory must be to work through and beyond the many individual representations in order to grasp and correctly represent the collective representation that is intimated in the partial and distorted individual representations, particular instances 'that serve to illustrate the idea but that would never have been enough to form it by themselves' (Durkheim 1995: 436).

Durkheim's method seeks to bring to light 'a whole world of stable ideals, the common ground of intelligence's' (Durkheim 1995: 437). Durkheim shares this theory, method and pedagogy with Socrates.

Socrates' Methods of Dialectic and Maieutic

Hannah Arendt helps us trace the continuity of Weber and Durkheim from Socrates' methods of *dialegesthi* and *maieutic*. According to Arendt (1990: 80), Socrates did not distinguish his methods from persuasion, nor did he make a strong distinction between the outcome of his methodical discourse from *doxa*, opinion. *Doxa* is the formulation in ordinary speech of the reality of the world. *Doxa* is not merely subjective fantasy, nor is it something absolute that is true for all; but it is the truth 'as it appears to me'. Arendt goes on to explain how the word *doxa* means not only opinion, but also splendour and fame, and so it is related to the political realm in which everyone can appear and show who he himself is, assert ones own opinion and be seen and be heard by others.

Socrates holds that the world opens itself up differently to every one, according to one's position in it, and that the 'sameness' of the world, its 'objectivity', resides in the fact that the same world opens up to everyone, and that despite all the differences between people and their positions in the world, and consequently their *doxai* 'both you and I are human' (Arendt 1990: 80). Socrates acknowledges that there is a multiplicity of perspectives (or 'standpoint epistemologies') on which *doxai* are constituted and defended, individual representations in which we express our opinions honestly and publicly in terms of 'this is the way things appear to me'. Socrates' way of theorizing begins in the very middle of these individual representations for he was convinced that there is a germ of truth, an illustration and intimation of a transcendental idea, immanent in every common opinion. The method for seeking the Beautiful, the True and the Good according to Socrates begins by attuning to the germs of transcendental ideals that are immanent in vernacular language and culture. 'What Plato later called *dialegesthai* Socrates himself called *maieutic*, the art of midwifery; he wanted to help others give birth to what they themselves knew already, to find the truth in their *doxa*' (Arendt 1990: 81).

Socrates' approach is premised on the fact that every person has one's own *doxa*, one's own opening to the world. Each of us sees the collective representation, the ideal, from our own particular point of view. Socrates cannot know beforehand what *doxa* the other possesses, his 'how-things-appear-to-me', as it were, so he begins with questions clarifying other's position in the common world. 'Just as nobody can know beforehand the other's *doxa*, nobody can know by himself and without effort the inherent truth of his own opinion. Socrates wanted to bring out this truth that everyone potentially possesses. If we remain true to his own metaphor of *maieutics* we may say: Socrates wanted to make the city more truthful by delivering each of the citizens of their truths' (Arendt 1990: 81). In Durkheim's terms, Socrates sought to enrich our moral-practical discourse by awakening us to the wealth of wisdom of the inherited commonwealth lying dormant in our collective representations. Socrates methods – *dialegesthai* and *maieutic* – 'brings forth truth *not* by destroying *doxa* or opinion, but on the contrary, reveals *doxa* in its own truthfulness' (Arendt 1990: 81).

Socrates' interlocutors attempt to recollect, exemplify and articulate, to correctly represent the idea, only to find that it eludes their grasp; that their representation is a pale approximation in which the idea, radiant but elusive, is only partially glimpsed, as through a glass darkly. Method seeks not an answer to the question, but its *raising*. The radiant idea lies submerged in deep water, in the tranquilized obviousness of the taken for granted common sense. By raising the question method initiates a creative reawakening by contemplation and reflection on things that are divine and sublime, on the fullness of the collective representation, on the transcendent idea that lies behind, and is implied by, alluded to, immanent in each person's individual representation. Socrates gives his interlocutors 'a glimpse of a whole intellectual world in which he participates but which is greater than he ... a first intuition of the realm of truth' (Durkheim 1995).

Socrates' dialogues, like all good methods of theorizing, characteristically end inconclusively, in *aporia*, (vertigo, bewilderment); his interlocutors (and indeed himself) are left addled and speechless: 'I don't know what more can be said!'. The eternal recurrence of *aporia* is not an obstacle in the way, something that method should overcome, but on the contrary, is an incentive to go on. The abysses that methods of theorizing lead to are in *béance* (Jacques Lacan): they call out for meaningful ideas. *Aporias* are 'clearings in the forest' in Martin Heidegger's sense; clearings wherein we may 'see the wood for the trees'. But arriving at a clearing does not mean that we are out of the woods yet, so to speak. Clearings are places where methods of theorizing lead us to, and also where methods of theory must begin-again. *Aporia* is the free space that theory methodically throws ahead of itself to clear a pathway that enables it to carry on. To bring into view the limit of what can be known, formulated, and correctly represented is the goal of methods of theorizing. Method acknowledges the limiting parameters of the human condition, and this is an ethical lesson that leads to wisdom. Socrates concedes to the Delphic Oracle that he may indeed be the wisest of men for at least he knows that he does not know.

James Joyce's Metaphors for Creative Methods

We will now try to collect some of the ideas outlined above by returning to a theme raised at the beginning, namely, the deep affinity between method, theory and poetry; an affinity exemplified in the creative art and life of James Joyce.

Joyce has several models and metaphors for his creative methods. One is Daedelus, the architect and inventor; another is Ulysses, the wily navigator negotiating his way through a mythic-modern city while menaced by giants and seduced by sirens; another is the Monastic scribe conveying the Word in illuminated manuscripts through Dark Ages; and another is the atomic physicist-fissionist, deconstructing and reassembling the elementary structure of the linguistic universe. In *Dubliners, Stephen Hero* and *A Portrait of the Artist* Joyce identifies with Daedelus, the engineer-artist-architect of the labyrinth built to corral the Minotaur and who subsequently invented wings with which he escaped. Daedalus stayed low, close to the earth. His son Icarus flew too near the sun; his wings melted and he fell to his death. When Joyce sets out 'to forge in the smithy of my soul the uncreated conscience of my race' (Joyce 1996: 288) he flies close to earth; he works with the mundane and the vernacular, the banal lives and the ordinary language of his fellow Dubliners. Another of Joyce's metaphors for his method is 'a priest of eternal imagination, transmuting the daily bread of experience into the radiant body of ever-living life' (Joyce 1996: 252). The artist-priest's vocation is to bear witness and record epiphanies – moments in ordinary life when the true, the beautiful and the good shine out as radiant ideals; and to shepherd his flock, to save them from the beast, to improve their souls and lead people to the good life. In *Ulysses* Joyce's character/avatar Stephen Dedalus identifies himself explicitly with Socrates' methods, explaining how Socrates learned dialectics from his argumentative wife, Xanthippe, and *maieutics*, the arts of midwifery, from his mother, Phaenarete, who was a midwife (Joyce 1997: 183). Like Socrates, Joyce takes it that the ideal is contained in the word from the street, in individual representations, and expressed in *doxai*, the opinions of ordinary people. 'I always write about Dublin', says Joyce, 'for if I can get to the heart of Dublin I can get to the heart of all the cities of the world. In the particular is contained the universal' (Joyce in Ellmann 1982: 505).

Like Giambattista Vico's *New Science* Joyce seeks methods by which to see and recognize *theoremata* – things divine and sublime on which to contemplate – encoded and dissimulated in the patrimony of language and culture. Joyce's methods, like Vico's, include mythology and etymology. For Joyce, radiant *theoremata* of Beauty, Truth and the Good appear as epiphanies – brief moments and instances in ordinary language and common life wherein we may glimpse the unity of beauty, truth and goodness. The artist must take care to correctly represent these epiphanies, seeing that they are the most delicate and evanescent of moments. Early in his work Joyce deliberately sets out his creative methodology so let us hear him directly. First in an undergraduate essay:[8] 'Beauty, the splendour of truth, is a gracious presence when the imagination contemplates intensely the truth of its own being or the visible world, and the spirit which proceeds out of truth and beauty is the holy spirit of joy. These are realities and these alone give and sustain life'. Three years later, in a draft of *Stephen Hero* he elaborates this methodology:

> This is the moment which I call epiphany. First we recognize that the object is *one* integral thing, then we recognize that it is an organized composite structure,

---

8 On one of his Irish literary heroes, James Clarence Mangan (1902).

a *thing* in fact: finally, when the relation of the parts is exquisite, when the parts are adjusted to the special point, we recognize that it is *that* thing which it is. Its soul, its whatness, leaps to us from the vestment of its appearance. The soul of the commonest object, the structure of which is so adjusted, seems to us radiant. The object achieves its epiphany. (Joyce 1955: 210)

A Portrait of the Artist explicates the methodology further, presented in the form of a quasi-Socratic discourse between Joyce and his friends as they walk through the city:

> An esthetic image is presented to us either in space or in time. What is audible is presented in time, what is visible is presented in space. But, temporal or spatial, the esthetic image is first luminously apprehended as selfbound and selfcontained upon the immeasurable background of space and time which is not it. You apprehend it as *one* thing. You see it as one whole. You apprehend its wholeness. That is *integritas* ... Then ... you pass from point to point, led by its formal lines; you apprehend it as balanced part against part within its limits; you feel the rhythm of its structure. In other words the synthesis of immediate perception is followed by the analysis of apprehension. Having first felt that it is *one* thing you now feel that it is a *thing*. You apprehend it as complex, multiple, divisible, separable, made up of its parts, the result of its parts and their sum, harmonious. That is *consonantina* ... When you have apprehended [beauty] as one thing and have then analyzed it according to its form and apprehended it as a thing you make the only synthesis which is logically and esthetically permissible. You see that it is that thing which it is and no other thing ... The radiance of which [Aqunias] speaks is the scholastic *quidditas*, the *whatness* of a thing ... The instant wherein that supreme quality of beauty, the clear radiance of the esthetic image is apprehended luminously by the mind which has been arrested by its wholeness and fascinated by its harmony is the luminous silent stasis of esthetic pleasure. (Joyce 1996: 241-2)

Joyce's method is of apprehending and correctly representing the *integratis, harmonia* and *claritas* of the radiant unity of the beautiful, the true and the good as it appears in epiphanic moments of immanent transcendence; moments wherein we 'see the light' as it were, and are thereby inspired and compelled to transform our lives. Joyce shows us is how creative *poiesis*, bringing forth ideas into the light, is a *glimpsing*. Artful – that is to say creative – methods of theorizing reveal truth in ordinary *doxa* by attending to the ordinary in such a way that its beauty is grasped and expressed. Its beauty is it perfect wholeness, its quiddity, its whatness: what it is that makes it what it is and not other than itself. The Absolute, unified ideal is impossible to grasp and express, but its brilliance may be glimpsed momentarily and correctly represented in the artist's poetic formulation. We do not see ideas directly. What we catch a glimpse of is not an ideal form from a transcendent realm of Forms; we encounter a collective representation, a social fact, and we encounter it as it is articulated through individual representations, the idea is re-presented through language. This is the ontology of social facts. Moreover, when we say that social facts exist in language, it is not Language in an abstracted, objectified sense or as fossilized in etymology. Original meanings give us important starting points and signposts, and this is one aspect of Vico's genius inherited by Joyce, but Joyce's creativity comes from his sensitivity to usage: the accretions, corruptions, fusions, resonances, the clustering of meanings in the genealogy of languages is even more important, for living language in everyday use is what we must attune to if we wish to be creative. This is what Joyce celebrates in *Finnegans Wake*: 'In the name of Annah the Allmaziful, the Everliving, the Bringer of Pluralities, haloed be her eve, her singtime sung, her rill be run, unhemmed as it is uneven!' (Joyce 2000: 104).

Joyce's affinities with Socrates as a philosophical ancestor and with Max Weber and Émile Durkheim as sociological contemporaries (and Joyce's difference from the transcendental formalism of Plato and Immanuel Kant's *a priori* categories) can be seen in the centrality of the metaphor of metempsychosis to his method. Metempsychosis -the transmigration of souls- is the quality of Proteus, the Greek god of primal matter, phenomena, the stuff of life that is difficult to pin down. Joyce's creative method of theorizing is to grasp and to correctly represent protean phenomena. Proteus is an aspect of Poseidon, descendent of the Titan Oceanus, the river of life that encircles the world. Proteus the 'Old Man of the Sea' has the gift of prophecy, but he changes form bewilderingly, from a lion into a snake, into a leopard, then into running water, then into a tree. But if one can catch hold of him, cling to him through his changes and pin him down, if he is grasped and held in spite of his metempsychosis, he will provide answers. But even then Proteus will not speak truth plainly, but answers questions circumspectly. In Joyce's idiom artful method renders knowledge from the stream of life by grasping and holding it even as it changes and flows through one's fingers. But even as it is grasped, and the truth that it contains rendered and correctly represented, the truth that is revealed by it is circumstantial and contingent.

In *Ulysses* and *Finnegans Wake* Joyce shows the protean quality of the social: the spirit of one word enters another, as does the spirit of one situation, or of one being; the doubling, punning movement of lives, histories, thoughts, actions, overlapping, intersecting, crossing over into one another; the recursive, playing out of themes in the circular movement of history, the multi-layered symbolic complexes that is the nature of the stuff of individual and collective existence. Ludwig Wittgenstein says, 'where our language suggests a body and there is none: there, we should like to say, is a *spirit*' (Wittgenstein 1983: 36). It is this Protean spirit that Joyce grasps and expresses, just as Weber's method shows us the spirit of capitalism. The truth that Joyce reveals is that ideal forms are themselves heteroclite. All forms proceed by incessant doublings and undoublings in which they remain enantiomorphous – that is, resembling each other but not superposable. This gives the world a wholeness that is not characterized by unity, but by adhesiveness (Ellmann 1977: 95). The world hangs together by elective affinities, contingencies, recurrences, and the desire of creative, poetic methods of theorizing is 'to bring into a world founded on discontinuity as much continuity such a world can sustain' (Bataille 1986: 19).

Joyce's empirical method for getting down into the Protean protoplasm of the social consists of his deliberately putting himself in exile. He wants to write about his membership, but to do this he needs some distance, estrangement, 'objectivity' in the language of conventional methodology. Joyce's approach is to leave his home and his city and take to the road to find his Delphi. His path takes him to Paris, to Ljubljana, Trieste, Rome, Zurich, home to Dublin and to Galway, briefly, and back to Paris, and again on to Zurich. He deliberately walks away from Dublin, while keeping it alive with him all the time. From these varying distances along the road Joyce can take parallax perspectives and methodically reflect on his autobiography. By this method, a path and a pilgrimage that winds recursively between home and away he hopes, he says, to Hellenize Ireland and to Hibernicize Europe.

Joyce's method of exile was a deliberate, self-conscious way of balancing the contradiction between being a theorist and a member; of cultivating a sociological imagination -an ability to think oneself away from the familiar, to disconnect oneself from the tranquillized obviousness of everyday taken-for-granted. The sociological imagination has three aspects, C. Wright-Mills (1959) says: a historical sensibility that discerns change and transformation, difference and development over time, and thus enables the imaginative reconstruction of the texture of forms of life. Joyce does this in *A Portrait* by self-reflectively recovering his experiences as a child, a schoolboy, and a student, and in *Ulysses* by recreating and re-membering in the condensation of 'Bloomsday' the life in Dublin that he left behind – his student days, his friendships, his meeting Nora, the trials of their love life, from the point of view of the man he has become – husband, father, his family's new friends, mature artist, the whole of his life now. Second, the sociological imagination requires an anthropological sensitivity, an ability to imagine the world from another's point of view, to be able to relativize one's own culture, to experience it as strange, as Joyce sees Dublin from Paris, Zurich and Trieste, and as he does his own lifeworld by the methodical hermeneutic quest to understand how Nora (Molly) and all of his characters in *Ulysses* see the world. At several points during his writing Joyce actively sought to contrive situations in which he would experience intensities – jealousy for example, so that he might represent them more correctly. When challenged that some of his methods seemed trivial, Joyce replied: 'Yes, some of my means are trivial, and some are quadrivial' (Joyce in Ellmann 1986: 75). He tried to keep the child in him alive as it gave him access to a universe which adults repressed. Joyce tells us that Leopold Bloom is the only character he invented; all the others are real people from his biography; and Bloom of course is a representation of his own ego-ideal as a modern ideal type, his reflexively self-formed self, the uncreated conscience that he forges in the smithy of his soul. Finally, Mills says, the sociological imagination is imbued with a critical sensitivity, and, as we know with Durkheim and Weber, critique requires a conception of the ideal. Through his Jesuit education Joyce is saturated with the ethical discourse of Judeo-Christianity, and also he has Celtic mythology at his disposal. But for a Catholic Irishman these are already too closely entangled with the prevailing power regimes that he wants to critically evaluate, (his mentor William Butler Yeats was already suffering for working in these registers) so Joyce sought divine measures in Greek myths.

By these methods Joyce wants to help people to take a new perspective on their own world, to reveal the truthfulness of what they already know, show what is good and virtuous in the familiar, ordinary, world; a life-world that however 'fallen', always already provides normative standards and measures, 'conceptions of the ideal by which we estimate and evaluate the world', as Durkheim says. Ordinary Dubliners already know what the beautiful, the true and the good are. Joyce's method, like Socrates, is to listen to them, and to attune and to awaken his readers to higher forms of life intimated but submerged and obscured in their everyday lives and their ordinary language and thereby to give us glimpses of the Beautiful, the True and the Good; so that 'once the mind is illuminated by a knowledge of what is highest, it will lead the spirit to choose what is best' (Vico 2000: 136).

Joyce says that imagination is nothing but the working over of the remembered, an idea he takes directly from Vico: 'Imagination is simply the resurfacing of recollections and ingenuity is simply the elaboration of things remembered' (Vico 2000: 315). The creative theorist/artist does not create something new from nothing, but he re-members (rearranges, reworks, rearticulates) elements that are already there: 'Problems are solved not by giving new information, but by arranging what we have always known' (Wittgenstein 1973: 109). Truth is already implicit in the *doxi* – the common language and opinions, individual representations of ordinary people. The method of the theorist as artist is to help people to re-member the wisdom distilled in collective representations that their own representations partake of and intimate, to give birth to the truths that they already know.

The working over and working out is the laborious work of *maieutics*. This method takes time and effort and is marked by intensities of reflexive self-transformation. 'In the intense instant of imagination ... that which I was is that which I am and that which in possibility I may come to be'. More than extrapolation occurs according to Joyce, and in so far as we may speak of 'creativity' it resides in the instant of intensive reflexivity occasioned by the moment of epiphany of the radiant ideal. Dialectic and maieutic are marked by a process 'erigenating from next to nothing ... to produce by fusion something that can never be quite what has been known and seen before' (Ellmann 1977: 4).

Leopold Bloom is a personification of the *phronimos*, the understanding man with an ability to put himself in others' shoes, to see the world from others' points of view, and thus to speak with insight into the realm of human affairs and enable good leadership (Arendt 1990: 76). The uncreated conscience forged by Joyce, Bloom –'the flower', representing the elusive ideal of human flourishing- is a poetic representation of a Weberian ideal-type hermeneutic actor, exemplifying *verstehen*; a person who tries to see the world from many, changing points of view. Bloom-Joyce is Protean himself: a stranger, a *flâneur*, an insider and an outsider to discourses of empire, nation, church and commerce; an ad-man; a civic-minded private man; a womanly man, a man who even tries to see things from a blind man's point of view. The multiplicity of views represented in *Ulysses* is always partial and imperfect. Joyce himself is partially sighted. Are we not all similarly handicapped? Such are the limits that the human condition places on knowledge/power, tempering it towards irony and wisdom.

And let us end this discussion of artful and creative methods of theorizing by asking how Joyce begins? 'With Joyce we are not beginning, we are resuming!' (Burgess 1987: 196). *Finnegans Wake* begins – resumes: 'riverrun past Eve and Adam's, from swerve of shore to bend of bay, brings us by commodious vicus of recirculation back to Howth Castle and Environs'. History is Vichian *ricorso*, a continuity of overlapping, spiralling circles and we have entered it in the middle of a sentence ... All beginnings are middles. We begin, unavoidably and necessarily *en medias res,* and our method is to pick up the threads of the conversation, attune to *doxai* – individual representations – in such a way as the collective ideas intimated in them and the wisdom distilled in them that may enable us to be wise are accessed. And all ends where creative *methodus* take us are Wakes; not ends, but more beginnings, *aporias*, food for more thought and more talk ...

References

Arendt, .73): *Theorizing*. London: Heinemann.
Blum, A.F. (1973): "Theorizing", in J.D. Douglas (ed) *Understanding Everyday Life.* London: Routledge and Kegan Paul, 301-19
Broad, W.J. (2007): *The Oracle: Ancient Delphi and the Science Behind Its Lost Secrets*. London: Penguin Books.
Burgess, A. (1987): *Here Comes Everybody: Introduction to James Joyce for the Ordinary Reader.* Cambridge: Arena Books.
Durkheim, É. (1974): *Sociology and Philosophy*. New York: Free Press.
Durkheim, É. (1995): *The Elementary Forms of Religious Life*. New York: Free Press.
Eisler, R. (1988): *The Chalice and the Blade*. San Francisco: Harper & Row
Ellmann, R. (1977): *The Consciousness of Joyce*. London: Faber.
Ellmann, R. (1982): *James Joyce.* Oxford: Oxford University Press.
Ellmann, R. (1986): "James Joyce in and out of Art", in *Four Dubliners*. London: Cardinal.
Graves, R. (1993): *The Greek Myths: Complete Edition*. London: Penguin Books.
Harrison, J.E. (1962): *Progelomena to the Study of Greek Religion*. New York: University Books.
Heidegger, M. (1977): *Basic Writings*. New York: Harper & Collins.
Joyce, J. (1955): *Stephen Hero*. New York: New Directions.
Joyce, J. (1996): *A Portrait of the Artist as a Young Man*. London: Penguin Books.
Joyce, J. (1997): *Ulysses*. London: Picador.

Joyce, J. (2000): *Finnegans Wake*. London: Penguin Books.

Konstantinou, I.K. (1957): *Delphi: The Oracle and its Role in the Political and Social Life of the Ancient Greeks*. Athens: Hannibal Publishing House.

Mills, C. Wright (1959): *The Sociological Imagination*. New York: Oxford University Press.

O'Neill, J. (1975): *Making Sense Together: An Introduction to Wild Sociology*. London: Heinemann.

Ricour, P. (1976): *Interpretation Theory: Discourse and the Surplus of Meaning*. Fort Worth: Christian University Press.

Slater, P.E. (1992): *Glory of Hera: The Study of Greek Religion*. New York: Princeton University Press.

Strabo (1927): *The Geography of Strabo: Book IX Chapter 3*. London: Loeb Classical Library.

Turner, V.W. (1969): *The Ritual Process: Structure and Anti-Structure*. London: Aldine/Transaction.

Van Gennep, A. (1961): *The Rites of Passage*. Chicago, IL: University of Chicago Press.

Vico, G. (2000): *New Science*. London: Penguin Books.

Weber, M. (1978a): *The Protestant Ethic and the Spirit of Capitalism*. New York: Charles Scribner's Sons.

Weber, M. (1978b): "Politics as a Vocation", in *Max Weber: Selections in Translation*, edited by W.G. Runciman. Cambridge: Cambridge University Press.

Wittgenstein, L. (1973): *Philosophical Investigations*. London: Wiley-Blackwell.

PART IV
Teaching

Chapter 10
Creativity in the Classroom: The Poetics of Pedagogy and Therapeutic Shock in Teaching Sociology[1]

Anders Petersen, Michael Hviid Jacobsen and Rasmus Antoft

Introduction

In his work *The Gay Science*, the great philosopher Friedrich Nietzsche amused himself with the statement: 'Is it not a very funny thing that the most serious philosophers, however anxious they are in other respects for strict certainty, still appeal to *poetical sayings* in order to give their thoughts force and credibility?' (Nietzsche 1910/2006: 65). Whether this fact is actually funny or not is a question to which there could probably be many different answers, but it is certainly interesting. Why? Because it shows that our scientific analysis and knowledge of the world has an unmistakably poetic edge – an aesthetic dimension or artistic element that goes beyond the slavish business of collecting so-called 'hard data', finding and calculating correlations, plotting positions on schemas or calculating neat slopes in graphs. It shows that sociology, too, is an art form, and can therefore be understood as a poetic scientific practice.

In the course of time, many people have claimed that we can learn a lot about science through art and literature, and vice versa (see for example Nisbet 1976/2002). Over the years, several books and articles have been published on this phenomenon, which, to use an umbrella term, might best be described as 'sociology through…'. We, for example, recall having come across titles such as *Sociology through Humour*, *Sociology through Science Fiction*, *Sociology through Popular Films*, *Sociology through Literature*, *Sociology through Rock Music*, *Sociology through Poetry* and *Sociology through the Projector* – and there are certainly a great many more. There is no doubt that sociology can learn a great deal, in many different contexts, from art and literature, although it is important to emphasize that, despite certain affinities, there is a world of difference between

---

1 This chapter is an abridged and revised version of a piece previously published in Danish in the edited volume *Den poetiske fantasi – om forholdet mellem sociologi og fiktion* (edited by Michael Hviid Jacobsen, Rasmus Antoft and Lisbeth B. Knudsen). Aalborg: Aalborg University Press, 2010.

the demands of the various sciences on the one hand, and those which apply to art and literature, on the other (Jacobsen and Antoft 2006). In this chapter, however, we will attempt to examine how the manner in which we teach and present our sociological knowledge and research in itself offers poetic potential.

University teaching can often seem to be a somewhat formal, dry and dusty affair, in which the lecturer, speaking in a large auditorium, provides compressed information to a number of students sitting in rows of chairs, in the expectation that the knowledge thus imparted will guide them as well as possible through their future examinations. The teaching often takes the form of monologue rather than dialogue, and of podium teaching rather than seminar activity, because the location and the actual form of the teaching do not permit more active involvement on the part of the students, or because curriculum pressures lead to everything being targeted and focused on providing relatively specific keywords or concepts that are easy to remember. Several years ago, the critical German social scientist Oskar Negt spoke of the phenomenon of 'exemplary learning' (Negt 1981), by which he meant that through experimentation with the form of learning – including group and project work – it should be possible for students (and in his perspective, particularly working-class students) to come to understand themselves as subjects in a wider social context, and thereby be made aware of their own (revolutionary) potential. The lesson we can draw in the context of this chapter from Negt's rather slogan-like concept is that it is also possible to learn about society through unusual, unconventional and at times provocative, challenging and boundary-shifting pedagogical means, such as film and literature. In this chapter we will examine several of these more creative forms of communication and sources of poetic inspiration, from which, in our view, sociological teaching and pedagogy can benefit.

Poetic Pedagogy and Pedagogic Poetry

In our many years of teaching experience, we have found that the use of literary and/or cinematic references as educational and analytical tools can help to concretise and communicate key sociological points to students in a creative and insightful way. But this is by no means our experience alone. The American sociologist Lewis Coser, in his classic work on 'sociology through literature', noted that the introduction of literature or literary parallels can help to break down students' initial resistance to often rather abstract sociological theory, because it affords 'an opportunity to clothe the dry bones of social theory with the living and plastic tissue which grows from literary imagination' (Coser 1972: 5). In a Danish context, in their book on poetic teaching, Susan Nårgaard and Ole Pedersen (1992) have described this effect with the picturesque expression that 'even a stone can bloom'. By this they mean that teaching sessions which might otherwise seem dull and lifeless can acquire experimental and alternative input which can inspire students to think independently and creatively, and which may ultimately also have a positive effect on their acquisition of the more conventional skills and competencies that the teaching seeks to promote. As they aptly write about poetic pedagogy or pedagogic poetry:

> Good teaching encompasses poetic elements. During a [lesson], moments may arise in which the normal experience of time ceases, and a space opens up in which sensual experience, emotion and the body are linked with intellect, and something that could not be said before finds its expression and maintains an impression that becomes an experience. (Nårgaard and Pedersen 1992: 32)

We are entirely in agreement with this assessment, and we regularly – and as often as possible – base our teaching on the idea that sensibility, facts and intellect can meaningfully be combined with sensual experience, intuition and emotion. In our context, this experience is expressed through the belief that social conditions and societal issues can usefully be examined from sources other than the more conventional empirical data such as the results of surveys or excerpts from interviews. The point is that literature and other types of poetic source material, such as films or art, can be exemplary and illustrative in introducing the basic concepts and issues of sociology and discussing these in an educational context. What such fictional descriptions may lack in precision, they make up for with stories that have an impact on the readers or listeners and call forth their understanding and empathy. The use of literature and other art forms can thereby awaken and stimulate the students' interest in sociology and convince them of the potential of their own discipline in conveying an understanding of social reality (Corbett 1994). Many years ago, Austin Porterfield (1957: 421) presented three ways in which literature can be used as a creative source to enrich the teaching of sociology to students. Firstly, it can exemplify and support key abstract concepts in theory; secondly, it can bring to life source material from various disciplines by breaking down conventional lines of demarcation between, for example, the humanities and the social sciences, and thereby facilitate learning; and thirdly, it can be used to localise the intimate relationship between the sociological issues that students are struggling with in their studies and those which are so vibrantly described in literature. This also applies to other types of poetic source material.

More specifically, some years ago, Alun Jones (1975) presented a useful overview of how a specific sociological textbook (Peter L. Berger and Birgitte Berger's *Sociology: A Biographical Approach* from 1975) could be supplemented in a teaching context with a number of excerpts from literary texts. The conclusion of the assessment of the teaching process was that the sociology students concerned overwhelmingly felt that the teaching of sociology through literature was a useful and valuable pedagogical technique, that the literary extracts were interesting, and that the choice of literature had been beneficial to their understanding of sociological problems. The point of mentioning Jones's experience here is to show that it is not important whether the examples used in teaching are drawn from fiction or reality, as long as they have a form and content that can stimulate and sharpen the students' sociological awareness, and thereby create room for exemplary sociological learning. In this way, extracts from literature, used in combination with sociological texts of both a theoretical and empirical character, can help to enable students to focus sharply on society or some aspects of it, and to confront and problematize their common-sense attitudes in a teaching context.

Film as a Teaching Tool

However, it is not only literature that can function as a source of inspiration for the sociological imagination of students in an educational context. Films, whether documentaries, historical depictions, portraits, thrillers, dramas, horror films, or extracts from these – and including those films which are sometimes called B-movies – can act as powerful communicators of fiction from which creative, original and thought-provoking parallels can be drawn with the realities that people actually experience. Whether such films are Charles Chaplin's *The Great Dictator* (1940), Thomas Vinterberg's *The Celebration* (1998) or Per Fly's trilogy *The Bench* (2000), *The Inheritance* (2003) and *Manslaughter* (2005) is not in itself the point. The important thing is that it is possible to draw parallels between elements of the film's depictions and sociological concepts and theories. The use of literature and film as source materials and exemplary case studies in teaching naturally demands that the teacher possesses some insight into the literary and cinematic field, so that the material used can constructively and creatively contribute to the students' understanding of the sociological categories, concepts and theories with which they work in their studies.

Experience with the use of film in educational contexts is now well-documented and tried and tested in sociology (for example, Anwary 2003; Berg 1992; Deflem 2007; Demerath III 1982; Livingston 2004; Miller 1990; Pescosolido 1990; Prendergast 1986; Rogers and Wolensky 1986; Smith 1973; Van de Poel-Knottnerus and Knottnerus 1994). Overall, film can serve many different functions in illuminating sociological issues, including distillation/condensation, dramatization, exemplification, providing evidence and support, problematization, provocation, catharsis and fact distortion. At the same time, films are in themselves also social artefacts which represent the specific social or cultural contexts – both in terms of values, and materially – in which they were produced (Diken and Laustsen 2008: 3). Most of us who study society and social issues are probably familiar with the feeling that arises when one watches a film that contains important sociological points or messages, and which one almost intuitively regards as academically relevant. We, too, have often had this experience. It is our view that, in principle, all films can be used as an analytical basis or as inspiration for sociological thinking – they do not need to be particularly intellectual or avant-garde. Even such popular animated series as *The Simpsons* or crime dramas like *CSI* or *The Wire* can be used to stimulate, inspire or enhance the sociological imagination (see, for example, Scanlan and Feinberg 2000; Penfold-

Mouce, Beer and Burrows 2011). In the following, we will therefore briefly outline some examples of films that have inspired us poetically, intellectually and pedagogically in our own actual teaching practice, and which may help to elucidate key sociological issues.

One Flew Over the Cuckoo's Nest

Elements of the so-called sociology of deviance deal with how people who are stigmatized and labelled as deviant experience institutionalization. It is however rare for concrete and in-depth studies to map and document life inside the institutions where those whom society has defined as deviant are kept. One exception is Erving Goffman's classic sociological study, *Asylums* (1961), in which, on the basis of long-term observations undertaken in a psychiatric hospital under a covert identity, he reveals the nature of everyday life in what he describes as 'total institutions'. Total institutions are total in the sense that the lives and identities of the patients or inmates are completely defined by the institution's framework, routines and rules. One of the most striking features of Goffman's analysis of total institutions is that 'mortification of the self' or depersonalization is an inherent characteristic – not only must detainees, upon arrival, be deprived of their personal belongings and clothed in institutional uniforms, but their entire identities from the world outside the walls must necessarily also be broken down in order to be rebuilt to suit life on the inside. Goffman also shows how the inmates, although they are deprived of most forms of freedom through constant monitoring and control, nonetheless manage to establish small pockets in which they can maintain a certain independence and personality, for example through petty thefts or breaches of the rules. Another feature of total institutions is the way in which 'looping' is a characteristic of some parts of psychiatric practice. Looping means that the actions performed by the inmates at the psychiatric hospital to demonstrate their improvement or normality – usually on the basis of the encouragement or instigation of the staff of the institution – are instead interpreted as an expression of their deviance and illness, which means that they can never, in principle, escape the institution's definition and treatment of them as people who need help and must therefore be hospitalized.

One of the most famous films of the 1970s – the decade after that in which Goffman's book was published – is undoubtedly Milos Forman's *One Flew Over the Cuckoo's Nest* (1975), an adaptation of Ken Kesey's well-known novel of the same name. In the film, Jack Nicholson, in particular, became famous in the role of Randle P. McMurphy, a man who – apparently on a dubious basis – is forcibly committed to a psychiatric hospital where the other patients are clearly in a considerably worse state than him, and which has characteristics that are strongly reminiscent of Goffman's 'total institution'. The film shows how McMurphy continually struggles to create a meaningful life for himself in the institution, how he in vain tries to prove his normalcy, how he particularly challenges the view of human beings and the world held by Head Nurse Ratched, who controls the ward, and how he foments rebellion and tries to help his fellow patients to achieve more freedom and win greater respect from the staff. At the end of the film, McMurphy, following repeated escape attempts and rebellions, is forcibly treated with electroshock and ends up as a living vegetable, after which his friend – the Indian Chief Bromden – delivers him from institutional life by smothering him with a pillow. The film – like the novel – can be used to illuminate and exemplify a variety of sociological themes, including institutionalization, the mortification of the self, the moral careers of inmates, the consequences of monitoring, and the human struggle for freedom. As Goffman himself points out, the characteristics of total institutions can also be applied to other types of total or totalizing institutions, such as prisons, refugee centres, concentration camps, etc.

In this way, using *One Flew Over the Cuckoo's Nest* in teaching the sociology of deviance or organizational sociology can help to cast a critical light on psychiatric practice, and can support and concretize many of Goffman's points and the theories of other critics from the same period (for example, Thomas Szasz, R.D. Laing and Michel Foucault). It can also serve as a contrast from the past to today's practices in the so-called 'people processing institutions', or as a caricature and corrective to a period in which such phenomena as lobotomy, electroshock and over-medication were commonplace in many of the institutions that took care of the mentally ill in our society (Faggen 2002; Lena and London 1979).

Girl, Interrupted (1999)

Another example of a film that provides an ideal pedagogical tool is *Girl, Interrupted* (1999). The film is based on Susanna Kaysen's autobiography of the same name, published in 1993. The core of the book is the following: Susanna is admitted to a psychiatric ward for teenage girls with a psycho-neurotic depressive reaction and personality disorder (Kaysen 1993: 4). The wording of the diagnosis alone is impressive, but the entire setup is actually so interesting that it is ideal for sociological teaching about the relationship between mental diagnoses and admission to what Goffman – as mentioned above – would call a total institution. As a reviewer wrote about the book in the journal *Teaching Sociology*: 'While the book certainly could be used in courses on mental illness and total institutions, its focus on self-perception and the role of perception in interaction makes it a valuable addition to courses in social psychology' (Potter 1996: 244). What the reviewer notes about the book certainly also applies to the film, for although an important ingredient in the film is the way in which the mental disorders of Susanna and the other patients are articulated and constructed as part of the total institution, the primary focus is on the girls' self-perceptions and their perceptions of others. This is reflected in the manner in which the film's dramaturgical techniques and suspense largely revolve around the interaction between the girls and their surroundings.

As an analytical approach to the film, and thereby in relation to the film as an educational tool, it would be obvious to focus on a central social psychological concept such as social interaction. The film makes it clear that it is through social interaction – that is, the relations between acting individuals – that the girls refine their views of themselves (their identities) and others. This social interaction is obviously not isolated from the environment in which the girls find themselves, and so the total institution forms an active part of the identity construction process. In a theoretical sense, the interaction sketched between the various parties can be illustrated through George Herbert Mead's concept of 'the generalized other'. According to Mead, when the self is being constructed, it is not enough merely to take over the role of the other: more is required. As Mead writes:

> If the given human individual is to develop a self in the fullest sense, it is not sufficient for him merely to take the attitudes of other human individuals toward himself and toward another within the human social process, and to bring that social process as a whole into his individual experience merely in those terms: he must also, in the same way that he takes the attitudes of other individuals toward himself and toward one another, take their attitudes towards the various phases or aspects of the common social activity or set of social undertakings in which, as members of an organized society or social group, they are all engaged. (Mead 1934/1967: 154-5)

But, as the title of the film *Girl, Interrupted* also implies, this is by no means a smooth process. The girls in the film are interrupted (to a disproportionate extent) in their construction of themselves, which leads to some serious consequences, including psychopathy and suicide. In this way, the film also opens up the possibility of a sociological analysis of the destructive nature of societal norms towards those individuals whom society regards as deviant.

Ressources Humaines (2000)

In the French film *Ressources Humaines* (2000), director Laurent Cantet creates a moving drama out of what might otherwise appear to be a somewhat unexciting theme: the introduction of the 35-hour week. The film is about a factory worker's son, Frank, a young, idealistic business school student, who returns 'home' from his studies in Paris to take on a white-collar position in the manufacturing company where his father has been employed for his entire working life.

In the film's opening scenes, Frank, who is a pattern-breaker in his blue-collar family, appears as a true boy scout, perhaps with a bit too much self-confidence: the perfect son. When he gets a job in the company's HR department, he is a conscientious, enthusiastic employee, full of new ideas for the development of the company. Frank's skill in desk work soon impresses the company management; the managing director is particularly enthusiastic about a study of another company that Frank describes. In this company, the management, using a questionnaire survey, had shown that the trade unions' objectives were out of touch with the actual wishes of the employees. Frank is given the task of following this example and conducting a similar survey. But Frank's hopes that the survey findings could be used as a starting-point for negotiations, and thereby help to resolve the dispute about the terms of the 35-hour week, turn out to be far removed from those of the managing director, who wishes to use the survey to split the unions representing the employees, and thereby enable staff cut-backs to be introduced. The managing director naturally achieves his goal, and the otherwise confident and conscientious Frank must concede defeat. When Frank then realizes that his own father is in line to be fired in the next round of redundancies, three years before reaching retirement age, he decides that he has had enough and goes on the barricades with the workers and the unions, who jointly regain their strength once the management's real intentions are exposed.

The film's story could be described as the unsentimental, practical education and introduction of a young, naive graduate to working life, company culture and corporate politics. Frank is so eager to prove his worth that he initially ignores the company's lines of communication and decision-making processes, and thus accidentally treads on the toes of key organizational actors. At the same time, the film's main character learns that his relationships with childhood friends who work on the assembly line are compromised by his new status, and he becomes feared and subject to suspicion because of his relationship with the company management. The film demonstrates in an exemplary manner how formal and informal organizational life operates at a workplace, and would therefore be a good educational tool for anyone who is entering the labour market for the first time and required to adapt to an organizational reality in which everyday life is often marked by conflicting interests, latent and manifest conflicts, the exercise of power, inclusion and exclusion mechanisms, complex cultural images, etc.

But the film is also interesting as a didactic tool to raise awareness of what exactly an organization is, and not least, the ways in which organizations function as social systems. As part of the teaching of organizational sociology in the sociology programme at Aalborg University in Denmark, an exercise was conducted in which the students were divided into groups and asked to analyse the film on the basis of key sociological organizational concepts that had been presented during the study programme, including (in)formal structures, (sub)cultures and processes, conflict and the exercise of power, communication and change. Through the film, by following Frank's entry into the company and his sometimes naive behaviour, the students achieved an insight into the organization which is reminiscent of the initial experience of a foreign, newly-arrived researcher in a new field of research. It is only by applying the concepts of organizational sociology that students are able to understand and interpret the drama that is played out in the conflict-ridden period of the company's life that the film depicts.

The interesting thing about this film as a pedagogical tool is that as the organizational drama unfolds, it reveals not only its formal organizational structure, authority and hierarchy, and thereby the legitimate exercise of power, but also the informal power structures, which are manifested as the ability to negotiate, lie and manipulate. Just think of the managing director's ability to hide the real intention behind Frank's survey. At the same time, the film also shows, in caricatured form, the major cultural differences between the employees on the shop floor and the management and HR staff, not just in the way they dress (artefacts and symbols), but equally in how they communicate. Language appears throughout the film as an important cultural marker which also illustrates the class differences between the employees in the company.

In addition to the students gaining an opportunity to analyse the film as a case study of life in organizations, they also obtain, through Frank, in the fictional story, a sense of just how complicated it can be for a researcher to penetrate organizational contexts and decode the norms, (in)formal rules and routines, structures and processes that form the basis of organizational life.

Pay It Forward (2000)

A final example we will provide of how films can enrich not only sociological teaching practice but also moral thinking among students is the film *Pay It Forward* (2000), based on the novel of the same name by Catherine Ryan Hyde. In continuation of the novel, the film shows how good and unselfish actions, performed among complete strangers that you randomly encounter, and for whom you are not in principle responsible, can spread like ripples in water and generate a veritable tsunami of goodness, of potentially global dimensions. In the film we meet the boy Trevor McKinney, who, as an experiment in his social studies class, is asked to carry out an action that will make the world a better place. He decides to do good deeds for three people, whom he at the same time – in true pyramid scheme style – asks to perform good deeds for other people. One of Trevor's good deeds is for a homeless man – someone who would normally be considered vulnerable and in need of care. He then subsequently performs more good deeds, which initially seem fruitless, but which later turn out to have sown the seeds of love, forgiveness and self-sacrifice. In the film, Trevor himself is a rather withdrawn boy who has a difficult life, with an alcoholic mother and an abusive and absent father, and his good deeds, which set so much goodness going, are therefore all the more unexpected, and illustrate how the sources of morality can be unpredictable and inscrutable. One of the film's main messages is that morality may ultimately lead to you having to pay the ultimate price – losing your life. Towards the end of the film, Trevor is stabbed to death when he tries to defend a friend who is attacked. Another of the film's essential messages is that Trevor's good deeds, and subsequently those of many others, are not expected to be returned or repaid, but are rather 'paid forward' to others who need help.

This film, which might perhaps at first appear rather saccharine, could be included as an inspirational and thought-provoking part of sociology courses focusing on such issues as morality, social cohesion or altruism. Specifically, it could complement and exemplify the remarkable view of moral understanding set out by the Polish sociologist Zygmunt Bauman in his book *Postmodern Ethics* (1993). The main point for Bauman – who in his development of a sociologically concise and postmodern morality draws inspiration from Emmanuel Lévinas,

Knud Løgstrup and Max Scheler – is that morality is not about obeying the law or acting in a way which will ensure your own well-being or survival. In Bauman's view, morality is rather about self-sacrifice and the courage to say no if you are subject to compulsion. For him, morality is not codified or universalized, as it is the unspoken but mandatory, continuous and unselfish expression of responsibility, *being-for* and solidarity with the 'Other' which is the locomotive of any form of moral action. For Bauman, humankind is always morally ambivalent – it can do both good and evil (however these may be defined), which means that human beings are always required, or have the opportunity, to choose – a choice that can at times seem overwhelming and burdensome, even life-threatening, and which creates uncertainty and anxiety. As Bauman writes about the morally ambivalent person and the inescapable responsibility he or she bears:

> It is moral anxiety that provides the only substance the moral self could ever have. What makes the moral self is the urge to do, not the knowledge of what is to be done ... One recognizes morality by its gnawing sense of unfulfilledness, by its endemic dissatisfaction with itself. *The moral self is a self always haunted by the suspicion that it is not moral enough.* (Bauman 1993: 80)

Trevor's death towards the end of *Pay It Forward* highlights such a Bauman perspective on morality. The morale of the film is thus that the willingness to die for 'the Other' (and thus to forfeit one's own life for the sake of someone else) represents the ultimate moral act. This rings a bell with and exemplifies Bauman's perspective because, as Bauman once stated, 'no principle or norm may claim to be moral, if it implies that my responsibility for the Other stops short of the gift of my life' (Bauman 1992: 210). Bauman's morality is thus a morality of responsibility, self-sacrifice and immediacy which is played out in concrete encounters between people and in the meeting with the 'face' of the weak, and which stems from a pre-social moral impulse that may from time to time find itself in opposition to both the law and the biased ethical atmosphere of a given period, as his study of the Holocaust has shown. In this way, an American film hit can be used to exemplify a concrete moral sociological approach and its practical applicability, problematize the prevailing moral attitudes of our society, and perhaps, ultimately, also inspire compassion among the students.

However, it is not only in the classroom or the lecture hall that the poetic imagination can stimulate and generate creative understanding of sociological issues and inspire different ways of thinking. Literature and film can ultimately also help to change the existing social and political reality by awakening the critical sense. The products of the fictional world, such as books and films, can prove agenda-setting for reality. Just think of how John Badham's controversial 1981 film *Whose Life Is It Anyway?* proved to be seminal in relation to discussions about euthanasia, or how entirely fiction-based films like *Lord of the Rings* or *The Da Vinci Code* have in recent years helped to stimulate popular and politico-religious notions of right and wrong, good and evil, among a worldwide audience. Similarly, a wide range of books have over time fundamentally changed our view of the world, as well as changing the world itself (Downs 1983). These films and books focus on the world – albeit through fiction – in a way that would be difficult for even the most profound or thorough sociology. Neither should there be any doubt that a deeper understanding of Danish society in the 20th century can be fostered both by conventional historiography and historical records and by television drama-documentary series such as *Matador* and *Krøniken*, not to mention the great Danish tradition of social realism, which in many ways also transcends the often artificially-maintained barrier between the factual and the fictional.

In their recommendable book *Sociology through the Projector,* the two Danish social scientists Carsten Bagge Laustsen and Bülent Diken demonstrate many of the analytical and social critical possibilities that can be traced in a number of recent films, as an expression of the possible or as yet unrealized potentials in society (Diken and Laustsen 2008). They do not, however, focus on the possible educational, communicational or learning benefits to be gained by training the sociological gaze through the visual impressions offered by film, or by acquiring an ear for music, or by shocking and provoking oneself in the direction of sociological understanding. In the following, via a series of case studies, we will illustrate how we believe that both sociological understanding and communication can benefit from drawing on various forms of poetic and creative techniques of presentation, performance and provocation.

Performance as Pedagogic Presentation

It is by no means new for sociologists to experiment with forms of presentation in an attempt to secure the best possible representation of the social reality they have studied, analysed and theorized about. Laurel Richardson, a sociologist, formulates, together with her husband Ernst Lockridge, a writer of fiction, analyses of qualitative interviews through poetry and personal travel accounts (Richardson and Lockridge 1991, 2004), while Johnny Saldaña (2003) transforms field studies into ethnodrama under the inspiration of the dramaturgical techniques of the theatre, and Regina Hewitt (1994) employs a dialogical form – a conversation between the sceptic and the enthusiast – in a discussion of the use of literary devices by postmodern sociologists. These are just a few examples among many, but common to all of these poetically-inspired forms of presentation is that they maintain the all-dominating communicative medium in science, namely the textual form. However, a minor revolution is currently taking place in the use of qualitative methods, not only in sociology, but in the social sciences as a whole. Performative sociology has become a focal point for sociologists who wish to move beyond the conventional textual forms of presentation, particularly in order to engage the recipients of the sociological knowledge, irrespective of the nature of the audience. The use of tools and methods borrowed from the arts and humanities in the representation of sociological knowledge is beginning to achieve critical mass, and photography, music, dance, poetry, visual art, video installations, dramatized monologues and theatrical performances have become part of the methodological toolbox and educational instruments available for the dissemination of research results. Elliot W. Eisner (1997) argues that the attempt to break with conventional forms of representation and the faith in the printed word as sacred is groundbreaking for the methodological aspirations of research. But if success in research springs from its ability to create meaning, expand awareness and enhance our understanding, there is a need to develop new ways to communicate and illuminate the social reality that we researchers analyse, construct and portray (Eisner 1997). As mentioned, a multitude of performative forms of representation exist, but here we will focus on drama and theatre, as these provide a good illustrative example of the new trends in qualitative sociology.

Drama and theatre have long been under development as means of research dissemination, particularly in ethnography. Here, the role of the ethnographer has undergone a transformation from a researcher who imparts knowledge via conventional forms of presentation to one who also plays the role of screenwriter and playwright, and sets the stage for research-based representations of ethnographic data through the medium of drama and performance (see Becker et al. 1989; Mienczakowski 1994, 1995; Paget 1990; Richardson and Lockridge 1991). It is not necessarily the researcher alone who stages and presents the dramatization of the data and its interpretation; there are several examples in the literature of collaborations with actors, playwrights and scriptwriters who are better able to translate sociological knowledge into a performance form and present it in a convincing manner. In this context, Howard S. Becker et al. (1989) developed a conceptual framework for a 'performance science' which is essentially a textual presentation that mediates ethnographic data through staged performances, but which can communicate emotions and moods as well as actual facts. The goal of these manuscripts is not to communicate research in a conventional manner, but rather to provide a basis for being able to perform this as drama in communicative contexts, such as at conferences (see Bagley 2008; McCall et al. 1990) and in educational environments (see Turner and Turner 1982; Pedelty 2001). It would be too broad in this context to expound the various arguments supporting the use of drama as a form in research communication and education. Consequently, our focus here is on the form of representation more generally: what can this contribute in a purely pedagogical sense?

The answer is obviously complex, but in very general terms, we could say that a dialogue is created between the researcher/actors and the audience, in which more subtle and precise descriptions and analyses of social phenomena can be presented. As Norman K. Denzin observes (2003: 13), a performance does not become authoritative by citing scientific texts, but through its ability to awaken and create common emotional experiences and empathy between the performer and the audience, in a situation in which memory, emotion, imagination and aspirations interact. This point is based on two central arguments. Firstly, the research becomes 'multi-vocal' (Eisner 1997); it is no longer the researcher's voice and opinion alone that are authoritatively present in the representation. The informants also play a role in the performance, as a consequence of which more voices are set in play. This means that the researcher's voice plays a less dominant role in the representation, in order to better leave the stage to the informants and their voices. Michael McCall et al. (1990) argue that the data thereby becomes clearer and less interpreted for the audience, and as the researcher's voice is not the only one in the manuscript, that voice becomes less authoritative, and the possibility is opened up for a dialogue on the interpretation of the data. At the same time the audience members achieve access, so to speak, to the data, and can on this basis construct their own analysis.

Secondly, it creates a space for the researcher to utilise several voices in the manuscript: voices which allow for the presentation of several and perhaps even competing interpretations. The opportunity to use several voices can allow the researcher to present his or her doubt and insecurity in relation to the interpretations. Space can thereby be created for alternative interpretations, and questions can be raised concerning the central argumentation of the analysis. At the same time, the audience members are given a more subtle picture of both the research process and the research results, and enter into a kind of conversation through which they can form their own images, categories and concepts, and thereby analyses of the social phenomenon or social reality presented by the performer(s).

This method of presentation is perhaps particularly interesting in relation to ethnographic and micro-sociological analyses. Christopher Wellin (1996) points out that there is a special coincidence of goals between ethnography and drama. Firstly, it is easier in this type of performance to present interactional and emotional dynamics that are difficult to capture in linear narratives in textual form. Secondly, both of these goals can be developed in an ethical and pedagogical manner when the choice of interpretations acquires a clear and explicit voice, and is thereby justified. Thirdly, ethnography and drama share a common frame of reference in their special interest in human interaction as a form of dynamic and contextualized experience. Although a major goal of ethnography is to create a detailed picture of human social life as it is experienced, the conceptual tools used to interpret the data have a tendency to filter out the human side of that experience (Bruner 1986). This tendency to overlook experience, particularly in field studies, is strongest among sociologists, as our understanding of validity essentially distances us from the people that we study, while the dominant metaphors we profess – structure and status – can blind us to the emotional and embodied elements in the enactment of social life. However, much qualitative research deals with episodes of social life, and not just with isolated perspectives and actions. Think of the importance of meaning and encounter in the sociology of Erving Goffman. The theatrical performance, as a form of representation which is structured around a number of 'scenes', creates new ways of apprehending and analysing the unfolding of social life, as it is designed precisely to capture episodes in human life and the meaning and experience constructed in this context (Goffman 1959; Jacobsen and Kristiansen 2006).

In the foregoing, we have advocated that it is in ethnographic studies of interaction and interactive dynamics, in particular, that performance can function as a mode of expression. One could debate whether it might also be a useful form of presentation in other contexts, but the answer to this must be derived from concrete experiments with the communication form and its potential. However, it is important to emphasize that a performance is more than just an aesthetic exercise. It is a method of cultivating the participatory character of qualitative research, and a means of minimizing the textual distance which is the usual result of the articles and monographs we write about the people we live with and make the objects of our sociological curiosity (Conquergood 1995). But there is also another important point to using this kind of pedagogical tool. Perhaps sociologists should try to relax, take themselves less seriously, understand their own role in the production of knowledge, and assume a less pretentious attitude towards the people they study – all of this in the context of improving the accuracy and quality of, in particular, ethnographically-inspired sociology (McCall et al. 1990).

Shock as Pedagogic Therapy

Earlier in this chapter we mentioned that fiction is capable of sharpening and stimulating the sociological imagination, and can help to throw a critical light on, or even help to change, the social or political reality. However, fiction can do more than that. It can also act as a shock, and thereby provide a kind of educational therapy. Let us explain. According to the dictionary, the concept of shock has three meanings: a sudden or disturbing physical or mental impression; a state of extreme weakness caused by a physical injury that impedes the blood from circulating properly; and last but not least, a powerful surprise. The latter meaning is especially interesting in this context, because it equates the concept of shock with a violent sense of surprise, and with terms like startling and chilling.

There can scarcely be a writer of fiction whose works have such a startling and chilling effect on the reader as those of the French writer Michel Houellebecq (see Petersen and Jacobsen 2012). It is not for nothing that Houellebecq has been called one of the most controversial writers of our time (Beránková 2006: 101). In our view, Houellebecq makes particular use of two techniques to achieve this effect upon his audience: cynicism, and a uniquely detached narrative style. With regard to the first of these, his novels *Atomised* (1998/2001), *Whatever* (1994/2002a) and *Platform* (2001/2002) can best described as acerbic and relentless dissections of the living conditions of the Western individual, or even as a kind of autopsy of normative developmental trends in the Western world. Houellebecq, in other words, pulls no punches when describing the current state of society (Petersen and Jacobsen 2012). Wielding an incisive pen, he cuts to the core of what he views as the Western normative framework, which, rather than providing the possibility of living a good life, creates the preconditions for the growth of individual suffering. From his perspective, the structure of society is such that it must inevitably rebound on the modern individual in the form of psychological disorders. In Houellebecq's universe, the symptoms of such disorders practically tumble over each other: powerlessness, languor, despair, mania and lassitude are just a few of the more diffuse kinds of disorder that haunt his characters. But one type of disorder that is especially characteristic for our society, namely depression, has a central place in Houellebecq's novels. In fact, depression is the form of pathology he most often utilizes to depict the dark side of society's nature. In *Whatever* (1994/2002a), for example, the principal character, Michel, describes a visit to the doctor as follows:

> At the end of an hour he pronounces a few phrases of general import on periods of blankness, extends my leave of absence and increases my dosage of medication. He also reveals that my condition has a name: It's a depression. Officially, then, I'm in a depression. The formula seems a happy one to me. It's not that I feel tremendously low; it's rather that the world around me appears high. (Houellebecq 1994/2002a: 115)

Examples abound in Houellebecq's novels of this kind of cynical observation, in which he points to depression as the direct consequence of social trends. This shocks the reader, precisely because we know he is spot on. With great power, Houellebecq thereby forces his way into a difficult sociological topic and provides a thought-provoking explanation of the enormous rise in our time in cases of depression and the consumption of anti-depressants (Petersen 2007: 11). However, as Axel Honneth (2003: 132) has quite rightly observed, while Houellebecq's novels may be an apt illustration of a particular social condition, they do not in themselves provide an adequately substantiated analysis from a sociological point of view.

His observations are also chilling. The narrative form utilized by Houellebecq is so consistently detached and ice-cold (see Beránková 2006: 102-4) that the reader is left with a quivering sense of inner turmoil. The term 'turmoil' is not in this context to be construed as Finn Skåderud does, namely as restlessness (Skåderud 1999: 18). Inner turmoil should rather be interpreted here as an insidious feeling of emptiness. This inner turmoil arises from the way in which Houellebecq portrays his characters as possessing an almost inhuman absence of genuine emotion, whether towards themselves or others. To provide a couple of examples: the above quote describes very well how this person, Michel, has an almost emotionless relationship with himself. Most people would probably not react in this way to being diagnosed with depression. Sex, on the other hand, is familiar to most of us. But although the act itself demands bodily contact, sex can easily be empty of intimacy. This of course is a banal observation if we relate it to 'one-night stands' or the porn industry. Houellebecq is not so banal. From his perspective, sex without intimacy cannot be reduced to porn, but should rather be seen as a serious symptom of the coarsening of society. One example of such a relationship devoid of intimacy is depicted in the following passage:

> Annabelle helped him off with his clothes and masturbated him until he could penetrate her. He felt nothing except the softness and the warmth of her vagina. He quickly stopped moving, fascinated by the geometry of copulation, entranced by the suppleness and richness of her juices. Annabelle pressed her mouth to his and wrapped her arms around him. He closed his eyes and felt the presence of his penis more acutely; he started to move inside her once again. Just before he ejaculated he had a vision – crystal clear – of gametes fusing followed immediately by the cell dividing. It felt like a headlong rush, a little suicide. (Houellebecq 1998/2001: 330)

Even without possessing further insight into these people, or knowing what they do or where they belong in the novel, this extract is disturbing, as it touches something fundamentally human, namely the fear of emptiness – the fear that life offers nothing beyond a large number of meaningless (ephemeral) contacts with the other, and thus a series of small suicides.

It is our belief that literary works such as Houellebecq's can have an excellent effect as pedagogical therapy; they are pedagogical, because Houellebecq, through the shock to which he exposes his readers, gives the teacher an opportunity to communicate sociological material in a manner that is provocative, entertaining and challenging for the students, and in this way, the literary material can function as a powerful eye-opener. To elaborate on this, it may be helpful to make use of the concept of epiphany, and particularly the view that Stephen Dobson elsewhere links with Walter Benjamin (Dobson 2010). The term 'epiphany' refers to a source of collective experience formation. If we relate this understanding to readings of, for example, Houellebecq – and the links from here to sociological concepts – the literature assumes the character of a starting-point for a feeling of collective awareness or eye-opening, which, we should note, extends far beyond the ordinary. Epiphany, in this sense, does not merely act as a corrective to or adjustment of a prevalent perspective, but breaks down the boundaries of the perspective itself and places it in a completely different light. The pedagogical element thus lies in taking advantage of the shock and the associated epiphany as a learning strategy, and utilizing this as an active part of the learning process, which can also help to support the students in achieving the academic goals of their sociological studies. If this succeeds, then the therapy – here to be understood as collective catharsis – is near at hand, quite simply because literature like Houellebecq's almost cries out for some kind of collective action. To put it in a slightly provocative manner: if Houellebecq's analyses do not get the students to open their eyes, get moving and respond, they must surely be buried in a deep, all-encompassing duvet.

Conclusion

A central aim of this chapter has been to demonstrate that the imparting of sociological knowledge can (and should) take advantage of a number of sources of inspiration and a wide range of diverse pedagogical tools which, in their separate ways, can help to identify and communicate information about social reality and human life to a wide audience. Irrespective of whether the material drawn upon consists of literature, films, performances, shock effects, etc., we base the use of these types of material on the assumption that, in their separate ways, they can each create an educational space in which we, as researchers, educators and teachers, can consciously enter into a dialogue with our sociological knowledge, art and the poetic imagination, as well as with the audience. It is the ability of art and fiction to illuminate and communicate our sociological investigations, categorizations, concepts and theories that forms the basis of interaction with the audience in the communicative situation, and it is our ability to creatively use these sources in close interaction with the audience that provides a range of opportunities for communication, learning and the creation of new insights. The communication of sociological knowledge is itself a form of performance, which means we must be aware of our communication tools, while recognizing that this performance is dependent on dialogue with the audience.

With this recognition, a more poetic approach to the communication of science in general, and to teaching in particular, will undoubtedly make these more empathic, subtle and precise, but also more fun and interesting. There should be no doubt that our interest primarily lies in the academic benefit, and thereby in the quality of the potential for sociological communication, that can be derived from providing sociological teaching and pedagogy with a poetic shot in the arm. It is also our experience that the audience (including students) can be inspired in their sociological perspective by a form that invites poetry in, and makes it a part of their independent academic interpretations and reflections.

We are extremely – almost painfully – aware that this creative way of thinking about and communicating sociology encompasses both possibilities and limitations. We have described some of the possibilities above, but there will also be information which is difficult to convey through the use of the poetically-inspired tools presented here. We are not arguing for the rejection of conventional forms of teaching and communication, but only for the exploration and testing of a range of more poetically-inspired forms of communication, to examine their potential in communicating various forms of sociological knowledge. This, however, demands sociological insight, perspective and, not least, the courage to break with conventional thinking about how sociological knowledge can be disseminated to an audience, and it requires the identification and analysis of the potential and possibilities of these many creative forms of presentation. In conclusion, we would also like to invite and encourage other sociologists to take the risk – or perhaps rather seize the opportunity – to cross the boundaries of conventional forms of teaching and learning, and to explore and experiment with new pathways in a more creative sociological practice.

Translated from Danish by Billy O'Shea

References

Anwary, A. (2003): "Teaching About South Asian Women Through Film". *Teaching Sociology*, 31(4): 428-40.
Bagley, C. (2008): "Educational Ethnography as Performance Art: Towards a Sensuous Feeling and Knowing". *Qualitative Research*, 8(1): 53-72.
Bauman, Z. (1992): *Mortality, Immortality and Other Life Strategies*. Cambridge: Polity Press.
Bauman, Z. (1993): *Postmodern Ethics*. Oxford: Blackwell.
Becker, H.S., M.M. McCall, L.V. Morris and P. Meshejian (1989): "Theatres and Communities: Three Scenes". *Social Problems*, 36(2): 93-116.
Beránková, E. (2006): "Les fureurs d'un physicien quantique – Quelques remarques sur le style de Michel Houellebecq". *Verbum Analecta Neolatina*, 8(1): 101-8.
Berg, E. Ziskind (1992): "An Introduction to Sociology Using Short Stories and Films: Reshaping the Cookie Cutter and Redecorating the Cookie". *Teaching Sociology*, 20(4): 265-9.
Bruner, J. (1986): *Actual Minds, Possible Worlds*. Cambridge, MA: Harvard University Press.
Corbett Jr., R. (1994): "'Novel' Perspectives on Probation: Fiction as Sociology". *Sociological Forum*, 9(2): 307-14.
Coser, L. (ed.) (1972): *Sociology Through Literature*. Englewood Cliffs, NJ: Prentice-Hall.
Deflem, M. (2007): "Alfred Hitchcock and Sociological Theory: Parsons Goes to the Movies". *Sociation Today*, 5(1) – online version.
Demerath III, N.J. (1981): "Through a Double-Crossed Eye: Sociology and the Movies". *Teaching Sociology*, 9(1): 69-82.
Denzin, N.K. (2003): *Performance Ethnography: Critical Pedagogy and the Politics of Culture*. Thousand Oaks, CA: Sage Publications.
Diken, B. and C. Bagge Laustsen (2008): *Sociology Through the Projector*. London: Routledge.
Dobson, S. (2010): "Sociologiske epifanier – at indkredse det eksistentielle og det monumentale", in *Den poetiske fantasi: Om forholdet mellem sociologi og fiktion*, edited by R. Antoft, M. Hviid Jacobsen and L.B. Knudsen. Aalborg: Aalborg Universitetsforlag.
Downs, R.B. (1983): *Books That Changed the World*. New York: Mentor.
Eisner, E.W. (1997): "The Promise and the Perils of Alternative Forms of Data Representation". *Educational Researcher*, 26(6): 4-10.
Faggen, R. (2002): "Introduction", in K. Kesey: *One Flew Over the Cuckoo's Nest*. New York: Penguin Books.
Goffman, E. (1959): *The Presentation of Self in Everyday Life*. Harmondsworth: Penguin Books.
Goffman, E. (1961): *Asylums*. New York: Doubleday.
Hewitt, R. (1994): "Expanding the Literary Horizon: Romantic Poets and Postmodern Sociologists". *The Sociological Quarterly*, 35(2): 195-213.

Honneth, A. (2003): *Behovet for anerkendelse*. Copenhagen: Hans Reitzels Forlag.
Houellebecq, M. (1998/2001): *Atomised*. London: Vintage Books.
Houellebecq, M. (1994/2002a): *Whatever*. Copenhagen: Borgen.
Houellebecq, M. (2001/2002): *Platform*. London: Vintage Books
Jacobsen, M. Hviid and R. Antoft (2006): "Sociologi og poesi – om affiniteten mellem samfundsvidenskab og skønlitteratur". *Sociologi i dag*, 36(4): 97-130.
Jacobsen, M. Hviid and S. Kristiansen (2006): "Goffmans metaforer – om den genbeskrivende og rekontekstualiserende metode hos Erving Goffman". *Sosiologi i dag*, 36(1): 5-33.
Jones, R.A. (1975): "The Use of Literature in Teaching Introductory Sociology: A Case Study". *Teaching Sociology*, 2(2): 177-96.
Kaysen, S. (1993): *Girl, Interrupted*. New York: Random House.
Lena, H.F. and B. London (1979): "An Introduction to Sociology Through Fiction Using Kesey's *One Flew Over the Cuckoo's Nest*". *Teaching Sociology*, 6(2): 123-31.
Livingston, K. (2004): "Viewing Popular Films About Mental Illness Through a Sociological Lens". *Teaching Sociology*, 31(1): 119-28.
McCall, M.M., H.S. Becker and P. Meshejian (1990): "Performance Science". *Social Problems*, 37(1): 117-32.
Mead, G.H. (1934/1967): *Mind, Self & Society*. Chicago, IL: University of Chicago Press.
Mienczakowski, J.E. (1994): "Reading and Writing Research: Ethnographic Theatre". *National Association for Drama in Education (Australia)*, 18: 45-54.
Mienczakowski, J.E. (1995): "The Theatre of Ethnography: The Reconstruction of Ethnography into Theatre with Emancipatory Potential". *Qualitative Inquiry*, 1: 360-75.
Miller, M.C. (ed.) (1990): *Seeing Through Movies*. New York: Pantheon Books.
Negt, O. (1981): *Sociologisk fantasi og eksemplarisk indlæring*. Copenhagen: Kurasje.
Nietzsche, F. (1910/2006): *The Gay Science*. London: Dover.
Nisbet, R.A. (1976/2002): *Sociology as an Art Form*. New Brunswick, NJ: Transaction Publishers.
Nårgaard, S. and O. Pedersen (1992): *Så selv en sten kan blomstre – om poetisk undervisning*. Århus: Kvan.
Paget, M.A. (1990): "Performing the Text". *Journal of Contemporary Ethnography*, 19(1): 136-55.
Pedelty, M. (2001): "Teaching Anthropology through Performance". *Anthropology & Education Quarterly*, 32(2): 244-53.
Penfold-Mounce, R., D. Beer and R. Burrows (2011): "*The Wire* as Social Science Fiction?". *Sociology*, 45(1): 152-67.
Pescosolido, B.A. (1990): "Teaching Medical Sociology Through Film: Theoretical Perspectives and Practical Tools". *Teaching Sociology*, 18(3): 337-46.
Petersen, A. (2007): *Depression – vor tidsalders vrangside*. Örebro Studies in Sociology, Örebro Universitet.

Petersen, A. and M. Hviid Jacobsen (2012): "Houellebecq's Dystopia – A Case of the Elective Affinity between Sociology and Literature", in *Utopia: Social Theory and the Future*, edited by M. Hviid Jacobsen and K. Tester. Farnham: Ashgate.

Porterfield, A.L. (1957): "Some Uses of Literature in Teaching Sociology". *Sociology and Social Research*, 41(6): 421-6.

Potter, A. (1996): "Review of: *Girl, Interrupted* by Susanna Kaysen". *Teaching Sociology*, 24(2): 244-5.

Prendergast, C. (1986): "Cinema Sociology: Cultivating the Sociological Imagination Through Popular Films". *Teaching Sociology*, 14(4): 243-8.

Richardson, L. and E. Lockridge (1991): "The Sea Monster: An Ethnographic Drama". *Symbolic Interaction*, 13: 77-83.

Richardson, L. and E. Lockridge (2004): *Travels with Ernest: Crossing the Literary/ Sociological Divide*. Walnut Creek, CA: AltaMira Press

Rogers, S. and R.P. Wolensky (1987): *Using Films in Sociology Courses*. Washington DC: American Sociological Association.

Saldaña, J. (2003): "Dramatizing Data: A Primer". *Qualitative Inquiry*, 9(2): 218-36.

Scanlan, S.J. and S.L. Feinberg (2000): "The Cartoon Society: Using *The Simpsons* to Teach and Learn Sociology". *Teaching Sociology*, 28(2): 127-39.

Skåderud, F. (1999): *Uro – en rejse i det moderne selv*. Copenhagen: Tiderne Skifter.

Smith, D.D. (1973): "Teaching Introductory Sociology by Film". *Teaching Sociology*, 1(1): 48-61.

Turner, V.W. and E. Turner (1982): "Performing Ethnography". *The Drama Review*, 26(2): 33-50.

Van de Poel-Knottnerus, F. and J.D. Knottnerus (1994): "Social Life Through Literature: A Suggested Strategy for Conducting a Literary Ethnography". *Sociological Focus*, 27(1): 67-80.

Wellin, C. (1996): "'Life at Lake Home': An Ethnographic Performance in Six Voices: An Essay on Method in Two". *Qualitative Sociology*, 19(4): 497-516.

Chapter 11

Inspiring 'The Methodological Imagination': Using Art and Literature in Social Science Methods Teaching

Julie Seymour

Introduction

It may not be 'a truth universally acknowledged' (Austen 1981: 179), but it does seem to be a prevalent discourse among students, of sociology and of other disciplines, that methods modules are less engaging than other substantive topics (Winn 1995). Undergraduate research methods modules in particular can be viewed by students as abstract and unrelated to the substantive topics which constitute, for them, the discipline of sociology. This view is also sometimes echoed by academic staff who consider their involvement in the delivery of such modules to be a chore rather than a challenge (Saunders 2012). However, there is an emerging tranche of pedagogical discussion through journals such as LATISS (*Learning and Teaching: The International Journal of Higher Education in the Social Sciences*), e-mail discussion lists, edited international volumes (Garner, Wagner and Kawulich 2009) and, in the United Kingdom, conferences held by the Higher Education Academy which aims to develop and disseminate innovations in the delivery of research methods modules. This chapter aims to contribute to this debate by showing how the use of art and literature in such modules can stimulate student involvement but, perhaps more importantly, lead to their greater intellectual understanding of the core principles of critically reading and carrying out social research. For the subject matters of the social sciences are human interactions and processes and researching these empirically, using high quality and systematic methodologies, is core to these disciplines and associated academic programmes. Students need to understand and utilize research methods modules and apply them to specific topics but, to develop as scholars, they also need to be engaged and be enervated by their content.

  The incorporation of artistic materials in social science teaching, particularly in introductory and theory modules to explain basic concepts, is not a new idea. In 1963 the American sociologist Lewis Coser (1963) published *Sociology through Literature: An Introductory Reader* and the US-based pedagogical journal *Teaching Sociology* has featured regular articles on this topic in each subsequent decade (Smith 1973; Special Edition on 'The Uses of Mass Media in Sociology Curricula' 1983; Hill 1987; Hendershott and Wright 1993; Weber 2010). Noticeably, the use of such media in sociology modules tends to be on theoretical (Sullivan 1982) or substantive courses including those concerned with race (Hill 1987; Fitzgerald 1992), technology (Hendershott and Wright 1993) or the sociology of literature (Hegtvedt 1991) rather than those explicitly on the social research process. In the United Kingdom, the use of literature (in particular) for pedagogical purposes is growing in social, political and educational research (Watson 2011) but again seems limited in discussions of the delivery of research methods modules. Drawing on personal experience of teaching research methodology at undergraduate and postgraduate level, I will discuss ways in which the incorporation of cartoons, television adverts, literature and music in such modules can both enliven the delivery of this topic and lead to greater theoretical and analytical understanding on the part of participants of the totality and interrelatedness of the research process.

This chapter will first briefly mention the use of art and literature as sources of data since this is covered more explicitly by other chapters in this volume. Thus television advertisements and songs can be raw material for lectures on artefact/documentary analysis and semiotics. It will then move on to discuss more thoroughly the use of fiction and cartoons as an aid to student understanding of the areas of epistemology, theory, methodology and research techniques, as well as the interlinkages between these elements of the research process. Hence, novels can be recommended to convey and illustrate the mind-set of epistemological positions (such as Pre-Enlightenment, Positivism or Feminism) or to illustrate debates about theoretical positions as in the Positivism 'vs.' Interpretivism debate. Stereotypical cartoons (the scientist, the anthropologist, the feminist) can stimulate discussion of the premises and lay discourses around a range of theoretical paradigms and methodological approaches. Finally there are fictional stories which can be critically compared with research studies to convey the experiences, dilemmas and ethical concerns of some research techniques such as covert ethnography.

Clearly, such literary and artistic material has to be read alongside more academic and methodological literature but the former can be used to enhance topics further and to intrigue students. Concurrently, students will be learning to develop their own critical faculties when engaging with art and literature to examine its expressed and semiotic significance (Sullivan 1982). This chapter then aims to illustrate how an engagement with contemporary literary and art forms can increase student enjoyment of research methods modules, confirm the academic and quotidian relevance of the research process to the social world but also, more importantly, develop students' critical *methodological* imaginations.

Using 'Artistic' Material in the Data Collection Process

The detailed examination of art and literature as a heuristic device to understand the society that produced it is often undertaken within Departments of Arts and Humanities as well as increasingly in media studies, organization and business studies and educational research (Watson 2011). Within an examination of the research technique of documentary (in its broadest sense) and media analysis however, there is scope to engage students on social science methods modules with contemporary forms of such material (Hegtvedt 1991). Other chapters within this volume will interrogate more fully this 'extrinsic approach to literature' (Hegtvedt 1991: 9) but I raise it here as one of the sessions within a methods lecture course which engendered significant student interaction and debate.

Following John C. Scott (1990), documentary analysis is presented as allowing both literal and symbolic interpretations of material. In an example considering the former approach, the annual Party Political Conferences of the largest political parties in the United Kingdom allow a comparative analysis of the key words and phrases in the speeches of the leaders of the three main parties, Conservative, Labour and Liberal Democrats. The recent introduction in some UK newspapers of Wordle diagrams of these speeches (where the key words in a speech are produced in a 'word cloud' where the size of the word reflects its prevalence (Feinberg 2011) has proved particularly useful as students have become accustomed to interpreting such visual presentations and may 'read' them as less dry than a list of numerical occurrences of words in a politician's speech.

This form of literal content analysis can be contrasted with a symbolic reading of advertising material which, almost by definition, will draw more fully on semiotic material (Slater 1998). The use of contemporary television advertisements as data for a Saussurian deconstruction of content can be literally 'eye-opening' for some students and for that reason I will outline an example of an exercise I undertook which, for some of them, constituted the most memorable element of their research methods module.

Using as data, a UK TV advert from the 1990s of the (now recently closed) Sellafield Visitors' Centre at Seascale in West Cumbria, UK, students repeatedly viewed this very short feature. Having outlined John C. Scott's (1990) distinction between intended meaning, received meaning and semiotic interpretations, students actively examined the material three times attempting to 'read' it with these three separate agendas. The advertisement proved exemplary for this purpose. Ostensibly acting as an inducement to attend the Visitors' Centre at the Sellafield Nuclear Site, it also acted as a reassuring message about the work of the company on the site, British Nuclear Fuels Limited. The presentation of the piece was almost synaesthetically whole. Reassuring cadences intoned the training and scientific endeavours of the company while not once utilizing the unsettling word 'Nuclear'. Predominantly blue and green images of the countryside and crystal clear coastal waters interspersed with a regionally appropriate, but also religiously reassuring, sequence of a shepherd with a crook seeking and finding a lost lamb. Male (only) children, in anachronistic 1950s long grey shorts and sweaters, played on nearby unpolluted beaches. The advertisement culminated in the children drawing on the sand the logo of the company in a symbolic representation of the future while the calmingly deep tones of the announcer reassured us about 'BNFL – Where Science Never Sleeps'. Students understood and became engaged with the iterative screenings of the same material whilst often animatedly contesting some of their classmates' interpretations of the data. In this way, the pedagogic points of multiple readings, biographical interpretations and cultural and generational scripts emerged in a discursive and interactive manner. As such, the use of material from popular culture served to convey and illustrate some conceptually difficult material in an inclusive and memorable way.

In addition, to first disassemble the students' expectations of how an academic methods lecture would proceed, this session opened with students entering the lecture theatre to the strains of 'The Flower Duet' by Delibes. They were asked whether they recognized the music and what associations it generated for them. While some cited the opera 'Lakme' as their source of recognition, many cited a UK television advert for British Airways which used this song to convey relaxedness, luxury and – with its classical music associations – 'high' class. Others, more familiar with film soundtracks, mentioned the 1983 vampire movie *The Hunger* which used it in a scene of same-sex seduction while further students name-checked Quentin Tarantino's apparently paradoxical use of this beautifully lyrical music during a brutal scene in which the main female character in the movie *True Romance* is violently beaten up but, equally violently, prevails. Finally, it was recognized, more recently, as being on the CD of classical music released to link into in the sensational success of the online/paperback novel *Fifty Shades of Grey* by E.L. James (2012).

This introduction to the lecture served not only to intrigue students but to also alert them to the way that symbols (visual, aural, oral and tactile) are used to convey messages from both 'high' and 'low' art (Fisher 2001) and, with Proustian resonance, how enduring and effective can be these triggers. Having shown how artistic materials were used to convey and practice a particular research technique, this chapter will now show how they can also be used in teaching to explicate and illustrate underlying theories and concepts in research methods.

Use of Art and Literature Sources to Understand the Elements of the Research Process

A second, less usual, way of using art and literature in research methods modules is to recommend them alongside academic and methodological readings to explain to students component elements of the research process. This section will discuss the use of fiction, television programmes and cartoons as an aid to student understanding of the areas of epistemology, theory, methodology and research techniques, as well as the interlinkages between these discrete parts of the research endeavour (Maynard 1994; Hesse-Biber 2007).

Introductory lectures to first year undergraduate modules stress that social research is a process which incorporates theoretical or epistemological underpinnings, methodological approaches and data gathering and analysis techniques (O'Connell Davidson and Layder 1994; Gilbert 2008). Each element of the process is necessary for the work to be considered academic social research (Gilbert 2008) and each element feeds into and off the two others (Figure 11.1).

Subsequent lectures explore in more depth epistemology, methodology and data techniques and while the number of research methods books which can be recommended to accompany this stage of the module are legion, the use of additional non-academic material can often serve to consolidate or reinforce learning and comprehension around these essential and interrelated concepts, as outlined below.

Epistemology/Theory
(Novels, Science Fiction, Cartoons, TV)

Techniques
(Media Adverts, Music, Fiction)

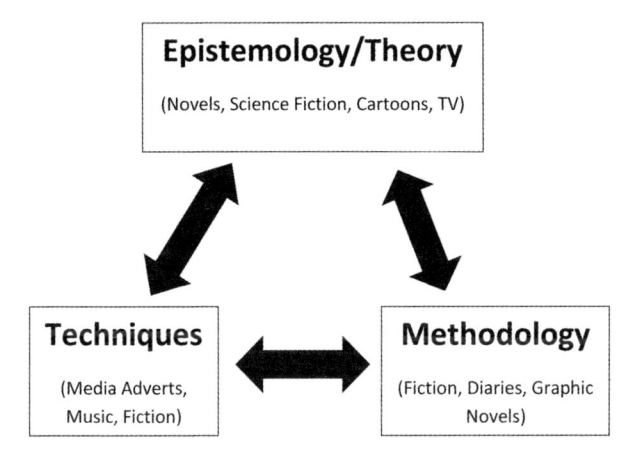

Methodology
(Fiction, Diaries, Graphic Novels)

Figure 11.1 The Components of the Social Research Process and Relevant Non-Methodological Material

Epistemology

In addition to the word itself, students sometimes struggle with the concept of epistemology or the investigation into the 'rules on what constitutes legitimate knowledge and what criteria establish knowledge of social or natural reality as adequate or valid' (Ramazanoglu and Holland 2002: 12). In the relevant lecture, the use of a prop from everyday life, such as a beach ball, can be used to suggest that the questions that may be asked of it differ with the position and interests of the questioner, as follows:

> Parent: Is it safe to be sucked?
> Materials Engineer: What is the strength of the plastic?
> Designer: What colour is it?

Yet it can take time for students to appreciate the manner in which mind-sets can vary and the extent to which we are ourselves still largely socialized into an Enlightenment approach that privileges science. As Janice W. Pascal and Grace A. Brown (2009: 72) say we need to reveal the 'embedded assumptions' in research methods. It can be helpful then to recommend novels which are staged in times and places where the protagonists' epistemological grounding is very different from those of a 21st century Western scholar (Negash 2004). Reading lists can include novels and science fiction recommendations which convey and illustrate such fundamental differences in lifeworlds.

Among these is included *The Name of the Rose* by the scholar Umberto Eco (1983) a pre-Enlightenment story of heresy, murder and mediaeval semiotics. In this novel, the 14th Century Benedictine abbey setting conveys intricately a period of European history during which it was believed by many that all knowledge in the world was already known and should only be made available to particular learned elites; what Theresa Colletti (2009) has described as a literary example of 'subaltern suppression'. Eco compares the deductive reasoning of the novel's main protagonist, William of Baskerville with the 'apocalyptic' thinking of the abbey's Librarian (Ford 2000). While the former considers knowledge should be extended, the latter believes it is static and should be preserved, not increased or transformed (Ford 2000: 101-3). In this way, the author exemplifies the way in which epistemological standpoints construct and are reflected in individuals' historical, political and religious positions.

Similarly, recommending Lindsey Davis' series on Marcus Didius Falco the 'Roman Detective' (2000) may again clarify this concept for students as, for Peter Hunt (2000: 32), the figure of the detective is the ideal narrator of a novel where 'a different world and mentality must be elucidated without the intrusion of patent lectures on social or cultural history'. The Falco novels set in the Roman Empire around 70-74 AD conjure up a society in which war and cruelty were valorized and brutality seen as an appropriate component of the rule of Law. While allowing students to consider contemporary comparisons, it also provides a fictional example of the epistemological position required to enact the violent exercise of sovereignty and of discipline on the body which occurred prior to the 'power of mind over mind' which Michel Foucault (1977) described as emerging with panoptical surveillance.

Such immersion in temporally and epistemologically varied narratives serves to make transparent to students the extent to which worldviews are essentially 'habits of thought' (Colletti 2009). For, as Peter Bondanella says in his review of Eco's novels, 'understanding a mind from the past involves clearing our own minds of any contemporary ideology and allowing the past to speak in its own language with its own technical terms and with its own ideology' (Bondanella 1997: 10). This requirement of epistemological transfer (and presumably return) then means that students are more attuned to the extent to which their own contemporary mindset is a socially constructed and 'historically circumscribed 'truth'' (Bondanella 1997: 10), and they should then appreciate more fully the concepts of discourse and epistemology. Crucially here, while most of the characters in such novels are fictional, the settings are historically and culturally accurate (Bondanella 1997; Hunt 2000; Ford 2000; Colletti 2009) thus serving as genuine examples to students of pre-existing societies. Sometimes however, as an aid to comprehension it can be useful to suggest that students extrapolate sociological concepts to their farthest point to imagine societies which have not yet come into being; essentially to enter the world of science fiction.

To pedagogically develop the impact of different epistemological standpoints on the subsequent formulation of research questions and ways of seeking sociological (and other) knowledge, science fiction can be cited alongside methodological textbooks. Here the particular case of the *Foundation Trilogy* by Isaac Asimov may coalescence with the wider interests of undergraduates. In the opening novel *Foundation* (1953: 16), Asimov describes in detail a society founded on the positivist tenets of the statistical science of 'psychohistory' which seeks to mathematically calculate 'the reactions of human conglomerates to fixed social and economic stimuli'. Here the protagonists calculate algorithms of human behaviour for many centuries into the future in an attempt to predict and engineer the nature of the society which will emerge. This fictional development of Auguste Comte's Science of Society – which sought to develop laws that explain the operation of social forces and provide an understanding of, and guide to, social change – clearly illustrates his famous comment *prevoir pour pouvour* (to predict is to be able to control) (Comte 1896/2000: 27). Notably, this novel is also used in organizational studies to discuss organizational theory and the role of the metanarrative (Phillips and Zyglidopoulos 1999). Such novels, particularly with the licence inherent in science fiction, can be useful in showing how, if followed to the extreme endpoint, theoretical positions can obscure the extent of both structure and agency that occurs in social life.

Science fiction can also be referenced to alert students to the emphasis on different social categories in epistemological positions and how this has led to a number of critical research approaches such as: feminist research, critical race and ethnic minority research and disability research (O'Connell Davidson and Layder 1994). Early *Star Trek* programmes featuring civil war between factions whose faces were half white and half black on different sides, or societies which censored heterosexual love, may lack the nuances we expect of contemporary social commentary in the media but their fantastic premises serve to emphasize the socially constructed nature of difference. Likewise, my methodological reading list contains the novel *The Left Hand of Darkness* by Ursula le Guin (1997). In this exploration of a world where gender categories are transitory, transmutable and interactive, Le Guin (the daughter of writer and anthropologist parents and a novelist of considerable ethnographic sensibilities) leads the reader to ponder both the arbitrary but extraordinarily persistent nature of divisions based on social characteristics and the lack of 'flexible boundary systems' (Sawhney 1995) which exist in contemporary terrestrial societies.

While dealing with imagined worlds, the science fiction examples cited above serve as a simultaneous reminder to students of the way in which authors (and researchers) are a product of their own epistemological, temporal and political standpoints (Negash 2004). This is illustrated by Asimov's post-war concern with science and technology, the writers' of the American TV series *Star Trek* focus on race relations and le Guin's centring of a feminist agenda in the late sixties. These topics can be linked with contemporaneous research foci such as Huw Benyon

(1973) on Fordism, Robert Blauner (1972) on *Racial Oppression in America* and Ann Oakley on housework (1974).

Finally, in this section on explicating the role of epistemology in research methods modules, Jose-Antonio Farfan et al. (2009) remind us of the importance of culturally responsive research methods and the need for the recognition of the heterogeneity of students. They discuss the requirement of engaging with what they call, in the UK context, 'non-traditional students' which incorporates those drawn from the widening participation agenda and those from 'national and ethnic cultural groups' (Farfan et al. 2009: 205).

Such responsiveness includes a recognition of the varied familiarity with literary and cultural 'canons' (of both 'high' and 'low' art) and acknowledgement of diverse epistemological standpoints. This can be illustrated to students by the recommendation of the work of Japan's 'Queen of Crime' Natsuo Kirino. As with other female writers in this genre, 'detective fiction by women was as much about the society in which these women live as it is about creating an entertaining mystery' (Seaman 2004: 185). Kirino's novel *Out* (2004) was described on its sleeve by the *New York Times Book Review* as 'a potent cocktail of urban blight, perverse feminism and vigilante justice'. A more sociological reading reveals it to be a novel of stark social exclusion based variously on gender, class, ethnicity and nationality and one which also explains, to a UK sensibility, the cultural importance of shame as a key foundation of Japanese social interaction and behaviour. As such, it allows the discussion of the concept of ontology or 'theory of being or existence' (Maynard 1994) and how this is culturally, historically and spatially as well as biologically constructed. Students can be allowed to ponder on the extent to which specific ontologies combine with epistemological foundations to impact on the co-production of research with research participants and to introduce the notion of the reflexive practitioner which will be developed further in lectures on methodology. Reference to actual accounts of such ontological and epistemological disjunctures in research endeavours can then be investigated. These include Catherine K. Riessman's (1991) response to feminist researchers regarding the situation in interviews 'When Gender is not Enough' or Kathryn Anderson and Dana C. Jack's (1991: 14) recognition of the former's return to culturally specific (but methodologically problematic) 'norms for conversation and interaction' when conducting 'insider' research with rural farming women in the American Mid-West.

Farfan et al.'s (2009) timely call for cross-cultural research methods, with its reminder of the variation in the underpinnings with which students approach a course, leads to the next section in which the teaching of the contrasting approaches to social theory which inform the research process is shown to benefit from the use of examples from art and literature.

Theory

As part of a research methods module, academic staff convey that 'theory should drive the research process from beginning to end providing a framework for action and for understanding' (Kawulich 2009: 37). They explain how different theoretical perspectives are rooted in specific epistemological underpinnings, how this leads to varying questions being asked by researchers about the social world which then have to be answered using evidence from suitable data which are collected using a range of appropriate techniques. Such theoretical perspectives are usually exemplified by the paradigms of positivism, interpretivism, critical sociology and postmodernism (O'Connell Davidson and Layder 1994). While these authors explicate these approaches in a particularly clear way, the initial introduction of students to these complex paradigms can be aided by the use, once again, of novels and, as I shall show later, cartoons.

The recommended reading list for the theory element of my introductory research methods module contains both methods textbooks and the 1974 novel *Zen and the Art of Motorcycle Maintenance: An Inquiry into Values* by Robert M. Pirsig. The latter is particularly useful when outlining the contrasting theoretical positions of positivism and interpretivism (it has also been used by Anne Hendershott and Sheila Wright (1993) to discuss the sociology of technology and concepts of alienation). This book is both an autobiographical account of a motorcycle journey taken in the late 1960s by the narrator with his son (and occasionally friends) and a reflection on the meaning of 'Quality'. Through a series of *chautauqua* or lectures on politics, morality or science, the author presents the apparently conflicting perspectives of objective classical thought and subjective romanticism. *Zen and the Art of Motorcycle Maintenance* outlines the basic concepts of positivism and interpretivism in a manner which may encourage preliminary student reading on the topic. Most usefully, while first appearing to be stressing the 'paradigm wars' between the two approaches, the novel goes on to show how an accommodation can be made between these apparently conflicting theoretical approaches. The book presents the argument that the 'central problem in contemporary Western culture is the dualistic thought process that dichotomises the classic modes of knowing art and science' (Hendershott and Wright 1993: 326). By outlining a potential middle way, Pirsig will hopefully contribute to the students' developing theoretical sophistication in which either/or theoretical standpoints are replaced with a more nuanced understanding of combined approaches which can give rise to research incorporating mixed methods. Prior to this however, students need to understand how methods are related to theoretical positions and the broad divisions between quantitative and qualitative research; cartoons can add to this pedagogic endeavour.

Linking Theory with Methodology

The use of cartoons to display 'ideal types' of the icons associated with positivism, interpretivism and feminism, namely the 'scientist', the 'anthropologist' and the 'feminist' can stimulate student discussion of the premises and lay discourses around different theoretical paradigms and how these lead to contrasting methodological approaches. They can also serve to initiate a consideration of the social construction of identity and labelling and how cartoons graphically display the 'pictures in our heads' which are used to categorise others (Lippman 1922). Cartoonists such as the North American Gary Larson and the artists at the UK comic *Viz* deliberately draw on stereotypical tropes to convey the 'collection of attributes believed to define or characterise members of a social group' (Moyle 2004: 15; Oakes 1994). These attributes can be examined to expose humorously the basic tenets of these theoretical perspectives and the resulting activities which they generate. Hence, in an introduction to positivism, Gary Larson's (1989: 151) image of the scientist – who is usually male, works in a lab wearing a white coat and may often be balding, bearded and wear glasses – can be interrogated for the symbolic messages conveyed about the use of the experimental method involving measurement and the position of the researcher as objective observer. These images could be updated for students with reference to the American comedy TV series about scientists, *The Big Bang Theory*. Here white coats are rarely shown but the mental labour of working through a theoretical physics equation is conveyed via a parody of the physically demanding training sequence in the film *Rocky* through the use of the same anthemic *Eye of the Tiger* backing music.

In comparison, Larson's cartoons of anthropologists show a more equal gender representation and feature researchers who wear shorts and pith helmets and write constantly in notebooks. One significant example, which I use to introduce a discussion of interpretivism and its associated emic qualitative and ethnographical methodologies shows such a figure sitting underground in a warren surrounded by small animals and entering the field note: 'March 5 1984: After several months I now feel that these strange little rodents have finally accepted me as one of their own' (Larson 1989: 156). Finally, the figure of 'Millie Tant', the radical feminist featured in *Viz* magazine can be used to introduce critical research and its associated emancipatory methodologies. This figure is female, angry and sports boots and a short haircut. She signifies the feminist challenge to gendered inequalities and resistance to the social construction of femininity. In keeping with the contemporary view of the potential availability of both qualitative and quantitative methodologies for feminist researchers (Maynard 1994; Hesse-Biber 2007), Millie Tant does not favour a specific form of data collection. Huxley (1998) has discussed the concerns that the presentation of women in *Viz* has evoked and all the stereotypical cartoons mentioned above can be used to introduce Pierre Bourdieu's (1984) concept of symbolic power/violence in language and images alongside the more light-hearted comparison of the embodiment of the three theoretical paradigms.

These cartoons with their visual representations of 'doing' research from within different theoretical perspectives make explicit the link between theoretical positions and methodological approaches. The images of the scientific laboratory or the fieldwork notebook signify the contrasting positions of each paradigm on what constitutes data, the researcher's relationship with those researched and the resulting data collection and analysis techniques which are used. As such, they illustrate to students that the methodological element of the research process is concerned with the 'process and procedure of knowledge production' (Ramazanoglu and Holland 2002). They also convey the relative position of methodology as drawing from theory and contributing to the choices and execution of specific data collection and analysis techniques. These introductory cartoons are then followed up by an in-depth academic exploration of the range of theoretical perspectives and a return to the research methods textbooks.

Techniques

The final element of the social research process consists of the research techniques themselves; that is the 'instruments' used for collecting and analysing data. These techniques are often referred to as methods but, as this can sometimes cause confusion for students due to the similarity with the word methodology, many use the former term (Hesse-Biber 2007). There are an extremely large number of research methods textbooks which outline the use and practice of data gathering techniques such as surveys, interviews, participant observation and documentary analysis as well as more innovative techniques involving visual materials, on-line interactions and walking interviews. In addition to this academic literature, fictional accounts can bring this, sometimes manual-like, textbook material to life. Novels can be critically read alongside research studies to convey the experiences, dilemmas and ethics of some research techniques.

An example frequently used in this way to introduce the issues relating to covert ethnography is *Imaginary Friends* (1967) by Alison Lurie. This novel, featuring a pair of sociologists who research covertly the dynamics of a group proclaiming the end of the world ('The Truth Seekers'), is widely believed to draw on Leon Festinger et al.'s (1956) study *When Prophecy Fails: A Social and Psychological Study of a Modern Group That Predicted the Destruction of the World*. Through Lurie's academic protagonists, the experienced McMann and the novice Zimmern, the difficulties of access, recording of field notes and relational issues with key contacts are all made transparent. Several times, the younger Zimmern is shown to be trying to adhere to a 'model' of pure research technique which is adapted and slightly ridiculed by the more pragmatic McMann. In this way, the novel allows students to consider the extent to which situations in the field require spontaneous adjustments to proscribed methods of data collection and, in particular, when ethical guidelines need a fluid interpretation (Bulmer 2001). That *Imaginary Friends* does this in a vivid and engaging way is shown by the fact that it is cited in more than 50 academic papers on pedagogic issues and the campus novel. The novel can then be compared with similar 'undercover' ethnographic research such as Nigel Fielding's (1981) study of the National Front or Simon Winlow's more recent exploration of the culture of nightclub bouncers *Badfellas* (2001).

A second artistic resource I recommend to enable students to contemplate the ethnographic issues of groups, boundaries and symbols of belonging is the beautifully illustrated 'silent' graphic novel *The Arrival* by Shaun Tan (2007). Through the use of drawings only (there is no text) the author powerfully conveys the strangeness of moving to a new land and culture. By depicting fantastic creatures and imaginative symbols which, by definition cannot be interpreted by the reader, he conveys the confusion, frustration and fear involved in learning to understand an unknown social world as well as the affirming impact of small acts of kindness by new acquaintances. This moving book can lead to discussions of the task of the ethnographer in grasping the 'symbolic world' of the society which their research is trying to understand and convey (Fielding in Gilbert 2001: 14). It also allows a comparison between the intellectual empathy of Max Weber's 'verstehen' and the assimilative but methodologically problematic behaviour of 'going native' (Fielding in Gilbert 2001: 148-9). The emotional impact of this graphic novel is a suitable reminder to students (and those who teach them) that social research is not some kind of academic exercise which takes place separately from 'real life'. It describes and theorizes people's social realities and quotidian activities and for researchers is also their work life.

Some students may be uncomfortable with the use of fictional material purporting to be from the researcher's point of view but this novel can be discussed instructively as being on the continuum of publications about methodology in which the researcher's voice is variously present and the socially constructed 'truth' of fieldwork accounts is acknowledged (Anderson and Jack 1991). Fictional novels may be at one end of this continuum but it can include autobiographies (Mead 1972), fieldwork diaries (the temporally 'infamous' Bronislaw Malinowski diaries 1967) through the more recent 'honest' accounts of conducting research (Shakespeare et al. 1993; Jamieson et al. 2011) as well as the extremely open reflexive methods textbook of Gayle Letherby (2003) to the apparently objective methods textbooks at the other extreme (Oppenheim 1992). This should result in the recognition that all researchers and authors have a personal and intellectual autobiography which influences their choice of topic and theoretical approach (Mauthner and Doucet 2003). This discussion can also serve to introduce to students the contexts in which the use of the subjective authorial standpoint and the academic use of 'I' can be employed in research reports. Indeed, I encourage students on my modules (and the reader of this chapter) to ponder on the literature and studies from which I construct my module reading list and chapter references. They represent my epistemic history, methodological training and practice, and intellectual and non-academic autobiography (Mauthner and Doucet 2003). Drawing from critical research standpoints, gendered topics, participatory methodology and media from (mostly) the last half century of Western popular culture, they represent one temporally bounded and spatially distinct use of illustrative material with which to teach research methods. The bibliography or reading list is then not only a reflection of the academic canon but also a record of a personal literary history.

This chapter has focused mainly on the use of artistic materials as an aid to student comprehension of methodological concepts and the interrelatedness of the social research process. For Michael R. Hill (1987: 39), however, such material, if used appropriately can directly inspire students to carry out empirical investigations. He considers that 'well-chosen novels not only illustrate major sociological insights and act as catalysts for classroom thought experiments but they also motivate subsequent research'.

Dissemination

The role of 'narrative fiction' in dissemination, especially as a rhetorical device, has been addressed by Cate Watson (2011). She describes how her whole-hearted adoption of the 'narrative turn' in the social sciences has led her to present conference papers and seminars as dramaturgical events with data reported as satirical 'Hogarthian scenes' (Watson 2011: 114) in which the audience play (scripted) roles. Such 'stories' in reporting research findings may be one literary step too far for students on an introductory methods module. They can, however, be encouraged to look at the use of descriptive or poetic language in research reports, especially those utilizing ethnography (Clifford and Marcus 1986). They can also be referred to specific authors such as Erving Goffman who are renowned for employing 'literary sensibilities and sociological rhetorics' (Smith and Jacobsen 2010: 119). Indeed, I have been conscious, when writing this piece about using artistic material, of adopting a more literary style especially through the use of adverbs and the employment of the occasional rhetorical flourish (such as that).

Conclusions

Caroline Ramazanoglu and Janet Holland (2002: 1) open their book on feminist research with the statement: 'Methodology is not generally taken to be an exciting area'. It is this perception which presents a challenge to doctoral supervisors and convenors of research methods modules and which has led Mark Garner et al. (2009: 3) to call for the establishment of a 'pedagogical culture' to develop research methods teaching. As part of this development, this chapter has shown that the use of material from arts and literature can be used to engage students and convey the key relevance of methodology to their social science studies. Elliot W. Eisner (1997: 7, here quoted in Watson 2011) also considers that such exemplars can help to 'enlarge understanding' of the concepts being presented. There is, of course, an implied assumption that students will be keen to approach this non-academic material and that it is not the process of reading *per se*, which limits their engagement with such modules. This is addressed to some extent by utilizing a range of media including films, music, TV, cartoons and graphic novels. Yet, in order to aid students to get the most benefit from this non-methodological material, it cannot be simply recommended but rather, space and exercises need to be created on the course for it to be interactively deconstructed. For, as Charlotte D. Fitzgerald (1992: 247) reminds us, academic staff have 'a responsibility to help students develop' critical thinking skills so they can better interrogate the module material. Tuition may be needed in recognizing the role of social structures in fictional work (Hendershott and Wright 1993) and in encouraging students' 'confidence in their ability to apply concepts to new situations and to reason by analogy' (Sullivan 1982: 110).

For, student satisfaction surveys notwithstanding, our role as co-facilitators of learning with students is not simply to be entertaining, it is also to encourage and develop critical academic faculties. Research methods modules are well placed to achieve this. As Martyn Hammersley (2012) notes about this topic: 'what is to be taught is not a set of rules to be simply applied but consists of skills, ways of thinking and intellectual virtues'. We should aim to be working with students to encourage them to become critical readers of all materials, academic and otherwise. By analysing the examples used in methods courses which incorporate artistic materials, students are both learning social theory and methodological skills but also developing their observational acuity and semiotic recognition when encountering non-academic material in their everyday lives. If students complete a research methods module with *just* a knowledge of the relevant academic canon and a grasp of research techniques, then it should be considered only a partial success. They also need to become skilled in 'identifying sociological content in new contexts (Sullivan 1982: 113). To paraphrase Erving Goffman (cited by Verhoeven 1993: 338 in Smith and Jacobsen 2010) we are not training researchers, we are developing scholars. Thus, there is much more to be gained from using art and literature in research methods modules than simply making the transmission of research skills more 'exciting'; there is also the possibility of inspiring, in those attending, 'The Methodological Imagination'.

References

Anderson, K. and D.C. Jack (1991): "Learning to Listen: Interview Techniques and Analysis", in *Women's Words: The Feminist Practice of Oral History*, edited by S. Gluck and D. Patai. London: Routledge.

Asimov, I. (1953): *Foundation*. London: Weidenfeld & Nicolson.

Austen, J. (1981): *The Complete Works*. London: Guild.

Benyon, H. (1973): *Working for Ford*. Harmondsworth: Penguin Books.

Blauner, R. (1972): *Racial Oppression in America*. New York: Harper & Row.

Bondanella, P. (1997): *Umberto Eco and the Open Text: Semiotics, Fiction, Popular Culture*. Cambridge: Cambridge University Press.

Bourdieu, P. (1984): *Distinction: A Social Critique of the Judgement of Taste*. London: Routledge.

Bulmer, M. (2001): "The Ethics of Social Research", in Nigel Gilbert (ed.): *Researching Social Life* (2nd edition). London: Sage Publications.

Clifford, J. and G.E. Marcus (eds) (1986): *Writing Culture: The Poetics and Politics of Ethnography*. Berkeley, CA: University of California Press.

Colletti, T. (2009): "Eco's Middle Ages and the Historical Novel", in *New Essays on Umberto Eco*, edited by P. Bondanella. Cambridge: Cambridge University Press.

Comte, A. (1896/2000): *The Positivist Philosophy of Auguste Comte, Volume 1*. Kitchener: Batoche Books.

Coser, L. (1963): *Sociology Through Literature: An Introductory Reader*. Englewood Cliffs, NJ: Prentice-Hall.
Davis, L. (2000): *One Virgin Too Many*. London: Arrow.
Eco, U. (1983): *The Name of the Rose*. London: Secker & Warburg.
Eisner, E.W. (1997): "The Promise and Perils of Alternative Forms of Data Representation". *Educational Researcher*, 26(6): 4-10.
Farfan, J.-A.F., M. Garner and B. Kawulich (2009): "Bridging Gaps: The Quest for Culturally Responsive Pedagogies in Collaborative Research Methods", in *Teaching Research Methods in the Social Sciences*, edited by M. Garner, C. Wagner and B. Kawulich. Farnham: Ashgate.
Feinberg, J. (2011): *Wordle Home Page*. (Online).
Festinger, L., H.W. Riecken and S. Schachter (1956): *When a Prophecy Fails: A Social and Psychological Study of a Modern Group that Predicted the Destruction of the World*. Minneapolis: University of Montana Press.
Fielding, N. (1981): *The National Front*. London: Routledge & Kegan Paul.
Fisher, J.A. (2001): "High Art versus Low Art", in *The Routledge Companion to Aesthetics*, edited by B. Gaut and D.M. Lopes. London: Routledge.
Fitzgerald, C.D. (1992): "Exploring Race in the Classroom: Guidelines for Selecting the 'Right' Novel". *Teaching Sociology*, 20(3): 244-7.
Ford, J.A. (2000): "Umberto Eco: The Name of the Rose", in *The Detective as Historian: History and Art in Historical Crime Fiction*, edited by R. Browne and L.A. Kreiser Jr. Bowling Green, OH: Bowling Green State University Popular Press.
Foucault, M. (1977): *Discipline and Punish: The Birth of the Prison*. London: Allen Lane.
Garner, M., C. Wagner and B. Kawulich (eds) (2009): *Teaching Research Methods in the Social Sciences*. Farnham: Ashgate.
Gilbert, N. (2008): "Research, Theory and Method", in *Researching Social Life* (3rd Edition), edited by N. Gilbert. London: Sage Publications.
Hammersley, M. (2012): "Is It Possible to Teach Social Research Methods Well Today?". Paper to the Higher Education Academy Social Sciences Teaching and Learning Summit: Teaching Research Methods, Radcliffe House, Warwick Conferencing Centre, University of Warwick, 21-22 June.
Hegtvedt, K.A. (1991): "Teaching the Sociology of Literature through Literature". *Teaching Sociology*, 19(1): 1-12.
Hendershott, A. and S. Wright (1993): "Bringing the Sociological Perspective into the Interdisciplinary Classroom through Literature". *Teaching Sociology*, 21(4): 325-31.
Hesse-Biber, S.N. (2007): "Feminist Research: Exploring the Interconnections of Epistemology, Methodology and Method", in *Handbook of Feminist Research: Theory and Praxis*, edited by S. Hesse-Biber. London: Sage Publications.
Hill, M.R. (1987): "Novels, Thought Experiments and Humanistic Sociology in the Classroom: Mari Sandoz and *Capital City*". *Teaching Sociology*, 15(1): 38-44.

Hunt, P. (2000): "Lindsey Davis: Falco, Cynical Detective in a Corrupt Roman Empire", in *The Detective as Historian: History and Art in Historical Crime Fiction*, edited by R. Browne and L.A. Kreiser Jr. Bowling Green, OH: Bowling Green State University Popular Press.

Huxley, D. (1998): "Viz: Gender, Class and Taboo", in *Because I Tell a Joke or Two: Comedy, Politics and Social Difference*, edited by S. Wagg. London: Routledge.

James, E.L. (2012): *Fifty Shades of Grey*. New York: Random House.

Jamieson, L., R. Lewis and R. Simpson (eds) (2011): *Researching Families and Relationships: Reflections on Process*. Basingstoke: Palgrave/Macmillan.

Kawulich, B. (2009): "The Role of Theory in Research", in *Teaching Research Methods in the Social Sciences*, edited by M. Garner, C. Wagner and B. Kawulich. Farnham: Ashgate.

Kirino, N. (2004): *Out*. London: Vintage Books.

Larsen, G. (1989): *The Far Side Gallery 2*. London: Futura.

Le Guin, U. (1997): *The Left Hand of Darkness*. London: Virago.

Letherby, G. (2003): *Feminist Research in Theory and Practice*. Buckingham: Open University Press.

Lippmann, W. (1922): *Public Opinion*. London: Allen & Unwin.

Lurie, A. (1967): *Imaginary Friends*. New York: Abacus.

Malinowski, B. (1967): *A Diary In the Strict Sense of the Term*, London: Routledge & Kegan Paul.

Mauthner, N. and A. Doucet (2003): "Reflexive Accounts and Accounts of Reflexivity in Qualitative Data Analysis". *Sociology*, 37(3): 413-31.

Maynard, M. (1994): "Methods, Practice and Epistemology: The Debate about Feminism and Research", in *Researching Women's Lives from a Feminist Perspective*, edited by M. Maynard and J. Purvis. London: Taylor & Francis.

Mead, M. (1972): *Blackberry Winter: My Earlier Years*. New York: Simon & Schuster.

Moyle, L. (2004): *Drawing Conclusions: An Imagological Survey of Britain and the British and Germany and the Germans in German and British Cartoons and Caricatures, 1945-2000*. Unpublished PhD thesis. University of Osnabruck.

Negash, G. (2004): "Art Invoked: A Mode of Understanding and Shaping the Political". *International Political Science Review*, 25(2): 185-201.

Oakes, P.J., A.S. Haslam and J.C. Turner (1994): *Stereotypes and Social Reality*. Oxford: Blackwell.

Oakley, A. (1974): *The Sociology of Housework*. Oxford: Martin Robertson.

O'Connell Davidson, J. and D. Layder (1994): *Methods, Sex and Madness*. London: Routledge.

Oppenheim, A.N. (1992): *Questionnaire Design, Interviewing and Attitude Measurement* (2nd Edition). London: Pinter.

Pascal, J.W. and G.A. Brown (2009): "Ontology, Epistemology and Methodology for Teaching Research Methods", in *Teaching Research Methods in the*

Social Sciences, edited by M. Garner, C. Wagner and B. Kawulich. Farnham: Ashgate.

Phillips, N. and S. Zyglidopoulos (1999): "Learning from Foundation: Asimov's Psychohistory and the Limits of Organization Theory". *Organization*, 6(4): 591-608.

Pirsig, R.M. (1974): *Zen and the Art of Motorcycle Maintenance: An Inquiry into Values*. London: HarperCollins.

Ramazanoglu, C. and J. Holland (2002): *Feminist Methodology: Challenges and Choices*. London: Sage Publications.

Riessman, C.K. (1991): "When Gender is Not Enough: Women Interviewing Women", in *The Social Construction of Gender*, edited by J. Lorber and S. Farrell. London: Sage Publications.

Saunders, C. (2012): "Making Methods Matter: Bringing Social Science Methods Teaching Alive with Audio-Visual Interviews with Methodologists". Paper to the Higher Education Academy Social Sciences Teaching and Learning Summit: Teaching Research Methods, Radcliffe House, Warwick Conferencing Centre, University of Warwick, 21-22 June.

Sawhney, S. (1995): "The Jewels in the Crotch: The Imperial Erotic in the Raj Quartet", in *Sexy Bodies: The Strange Carnalities of Feminism*, edited by E. Grosz and E. Probyn. London: Routledge.

Scott, J.C. (1990): *A Matter of Record: Documentary Sources in Social Research*. Cambridge: Polity Press.

Seaman, A. (2004): "Cherchez la Femme: Detective Fiction, Women and Japan". *Japan Forum*, 16(2): 185-90.

Shakespeare, P., D. Atkinson and S. French (eds) (1993): *Reflecting on Research Practice: Issues in Health and Social Welfare*. Buckingham: Open University Press.

Slater, D. (1998): "Analysing Cultural Objects: Content Analysis and Semiotics", in *Researching Society and Culture*, edited by C. Seale. London: Sage Publications.

Smith, D.D. (1973): "Teaching Introductory Sociology by Film". *Teaching Sociology*, 1(1): 48-61.

Smith, G. and M. Hviid Jacobsen (2010): "Goffman's Textuality: Literary Sensibilities and Sociological Rhetorics", in *The Contemporary Goffman*, edited by M. Hviid Jacobsen. London: Routledge.

Sullivan, T.A. (1982): "Introductory Sociology through Literature". *Teaching Sociology*, 10(1): 109-16.

Tan, Shaun (2007): *The Arrival*. London: Hodder Children's Books.

Verhoeven, J.C. (1993): "An Interview with Erving Goffman". *Research on Language and Social Interaction*, 26(3): 317-48.

Watson, C. (2011): "Staking a Small Claim for Fictional Narratives in Social and Educational Research". *Qualitative Research*, 11(4): 395-408.

Weber, C.D. (2010): "Literary Fiction as a Tool for Teaching Social Theory and Critical Consciousness". *Teaching Sociology*, 38(4): 350-61.

Winlow, S. (2001): *Badfellas: Crime, Tradition and New Masculinities*. Oxford: Berg.

Winn, S. (1995): "Learning by Doing: Teaching Research Methods through Student Participation in a Commissioned Research Project". *Studies in Higher Education*, 20(2): 203-14.

Chapter 12

Imagining the Outsiders: Exploring Literary Representations of 'the Other' as Pedagogic Practice

Louise Sturgeon-Adams

> Thou shalt not sit with statisticians nor commit a social science
> W.H. Auden, *Under Which Lyre* (1946)

Introduction

The aim of this chapter is to explore an issue arising from traditional teaching methods within the social sciences which, at its core, aims to address how lecturers can perform a 'balancing act' within their teaching practice. On one hand, the task of the social scientist is to bring order to chaos; to clarify and attempt to explain complex social problems, using theoretical perspectives and research evidence to support these understandings. On the other hand, there has to be an acknowledgement that complex social problems are experienced by individuals in specific contexts, and that these individual experiences can illuminate these problems and provide a level of understanding that a codified social science based approach cannot. This chapter aims to reflect upon this issue as it pertains to current teaching practice, within a particular context, which it is argued, is constructed in such a way as to provide a somewhat stilted version of what brings students to the study of subjects such as sociology and criminology in the first place, which is an interest in, and fascination with, human behaviour within its social context.

The current social context brings with it a number of ideas which compete for our attention. For example, the rise of the 'risk' society and our concern for protection from a range of possible harms (the prevalence of which is often amplified by the popular press) which sits somewhat uncomfortably alongside our desire to understand the lives of those whom we may deem to be very different from ourselves; those we may term 'outsiders'. It is my contention that there is a balance to be achieved, between the focus of social science disciplines (and the kinds of knowledge that they are able to provide, or at least in the way such knowledge is currently presented) with what might be termed the more individual, human, existential experiences which – as the opening quotation by W.H. Auden above indicates – are to be found in alternative forms of knowledge outside the social sciences and their world of statistics, notably in the representations of the self which are found in literature, in which the realm of human experience can be explored and laid bare by opening ourselves to these alternative forms of knowledge, such as the first person narrative. It is argued here that to explore the ways in which social problems are explained and conveyed within such narratives, adds an extra dimension to our understanding of those social problems, and a richness to those understandings that social science itself finds it difficult to convey.

Debates regarding the construction of knowledge are taking place in the field of sociological inquiry. Carol Smart (2009) cites the example of John Law (2006) 'who has been critical of sociological methods for the way in which they turn 'mess' into order. He has argued that everyday life is both messy and complex and, as a consequence, methods must be developed which can both grasp the mess and then find ways to represent messiness without forcing a coherence and kind of logic on to lived experience' (Smart 2009: 2). A similar point has been argued by Margaret S. Malloch (2007) in terms of expanding the criminological imagination which 'requires the development of different forms of knowledge, different experiential accounts, which may challenge the status quo and provide a different way of looking at social life' (Malloch 2007: 247). This debate is primarily focussed on the ways in which research is undertaken and represented, and yet it is argued here that it applies equally to our teaching endeavours if we hope to foster depth of understanding in our students, of the essential 'messiness' of what we are attempting to understand and explain.

This chapter, therefore, aims to bring together several strands of discussion which are applied to an example of teaching practice, focussed on a particular undergraduate module entitled 'Drugs and Drug Use'. Firstly, the chapter argues that a problem can arise within the traditional model of teaching practice, in which creative approaches to exploring knowledge are difficult to incorporate, and something of value is therefore absent – which, it is argued here can tell us something essential about the human experiences we are attempting to explore. It is then suggested that developments in different ways of approaching and understanding pedagogy allow for a more flexible approach to teaching practice, which entails viewing the task of the educator from a different perspective, which, in turn, enables exploration of alternative sources of knowledge, for the ways in which they can deepen our understanding of social problems.

This chapter therefore argues that what is required is a pedagogic model which enables and encourages an exploration of existential issues, within which students are encouraged to explore, in this particular case, first person narratives of drug use in order to address the visceral and human elements of such behaviour. It is in literature that vivid and powerful examples of such existential narrative accounts can be found, and an example of such will be explored here; Thomas De Quincy's *Confessions of an English Opium Eater* (1821/1971) which was first published in 1821 was the first (and arguably most influential) account of drug use in literature. The chapter will explore the ways in which drug use is discussed, explored and explained in this highly individual and personal account that exists in a different sphere from the traditional social science approach, but which can bring the human experience of drug use to life in a way that other forms of knowledge cannot.

Identifying the Problem

Current pedagogic practice, especially in the traditional lecture/seminar format of Higher Education, arguably focuses upon a 'transmission' model of teaching and learning whereby 'pre-existing fixed ideas are transmitted to the learner' (Kolb and Kolb 2005: 5). Within this model, the academic is viewed as 'the expert' or 'the sage on the stage' and the learners are viewed as the recipients of this wisdom and knowledge. Such an approach can achieve a range of learning outcomes, but it has a number of limitations. The discussion in this chapter arises from personal experience of developing and teaching an undergraduate module entitled 'Drugs and Drug Use' to B.A. Criminology students, within such a model. The aim of the module is to problematize the notion of 'drugs' and, in some sense, to critique and challenge popular discourse about the ways that drugs and drug users are currently understood. In teaching the module I have become aware that most students come to the module with some fairly fixed preconceived notions about what drugs are (for example, they do not generally view alcohol as a drug) and the effects that they have (for example, they tend to have firm ideas about drug users as 'crackheads' or 'junkies' with no job, poor health and an accompanying compulsion to commit crime to feed their habit, a view which does not speak to the reality of a wide range of drug use within our society). What the students always have in common, however, is a fascination with the subject, which is what brings them to the module in the first place, and that this fascination is based to a large degree on what they perceive as the 'otherness' of drug using behaviour that is, in that it is concerned with experiences that most of the students cannot imagine themselves having. Experience of teaching the module over several years has shown that it is difficult to maintain this level of fascination over the course of a semester, and that this seems somehow to be related to the 'academicization' process in which the subject as a whole must necessarily be broken down into topics which are then explored in detail, within the traditional pedagogic model.

So, for example, this particular module begins by examining definitions of drugs (in which students begin to question what is and is not a 'drug'); it explores how certain drugs have come to be outlawed; it moves on to look at measuring the extent of drug use (which is problematic due to the illicit nature of drug use and so statistics tend to focus on crime); ways in which drug use has been explained are explored (the key theories being social learning theories and disease models); the complex links between drugs and crime are then explored in some detail (by means of statistical associations and explanatory theories). All of these topics are necessary elements of a module which seeks to encourage depth of understanding among the students, within a critical framework, but there is a significant weakness in this pedagogic approach, and that is that it does not seem to speak directly to the fascination that brought the students along to the module in the first place. It could be argued that the traditional pedagogic approach is essentially reductionist in nature, in attempting to break 'the drug problem' down into its constituent parts, and providing evidence for the ways in which we might understand those constituent parts, but in doing so the subject itself is in danger of becoming bland, and therefore losing something of the original enthusiasm of the students. What such an approach does not do, in other words, is to speak to the issue of drugs as an existential issue, an endlessly complex human issue, one in which all of human experience can be located – from joy to misery and beyond. There is a lingering sense, at the end of each delivery of the module, of unrealized promise, which could also be characterized as a failure of imagination.

There is no doubt that drug use is seen as an increasing social problem. Undergraduate students (studying social sciences in general, and criminology in particular) come to the study of drug use accompanied by all the social and cultural associations with having been exposed to various ideas about the nature of this problem, one that is so serious that it is in need of 'almost constant attention' (Barton 2003: 24). One of the key areas that students have been exposed to is the popular press, in which drug use has often been sensationalized and glamorized (examples of this often arise from reporting of the lives of celebrities such as Amy Winehouse and Pete Doherty). Indeed, it has been said that 'exaggeration, distortion, inaccuracy, sensationalism; each of these labels has been consistently applied to the reporting of drug related issues in the print and other media over the past 40 years and beyond' (Coomber et al. 2000: 217). In addition to this, is the popular conception that drugs are linked inexorably with crime (in the increasingly amplified mantra of the unquestioned 'fact' that 'drugs cause crime').

The task for a lecturer in the field of criminology is to enable students to begin to disentangle these ideas and begin to question their origins and authenticity by exploring the range of evidence that is available. In some ways, it could be argued that criminology is uniquely placed for such an undertaking, given that 'crime' itself is viewed as a set of socially constructed categories, in which 'the concept of crime is meaningful only in terms of certain acts being prohibited by the state, and a problem can only be a problem to somebody' (Cohen 1971: 17). This is particularly apposite when applied to drugs, given that a 'substance's meaning or reality, its capacity to attract or repel, varies according to the cultural context in which it is placed' (McDonald 1994: 11). It is on this premise that the module upon which this discussion is based is constructed. When it comes to pedagogic practice, however, it begins to feel as though something of value has been left unexplored, resulting in a vague sense, at the end of each delivery of the module, of dissatisfaction at the levels of interest maintained and inspired in each student group. This has led to questioning the way in which this module is structured, and by extension, to explore ways in which it could be different. The notion of reflective practice can be instructive here, in undertaking such an examination, where reflective practice is taken to be a willingness to subject every action and thought both to reflection *in action* and self-respectful effective reflection *upon action* (Schön 1983). It has also been described as 'a process of learning and developing through examining our own practice, opening our practice to scrutiny by others, and studying texts from the wider sphere. It is a focusing closer and closer' (Bolton 2001: 4). It is within such a model that the author's current practice is explored.

Of central importance here is the fact that the module under discussion was (despite several years of teaching experience), the first module constructed entirely by the author of this chapter. Herein, however, lies a problem which is not readily addressed within academic teaching practice, and which relates to relative inexperience of constructing modules:

> When a practitioner makes sense of a situation he perceives to be unique, he *sees* it *as* something already present in his repertoire. To see *this* site as *that* one is not to subsume the first under a familiar category or rule. It is, rather, to see the unfamiliar, unique situation as both similar to and different from the familiar one, without at first being able to say similar or different with respect to what. The familiar situation functions as a precedent, or a metaphor, or ... an exemplar for the unfamiliar one. (Schön 1983: 138)

In other words, the novice at module construction looks to what they have already learned about such a task which, in the academic sphere arises, on the whole, from personal experience of the ways in which academic subjects have been presented to them. This is based upon experiences they themselves had as students, as well as on learning from more experienced colleagues. It is argued here, that learning from experience, within the academic sphere, guides the novice towards employing 'the 'transmission' model on which much current educational practice is based where pre-existing fixed ideas are transmitted to the learner' (Kolb and Kolb 2005: 5). It is within this model that the module was originally developed, given that it was arguably the only model that I was aware of, or had been exposed to. The stated aims of the module, as originally constructed, are as follows:

1. To introduce students to the application of a range of social science concepts to the issue of 'the drug problem', drug-using behaviour and the range of available responses.
2. To examine the nature and extent of 'the drug problem' employing a range of empirical data.
3. To explore the range of theoretical perspectives used to explain drug-using behaviour.
4. To examine the links between drugs and crime.
5. To explore the range of responses that has been employed historically.
6. To examine current responses to what is seen as a significant social problem.

Experience of having delivered the module over several years has led to a more questioning stance regarding these aims. In many ways, they are perfectly sensible, in that they address aspects of what we would commonly call 'the drug problem', but reflecting on those aims with the benefit of experience, the first question that springs to mind is; where are the human beings to whom we are necessarily referring when we discuss aspects of 'the drug problem'? This issue speaks directly to the sense of dissatisfaction felt at the end of the delivery of the module, whereby it is felt that something of value has not been realized; it would seem that human beings and their experiences are missing – in other words, precisely that aspect of the issue that brought students to the module in the first place. Shad Maruna and Amanda Matravers have argued for the value of the single-person case study within criminology on the grounds of 'the complexities, the conflicts, the contradictions, the insecurities and confusions that all of us struggle with as vulnerable, sensitive, emotional beings', and argue that such complexity has been 'replaced by a sort of 'stick figure' of the over-socialized individual or the rational actor' (Maruna and Matravers 2007: 430). In other words, it could be said that such a model almost primes the students for disappointment. Alongside this realization of having identified a gap in the knowledge that is being conveyed in this particular module is the identification of the ways in which pedagogic practice is developing, which attempt to view pedagogy from a much more humanistic perspective than has traditionally been the case with what has been described as the transmission model. Such developments have arisen from the realm of online learning, in the main, but they are instructive here in the sense that the focus on the place of the student in the learning process is seen from an alternative perspective. It has been said that '[c]onstructivist theorists do not believe that knowledge is a constant for each object or event, but rather that it is constructed by individuals as they interact with an object or event in relation to their past experiences, their beliefs and their current mental structures' (Stacey 2003: 3). The role of the educator is therefore is focussed on 'promoting human interaction' (Salmon 2004: 4) within a constructivist pedagogy and there is a move away from knowledge being viewed as 'structured ... managed ... and hierarchical (Van Dusen 2008: 3) within which critics such as Paulo Freire (2007) have argued that the critical imagination is suppressed. A critical constructivist approach, it is argued, can enable educators to experience an increased sense of freedom to explore the range of knowledge that is open to them, and the ways in which different types of knowledge can illuminate the social problems that they, as social scientists, seek to explore, and to contribute to what David Smith (2006: 361) has referred to as 'the revival of complex subjectivity' within criminology. It is argued here that such an approach can enable educators to move more freely towards education's 'potential to personally, socially and politically reward, enlighten, and empower' (Barton et al. 2010: 24).

A critical constructivist approach can engage more fully than traditional approaches with ideas of what it means to be human in a complex social word, in other words, existential ideas in a world in which (as is argued in the module in question) 'there is no single entity that can be described as the drugs problem and therefore no simple solution' (Davidson et al. 1997: 2). The area of study that has been described here as 'the drug problem' naturally encompasses important areas of human experience, which also often tend to be particularly interesting to younger adults: areas of authority, conformity and rebellion, identity (who am I really if my emotional state and my sense of myself can change profoundly just because my body absorbs a few milligrams of a certain chemical?), escape from social roles and pressures, self-control versus being a slave to constantly renewed desires; in other words, a whole set of tensions which map out what it means to exist. There are a few subjects which have the capacity to travel freely over the entirety of this map, and the 'drug problem' is one of these privileged subjects. It is argued here that literature engages with the issue of drugs on this level of human experience, especially when viewed in the context of the construction of a critical pedagogical approach which 'is underpinned by a myriad of narratives and is an ongoing process which responds to specific contexts and conditions' (Barton et al. 2010: 28).

It is my position here that there exists a general cultural fascination with drugs, their use, and those who take them. It is argued that there is a level of cultural 'hysteria' associated with drugs and their use, which speaks to simplistic understandings of drug-using behaviour which is limited by the public discourse that starts with an aggregate notion of 'drugs', as though the substances all have a key element in common (which, in fact, they do not); as though there is something that makes them inherently different from other (for example, legal) substances, (when there is not); and fails to address a number of factors that underpin and contextualize any debate about 'the drug problem'. Much of the current debate surrounding drugs centres on the 'fact' that 'drugs cause crime' because it is taken as axiomatic that drug users commit crime in order to fund their drug habit (Hammersley 2008). Criminology, as a discipline, has engaged with elements of this debate: for example in exploring the ways in which the media acts against 'a more complex discussion to the detriment of a holistic drugs discourse' (Taylor 2008: 369); in problematizing the distinction between legal and illegal drugs (Boland 2008), and in exploring the highly complex links between drugs and crime (Bennett and Holloway 2005).

However, it is my contention that social science can also seek to engage with the fundamental issues of the experience of being human; exploring experiences of drug use can bring us onto contact with notions of 'coping' with human existence, and indeed raises fundamental questions about such 'coping', and that this is crucially related to society's 'intolerance of different fundamental structures of experience' (Laing 1967: 65). This has been expressed by Jock Young (1971: 99) as a 'clash between groups stressing productive and hedonistic values', but it is more than that: the criminal law, as it applies to a range of illicit substances, both justifies and amplifies our ability to set ourselves against such difference in values. The idea of self-transcendence can be illustrative here, as a means by which we can explore those different fundamental structures, as we attempt to identify what the fundamental nature of 'the drug problem' really is. It is argued here that certain drugs (notably opiates) enable users to forget the past, have no concern for the future and reposition themselves with regard to other people's expectations of them. It is argued that, for this reason 'the normal person simultaneously both covets and castigates the deviant action' (Young 1971: 101).

So, is the perceived diminishing enthusiasm in the students necessarily 'a bad thing'? If this enthusiasm is fuelled by sensationalist stereotypes and media discourse around drugs and their use (and part of the purpose of the module is to question such stereotypes), what has been perceived as diminishing enthusiasm could be seen as a measure of success, that is, that the students have been through a process of learning and development which enables them to question the 'taken for granted' notions of drugs and drug use. However, remaining is the issue of the failure to provide a single, overarching theory of drug use. There is no totalizing theoretical explanation that can answer the question 'why do people take drugs'? Furthermore, there is no totalizing explanation of the question that necessarily follows, which is, given that taking drugs causes some people so many problems, 'why don't they just stop'? Therefore, there is a failure to provide an overarching intellectual idea which allows students to grasp the subject. A broad social science perspective on theories of drug use results in positing a range of theories which attempt to explain drug use, but which fail to answer the fundamental questions adequately. It is argued here that students need to be encouraged to come to their own view regarding the adequacy of the theoretical positions, and that the educator can encourage students to do this within a critical constructivist model of pedagogy which moves from the general to the specific. It is in this context that a literary text, such as *Confessions of an English Opium-Eater*, can stand as a case study, a first person narrative that can address questions of the particular, given that 'narratives are interpretive tools, that constitute a practical but also highly selective, perspective with which we look at the world around us and give it purpose' (Shekedi 2005: 11).

It is instructive to look at the work of Jerome Bruner (1985) here in order to further our discussion. He distinguishes between the positivistic and the narrative modes of thought, which are two distinct ways of knowing and thinking about the social world. Each provides a 'system for ordering experience and constructing reality' (Shekedi 2005: 8). The positivistic mode (characterized by Bruner as paradigmatic or logico-scientific) is 'centred around the narrow epistemological question of how to know the truth' (Bruner 1985: 98). The narrative mode addresses 'the broader and more inclusive question of the meaning of experience' (Bruner 1985: 98) in which reality is constructed. The position of the narrative mode of thought is based upon on the assumption that the complicated and rich phenomena of life are better represented in stories or narratives than in the logico-scientific model, which presents the social world from the assumption that 'the social sciences can and should proceed on the model of the natural sciences, and the closer they can get to this model the better ... they will be' (Smith 2004: 39). Within this model, facts are obtained by meticulous collection and analysis of data. In summary, positivism holds that 'there is a world out there that we can record and we can analyse independently of people's interpretation of it' (May 1997: 11). There are two central reasons, therefore, for our purpose of exploring the issue of drugs and drug use from a narrative, interpretivist perspective; the first of these is that 'the study of narrative is the study of ways humans experience the world' (Grimmett and MacKinnon 1992: 404); the second is that the epistemological stand-point of the constructivist is existential or non-determinist (Shekedi 2005). My argument here is essentially that the transmission approach to teaching begins with a limited, positivistic view of exploring the social world, and what is essential is to broaden this out. It is therefore argued that a critical constructivist view, which incorporates narrative accounts of lived experience, will result in depth of understanding such that 'the poetic imagination in alliance with the sociological imagination may stir the stagnant waters of doxical methodological assumptions in sociology' (Jacobsen and Marshman 2008: 800).

Confessions of an English Opium-Eater

In the opening section of *Confessions of an English Opium-Eater*, Thomas de Quincey states: 'I here present you, courteous reader, with the record of a remarkable period in my life: according to my application of it, I trust that it will prove, not merely an interesting record, but, in a considerable degree, useful and instructive' (De Quincey 1821/1971). The renowned novelist William S. Burroughs stated that De Quincey's *Confessions* was 'the first, and still the best, book about drug addiction', and that 'no other author since has given such a completely analytical description of what it is like to be a junky from the first use to the effects of withdrawal' (Burroughs 2001: 507). Indeed, Burroughs should know; he was himself an opiate addict, his drug of choice being heroin, a derivative of opium (Burroughs' text *Junky* also arguably stands as one of the seminal accounts of drug use, and is eminently worthy of exploration in its own right). It is for its descriptive and analytical power, as well as being a first person narrative, that De Quincey's text has a place within the kind of module that has been outlined in this chapter.

The argument so far throughout this chapter has been, essentially, that literary representations of human experience, as conveyed through the first person narrative, can add something of considerable value to a social science based approach to understanding social problems. This view, in no small part, rests on the assumption that narrative approaches are based upon the epistemological assumption that human beings make sense of random experiences by employing story structures (Bell 2002). It is the social scientist's task then, not to approach literary narrative accounts of individual experience from the perspective of a literary critic; this would result in something other than social science. It is possible however, to read such texts from the perspective of gaining insight and understanding of particular instances of what we have termed 'social problems'. In taking such an approach to reading De Quincey's text, it could be argued that two levels of understanding and meaning arise: the first of these lies in developing an understanding of De Quincey's world as he experienced and understood it; the second lies in the students' incorporation of such meaning and understanding into their own narratives (or understandings of) drug use. In other words, such texts can address a key weakness that has already been identified in this chapter – whatever social science perspectives state about the theoretical explanations for drug use (and we have already discussed student dissatisfaction with the inadequacies of such perspectives) they fail at really answering two key questions: why do people take drugs and why do they not just stop? The first person narrative is able to address such questions in its particular focus on the individual.

In this particular example, as can be seen from the quotation above, De Quincey himself states his hope that reading his *Confessions* will not only prove interesting, but also 'useful and instructive'. The view taken here is that the full and rich account that De Quincey sets before us can indeed provide us with a level of understanding that takes us beyond the range of understandings that social science can provide. Literature can act, and does in this instance, as a means by which we can question common ideas about human experience. Literature often deals with the aberrant and uncharacteristic; there is a resistance to categorization that is a feature of good literature. It is argued here that such work, when incorporated into a constructivist pedagogical approach (in which students are encouraged to develop their own understandings of social problems from a range of possible sources of knowledge, including those outside of traditional social science material), can serve to enrich the students' learning experience, by giving them a window onto another world, in which they are able to address questions of: individual motivation within the social, cultural and historical context; how the individual makes sense of their own experiences within the narrative; how this narrative might compare with other life narratives; contradictions felt concerning particular life events; and feelings of ambivalence and contradiction which are a common feature of the human experience.

An initial approach to a reading of De Quincey with students could be to consider the ways in which it departs from or adheres to student expectations of the ideas, feelings and experiences they might expect to find in drug users' 'confessions' or 'survivor's memoirs', in other words, a drug user's narrative. Students form their ideas and expectations from numerous sources: most commonly they form them from films and television drama, references in popular culture or in media accounts of celebrities, second or third-hand accounts from friends, occasionally from personal experience as a family member or friend of a drug-user, and, less frequently, from personal use of opiates. Of key importance here, for our purposes, is the notion that narratives incorporate experiential and quest-like qualities (Conle 2000), to which students have been regularly exposed. De Quincey, in laying his life bare before us, presents us with a complex version of the quest narrative, thereby addressing the existential elements of drug-using behaviour. Traditionally, within the quest narrative, the hero is led astray by temptation or by false friends. In terms of such a narrative related to addiction, a long-drawn out deterioration in moral character and integrity usually takes place as the addiction takes hold; a state of utter degradation and dependence arises; an epiphany is prompted by a sense of crisis; a process of self-discovery takes place; a slow and painful journey back to the light follows, leading finally to redemption through self-knowledge, strength of will, and possibly the support of others. Along the way there may be, of course, failed attempts to live without the drug – these cycles of relapse are never simply mere repetitions – each one functions to intensify the downward spiral and the addict's awareness of his divided consciousness: the urgency of the need for the drug against the increasing sense of waste, apathy, and worthlessness. Against the neatness of this kind of narrative, De Quincey's *Confessions* are a useful corrective. There are four key areas where student discussion can begin to focus:

1. *The lack of finality*: De Quincey wrote the first edition of *Confessions* in 1821 whilst still having an opium addiction. He states that he has broken 'almost to the last link' the chains of opium addiction which bind him. There has been no neat resolution to his problem. When we read the final edition, we realize that, by 1856, De Quincey has been taking opium for *over 50 years*, and daily for over 40 years.

2. *The effects of opium*: There is no simple account given of the effects of opium. Both the pains and pleasures of opium are considered, but in a manner far removed from a utilitarian cost-benefit analysis, or indeed from the position of the rational actor. Instead, one elides into another. De Quincey, in describing the pleasures of opium, states that, on first taking the drug, he found opium to be 'a panacea ... for all human woes' (De Quincey 1821/1971: 72) and far from dulling the mental faculties 'introduces upon them the most exquisite order, legislation, and harmony' (De Quincey 1821/1971: 72). He contrasts this with wine which 'unsettles and clouds the judgment' and 'disorders the mental faculties'. De Quincey's view was that 'having once tasted the divine luxuries of opium' no man would 'afterwards descend to the gross and mortal enjoyment of alcohol' (De Quincey 1821/1971: 32). Of course, what is not acknowledged here by De Quincey is that he was, in fact, consuming some considerable quantity of alcohol within the laudanum and would therefore now be categorized as a 'polydrug user' (a situation which could only have served to complicate his condition in terms of his intermittent attempts at withdrawing from laudanum).

3. *Ambivalence and self-awareness*: His own pariah status, isolation, and status as a rebel is pitted against De Quincey's own awareness of himself as what he views as an exceptional being. He describes himself as 'the best living Grecian', the biggest opium user (possibly excepting Coleridge), the first person ever to wean himself off opium (almost), an exceptional philosopher who plunges 'fathoms deep' into metaphysical questions. De Quincey almost accords himself heroic status, which perhaps acts a means by which he can allow himself an (almost) fatal flaw. At various points, he makes heroic attempts to cease his use of opium, and yet always returns to it.

4. *Morality*: There is an enormous sense throughout the *Confessions* of frustration, waste, apathy, self-destructiveness and yet no simple idea of self-blame or personal responsibility. De Quincey attempts to evade responsibility by tracing a causal link for his addiction back to his first use of opium (to relieve the 'excruciating pain' of facial rheumatism). De Quincey feels compelled to even trace the origin of this pain to his habit of dousing his face in icy cold water before sleeping. His recreational use of opium continued for almost ten years, until intense stomach pains (traced back to the period immediately after running away from school, when he suffered semi-starvation) are said to force him into regular use.

In *Confessions of an English Opium-Eater* De Quincey provides us with the first written account of a life of what we might now call 'addiction'. In fact, in terms of drug use, it could be argued that De Quincey produced a portrait of the original outsider, in the sense that Howard S. Becker (1963) describes it, whereby 'deviance is *not* a quality of the act the person commits, but rather a consequence of the application by others of rules and sanctions to an 'offender" (Becker 1963 9). The *Confessions* can therefore be read as a narrative case study of deviance, as well as a life laid bare, in which De Quincey posits the question 'how came any reasonable being to subject himself to such a yoke of misery, voluntarily to incur a captivity so servile, and knowingly to fetter himself with such a sevenfold chain?' (De Quincey 1821/1971: 33).

Of particular interest for our purposes is the fact that opium was a legal drug at this time, and was readily available to those who wished to use it. During the nineteenth century, laudanum (tincture of opium, which is opium dissolved in alcohol) was sold openly in pharmacies and marketed as a pain-killer for both adults and children, under such names as 'Mother Bailey's Quieting Syrup' and 'McMunn's Elixir' (Morrison 2011). There were no attempts to control the consumption of opium until the Pharmacy Act of 1868. It was socially acceptable to take opium and its use was widespread as a cure-all for a range of diseases, its use being viewed by the population as not much more than a 'bad habit' (Berridge 1979: 68). De Quincey observes that 'some years ago, on passing through Manchester, I was informed by several cotton-manufacturers, that their work-people were rapidly getting into the practice of opium-eating; so much so, that on a Saturday afternoon the counters of the druggists were strewed with pills … in preparation for the known demand of the evening' (De Quincey 1821/1971: 31). What is more, frequent users of laudanum in De Quincey's time faced social criticism but not legal sanctions. Related to this is the fact that at no point in his narrative does De Quincey have any need to become involved with criminal behaviour in order to be able to buy opium. Opium is readily available to him, and it is relatively cheap. De Quincey's *Confessions* therefore turn our attention away from considerations of crime and legality, and invite us to consider more complex issues of morality within the social context. For De Quincey, and those around him, opium use was 'a moral issue, a question of character' (Morrison 2011: 271). This is an important point; much of our current concern with drugs and their use rests on the assumption that they 'lead to crime'. This was not a relevant frame of reference for De Quincey, and yet he still experienced an enormous sense of social opprobrium. This is illustrated by a strand of self-blame and moral judgement that runs throughout the work. For example, De Quincey states that he brought upon himself 'all the sufferings which I shall have to record' (De Quincey 1821/1971: 34) and indeed, he records many – large sections of the *Confessions* are dedicated to the dreams, many of which were disturbing, that he experienced whilst under the influence of opium. He emphasizes throughout how earnest his attempts to cease the habit were: 'the temptations to it were potent from the first, and the resistance to it, in act or in effect, was earnest to the last' (De Quincey 1821/1971: 30). De Quincey is at pains to stress how others have been unable to cease: 'If opium-eating be a sensual pleasure, and if I am bound to confess that I have indulged in it to an excess … it is no less true, that I have struggled against this fascinating enthralment with a religious zeal, and have, at length, accomplished what I never yet heard attributed to any other man – have untwisted, almost to its final links, the accursed chain which fettered me' (De Quincey 1821/1971: 30).

Conclusion

This chapter has sought to discuss an issue arising from traditional teaching practice, one which is based on a 'transmission' model of knowledge transfer and which adheres strongly to disciplinary boundaries. It was argued that, in the context of a particular module entitled 'Drugs and Drug Use' adherence to such a model can result in a sense of dissatisfaction, which could be characterized, amongst other things, as a failure of imagination. It was argued that an approach based entirely upon such a model, within the social sciences, fails to address an important area for exploration, namely the existential, human element of what it might feel like to be a drug user. The chapter proceeded to argue that it is possible to take an approach to teaching which begins from constructivist principles, which in turn encourage the exploration of a wider range of sources of knowledge which may be able to address some of the weaknesses of a stratified social science based approach to developing knowledge, issues that are being identified more broadly in the social science community, particularly within sociology and criminology.

The chapter then went on to argue that an element of the perceived weakness of a social science based approach to gaining knowledge and understanding, in certain areas, can be addressed to some extent by turning to literary texts as an important source of knowledge. It was argued that certain works are able to stand as narrative case studies that speak directly to the existential, human elements of social problems, in this case, drug use. Thomas De Quincey's *Confessions of an English Opium-Eater* (1821/1971) was used as the example in this particular case, given its status as the first literary account of drug use, many elements of which still resonate today. It was argued that this text is able to address complex questions with which students may struggle for satisfactory resolutions, within the traditional social science model, such as questions of continuing drug use in the face of personal suffering and social opprobrium. A brief analysis of the text was undertaken in order to begin to demonstrate the ways in which such a text is able to enhance our understanding of what is seen currently as a significant social problem.

References

Barton, A. (2003): *Illicit Drugs: Use and Control*. London: Routledge.
Barton, A., K. Corteen, J. Davies and A. Hobson (2010): "Reading the Word and Reading the World: The Impact of a Critical Pedagogical Approach to the Teaching of Criminology in Higher Education". *Journal of Criminal Justice Education*, 21(1): 24-41.

Becker, H.S. (1963): *Outsiders: Studies in the Sociology of Deviance*. New York: Free Press.
Bell, J. Sinclair (2002): "Narrative Inquiry: More Than Just Telling Stories". *TESOL Quarterly*, 36(2): 207-13.
Bennett, T. and K. Holloway (2005): *Understanding Drugs, Alcohol and Crime*. Berkshire: Open University Press.
Berridge, V. (1979): "Morality and Medical Science: Concepts of Narcotic Addiction in Britain". *Annals of Science*, 36: 67-85.
Boland, P. (2008): "British Drugs Policy: Problematizing the Distinction between Legal and Illegal Drugs and the Definition of the 'Drugs Problem'". *Probation Journal*, 55(2): 171-87.
Bolton, G.E.J. (2001): *Reflective Practice: Writing and Professional Development*. London: Sage Publications.
Bruner, J. (1985): "Vygotsky: A Historical and Conceptual Perspective", in *Culture, Communication and Cognition: Vygotskian Perspectives*, edited by J.V. Wertsch. Cambridge: Cambridge University Press.
Burroughs, W.S. (2001): "Trip to Hell and Back", in *Burroughs Live: The Collected Interviews of William S. Burroughs, 1960-199*, edited by S. Lotringer. Los Angeles, CA: Semiotext(e).
Cohen, S. (1971): *Images of Deviance*. Middlesex: Penguin Books.
Conle, C. (2000): "Narrative Inquiry: Research Tool and Medium for Professional Development". *European Journal of Teacher Education*, 23(1): 49-62.
Coomber, R., C. Morris and L. Dunn (2000): "How the Media Do Drugs: Quality Control and the Reporting of Drug Issues in the UK Print Media". *International Journal of Drug Policy*, 11(3): 217-25.
Davidson, N., L. Sturgeon-Adams and C. Burrows (1997): *Tackling Rural Drugs Problems: A Participatory Approach*. Police Research Group Crime Detection and Prevention Series, No. 81. London: Home Office.
De Quincey, T. (1821/1971): *Confessions of an English Opium-Eater*. London: Penguin Books.
Freire, P. (2007): *Pedagogy of the Oppressed*. London: Continuum.
Grimmett, P.P. and A.M. MacKinnon (1992): "Craft Knowledge and the Education of Teachers". *Review of Research in Education*, 18: 385-456.
Hammersley, R. (2008): *Drugs and Crime*. Cambridge: Polity Press.
Jacobsen, M. Hviid and S. Marshman (2008): "Bauman's Metaphors: The Poetic Imagination in Sociology". *Current Sociology*, 56: 798-818.
Kolb, A.Y. and D.A. Kolb (2005): "Learning Styles and Learning Spaces: Enhancing Experiential Learning in Higher Education". *Academy of Management Learning and Education*, 4(2): 193-212.
Laing, R.D. (1967): *The Politics of Experience*. London: Penguin Books.
Malloch, M.S. (2007): "Changing Focus: 'Drug-Related Crime' and the Criminological Imagination", in *Expanding the Criminological Imagination: Critical Readings in Criminology*, edited by A. Barton, K. Corteen, D. Scott and D. Whyte. Cullompton: Willan.

Maruna, S. and A. Matravers (2007): "N=1: Criminology and the Person". *Theoretical Criminology*, 11(4): 427-42.

May, T. (1997): *Social Research: Issues, Methods and Process*. Buckingham: Open University Press.

McDonald, M. (ed.) (1994): *Gender, Drink and Drugs*. Oxford: Providence.

Mendelson, E. (ed.) (2004): *W.H. Auden: Collected Poems*. London: Faber & Faber.

Morrison, R. (2011): "De Quincey's Addiction". *Romanticism*, 17(3): 270-7.

Schön, D.A. (1983): *The Reflective Practitioner: How Professionals Think in Action*. London: Temple Smith.

Shekedi, A. (2005): *Multiple Case Narrative: A Qualitative Approach to Studying Multiple Populations*. Amsterdam: John Benjamin's Publishing Company.

Smart, C. (2009): "Shifting Horizons: Reflections on Qualitative Methods". *Feminist Theory*, 10(3): 1-14.

Smith, D. (2004): "The Uses and Abuses of Positivism", in *What Matters in Probation*, edited by G. Mair. Devon: Willan.

Smith, D. (2006): "Making Sense of Psychoanalysis in Criminological Theory and Probation Practice". *Probation Journal*, 53(4): 361-76.

Stacey, P. (2003): *Online Pedagogies for Active Learning: October 17th 2003*. Available at: www.bctechnology.com/statics/pstacey-oct.html.

Taylor, S. (2008): "Outside the Outsiders: Media Representations of Drug Use". *Probation Journal*, 55(4): 369-87.

Van Dusen, E. (2008): *Connectivism: Teaching and Learning*. Available at: http://design.test.olt.ubc.ca/Connectivism:_Teaching_and_Learning.

Young, J. (1971): *The Drugtakers: The Social Meaning of Drug Use*. London: Judson, McGibbon & Kee.

Chapter 13

The Uses of Literary and Cinematic Characters in Teaching Sociology

Lisbeth B. Knudsen

Introduction

Studying sociology means training to become a sociologist. *Sociologist* is a title indicating a person's profession; that the person has completed a specific type of education. However, a person may also be described as a sociologist if his or her research interests lie within the sociological field; when established, the Danish Sociological Society stated in its Articles of Association that membership is open to all persons working sociologically. For most people, studying to become a sociologist means embarking on a process of personal development as well – a process implying that the sociologist graduating will be a very different person from the student enrolling a few years before, not only from a professional or knowledge perspective but also from an attitudinal perspective. In my opinion, it is virtually impossible not to be influenced and shaped as a human being by the knowledge of society acquired through sociological studies.

An essential element in the training to become a sociologist is learning and mastering sociological concepts that can be used to conceptualize and understand overall social structures, as well as more mundane everyday occurrences and personal experiences, present as well as *past*. A colleague, looking back on her career, once described how her research interests and priorities had been influenced by her own experiences of growing up in a village, and how the sociological concepts she later acquired helped her get a deeper understanding of the community she grew up in, social mobility and social relations (Drewes Nielsen 2010).

What I personally remember most clearly from my early student days is not a gradual emergence of a sociological consciousness or sociological imagination. On the contrary, what I remember most vividly is a string of unrelated events, fragments of inspiring and thought-provoking lectures, teachers' interpretations and explanations, texts I read, and, above all, spending time with my fellow students, the general atmosphere and my new life in the city – and that is what eventually turned me into a sociologist.

During my studies, I was introduced to statements and documentation that challenged, provoked and nearly upended my Christian middleclass upbringing. I was presented with new and completely different angles on social correlations which I had believed to be obvious and interpreted within a generally accepted frame of reference. And class and social inequality became apparent. Actually, it was this growing realization that the world could be perceived differently from what I had previously taken for granted that was the most challenging and exhilarating about the studies I had embarked upon. My old foundation was shaken and I had to build a new one, one that was capable of bridging my most fundamental, deeply personal beliefs and all the new understandings and explanations I was introduced to. I had to find a perspective from which I was able to view both my present and previous experiences.

This – for me – new sociological interpretation happened as a mixture of very personal and purely professional sociological conceptual understandings. Sociological interpretation often finds itself in this kind of hybrid or overlapping area – sometimes marked by inherent conflict and sometimes by 'eureka-moment' agreement. This 'struggle' between the conceptual understandings of sociology and the more personally rooted and often more common sense-based understandings can be both uplifting and painful, but nearly always highly rewarding.

However, there were also interpretations of reality outside the academic world that offered inspiration or input for sociological analysis. 'Start by reading old social realistic novels if you need a good starting point for an understanding of that certain period in history – the living condition of a certain class, a specific geographical area or gender relations at that specific time' was the advice (or at any rate the essence of it) of Kaare Svalastoga, the Norwegian historian who was a professor at the Institute of Sociology in Copenhagen, which had existed for less than ten years when I enrolled in 1967.

His advice was an eye-opener for me. It enabled me to find a place for the world of fiction I had always loved within the academic understanding of the world; and in reality it also gave me permission, within the framework of social science, to look for inspiration elsewhere and to make use of a variety of sources and methods: in fact, to use the approach termed *mixed methods research* in recent sociological jargon (Bryman 2004). Most importantly, his advice served as recognition that also personal accounts and conditions and events described in works of fiction can be considered serious and substantial enough to be useful in a scientific context and thus as a means of gaining an understanding of society.

The inspiration for the reflections in this chapter stems from Kaare Svalastoga's welcome advice and my own subsequent experiences from teaching sociology. In this chapter, I will give some examples and discuss the use of stories and characters from for example novels and films to depict or create a mental picture of social conditions, in order to demonstrate how especially images created by fiction can provide a valuable and sometimes necessary illustration of facts when teaching sociology. Also, it is relevant to point out that, as a main rule, sociology needs some empirical basis, even when developing the concepts, in order for the concepts to be applicable in understandings and explanations of social phenomena. To benefit research, concepts need to reflect and be recognizable in everyday occurrences and empirical findings. Exemplifying important concepts by referring to fiction is one of the advantages pointed out by the American sociologist Robert Alun Jones (1975) in his early reflections on the benefits of using fiction in the teaching of sociology, and which some of my Danish colleagues have referred to as 'a pedagogical tool in sociology teaching' (Antoft, Jacobsen and Petersen 2010).

In this chapter, I will focus on the teaching perspective – in other words, on subject areas I have taught by using the examples below, and not on how the examples have inspired or been used in my research.

Historical Stories

A couple of years ago, Karin Esmann Knudsen edited a book in Danish entitled *Historiske fortællinger* [*Historical Stories*] (2008) with the subtitle "Historieformidling og litteratur" [Dissemination of Historical Facts and Fictitious Historical Literature"]. In some ways, this book seeks to shed light on the topic I am exploring here, although with a different purpose: in a history-profession context, the question is whether *historical facts* are lost in texts dealing with historical events but presented in the form of works of fiction. The reasons stated in the editor's preface for publishing the book were 'the modern challenges we face when communicating history' (Knudsen 2008: 8), and thus, as the editor points out, it can be seen as a contribution to the debate surrounding the literary, cultural, historical and democracy canons published in Denmark in 2004, 2006, 2006 and 2008 respectively (the concept of the 'canons' are explained more in detail regarding literature later). In the light of the ongoing national vs. global discussion, the way history is communicated has acquired a new meaning, and Knudsen's anthology is an important contribution to the attempts to define the conditions, practices and opportunities of 'the broad and overlapping fields of history and literature' (Knudsen 2008: 8).

When history is transformed into modern-day fiction, it is crucial not to mistake the apparent authenticity of for example a thriller or a coming-of-age novel with genuine historical facts, but to have the knowledge required to balance the impression left by docu-fiction against a facts-based understanding of the real-life events that the work of fiction is based on. Some of the examples mentioned in the book include James A. Mitchener's novels on the history of nations or geographical areas (for example the multi-facetted history of Poland with its divisions, invasions and reunifications, or of the various groups populating Hawaii), and Fredrick Forsythe's thrillers (for example *The Day of the Jackal* from 1971 about the attempted assassination of Charles de Gaulle, the President of France). The detective stories written by Swedish novelists Maj Sjöwall and Per Wahlöö in the 1970s put the spotlight on the changes happening in the Swedish police and the police executives' belief in increasing militarization, and they no doubt had an effect on, but also reflected, the mounting criticism of the Swedish police, especially its upper echelons. Henning Mankell's more recent novels, featuring detective inspector Kurt Wallander, are set in Ystad, a town in Southern Sweden. One of his most recent novels takes place in 2008 and involves espionage with connections back to a real-life episode involving Soviet submarines in the Swedish archipelagos in the 1980s (Mankell 2009). Wallander is yet another decent, usually low-ranking, police officer so typical of this genre. These novels rely on balancing the credibility of made-up stories involving real persons (deceased or present) in an overall plot made all the more exciting and relevant by being rooted in 'reality', but not necessarily historically correct in terms of characters and conversations. A number of the novels have been turned into TV series in Sweden, and even an English version featuring Kenneth Branagh as Wallander, but still set in the Swedish town bearing the almost unpronounceable (at least for people with English mother tongue) name: Ystad.

The contributions in Knudsen's anthology revolve around the relationship between literature and history but, as stated earlier, my chapter aims to explore and establish a relationship between sociology and literature (or fiction in general). What sociology stands to gain by involving fiction is, above all, the ability of fiction, with its rich, textured and plausible examples, to inspire the theoretical/conceptual and the historically empirical aspects of sociological analysis of society.

An example of such theoretical/conceptual aspects could be a demonstration of the implications of Max Weber's concept of bureaucracy in its most extreme Kafkaesque sense, depicted almost as a parody in the novel *The Castle* (Jørgensen 2010). In this context, it is not relevant whether the castle described by Franz Kafka ever existed, or whether the events described in the novel did in fact take place; what matters is that the ideal type *bureaucracy* is recognizable in a perverted – some might say pure – form. *The Castle* can be read as a supplement to the curriculum sociological literature – but it will also be immediately recognizable for people without any knowledge of sociology because anyone can see that this is red tape run riot!

I will return to the other aspect later – how fiction can illustrate what I have called *the historically empirical aspect*. What matters in this chapter is the exact opposite: an example is good because the director and/or writer manages to capture the essence spot-on. What is described is not new or unknown phenomena, but the example manages to flesh out a character or a course of events and bring them to life in a way that is consistent with statistics or the reality described in research. Referring to such a fictional character or situation when teaching makes the facts studied in statistics and textbooks come alive for the students.

Unless we are dealing with periods or conditions we have intimate knowledge of, sociologist are sometimes unable to evaluate the empirical, historical correctness of fiction – and to be honest, we may not always be as concerned about it in our profession as a professional historian would be (Jensen 2005); but correctness is relevant if we choose to use fictional examples in our teaching. As sociologists, we can also use fictional descriptions of society, human relations and the living conditions and life courses of fictional characters as inspiration for both our research and as illustrations of the life we are trying to describe and capture with our sociological tools. As mentioned, it is the teaching of sociology I will focus on in this chapter.

When using examples from fiction in a teaching context, it is important to choose examples that draw on a shared frame of reference; in other words, films or novels well-known to both students and the teacher and thus capable of constituting this shared frame of reference. There are works of fiction which I (born in 1948) and others of my generation consider to be (or think ought to be) common knowledge, but which the students of today have not studied or even heard about. That even standard and universally praised works of Danish literature are unknown even to people who hold a degree was really brought home to me when I was watching the Danish version of the game show "Who Wants to Be a Millionaire?" in the spring of 2009. In one of the variations of the show (in Denmark), the participant is allowed to bring along another person to help answer the questions – in this particular show one of the two persons was a schoolteacher. One of the questions related to a novel written by a famous Danish writer, and the question stated that it was a novel by Herman Bang (1857-1912), and more specifically it included the name of one of its main characters, the station master. The four choices of titles included: *Hærværk*, *Livsens ondskab*, *Ved vejen* and *Løgneren* – all works that were compulsory reading when I went to school. The teacher was absolutely clueless! She literally did not have a clue about any of them! The other said it would have to be *Ved vejen*, because he had read that one at school, and it was the most boring book he had ever read – that was the reason he remembered it.

Neither of the participants seemed to be aware that of the four choices, only *Ved vejen* was written by Herman Bang. The other three novels are all major works in Danish literature, but the schoolteachers failed to recognize both the titles and the writers of them. Poor Tom Kristensen, Gustav Wied and Martin A. Hansen, all distinguished writers! It needs to be added that of the four writers, only Gustav Wied is not included in the canon of Danish literary writers, and 'students *must* have read at least one text written by these authors in Danish classes taught in primary, secondary as well as upper-secondary education', as stated by the committee compiling the canon under the Ministry of Education (Undervisningsministeriet *2004).*

Any interpretation and use of fictional examples will inevitably be coloured by the teacher's own history and subjective knowledge, especially in the case of examples from periods the teacher has first-hand experience of. To illustrate my point, I will mention a couple of films about the 1970s, but made in the last two decades. In both cases, the director grew up in the environment portrayed, which already in the reviews of the films lent them an air of authenticity. But the outcome of the personal experiences was very different. Peter Bay's film *Fede tider* [*Groovy Times*] from 1995 is about a family moving into a hippie commune established in a spacious house in a wealthy suburb in the northern outskirts of Copenhagen. This is a historical fact: some of these houses were legitimately purchased and turned into hippie communes by their inhabitants in the 1970s. The film was marketed as a 'humorous description of life in a Danish hippie commune in the 1970s. Shared economy, women's liberation and communal bedrooms were all parts of the shared ideology. But walking the talk was not always as easy as it sounds' (Scope 2010). The hippie lifestyle, no inhibitions about being naked, free love (meaning free sex), dabbling with revolutionary parenting and education – everything is portrayed in the film as great fun, bordering on the ridiculous. Using this film as an example of real life thus poses a dilemma: students, and even younger teachers, will probably see the description as funny and entertaining, and as giving a fairly accurate picture whereas the 'older' teacher will note the inaccuracies and exaggerations (albeit to some extent depending on political beliefs).

Niels Arden Oplev's film *Drømmen* [*The Dream*] from 2006 is a very different film; in my opinion the exact opposite of *Fede Tider*. Through a story about rebellion against the traditional way of life in rural Denmark in the 1960s and 1970s, and in particular against its authoritarian structure represented by a hidebound and despotic headmaster, the film manages to demonstrate the necessity of the rebellion against the norms at the time, political as well as moral (and not 'just' sexual), and the liberation that this rebellion brought with it. The young schoolteacher in the film introduces, along with the music of the 1960s, a new humane 'equality-based' way of interacting with his students. Both he and the political upheaval in the rural community are described within a frame of everyday life in which the big changes in society are firmly rooted and played out.

These two Danish films show (at least) two sides of the major changes happening in the wake of the student protests in 1968, but from a sociological point of view *Drømmen* is by far the most relevant. However, both films describe only a segment of reality – not all headmasters were as cruel as the one in *Drømmen*, and not all hippie communes were as extreme and silly as depicted in *Fede tider*.

In a teaching context, the two films are valuable because they were produced within the same decade and because they are recent enough for the majority of students to be familiar with them, to a much large extent than the works and characters I am going to discuss below.

Fields of Research and Teaching

The primary focus in my own research and teaching has been the family and biological reproduction – fertility, abortion, contraception, and the circumstances surrounding them. I have found it inspiring to approach my research from different angles: demographic, sociological and medical-sociological and focusing on planned fertility, controlled fertility and the conditions and consequences of the increasing possibilities for women and couples to avoid having children at times when they do not want them. In Denmark, abortion on demand in the first twelve weeks of pregnancy and easily accessible contraception have been available since the early 1970s and late 1960s respectively (Knudsen et al. 2003), which has made it possible to choose not to have children and thus not to be forced into unwanted co-parenthood with a casual partner. As Anthony Giddens (1992) has expressed it, today reproduction has become subject to the individual's strategic life planning, and sex disengaged from biological reproduction. In this context, individualization and reflexivity are seen as positive things. Lots of articles and papers have been written – and will continue to be written – on these phenomena, and what happened when they emerged and became dominant characteristics of society. However, their findings are often marked by a surprising lack of understanding of the conditions people lived under 50-100 ago.

'Today we strongly prefer to just live together without getting married', is one of the statements I often hear from students, who are, as a starting point, convinced that there is a pronounced difference in perceptions and attitudes towards families compared to the 1950s (and before that). But they are not aware that this difference (which *is* real) is only realizable because material conditions are different today, which has resulted in social structures and frameworks within which it is possible to make different choices. Young students, who have grown up in a society in which it is a given fact that biological reproduction and family formation is subject to the individual's self-determination, find it difficult to understand or even imagine a world without these opportunities and the consequences this had for people living without them. Below, I will give some examples of how I have used literature or films to illustrate such conditions.

Family Pictures

As mentioned above, the material and attitudinal background of the general characteristics of an individual's life course in Denmark and other western countries today is very different from the background of the corresponding characteristics 50-100 years ago. This applies to for example the reasons for living alone, for not marrying, how old you are when you have your first child, or for not having children at all.

When these characteristics are interpreted within a framework of infinite choices and a reflexive approach to life, it can be difficult to make students understand that the desire to be able to choose and the reflections on choices may have been just as strong in previous times, but that the people living then were unable to exercise the choices because the material and legal conditions of their lives were different. To give an example: it was not until the 1920s that women were allowed to have custody of their own children in case of divorce (Knudsen 2004). This fact – together with the limited financial opportunities of women – goes a long to explain why women 'chose' not to divorce their husbands. It is in a context like this that literary and cinematic images can be used as a teaching tool to render historical conditions intelligible. Using situations or characters that are relatively unambiguous and known from novels, films or TV series that students are familiar with has the obvious advantage of creating a frame of reference that is readily established, shared and not subject to discussion.

Students' knowledge of earlier decades can be somewhat inaccurate, just as they sometimes fail to place major theoretical and empirical works in terms of time as well geography when they use them. An example of this could be American theories on family relations; it is important to bear in mind that for example the theories of Talcott Parsons were heavily influenced by the family pattern prevalent in the 1950s in the aftermath of World War II in the USA. Or that Ulrich Beck's more recent statement that women are 'only a husband away from poverty' is based on conditions in Germany in the 1980s that are not at all similar to Danish gender roles at the time. In the 1980s, Danish women had already achieved widespread financial independence as a consequence of changes in women's legal, labour market, social and moral conditions; facts that need to be taken into consideration when applying Beck's theory in a Danish context, and which need to be communicated clearly in a teaching situation. The concepts and theories may be still be very useful, but the individual researcher or student will have to be aware of, and take into account, the time aspect and cultural differences, and consider whether and how they may affect the validity of a concept in a modern Danish context. Needless to say, some knowledge of history is required to do so.

Family and the relationship between family members are recurring topics in literary and cinematic projects – sometimes as the main theme, sometimes as the backdrop to the overall plot, or used to add a little spice to it. The development in relations between family members or of an individual character may run in parallel with the main plot or may be so interwoven with it that they are impossible to tell apart. A Danish TV series, *Krøniken* [*A Chronicle of a Family Business*], was shown on Danish TV in 2004 (with reruns in 2009 and 2010), receiving mixed reviews and comments. Prior to its release, the series had been proclaimed a sort of sequel to the earlier and very popular series *Matador* (meaning both *tycoon* and the board game *Monopoly*) (see below), which would, admittedly, be a tall order for any series. The plot revolves around a family business and the conflict between a father and his son, in particular their differences of opinion about the future course of the company created by the father. The father-son conflict is at least as important to the overall plot as the description of the fate of the radio manufacturing company Bella in post-war Denmark. In fact, the father-son conflict may have been intended as the main plot, a personification of the emergence of modern society and new structures and attitudes, represented by the son. The series portrays a strong contrast between this upper-class father-son relationship and a working-class father-son relationship, a parallel plot in which the latter son comes to represent the new generation of working-class children turned academics, thanks to the social democratic welfare model.

The individual stories of the characters in *Krøniken* unfold against a (sketchy) backdrop of external events and developments: rural migration and women's fight for higher education are illustrated by the young girl Ida, who leaves her provincial town, Ringkøbing, in western Jutland to start a new life in the capital, Copenhagen. The series occasionally shows how this affects her relationship with her hometown and her parents.

When watching this series, or similar series, you cannot help wonder if this was how it really was, if the course of events you have just seen represents facts or if they were just an approximation of reality. Was this an accurate description of what life was like then? And how are we to find out if we, as non-historians, have not experienced the events ourselves or know people who lived at the period in question? And what happens if you use fiction in a professional academic context? Who and what can we trust?

One solution to this problem is to consult a number of sources; perhaps others have written about the same events, seen from different class or gender perspectives, because fictional stories are always subjective.

The Recent History of the Family

As already mentioned, in post-modern Danish society family formation and family forms are different from what they were 50-100 years ago. In the family sociological field, some of the developments in the 1900s follow a J- or U-shaped course. This is for example the case with the proportion of a Danish female birth cohort who does not give birth to a child: 25 per cent of the women born shortly before 1900 remained childless, compared to 12-13 per cent of women born in the late 1950s (*Befolkningsudvikling og Sundhedsforhold* 1966; *Befolkningens udvikling* 2008). Nevertheless, there is a lot of talk these days about childlessness being on the increase, probably heavily influenced by the improved possibilities of planning births.

Students, whose historical perspective usually only stretches back to the 1970s or perhaps the 1950s, often choose the family of the 1950s in Denmark as their image for analytical comparison of the *traditional family*, or the family 'in earlier times'. In the 1950s, the dominant family model was a single-breadwinner nuclear family: a stay-at-home mother, perhaps working part-time, a couple of children and a father working outside the home. The Danish National Centre for Social Research (see, for example, Bertelsen 1981) interpreted a questionnaire-based survey on families showing a statistical decrease in fertility as women's reactions to increasingly working outside the home. And Maria Marcus (1964) and other (female) writers of fiction have written poignantly and ironically about family life and gender roles, portraying especially the role as housewife as a relic of an old patriarchal society that had to be overturned. While students today may think Marcus an outdated curiosity (that is, if they have ever heard of her), there are many more recent images available in fiction that demonstrate that *in earlier times* 'family' was not synonymous with the standardized 1950s image, and that far from all families fitted this ideal type of a family.

One such example, which can still be very useful, is the Danish TV series *Matador*, which premiered about 30 years ago. It was immediately a huge success, and when the 24th and last episode was shown in 1982, 83 per cent of the Danish population was watching (Grubb, Hemmersam and Jørgensen 2004). Since then, the series has become iconic as a unifying force of the nation – a status confirmed through stories about how the brides-to-be of the Danish princes have watched *Matador* as an introduction to Danish society: fiction elevated to royal teaching material. The series has had a number of reruns, most recently in the winter of 2013, plus sold about 800,000 videotapes and 400,000 DVDs. 'This proves the series' universal appeal in Denmark, and the Danish Broadcasting Corporation does not hesitate to call it part of the Danish national heritage' (Grubb, Hemmersam and Jørgensen 2004: 1). Due to its immense popularity and the many reruns, even students now in their mid-20s (born years after the series was shown for the first time) will have had ample opportunity to familiarize themselves with the characters of *Matador*, and the series is therefore useful as a shared frame of reference. Another advantage is that as the viewers grow older, they discover more facets of the series; those who first saw it as children will discover new aspects of it and understand them differently when seeing it again as young adults.

Ulrik Grubb and his co-authors give several examples of the authenticity of the props used in the series, for example clothes and beer bottles, and they maintain that an essential part of the fascination that *Matador* exercises, over and over again, lies in this painstaking recreation of the external framework. Furthermore, they emphasize that *Matador* is neither facts nor docudrama, but that all characters are purely fictional. But they also emphasize that 'the series is set in the framework of Danish history 1929-1947. Matador is a typical historical TV series' (Grubb, Hemmersam and Jørgensen 2004: 3). The main scriptwriter, whose idea the series is based on, set her series in a provincial town not far from Copenhagen which she has also described in other autobiographical novels. However, it is the series' characters and the relations between the individual characters that I find particularly useful in my teaching. 'It is the plot, the fictional story in *Matador*, which is the central element. The historical reality is used mainly as a backdrop but still plays a role as part of the plot, in line with the characteristics of its genre' (Grubb, Hemmersam and Jørgensen 2004: 3). That is the reason why I find it so useful and valuable when trying to illustrate a sociological phenomenon for my students – the fact that the series revolves around individuals, but that the everyday life of these fictional characters is obviously influenced by the current social context and the prevalent material conditions at the time.

The most difficult balance here is probably maintaining the distinction between what are documented facts and what is fiction. The very fact that several generations are familiar with and have experienced *Matador* may give the interpretation of the series a dominant position in the conception of history, which has actually caused some debate. On the TV series' website, it says: 'All in all, there can be no doubt that *Matador* has influenced the way Danes look at Danish history in the period 1929-1947 which provides the setting for the plot of the series'.

But let us return to the sociology of the family. *Matador* is useful in this respect because the main plot centres on two families and their households. The concept of household is important in my context. We are often told in the press, and even in some research papers, that many more people live as singles today than before.

And it is true that in *Matador* we see larger households and fewer people who *live* on their own than today; but what Matador's plot, spanning several decades, also shows us is characters whose position in the household reveals profound differences. The household of the old distinguished and very traditional banking family Varnæs, gradually ousted from its position of power by the innovative newcomer in town, Mads Skjern (the modern-time capitalist), includes Mr. and Mrs. Varnæs, their two children, Mrs. Varnæs' sister, the unmarried aunt Elisabeth, who looks after the children when the lady of the house takes to her bed, yet again, in the wake of some minor disaster. The unmarried Elisabeth causes quite a scandal (in the family as well as among its old local friends) when she decides to leave her sister's household to live in an apartment on her own (and of course even more so when she starts a love affair with the manager of the competing bank, who is the brother of Mads Skjern, to boot). Until then, she has been part of her sister's household – but she is still *single* in that she is not married, neither does she have her own children nor her own household; but she is not single in today's sense of the word, which usually implies a person living on their own. In her sister's household, Elisabeth is considered a fixture of the household, somebody who is was part of – even indispensable to – the family's everyday routine; but entirely on her married sister's terms.

The family's cook, Laura, is another (indispensable) part of the household, but in a different way than Elisabeth, as she is an employee. But downstairs in the kitchen, and her room adjacent to it, she follows the family through thick and thin. Her only act of rebellion is hiding a dog left behind by the Germans stationed in Varnæs' garden during the Occupation, and insisting on being allowed to keep it.

Elisabeth and Laura are both images of family and household relations that are different from today's norms. Although they did not live alone by today's standards, they were both single and alone, and no doubt lonely at times. Their situations also reveal pronounced class differences. But both had limited self-determination: it was not up to Laura, for example, to decide whether she could keep the dog – the family upstairs had to be asked permission and was able to dictate the terms!

Going further back in time, the novels written by Martin Andersen Nexø about *Pelle Erobreren* [*Pelle the Conqueror*] (written 1906-1910) and *Ditte Menneskebarn* [*Ditte, Child of Man*] (written 1917-1921) are examples of classical, social realistic novels, written with the clear objective of demonstrating poverty and social inequality. However, both novels also contain examples of how family life *in earlier times* or *traditionally* (as students often refer to it) was very different from the model of the nuclear family of two parents, one staying at home, the other working outside the home and 2-3 children often presented as the *Family*.

Pelle migrates to Bornholm (the easternmost island in Denmark), with his farther, Lassefar, from Småland (a region in southern Sweden from where many emigrated to America). Later he moves to Copenhagen on his own to become a part of the early labour movement. It is this second part of the novel, with its descriptions of the horrible housing standards, the miserable living conditions of families and the appalling conditions of single mothers that made the biggest impression on me when I read it. Nexø described the suffering and debasement of the urban proletariat in Copenhagen, and in doing so helped pave the way for a dawning understanding that change was long overdue and eventually a reorganization of the living conditions of working people.

In *Ditte Menneskebarn* we meet the rural proletariat, described in a way that very effectively dispels any myths about the idyll of country life – that of a large household of family members, each making their contribution towards the livelihood of the family: the menfolk working in the fields and the women in the house. Some students actually describe 'country living' by an image of a husband and a wife and their children, plus a number of farmhands and maids, without even pausing to consider whether the farmhands and maids had their own family, and if so, where they lived. In the account of Pelle's first years on Bornholm, *Pelle Erobreren* describes how the households of big farms also included many farmhands who were either single or had had to leave their family behind to come and work at the big farm, to earn a living (Nexø 1933). In *Ditte Menneskebarn*, we meet these broken families, women living alone, whose children have to go into service on a big farm at a young age, fathers absent for long periods of time, or perhaps permanently. Ditte has 'Bedste', her beloved grandmother, to comfort her when her mother is working her too hard: 'On the days Ditte did not go to school, there were a thousand chores for her to do' (Nexø 1976, Bind I: 107). After her Lutheran confirmation (at 14), Ditte leaves home to go into service full-time – but it was not unusual for children to be sent to work in a strange household at an even earlier age.

Sexuality, Unplanned Pregnancies and Wished-for-Children

Today, having a child – when, how many and with whom – is subject to reflexive consideration, negotiation and (more or less) conscious decision (Giddens 1992). Easy access to safe contraceptives and legally induced abortions has made it possible to choose not to have children or to choose not to share parenthood with a person considered not desirable as a permanent partner (Knudsen and Wielandt 1996). One consequence of these choices and rejection of choices is that the children actually born will usually be wanted and often carefully planned children.

In Denmark, the Pill became available in the late 1960s, the right to have an induced abortion was liberalized in 1970, and the act allowing abortion on demand in the first 12 weeks of pregnancy was passed in 1973. The possibilities of choosing not to have a child – by using contraceptives or by having a pregnancy terminated – made it possible to start focusing on enjoying sex. Sex outside marriage, obviously, but also sex within marriage: men and women were free to enjoy sex, without the fear of getting pregnant or having (another) child or resorting to an expensive and perhaps dangerous illegal abortion. A woman no longer had to marry a man she barely knew because she got pregnant, and a man no longer had to face up to his responsibilities and 'make an honest woman' of a girl if he got her pregnant (Knudsen and Wielandt 2000).

'But it's Wednesday!', the father says to the mother, who, with a sigh of resignation, lets him 'have his way with her', overheard by their increasingly sexually aware teenage daughter sleeping in the same bedroom and desperately trying to shut out the sounds from the marital bed (that is how I recall the scene from the film adaptation (1986) of the autobiographical novel about growing up in a poor neighbourhood in Copenhagen, *Barndommens gade* [*Childhood's Street*] written by Tove Ditlevsen in 1943). That is a very poignant description of the fear of yet another pregnancy and sex as a joyless marital duty. And a situation almost impossible to imagine for young people, born post-1973 and living in a world of easy access to contraceptives. But it is nevertheless a necessary interpretation to include when analysing family and fertility over time.

It is also possible to find descriptions of young people's first sexual experiences in literary fiction from that time. A quick, embarrassed coupling in a dark alley or behind the bike shed, the constant fear of unwanted pregnancy. A young girl's first time, letting him 'go all the way'; him chivalrously taking out his chewing gum while 'making love', to save it for later. Harald Herdal's urban collective novel *Løg* [*Onions*] from 1935 tells the individual stories of seven young people. Due to its very direct descriptions of their first fumbling sexual experiences, the novel was above all considered immoral and pornographic when first published, but the novel is not only about sexuality: it also gives a critical, social realistic description of the problems facing young people living in the city in the 1930s: unemployment, a shortage of affordable housing, the relationship with their parents. If young people read his novel today, they will probably think that the conditions described are typical of a period much further back in history than just a few generations from their own.

Conclusion

Using my own personal experiences, first as student of sociology trying to grasp the new world revealing itself through my studies and later as a teacher of sociology, I have attempted to illustrate, with a few examples, how it is possible to use literary and cinematic images to teach and flesh out sociological phenomena. As should be clear from the chapter, my aim and objective in doing so is to make empirical reality come to life, as it were, for my students through references to shared knowledge of fictive characters and stories, provided the description of them are somehow rooted in reality. Within my own field of research, reproductive sociology and the sociology of the family, material conditions have changed considerably over the last 100 years. The choices people have today when it comes to partners, pregnancy and family formation are strongly connected with gender equality, that women have financial independence, and that it is possible to avoid pregnancy and 'unwanted' children. In this context, literary and cinematic images can help explain that the differences in present-day way of life cannot be seen merely as an expression of changes in attitudes. The differences must also be seen as an expression of the fact that it is political changes, usually anchored in the actions and values of the population, that have resulted in the changed framework conditions that are the preconditions for the realization of the choices we have today.

I have pointed out some of the obvious advantages of using literary and cinematic images, but also some of the problems and potential pitfalls involved, especially if the examples used are interpreted differently by the teacher and the students. However, in my experience, using examples from fiction can be a valuable tool when teaching sociology.

Translated from Danish by Lis Sand.

References

Antoft, R., M. Hviid Jacobsen and A. Petersen (2010): "En lyskile ind i læringsrummet – om poesi, performativitet og terapeutisk chok i pædagogik og læring", in *Den poetiske fantasi – om forholdet mellem sociologi og fiktion*, edited by R. Antoft, M. Hviid Jacobsen and L.B. Knudsen. Aalborg: Aalborg Universitetsforlag.
Befolkningens udvikling 2008 (2009): Copenhagen: Danmarks Statistik.
Befolkningsudvikling og Sundhedsforhold (1966): Copenhagen: Det Statistiske Departement.
Bertelsen, Ole (1981): *Det faldende fødselstal: Belyst ved familiestørrelsens sammenhæng med kvindens uddannelse og erhvervsarbejde*. Copenhagen: National Institute of Social Research, Publikation 104.
Bryman, Alan (2004): "Combining Quantitative and Qualitative Research", in *Social Research Methods*, edited by A. Bryman. Oxford: Oxford University Press.
Drewes Nielsen, L. (2010): "Ved landsbyens gadekær – bondesamfundet som vugge for den sociologiske fantasi", in *Den poetiske fantasi – om forholdet mellem sociologi og fiktion*, edited by R. Antoft, M. Hviid Jacobsen and L.B. Knudsen. Aalborg: Aalborg Universitetsforlag.
Giddens, A. (1992): *The Transformation of Intimacy: Sexuality, Love and Eroticism in Modern Societies*. Stanford, CA: Stanford University Press.
Grubb, U., K-J. Hemmersam and J. Riskær Jørgensen (2004): "Matador – den vellykkede historiske fiktion". *Historie-nu*. Available at: www.historie-nu.dk/matador1.pdf.
Herdal, H. (1935): *Løg*. Copenhagen: Skandinavisk Bogforlag.
Jensen, A. (2005): "Anmeldelse af Mogens Nygaard Christoffersen: *Familiens udvikling i det 20. århundrede: Demografiske strukturer og processer*". *Dansk Sociologi*, 16(1): 170-1.
Jones, R.A. (1975): "The Use of Literature in Teaching Introductory Sociology: A Case Study". *Teaching Sociology*, 2(2): 177-96.

Jørgensen, T.B. (2010): "Bureaukratiet hos Max Weber og Franz Kafka – fra idealtype til tragedie – eller komedie", in *Den poetiske fantasi – om forholdet mellem sociologi og fiktion*, edited by R. Antoft, M. Hviid Jacobsen and L.B. Knudsen. Aalborg: Aalborg Universitetsforlag.

Knudsen, K. Esmann (ed.) (2008): *Historiske fortællinger: Historieformidling og litteratur*. Odense: Syddansk Universitetsforlag.

Knudsen L.B. (2004): "Nye familieformer og færre børn", in *Den danske velfærdsstats historie*, edited by N. Ploug, I. Henriksen and N. Kærgård. Copenhagen: National Institute of Social Research.

Knudsen L.B. et al. (2003): "Induced Abortion in the Nordic Countries: Special Emphasis on Young Women". *Acta Obstricia et Gynecologia Scandinavica*, 82(3): 257-68.

Knudsen, L.B. and H. Wielandt (1996): *På vej mod ønskebarnet*. Copenhagen: Frydenlund.

Knudsen, L.B. and H. Wielandt (2000): "Fri abort", in *Kvinder – køn, krop og kultur*, edited by K. Helweg-Larsen, B.L. Pedersen and A. Tønnes Pedersen. Copenhagen: Gyldendal.

Mankell, H. (2009): *Den urolige mand*. Copenhagen: Gyldendal.

Marcus, M. (1964/1979): *Kvindespejlet*. Copenhagen: Lindhardt & Ringhof.

Nexø, M. Andersen (1933): *Pelle Erobreren*. Copenhagen: Gyldendalske Boghandel/Nordisk Forlag.

Nexø, M. Andersen (1976): *Ditte Menneskebarn, Bind I og II*. Copenhagen: Gyldendals Tranebøger.

Scope (2010): http://www.scope.dk/film/985-fede-tider.

Undervisningsministeriet (2004): Dansk litteraturs kanon – Rapport fra Kanonudvalget. Copenhagen: Undervisningsministerriet/Ministry of Education. Available at: http://pub.uvm.dk/2004/kanon/kap06.html.

Index

Bold page numbers indicate figures, *italic* numbers indicate tables.

44 Letters from the Liquid Modern World (Bauman) 66

Abbott, Andrew 148-9
addiction to drugs 243-7
advertisements 219-20
After the Bath (Degas) 65
"Alice in Computerland" (Richardson) 121-9
All the Names (Saramago) 80-1, 82-7
allegory 74, 76-9
Andreski, Stanislav 2, 28
anecdotal sociology 35-6
anthropology 226
    as art 5-6
    turns towards poetics 4
aporia 187
apple eating as example of presence 149-51
Arendt, Hannah 186
Arrival, The (Tan) 228
Art of the Novel, The (Kundera) 63-4
Art Worlds (Becker) 46-7
art(s)
    film as teaching tool 200-7
        lessons for sociology from 197-8
    presence in 145-8
    social science as 5-9
    turn towards 3-5
    used alongside textbooks in teaching 220-9, **221**
    see also literature
Asimov, Isaac 223
Asylums (Goffman) 41, 201
Attali, Jacques 114
Auden, W.H. 235
authorship 73-4

autobiographies 228
autonomy 116-17
    illusion of 165-6
autopoiesis 110

Bacon, Francis
    accidents, reliance on 65-6
    aims for *Two Figures* 55-6
    crucifixion motif 60-1
    distortion in portraits 64-5
    face and feelings of the Other 56-8, 57n2
    links with Bauman and Kundera 56-8
    locking the valves of feeling 58-62
    meaninglessness of life 59-60
    narrative, repudiation of 61-2
    nostalgia, refusal of 61
    respect towards the Other 59
    unlocking the valves of feeling 63-6
Barndommens gade (Childhood's Street) (Ditlevsen) 263
Bateson, Gregory 162-3
Bateson, Mary Catherine 1
Baudelaire, Charles 6
Bauman, Zygmunt
    and *Crucifixion* (Bacon) 61-2
    face and feelings of the Other 56-8
    Holocaust, the 62-3
    links with Bacon and Kundera 56-8
    locking the valves of feeling 59
    morality 205-6
    multiplicity of meanings in work 66
    nostalgia, refusal of 61
    piercing through the curtain, sociology as 56
    unlocking the valves of feeling 65, 66
Bay, Peter 155-6

Beck, Ulrich 115-16
Becker, Howard S. 27, 208
    influences on 45
    performance, society as 47-9
    representation of society 47
    style of writing 46-7
    voices, multiple in communication of research 48
Beethoven, Ludvig van 6, 7
being, theory of 224
Benjamin, Walter 6, 7, 74
Bentham, Jeremy 169-70
Berger, Peter L. 1, 3, 16-17
Between Literature and Science (Lepenies) 25
bildungsroman 169-74
biopolitics 83-6
Blindness (Saramago) 77-9, 80
Blumer, Herbert 40
Boat Race 144
body, the 140
Bohr, Niels 7-8
Bondanella, Peter 222
Bourdieu, Pierre 118
broadmindedness in social sciences 1-2, 17
    see also Chicago School of Sociology
Brooke-Rose, Christine 113-14
Bruner, Jerome 242
Bulmer, Martin 23-4

Cannatella, Howard 9-10
capitalism 77-9
    spirit of 182-4
Cappetti, Carla 27
cartoons 226-7
Castle, The (Kafka) 254
Castoriadis, Cornelius 117, 118
Cave, The (Saramago) 76
Chicago School of Sociology
    aversion to abstract intellectualism 27-8
    basis for sociology at 26
    characteristics of 26-8
    duality of approach 23-4
    Erving Goffman 37-45
    Everett C. Hughes 33-6
    Howard S. Becker 45-9

humanism of approach 28
inter-disciplinarity of 27
members of 26
openness to diverse materials 27
origins of 26
Robert E. Park 28-33
as shared mind-set 27
super-journalism 28-33
for today's sociologists 50
choice, freedom of 115-16
Citati, Pietro 172
'city as social laboratory' 31-2
civil society 77
Collins, Randall 40
common sense 69, 87-8
communication
    Erving Goffman 38
    influence of the Chicago School 50
    materialities of 137-8
    society as 29-31
    as story-telling/narrative 32-3
    teaching sociology 229
Communist Manifesto, The (Marx) 8
community and the state 77
confession, novels of 168-9
Confessions of an English Opium Eater (De Quincey) 238, 242, 243-7
constructivism 240-1
contextualization 73, 75
Contre-allée (Derrida) 112
creativity, problems with need for 155-6
criminology, drugs and drug use in 237-47
crisis situations
    exterior position in observing 160-2
    knowledge of 159-60
critical constructivism 240-1
cross-disciplinarity in social sciences 1-2
    see also Chicago School of Sociology
Crucifixion (Bacon) 61-2
crucifixion motif, use if by Bacon 60-1
cubism 7
cultural turn in social sciences 4-5
culture and presence and meaning 140-1

Danish literature 255
Davis, Lindsay 222
de Musset, Alfred 110-11
De Quincey, Thomas 238, 242, 243-7

de Rond, Mark 144
de Tocqueville, Alexis 117
Degas, Edgar 65
Deleuze, G. 57n2
Delphic Oracle 178-81
Denzin, Norman K. 208
depression 211
depth and surface 140
Derrida, Jacques 112
desire 165
detective novels 253-4
deviance, sociology of 201-2
dialectic 186-7
Diken, Bülent 207
Ditlevsen, Tove 263
Ditte Menneskebarn (Nexø) 262
documentary analysis 219
Double, The (Saramago) 76-7, 81-2
doxa 186
drama in teaching 207-10
drugs and drug use 236-47
Durkheim, Émile 24, 177, 184-6

Eco, Umberto 222
Edmondson, Ricca 43-4
Eisner, Elliot 208, 229
Elias, Norbert 159, 160
Emerson, Ralph Waldo 114
Encounter (Kundera) 63
enlightened disenchantment 86-7
epiphany 212
epistemology 221-4
essays as preferred style
    Goffman 39-40
    Hughes 34-5
ethnography 208, 209
executive power 77
exemplary learning 198
exile
    Joyce's method of 191
    and language 112-13
    refusal to be integrated 113-14
existence, theory of 224
experimental sociology, fiction as 70-1
experimental texts
    centre/margin 94
    criteria for 95-6
    criticisms of 97

difficulties with 95
editorial resistance to 97-8
future for 105-6
lessons from critics 99-100
"Louisa May's Story of Her Life"
    (Richardson) 100-2
one-scene play 102-4
optimism as premature 104-5
poetic exemplar 100-2
Qualitative Health Research response
    to 97-9
reading 96-7
resistance to 93
expressive/symbolic language 32-3
exteriority
    in observation 160-2
    and the theatre 163

Falco series of novels 222
families and reproduction 256-63
Farfan, Jose-Antonio 224
fatalism 115
Faulkner, Sandra L. 95-6
Fede tider (Groovy Times) (Bay) 155-6
fiction. *see* literature
fictionalization of mankind 168
film as tool for teaching 200-7, 255-6
'*Flower Duet, The* ' (Delibes) 220
Forster, E.M. 135
Foucault, Michel 157
Foundation Trilogy (Asimov) 223
fragile individuals 114-15
Frame Analysis (Goffman) 42
free association 35
freedom, human 115-16
Friedson, Eliot 38

Gadamer, Hans-Georg 138
game metaphor 42
Gasset, José Ortega y 34
Geertz, Clifford 5-6, 133
geography, turns towards poetics in 4
geology 158
Girard, René 164-7, 169
Girl, Interrupted (Mangold) (film) 202-3
global condition of literature 71-3
Goethe, Johann Wolfgang von 169-74
Goffman, Erving 201

characteristics of work 38-9
and the Chicago School 37
communication of findings 38
comparison with Saramago 87-8
concepts generated by 40
essayistic style 39-40
frame metaphor 42
game metaphor 42
humour and irony in work 43-4
influence of 37-8
metaphors, use of by 41-3
poetic style 38-9
relevance of work to readers 44
as rhetorical genius 44
ritual metaphor 42
Simmel as inspiration for 39
source material 41
as teacher 45
theatrical metaphor 41-2
Gold Coast and the Slum, The (Zorbaugh) 24
Goytisolo, Juan 111-12
Grubb, Ulrik 260
Gumbrecht, H.U. 137-8, 140-1

Habermas, Jürgen 69
Hamvas, Béla 167-9
Hegel, G.W.F. 6
Heidegger, Martin 9, 139-40, 141-2
Hewitt, Regina 207
historical stories 253-6
Historiske fortællinger (Historical Stories) (Knudsen) 253
Holocaust, the 62-3
Honneth, Axel 211
Houellebecq, Michel 210-12
Hughes, Everett C.
    anecdotal sociology 35-6
    free association 34, 35
    influence and writings of 33
    lecturing style 36
    as Park's student 33
    and Simmel, comparison of 34-5
    style of writing 34-6
humanism of Chicago School of Sociology 28
humour, use of by Goffman 43-4

identity
    construction of 202-3
    as forensic 80
    in a mediated age 76-7
    social aspect of 80-2
    social construction of 226
Žižek, Slavoj 143
images, sociologists' use of 8
imagination, methodological 3
individuals, fragile 114-15
inhibition, methodological 2
innovation, problems with need for 155-6
institutionalization 201
intellectual craftsmanship 3
inter-disciplinarity
    in social sciences 1-2
    see also Chicago School of Sociology
Interaction Ritual (Goffman) 42
interpretation of meaning 133, 143
    see also presence
ironic distanciation 71
irony, use of by Goffman 43-4

Jones, Alun 199
journalism
    New Journalism 31
    and social science 25
    and sociology 31-2
    super-journalism 28-33
journey, methodology as 8-9
Joyce, James 187-93

King, Anthony 144
Kirino, Natsuo 224
knowledge
    of the out-of-ordinary 159-60
    outsider's 161-2
    and truth 141-2
Knudsen, Karin Esmann 253
Kristeva, Julia 117-18
Krøniken (A Chronicle of a Family Business) (Danish TV series) 258-9
Kundera, Milan
    aims for *The Curtain* 55
    and *Crucifixion* (Bacon) 61
    face and feelings of the Other 56-8
    links with Bauman and Bacon 56-8

locking the valves of feeling 59, 61-2
memory 61
multiplicity of meanings in work 66
nostalgia, refusal of 61
revealing the hidden as the poet's task 109-10
unlocking the valves of feeling 63-4

laissez-faire 119
language
    exile and 112-13
    and self-distantiation 111-12
    symbolic/expressive 32-3
Larson, Gary 226
Laustsen, Carsten Bagge 207
Law, John 236
Le Guin, Ursula 223
learning, exemplary 198
    see also teaching sociology
lecturing style of Hughes 36
Left Hand of Darkness, The (Le Guin) 223
Léger, Ferdinand 7
Lepenies, Wolf 25, 69, 70
Leth, Jørgen 145-8
linguistic universe 113
literary criticism and social science 6
literary social science
    Alice in Computerland 121-9
    centre/margin 94
    criteria for 95-6
    criticisms of 97
    difficulties with 95
    editorial resistance to 97-9
    future for 105-6
    lessons from critics 99-100
    "Louisa May's Story of Her Life" (Richardson) 100-2
    one-scene play 102-4
    optimism as premature 104-5
    poetic exemplar 100-2
    Qualitative Health Research response to 97-9
    reading 96-7
    resistance to 93
literature
    autobiographies 228
    confession, novels of 168-9
    Danish 255

    detective 253-4
    as early influence on sociology 24-5
    as experimental sociology 70-1
    global condition of 71-3
    lessons for sociology from 197-8
    reality, use of for understanding 164-74
    science fiction 223-4
    sociology of 164
    teaching, use of in 198-200, 206-7, 261-2
    translation of 71-3
    truth, novels of 168
    turn towards 3-5
    used alongside textbooks in teaching 220-9, **221**
    see also Saramago, José
Lockridge, Ernst 207
looping 201
"Louisa May's Story of Her Life" (Richardson) 100-2
Luhmann, Niklas 110
lyrical sociology 148-9

Macbeth (Shakespeare) 135-6
Maffesoli, Michel 114
magical realism 71
maieutics 186-7, 192
Malloch, Margaret S. 236
Mankell, Henning 253-4
Maruna, Shad 240
Marx, Karl 8, 24
Matador (Danish TV series) 259-61
Matravers, Amanda 240
Matthews, Fred H. 27-8
McCall, Michael 209
McGuigan, Jim 69
Mead, George Herbert 203
meaning
    as central to human lives 133
    presence, contrast with 137-8, 139-42
    in qualitative research 133-4
    questioning of approaches based on 134
    see also presence
meaninglessness of life 59-60
memory 61
Merleau-Ponty, Maurice 140

messiness, representation of 236
metaphors
   frame metaphor 42
   game metaphor 42
   Goffman, use of by 41-3
   Hughes, unconventional use of by 36
   ritual metaphor 42
   sociologists' use of 8
   theatrical metaphor 41-2
metempsychosis 190
methodological imagination 3
methodological inhibition 2
methodology
   defined 2
   expansion of understanding of, need for 2-3
   as a path 8-9
   as strait-jacket 2
methods of theorizing
   defined 177
   dialectic 186-7
   Durkheim's approach to representation 184-6
   Joyce 187-93
   maieutics 186-7
   Oracle at Delphi 178-81
   Socrates 186-7
   spirit of capitalism 182-4
   theorai 17981
   Weber 182-4
micro-sociology 209
Mills, C. Wright 2, 3, 7
modernity, solid 117
Mol, Anne-Marie 150-1
morality 205-6
Müller, Peter 169
multi-disciplinarity in social sciences 1-2
   see also Chicago School of Sociology
multi-perspectivalism 7-8
multiple voices in communication of research 48, 208-9

Name of the Rose, The (Eco) 222
names and naming 79-80
Nårgaard, Susan 198-9
narrative
   communication 32-3
   and presence 135
   repudiation of by Bacon 61-2
   see also literature
narrative/positivistic modes of thought 242-3
Negt, Oskar 198
neoliberalism 77-9
New Journalism 31
Nexø, Martin Andersen 261-2
Nichols, Bill 2-3
Nietzsche, Friedrich 163, 197
Nisbet, Robert 2n1
nonsocialization of exiles 113-14
nostalgia, refusal of 61
Notebooks (Saramago) 73
novels. *see* literature

One Flew Over the Cuckoo's Nest (Forman) (film) 201-2
ontology 224
openmindedness in social sciences 1-2, 17
   see also Chicago School of Sociology
opium addiction 243-7
Oplev, Niels Arden 256
Oracle at Delphi 178-81
organizational sociology 201-2
organizations as social systems 204-5
Other, the
   face and feelings of 56-8
   generalized 203
   locking the valves of feeling towards 58-62
Out (Kirino) 224
outsiders 161-2
Outsiders: Studies in the Sociology of Deviance (Becker) 47

paleoanthropology 8-9
Panopticon (Bentham) 169-70
Park, Robert E. 23
   aversion to abstract intellectualism 27-8
   'city as social laboratory' 31-2
   communication
      society as 29-31
      as story-telling/narrative 32-3
      contradiction in ideas of 32-3
      debt owed to literary writers 25
      Hughes as student of 33

journalism and sociology 31-2
super-journalism 28-33
path, methodology as 8-9
Pay It Forward (Leder) 205-6
Pedersen, Ole 198-9
Pelias, Ron 142
Pelle Erobreren (Pelle the Conqueror) (Nexø) 261-2
performance, society as 47-9
performance science 208
'Performance Science' (Becker) 47
performative sociology 207-10
phenomenology 139-40
Phenomenology of Spirit (Hegel) 6
Pirsig, Robert M. 225
Pizzorno, Alessandro 161
Plato 155-6, 158, 163
plot and presence 135
Plummer, Ken 28
poetics
  turn towards 3-5
  see also art(s); literature
poiesis of the spirit of capitalism 182-4
Porterfield, Austin 199
Portrait of the Artist, A (Joyce) 189
positivism 226
positivistic/narrative modes of thought 242-3
Postmodern Ethics (Bauman) 205-6
postmodernism 5
poverty 83
pregnancy, fear of unplanned 262-3
presence
  apple eating example 149-51
  approach centred on 137
  in the arts 145-8
  characteristics of *139,* 139-42
  criticism of conservatism 142-3
  in cultural phenomena 144-5
  defined 134, 136
  in human life 137-9
  lyrical sociology 148-9
  meaning, contrast with 137-8, 139-42
  and narrative and plot 135
  poetic, connections with 135
  in social sciences 148-9
Presentation of Self in Everyday Life (Goffman) 41-2

primal shelter, yearning for 118
Proteus 190

Qualitative Health Research (QHR) (journal) 97-9

Radin, Paul 161
reality
  bildungsroman as theatricalization 169-74
  character of 156-9
  exterior position in observing 160-2
  knowledge of the out-of-ordinary 159-60
  novels, use of for understanding 164-74
  recognition rather than cognition 158
  schismogenesis 162-4
  as series of layers 157-9
  significance of 155-6
  theatricalized 163-4
Rembrandt 6-7
representation
  Durkheim's approach to 184-6
  of messiness 236
  of society, Becker on 47
reproduction and families 256-63
Ressources Humaines (Cantet) (film) 203-5
Richardson, Laurel 100-2, 207
Ricoeur, Paul 133
ritual metaphor 42
rootedness 114
Rorty, Richard 96, 151-2
Rosanvallon, Pierre 118

Saldaña, Johnny 207
Saramago, José
  allegory 74, 76-9
  and authorship 73-4
  biopolitics 83-6
  common sense 69, 87-8
  contextualization 73, 75
  critical sociology, novels as 69
  enlightened disenchantment 86-7
  experimental sociology, fiction as 70-1
  global condition of literature 71-3
  Goffman comparison 87-8

identity 76-7, 80-2
ironic distanciation 71
literary correlates to 71
names and naming 79-80
neoliberalism 77-9
research 87-8
selection of novels for analysis 75-6
speculative social thought, novels as 70
state and bureaucracy 82-3
states, opposition to 77
Scheler, Max 115
schismogenesis 162-4
Schön, D.A. 239
science fiction 223-4
 see also literature
Scientific Method 2, 2n1
Seeing (Saramago) 77
self-distanciation 111-12, 114-15
self-perception 202-3
Sellafield Visitors' Centre advertisement 219-20
sex and sexuality 211-12, 262-3
shock as pedagogic therapy 210-12
Simmel, Georg 6-7, 9, 24, 34-5, 39
Sjöwall, Maj 253
Skinner, Quentin 74-5
Smart, Carol 236
Snow, Charles P. 1
Sociological Imagination, The (Mills) 7
sociology
 early literary influences 24-5
 turn towards poetics 4
 see also Chicago School of Sociology
Sociology as an Art Form (Nisbet) 2n1
Sociology as Sorcery (Andreski) 28
Sociology Through the Projector (Laustsen and Diken) 207
Socrates 186-7
solid modernity 117
spirit of capitalism 182-4
Star Trek 223-4
states
 biopolitics 83-6
 the body and memory 83-6
 and bureaucracy 82-3
Steiner, George 113
Stephen Hero (Joyce) 188-9

story-telling/narrative communication 32-3
 see also literature
Strategic Interaction (Goffman) 42
super-journalism 28-33
surface and depth 140
symbolic/expressive language 32-3
symbols and high and low art 220
Symphony No. 9 (Beethoven) 6

Tambling, Jeremy 74
Tan, Shaun 228
teaching sociology
 advertisements 219-20
 art/literature alongside textbooks 220-9, **221**
 autobiographies 228
 balancing act in 235
 benefits of using art/literature 230
 cartoons 226-7
 creativity in 9-10
 criminology 237-47
 critical constructivism 240-1
 dissemination 229
 documentary analysis 219
 drug use in literature 236-47
 epiphany 212
 epistemology 221-4
 families and reproduction 256-63
 film as tool for 200-7, 255-6
 Goffman 45
 historical stories 253-6
 lecturing style of Hughes 36
 literature used in 198-200, 206-7, 261-2
 messiness, representation of 236
 ontology 224
 performance in 207-10
 sex and sexuality 262-3
 shock as pedagogic therapy 210-12
 techniques 227-9
 television programmes 258-62
 theory 225
 theory and methodology, linking 226
 university 198
techniques, teaching 227-9
television programmes 258-62
theatre in teaching 207-10

theatrical metaphor 41-2
theatricalized reality 163-4
   bildungsroman 169-74
theorai 17981
theoremata 179
theorizing, methods of
   defined 177
   dialectic 186-7
   Durkheim's approach to representation 184-6
   Joyce 187-93
   maieutic 186-7
   Oracle at Delphi 178-81
   Socrates 186-7
   spirit of capitalism 182-4
   theorai 17981
   Weber 182-4
thought, positivistic/narrative modes of 242-3
Three Studies for a Crucifixion (Bacon) 60-1
total institutions 201
tradition
   respect for 156
   significance of 155-6
translation of literature 71-3
Tricksters 161-2
truth, novels of 168
truth and knowledge 141-2
Turner, Bryan S. 78-9
Two Figures (Bacon)
   artist's aims for 55-6
   described 55

Ulysses (Joyce) 191
universe, linguistic 113
University of Chicago. *see* Chicago School of Sociology

Vico, Giambattisto 178-9, 181, 192
Viz comic 226
voices, multiple in communication of research 48, 208-9

Wahlöö, Per 253
Wallraff, Günther 25
Watson, Cate 229
Weber, Max 8, 24-5, 177, 182-4
Wellin, Christopher 209
Whatever (Houellebecq) 211-12
Wilhelm Meister (Goethe) 170-4
Williams, Robin 42
workplace, life at the 204-5
Wright-Mills, C. 191
Writing for Social Scientists (Becker) 46

Young, Jock 241

Zen and the Art of Motorcycle Maintenance (Pirsig) 225
Zorbaugh, Harvey Warren 24